Acceptance and Commitment Therapy for Behavior Analysts

This book provides a thorough discussion of acceptance and commitment therapy or training (ACT) and a guide for its use by behavior analysts. The book emphasizes how the intentional development of six core behavioral processes – values, committed action, acceptance, defusion, self-as-context, and present moment awareness – help establish the psychological flexibility needed to acquire and maintain adaptive behaviors that compete with maladaptive behavior patterns in verbally able clients.

Split into three parts, the book discusses the history and controversy surrounding the rise of acceptance and commitment strategies in behavior analysis and shows how the processes underlying ACT are linked to foundational behavioral scientific principles as amplified by stimulus equivalence and relational learning principles such as those addressed by relational frame theory. In a careful step-by-step way, it describes the best practices for administering the acceptance and commitment procedures at the level of the individual client, organizational systems, and with families. Attention is also given to the ethical and scope-of-practice considerations for behavior analysts, along with recommendations for conducting on-going research on this new frontier for behavior analytic treatment across a myriad of populations and behaviors. Written by leading experts in the field, the book argues that practice must proceed from the basic tenants of behavior analysis, and that now is the opportune moment to bring ACT methods to behavior analysts to maximize the scope and depth of behavioral treatments for all people.

Acceptance and Commitment Therapy for Behavior Analysts will be an essential read for students of behavior analysis and behavior therapy, as well as for individuals on graduate training programs that prepare behavior analysts and professionals that are likely to use ACT in their clinical practice and research.

Mark R. Dixon is a clinical professor in the Department of Disability and Human Development at the University of Illinois Chicago, USA.

Steven C. Hayes is Nevada Foundation Professor in the Behavior Analysis program at the Department of Psychology at University of Nevada, USA.

Jordan Belisle is an associate professor in the Psychology Department of Missouri State University, USA.

Behavior Science: Theory, Research and Practice
Series Editor: The Association for Behavior Analysis International

Applied Behavior Science in Organizations: Consilience of Historical and Emerging Trends in Organizational Behavior Management
Edited by Ramona A. Houmanfar, Mitch Fryling & Mark P. Alavosius

A Programming Contingency Analysis of Mental Health
By Israel Goldiamond

Acceptance and Commitment Therapy for Behavior Analysts: A Practice Guide from Theory to Treatment
By Mark R. Dixon, Steven C. Hayes and Jordan Belisle

Women in Behavior Science: Observations of Life Inside and Outside of the Academy
Edited by Ruth Anne Rehfeldt, Traci Cihon and Erin Rasmussen

For more information about this series, please visit: www.routledge.com/Behavior-Science/book-series/ABAI

Acceptance and Commitment Therapy for Behavior Analysts

A Practice Guide from Theory to Treatment

Mark R. Dixon, Steven C. Hayes and Jordan Belisle

NEW YORK AND LONDON

Cover image: © Getty Images

First published 2023
by Routledge
605 Third Avenue, New York, NY 10158

and by Routledge
4 Park Square, Milton Park, Abingdon, Oxon, OX14 4RN

Routledge is an imprint of the Taylor & Francis Group, an informa business

Library of Congress Cataloging-in-Publication Data
Names: Dixon, Mark R., 1970- author. | Hayes, Steven C., author. | Belisle, Jordan, author.
Title: Acceptance and commitment therapy for behavior analysts : a practice guide from theory to treatment / edited by Mark R. Dixon, Steven C. Hayes and Jordan Belisle.
Description: New York, NY : Routledge, 2023. | Series: Behavior science: theory, research and practice | Includes bibliographical references and index. |
Identifiers: LCCN 2022039402 (print) | LCCN 2022039403 (ebook) |
ISBN 9781032168081 (pbk) | ISBN 9781032168098 (hbk) |
ISBN 9781003250371 (ebk)
Subjects: LCSH: Behavioral assessment. | Acceptance and commitment therapy.
Classification: LCC BF176.5 .D59 2023 (print) | LCC BF176.5 (ebook) |
DDC 150.28/7--dc23/eng/20221230
LC record available at https://lccn.loc.gov/2022039402
LC ebook record available at https://lccn.loc.gov/2022039403

ISBN: 978-1-032-16809-8 (hbk)
ISBN: 978-1-032-16808-1 (pbk)
ISBN: 978-1-003-25037-1 (ebk)

DOI: 10.4324/9781003250371

Typeset in Minion Pro
by Deanta Global Publishing Services, Chennai, India

Contents

PART 1

History and Theory Underlying ACT

1

Behavior Analysis and the Functional Approach to Intervention

Behavior analysis is at a choice point of its own making. Our own data make it plain that once people start to speak, listen, and reason in a sophisticated way, the contingencies of reinforcement are no longer the sole ontogenetic causes of our behavior.

Pause to think about your own thinking and how dominant it can be. If an important meeting is coming up, you are thinking about how to handle it. If you are feeling anxious, lonely, or sad, or if you are pondering why you feel this way – what are you going to do about it? If your coworkers fail to appreciate you, or your friends let you down, thoughts about who you are, or ruminations about past wounds and betrayals, can come to dominate these moments so thoroughly that they drown out attention to the present environment and what is really happening – here and now.

These are the kinds of creatures we are.

Most psychological approaches start here, and as they attempt to get a toe hold on the scientific analysis of human functioning, they soon succumb to the strong tendency to chase lay language concepts and their apparent extensions into applied affairs using the tools and methods of top-down normative, nomothetic science. Personality types. Cognitive styles. Stages. Mental disorders. Syndromes. Mental and, most of all, *normative* causes of all kinds.

Behavior analysis started in a very different place – in the study of individual non-human animals as a kind of preparation to find high precision and high scope principles that would allow human functioning to be addressed and human well-being to be advanced. Behavior analysis was not designed to stop at the water's edge of complexity, nor to be concerned about "the behavior of the rat for its own sake" (Skinner, 1938, p. 441). The whole point was to develop such powerful functional principles that, say, a Walden II (Skinner, 1948) could be imagined and then sought, step by step.

These principles would be developed and vetted using idiographic methods that stayed true to a psychological level of analysis – the whole organism interacting in and with a larger context described historically and situationally. The approach would be bottom-up, not top-down: inductive, empirical, and experimental. Concepts would be functional, not topographical. They would be generalized to the nomothetic level gradually, as the data warranted, through replication, systematic extensions, and applications.

Everyone developing this field that way (and Skinner in particular) knew it was a strategic gamble and there may be kinds of situated actions that required accounts that went beyond what could be seen in the behavior of non-human animals due to a factor beyond the obvious one of complexity. Skinner himself said that the "differences I expect to see revealed between the behavior of a rat and man (aside from enormous differences of complexity) lie

DOI: 10.4324/9781003250371-2

in the field of verbal behavior" (1938, p. 442). In the bottom-up approach, that would only be revealed if it occurred. Meanwhile the field pushed on, refining its concepts while looking for evidence of clear functional differences.

Arguably, no animal has actually ever been taught to perform an entirely new behavior in these early contrived experimental arrangements. Pigeons peck. Rats forage and push on objects in their environment. That is the kind of creatures they are. Behavior scientists were able to bring these behaviors under stimulus control. The peck response was brought under the control of a disc and spatial patterns. Pushing and foraging responses were made to occur with a mechanical lever and in response to lights and other gadgets. Yet, in some form, the response is something these animals already do to survive. What, then, is uniquely human behavior?

By 1957 Skinner had described a theoretical approach to verbal behavior that did *not* force behavior analysis into that choice point that the field now faces. Although verbal behavior was said to be mediated by social reinforcement that required special training of an audience, the implications of that adjustment were not disruptive to the existing strategy of behavior analytic research. Indeed, by that definition the interactions between an experimenter and a laboratory animal comprised "a small but genuine verbal community" (Skinner, 1957, p. 108, footnote 11), so nothing fundamentally had changed in the analytic approach.

A few years later, Skinner (1966) introduced the distinction between contingency-shaped and rule-governed behavior, but this too did not fundamentally alter the trajectory of a behavior analytic account. Some argued that it did so if it could be said what "specification" meant in the definition of rules as a "contingency specifying stimulus" (Hayes & Hayes, 1989), but that never happened.

In the latter part of the last century the indications that change had arrived were there in multiple forms, but professional changes in applied behavior analysis (ABA) blunted their impact. Research on rule governance uncovered findings that were hard to explain using only direct programmed contingencies (Hayes, 1989). Stimulus equivalence showed how early and how profoundly derived stimulus relations could alter human behavior in the absence of direct reinforcement (Sidman, 1994). And the study of multiple stimulus relations and relational framing showed how widely the concept of derived stimulus relations applied (Hayes et al., 2001).

None of these developments hit mainstream applied behavior analysis with full force because the even more enormous impact of the professionalization of applied behavior analysis was taking center stage during this same era. There was much to do to specify how to work with applied populations from within the purview of Board-Certified Behavior Analysts (BCBAs), and by far the population most of relevance to these professional standards was people with developmental disorders. Master's level training programs proliferated, the profession dramatically expanded, and the field demonstrably narrowed its focus to these populations (Axelrod et al., 2012). Research that might have expanded the scope of the field, especially in the area of verbal behavior, instead itself became very dominantly focused on persons with autistic spectrum disorders or other developmental disabilities, some of whom did not show stimulus equivalence (Dixon et al., 2007). The point of emphasis became the teaching of elementary verbal operant abilities, like tacting and manding, and extending accounts based on them, even if those accounts were exclusively conceptual.

What has changed in the last decade is that as this process of professionalization has settled in for the long haul, young BCBAs who feel less connected to old theoretical wars are looking for help, with full awareness that more is needed in order to step up to the challenges that they and their clients face. The presence of even the simplest derived stimulus relations enormously reduces the clarity of answers provided by traditional functional analysis (Belisle et al., 2017). Every practicing BCBA is well aware of that fact – they just do not know what to do about it. Similarly, BCBAs know that parents and staff alike need additional support in dealing with their own psychological events in order to implement traditional behavioral programs. Simply insisting that they follow behavioral programs is hardly an adequate response.

What, however, is the alternative?

Even within the narrow range of current BCBA practice, the data are accumulating that relational frame theory (RFT) (Hayes et al., 2001) and acceptance and commitment therapy or training (ACT, said as a single word, not initials) (Hayes et al., 1999, 2012) can be of use to applied behavior analysts. They do provide an alternative. This is true in areas such as staff management (Bethay et al., 2013; Little et al., 2020) or parent training (Hahs et al., 2019). Perhaps even more telling, these methods significantly improve outcomes in the areas of verbal development (e.g., Dixon et al., 2017) and behavioral management (e.g., Eilers & Hayes, 2015) that remain the core focus of the field.

In what may well be seen in hindsight as a milestone marking a change in the direction of the field, in 2018 a full extra day was provided at the annual conference of the Association for Behavior Analysis International (ABAI) on ACT and RFT, in effect announcing that behavior analysis had now reached the choice point we referred to as we began this book. If it really is the case, and we believe it is, that once people start to speak, listen, and reason in a sophisticated way, direct contingencies of reinforcement are no longer the sole ontogenetic causes of our behavior, then behavior analysis needs to change in very important ways order to serve humanity. As difficult as that will be, we need to move forward with an analysis that addresses and deals with the private events that modulate contingency control. We need to expand on what we have traditionally defined within behavior analysis as a functional analysis. And at the same time, for the sake of the coherence of our field and the progressivity of these developments, we need to make these changes in a way that fits with the most fundamental feature of our discipline, embracing and strengthening its functional approach, idiographic focus, evolutionary coherence, and empirical accountability.

In these first four chapters we intend to put ACT in context. We mean to describe more about what functionalism means and how to gird ourselves for the difficult task of addressing private events without succumbing to the lure of mentalism. Our intent in Part 1 of the book is to lay a firm foundation for ACT and to explore the processes of change that are inside it. In Part 2 we will show how ACT addresses such dimensions of behavior as affect, cognition, attention, sense of self, motivation, and overt habits of values-based action. Relying on behavioral principles as expanded by RFT and evolutionary science, we argue that these processes can be addressed without ever leaving behavior analysis as a field, nor the best of its philosophical, theoretical, methodological, and empirical traditions. Finally in Part 3 of the book, we will focus on the practical steps that need to be taken to put ACT into behavior analytic practice.

In this chapter we begin this journey with the topic of functionalism and why it is the defining feature of our field.

FUNCTIONALISM AND THE SCIENTIST PRACTITIONER

Functionalism is at the heart of behavior analysis. It is one of the features that most distinguishes ABA and other human service fields.

The distinction between functionalism and structuralism exists across scientific disciplines, such as anthropology, sociology, physiology and anatomy, and fields of psychology and behavioral biology. On the one hand, structuralism seeks to identify causation solely in terms of underlying proximal structures or mechanistic arrangements that are assumed to be present that account for the actions of systems. For example, what "is" a clock? From a structuralist perspective, a clock is a device with two arms, numbers, and gears that when given energy through a battery or another source moves the arms at a set rate and location. This is all true – and likely provides some information that is necessary to fix a broken clock if so desired. An interest in structure is fundamental to all science. But when it becomes an "ism" in describing behavior, it is hard to go beyond these topographical and mechanistic features into issues of history, context, purpose, and impact, both for the behavioral scientists and for those organisms the behavioral scientist studies. Part of the problem is that structuralism can lead to a diminished sense that an examination of history, development, and function is even needed since structural accounts appeal to the commonsense elemental realism that resides within language itself: metaphorically, structuralist studies purport to answer what a clock – or anything else you can name – "*actually is*." That interest can easily lead to a false sense that there is little else to know. In the behavioral sciences particularly that idea has at times been toxic because behavior is a verb and the subject matter can slip away when history, development, and function are not at the fore.

Functionalism, on the other hand, seeks to identify relationships between interacting variables over time that have led to the development and selection of behavioral features. That is, functional accounts ask about what the various behavioral forms have produced historically, how that impact may have altered development, how they are functioning currently, and why that might be of importance. When a functional approach of that kind is extended in time, it blends into the contextually bound histories of variation and selective retention that are defining features of an evolutionary account that can be applied to genetic, epigenetic, or cultural development. When it is limited to the lifetime of the individual, the same approach becomes a defining feature of a functional and contextual psychological approach.

If we return to our example of a clock, from a functional perspective, a clock is a device that is used by people to tell time. When a clock hand strikes a specific number such as "6," this can lead to temporally reliable patterns of behavior, such as preparing dinner or taking a walk. A clock could be an analog clock as described above, a digital clock, or a sundial. Often many different forms can serve any given function. At the same time, any given structure could serve different purposes. By way of an example, if a person chose to use a wall clock as a dinner plate, the physical structure of the clock would remain the same, but the function of the clock would now be entirely different. If that function came to dominate over time, the structure might be modified to better serve the new function – in this example a dome like lens might now be avoided in favor of concave one that better retained the food.

The "double headed arrow" in Figure 1.1 helps explain one reason we are more interested in a functional analytic perspective than a structural one alone. Structure can be important, but evolution itself suggests that structure is generally driven by function in the long run, and functional accounts tell us more about how to change conditions now that can influence the structure (i.e., what behavior looks like). Practically speaking, these benefits are why behavior analysts are more interested in what something *does* than what it looks like. To change what it looks like, we have to change what it does or how it operates within an

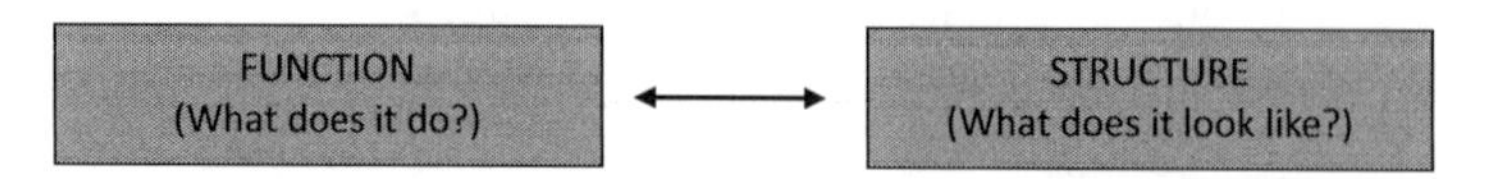

FIGURE 1.1 Evolution and adaptation diagram.

environment, to understand why it emerges as an adaptation within the environment and to change the environment accordingly.

Because language and cognition are at the heart of what we seek to predict and influence through ACT-based approaches, it's worth reminding readers how these two different approaches might apply to language and cognition. Consider a classical structural approach to psycholinguistics. Spoken words are thought to reflect underlying structures that are often considered universal, such as deep grammatical structures. According to the early and classical ideas of Noam Chomsky (a famous linguist and notable in behavior analysis for disagreeing with Skinner's account of language), universal grammar must be due to underlying structures that exist in the "mind/brain" of the person (1972). The result is a hypothetical "device" called a Language Acquisition Device that is thought to be the hidden or latent structure that produces language, much as an idealized circle in Plato's system produces circles. Whether such a device exists as such is inconsequential – it is a way of describing how likely deep-seated and multiple interacting neurological structures participate in the development of generally uniform grammatical patterns as they exist for humans – and not other animals. This is a much more sophisticated way of saying "pigeons peck." Humans "language." The challenge becomes one of causation. Do these inferred underlying structures cause the development of grammar and syntax any more than the beak, brain, and neck muscles of the bird cause it to peck? A lack of clarity on that front is why it is so hard to turn structural accounts into successful intervention programs.

To Skinner (1953), this *formistic* or *mechanistic* approach can lead to the proliferation of explanatory fictions, where we attribute cause to hypothesized forms and structures inside the person, without adequately considering the context that gave rise to those structures and resulting behaviors in the first place. In 1957, Skinner provided the first comprehensive functional analysis of human language as verbal behavior, or verbal behavior theory. He proposed that, rather than focusing solely on the structural characteristics of language, a functional approach must consider the context within which language emerges. Given Skinner's work on operant conditioning, it comes as no surprise that his approach emphasized patterns of reinforcement that support the development of language. For example, a mand can take on many grammatical forms, or can include nouns, verbs, and adjectives. What is important is that a mand occurs in the context of consistent establishing operations (EO) and results in the acquisition of a specified reinforcer from the listener. The same set of sounds could serve different functions in different contexts. For example, the word "cat" can serve as either a mand (i.e., asking for a cat) or a tact (i.e., identifying a cat) depending on the context. Skinner's account extends to private events such as problem solving, thinking, and reasoning that are more often accounted for within structuralist cognitive models.

The details of Chomsky's criticism of Skinner's approach (1959) are not of primary interest to us more than half a century later, but his criticism can largely be understood as the difference between structural and functional approaches to scientific inquiry. Seen in hindsight, some of Chomsky's criticisms did point to holes in the functional analysis of human language and cognition. For example, it is hard to use Skinner's account to address fully the seeming self-organization and complexity evident within the structure of human language and cognition. More recent advances that we discuss in this book make a functional explanation more plausible than Skinner's early accounts. Furthermore, Chomsky seemed to correctly acknowledge the lack of Skinner's analysis of the listener – as comprehension of language is perhaps even more important than speaking. Conversely, Chomsky's strategy left unanswered how such complex structures arrive so uniquely for every single person on the planet. Equally unique is the environment, past and present, that surrounds each person throughout their life. And it is by understanding the environment that we can start to understand complex behavior.

A FUNCTIONAL APPROACH TO BEHAVIOR-BEHAVIOR RELATIONS

Behavior analysis has made considerable progress since Skinner's initial account. In the next chapter we will touch on the topic of stimulus equivalence and we will show how it led to the RFT account of multiple derived stimulus relations and more recent extensions. We are going to avoid those details now because we want to focus instead on what a functional approach is and how it is different than more traditional accounts – and why ACT and RFT requires a clear understanding of how one action can relate to another.

Take a neurotypically developing English-speaking child who generally responds to social praise and criticism as social reinforcement and social punishment respectively. If that child learns that "mal" is the opposite of "bon" and "bon" is the same as "good," you can now likely train behavioral performances by using the word "mal" as a negative consequence. Let's just assume for now that what has just been said is what happened. RFT will ultimately explain how and why, but for now we do not need to explain how or why – we can stay with a more commonsense description for the purposes of the example.

Now imagine that two analysts who do not know the child's history, one a cognitive structuralist and one a behavior analyst, are both wondering why the child avoids repeating actions that are followed by the sound "mal." The cognitivist may claim that is because the word "mal" is in a semantic network that gives it an aversive meaning. The behavior analysts suggest that it is a conditioned punisher because it likely has been associated with the word "bad."

In fact, it cannot be a conditioned punisher because it's never been associated with primary or conditioned punishers – it has never even been heard or seen in the same context as anything bad. It shares no formal properties with existing punishers either – it cannot be stimulus generalization. As a result, if this "conditioned punishment" analysis were to be applied to other children, we would soon be applying conditions that were far from those that actually led to the performance.

The cognitivist has a very different problem. The concept of a "semantic network" does not tell the analyst what to try to do in the first place to try to establish the performance. "Semantic networks" describes a result, but not how to produce it.

The promise of a functional account is that it *does* tell the analysts what to do to establish or maintain the behavior of interest … but it can do that only if the functional account is adequate. To understand functional relations of the kind that led to this child's performance, it would be necessary to know how one behavior relates to another.

In this case, we would need to understand how "mal" came to be related to "good" in a particular way and how and why using the word "mal" acted as a consequence for another behavioral performance. We are describing a "behavior-behavior" relation. If your goal with behavioral concepts is to use them to predict and influence behavior, when dealing with behavior-behavior relations it is important to understand the contexts in which each of two related actions occur, and the context in which the interrelation between those actions occurs. Concepts need to be both functional *and* contextual (Hayes & Brownstein, 1986), whereby each has influence on the other.

In order to apply a functional and contextual understanding in this case we would need to know the history and circumstances (the "context") that led to each behavioral event *and their interrelationship* (Figure 1.2). We have italicized that last point because it is so commonly ignored. Understanding these three contextual features is precisely what RFT, and ACT, proposes to do idiographically, but even before we get there it is worth noting that when behavior analysts ask why certain events have the function that they do, in some circumstances we need to understand behavior-behavior relations involved before it is possible to give an answer that is practically useful and scientifically adequate.

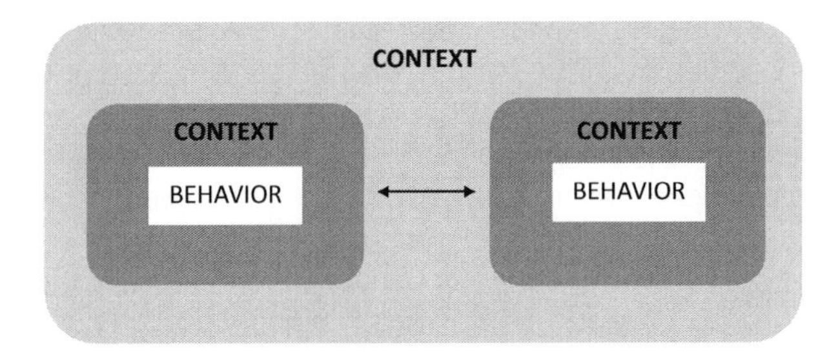

FIGURE 1.2 Context and behavior.

The reason knowledge of that kind is key is that behavior analysts utilize scientific methods functionally – to isolate idiographically sensible functional interactions between environmental variables and behavior. Functional interactions are discovered through a process called functional analysis, which literally means to observe or analyze behavior-environment interactions at the level of the behaving organism. Interventions are then designed to influence environmental variables to bring about behavior change.

Most concepts in other applied psychological traditions are vetted by normative consistencies between people. Psychometrics is a classic example. Psychometric analysis applies not to the functional contextual reality of people – the history and circumstances of individuals – but to structural consistencies in language use *between* people. The problem is that variability between people and variability within people are not the same thing. Statistical physics has known for over a century that it is not possible to move reliably from the behavior of a collection of things to predicting the behavior of an individual thing that is inside that collection over time, except in a few very extraordinary circumstances described by the ergodic theorem (Birkhoff, 1931; von Neumann, 1932). None of those circumstances (namely stationarity and that all elements show the same dynamic properties) apply to people. We can say it in a simpler way for now: it is scientifically necessary for functional analysis to be done idiographically and then gradually generalized to nomothetic statements. We will do a somewhat deeper dive into why later in the book.

The uncertain relationship of between-person variability to within-person variability is part of why the normative approach is so hard to turn into reliable interventions. It is easy, for example, to use psychometrics to assess emotions, thought, and overt behaviors, without ever even inquiring about the history of these events, nor the contexts in which they occur for the individual. That situation means that we can be left with latent constructs that "explain" action without telling us what to do to *change* those actions. That's a major problem.

If a new functional analytic strategy can emerge, the scope of our field can expand dramatically, and the depth of our interventions can improve notably. We have already seen that this is true with the example of the commonly used applied behavior analytic technique termed the "experimental functional analysis" (EFA) (Iwata et al., 1989/1994). EFA proved to be an evolutionary cusp in our field (like a behavioral cusp but experienced by all members of the community through a collective change in behavior). Prior to the EFA, behavior was largely assumed to be under the influence of reinforcement and punishment – a relatively simple model to inform the development of behavioral intervention. If the analyst wants the behavior to occur more frequently, they must reinforce the behavior. High quality reinforcers that are delivered immediately and contingently will bring about the greatest increases. Most of the time, clients are not referred to behavior analysts or seeking services to increase a behavior. Rather, many clients come seeking services to decrease a behavior, such as vocal stereotypy or self-injury, that is considered disruptive or harmful. Again, the solution is quite simple, high magnitude punishers that are delivered immediately and contingently will bring about the greatest decreases.

Given what we know now, this simple model can be harmful. Overuse of punishment can lead to long-term negative social, emotional, and behavioral outcomes for clients. Nonfunctional reinforcers are unlikely to maintain positive behavior once they are withdrawn. Behavior analysts are still trying to extricate themselves from this era of behavior science, and many of these practices are still used today by some with autistic learners and given more palatable descriptions (e.g., "reflection area" operating as a time-out/social exclusion zone, reinforcement withdrawal incorrectly labeled "extinction").

The EFA provided a functional analytic method to move past a very limited model of behavior change. Behavior serves a function. To change behavior, we must start by determining the function that behavior serves *for the individual*, and we need to do so longitudinally and empirically, not just conceptually. The initial work utilizing EFA focused on self-injurious behavior exhibited by autistic children. Consider that self-injurious behavior is a description of structure (i.e., what the behavior looks like) not of function. In the EFA, functional conditions are manipulated, and their influence on relative rates of behavior are ascertained. For example, if self-injury occurs most readily in the condition where contingent escape from a demand is delivered following the behavior, then we can assume the function of the behavior is escape. A functional intervention to decrease self-injury therefore requires that a new behavior be established, such as a functional communicative response, that serves the same function and is more efficient. No punishment is needed, and the behavior we are promoting is maintained by functional reinforcers.

The EFA also provides an illustrative example of the importance of expanding our scientific models of behavior change. A model that exclusively assumed reinforcement and punishment as functions will necessarily result in analytic strategies to ascertain relative rates of reinforcement and punishment. Moreover, interventions will attempt to influence behavior utilizing these processes exclusively. Adding establishing operations to our scientific model (e.g., demands, attention deprivation) opened the door for a more functional approach to intervention that sought to establish new behaviors that address these EO/AO (establishing/abolishing operations) functions. It is also true that this now "traditional" approach to EFA hit a barrier with derived stimulus relations, but we should celebrate it as a great advancement nevertheless. Now it is time to take the next step – to discover our next evolutionary cusp – that will allow derived relations to be addressed through additional development of functional analytic methods that tie directly to those challenges that are uniquely human.

We believe that ACT and RFT represent a new functional strategy that has emerged within the field of behavior analysis and will permanently change the types of applied problems we are able to solve and the clinical populations we are able to serve. It will also change considerably how we serve those who have traditionally benefited from behavioral intervention. To see how it might do so, we need to step forward from how we will study and change behavior-behavior relations to a science of private events.

A FUNCTIONAL APPROACH TO PRIVATE EVENTS

Behavior analysts are used to focusing on overt behavior, but their use of the term "behavior" is quite broad. Early in his career Skinner defined behavior in two different ways. He defined behavior topographically as behavior as "the movement of an organism or of its parts in a frame of reference provided by the organism itself or by various external objects or fields of force" (Skinner, 1938, p. 6). This is not yet a functional definition: raising a hand to get attention and raising a hand to stretch a muscle is the same behavior by this definition. Just a few sentences later Skinner defined behavior as "the functioning of an organism which is engaged in acting upon or having commerce with the outside world" (1938, p. 6). From this perspective, behavior and the circumstances that impact it are two aspects of a single event, and anything that involves commerce with the world is part of behavior analysis. Skinner never revisited the definition, but as his career evolved that second sense became more and more dominant. He talked of thinking as behavior; remembering as behavior; feelings as behavior; and so on. Any and all of the ways that we interact with the world, publicly or privately, was "behavior."

What is "radical" about Skinner's behaviorism is that he applied contingency thinking to the behavior of scientists themselves (1945). In so doing, traditional methodological behaviorism was turned on its head, and Skinner took behavioral thinking in a new direction.

In the case of behavior analysis, the same functional contextual model of behavior used to produce the desired change in behavior is applied to the scientist as well. From a strictly functional analytic and contextual perspective, "science" is just a term that represents the behavior of scientists in context: as a social enterprise that has as its desired function the development of increasingly organized statements of relations among events so as to allow analytic purposes to be accomplished with precision, scope, and depth. Said in another way, developing and utilizing models of behavior change is simply a pattern of shared verbal behavior of scientists and practitioners that may be effective in solving socially important behavioral challenges (Belisle, 2020). In the unique case of behavior analysis, the scientist and the practitioner are inseparable in what is called the scientist-practitioner model (Belisle et al., 2021), and they in turn are approached in the same way as the clients we analyze.

This approach fundamentally delinks the "public-private" distinction from the "objective-subjective" one. Yes, behavior needs to be directly observed, Skinner (1945) argued, but that can occur with private actions such as thinking and feeling as well. What makes an observation scientifically valid, he argued, was not that it is public, but that the contingencies controlling the observation by the scientist ensure tight stimulus control on what was observed. According to this view, the mere number of potential observers should not be the primary factor driving what we consider to be behavior and therefore accessible to behavior analysis.

Take an example of a speech that is being rehearsed privately. A person can speak and listen without external signs of doing so; noticing even when words do not come easily and thus must be practiced more, or "hearing" pauses for effect, or how to say particular words of emphasis. This private speaking is behavior – or so Skinner argued. It is being directly observed.

If the contingencies controlling an observation are loose, errors will occur whether or not the observation is of a public event or a private event. For example, a child may claim to have a stomach ache to avoid a math test. This same process readily occurs publicly too, however. Suppose an undergraduate class is shown a slide for only one-third of a second that says.

Paris in the

the Spring

If the entire class is then asked to write down what they saw, they will report that they saw the words "Paris in the Spring." Inter-observed agreement will be very high. Now put the same slide up for a minute at a time and a ripple of laughter will spread across the room as the class realizes that a more extended observation proves that this "observation" is due to the history of the class with a familiar phrase and where line breaks are placed – it is not solely due to the actual words and the current stimulation they provide. That is why what Skinner claimed that "truth by agreement" is not a reliable guide to scientific objectivity.

Applied behavior analysts rightly want to see a focus on overt behavior, and that should not change, but it is very much in the functional and contextual behavioral tradition to want to address the various features of human action, even those that are private, if there are conceptual or applied reasons to do so. In short, behavior analysis "does not insist upon truth by agreement and can therefore consider events taking place in the private world within the skin" (Skinner, 1974, p. 16). How to best divide private actions into units is a challenge, but this is not unique because "any unit of operant behavior is to a certain extent artificial. Behavior is the coherent, continuous activity of an integral organism although it may be analyzed into parts for theoretical or practical purposes" (1953, p. 116).

These are *dramatically* functional ideas: the functional analysis of the scientist who opens the door to private events. We can divide up the stream of actions of a person if it helps us understand what to do to serve that person. Distinctions are viewed as being merely useful tools rather than ontological statements. Every time a person is asked "what do you think?" or "what do you feel?," that behavioral stream is divided to a degree, and the only issue is how best to analyze human complexity functionally.

To see how this way of thinking leads us back to behavior-behavior relations, consider the question "why did you do that?" When a person responds by formulating a rule, that social "reason giving context" is an example of exactly how behavior-behavior relations might be altered. A person with "a good reason" for, say, missing a meeting is more likely to miss that meeting not just because of the external situation but also because she knows that one behavior (being able to explain away the failure to keep a promise) alters the context of another behavior (if the meeting is missed, negative consequences are less likely once the "reason" is deployed); see Figure 1.3.

In this case, a social/verbal context of reason giving is a historical and situational cue in which a particular verbal network can serve as a discriminative stimulus (S^D) for another behavior. But note that the person missing the meeting will need to generate the rule (the "excuse" or "reason") and self-detect its plausibility. A young child might say "just cuz" when asked "why did you do that?," but a verbally able adult will not. Being able to self-detect good reasons is a highly skilled performance. "Because the dog ate my work schedule" does not look topographically weaker than "because my car broke down," but it is far less likely to reliably alter social consequences. In some environments (e.g., military boot camps), literally NO excuse will be given credence, regardless of its plausibility or even its factual basis. It is usually considered rude, however, to try to establish such contexts. The next time someone tells you they missed a meeting with you because they forgot, try replying "why did you forget?" and you will sense that you are stepping into a new and dangerous social territory.

These are the kinds of relations that make functional analysis of verbal humans so hard, but they also help describe how ACT works. ACT alters the very social/verbal contexts that glue

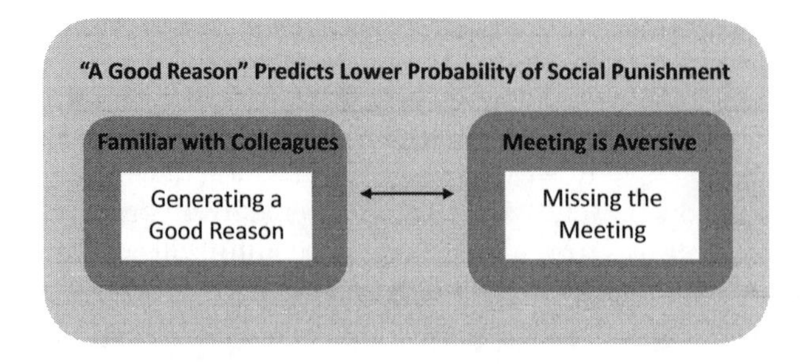

FIGURE 1.3 Social punishment diagram.

behavior together, including public and private behaviors – undermining those contexts when they lead to self-defeating behavior-behavior relations and augmenting them when that helps the person forego smaller, sooner reinforcers in the service of larger, later ones.

Parenthetically, this approach avoids the functional error of mentalism, which is to ascribe causal properties to actions over other actions without addressing the contexts that lead to functional relations among behaviors. "Mentalism" occurs more readily when a private behavior is said to cause a public one (thus its common name), but the error comes from the analysis, not from privacy. While context can be directly manipulated, behaviors are inherently "dependent variables" – they depend on context. Treating behavior-behavior relations as causal without specifying context is the very core of mentalism. It would be odd to make that error with entirely overt behavior, but you could. "Joe throws a baseball well because he can shoot baskets well" would be the same error – it's just rarely made when everyone realizes you are dealing with two behaviors. Indeed, that is part of the reason why behaviorists insist on calling all forms of human action by that term. Rigidly doing so has far too high of a cost in mainstream culture to be the only way for behaviorists to speak, but it's helpful that almost all behavior analysts have been in learning environments that insisted on calling all psychological events by a single and appropriate name: behavior.

FUNCTIONAL ANALYSIS AND THE FIELD OF ABA

A shared vernacular and approach is arguably what defines a field. For us, that is much more than just "calling everything behavior." Applied behavior analysis is a field that is defined by idiographic functional analysis. The term does not pertain to any single procedure, technology, or family of technologies. BCBAs too often use the term "functional analysis" interchangeably with Iwata's EFA, which is problematic for a number of reasons, and a review of the history of behavior analysis shows why.

The original use of the term was by Skinner in reference to his experimental analyses with non-human organisms (Dixon et al., 2012; Schlinger, 2017). These analyses did not include Iwata's "four functions," and many early experiments did not even include a control condition. Until much later in this line of research, the functional analysis of behavior did not actually involve humans at all.

One of the first research studies to apply functional analytic methods with a human subject was conducted by Fuller – 40 years before Iwata and colleagues developed the EFA (Sturmey, 2020). The intervention and target behavior would seem quite benign by today's standards, where positive reinforcement was used to teach an 18-year-old male with a profound intellectual disability to raise his hand. However, consider that prior to this N-of-1 study, it was widely believed that individuals with profound disabilities were simply incapable of learning. This functional analytic strategy – at that time focusing exclusively on a somewhat arbitrary reinforcer (sugar water) – set the stage for the development of a functional analytic field.

The first robust line of applied work with human subjects also did not take place in the field of autism treatment. Lindsley and colleagues (including Skinner) extended this work in the 1950s to hospitalized psychiatric patients to address a variety of behavior challenges experienced by this population (Sturmey, 2020). This involved the systematic collection of behavioral data and the development of techniques that utilized reinforcement contingencies to influence behavior.

The earliest usage of the term "functional analysis" therefore emphasized the experimental analysis of behavior and at the idiographic level. It was immensely important in the broader field of psychology that Skinner and his colleagues were able to effectively turn behavior "on and off" by manipulating variables within a highly controlled environment (i.e., operant chamber). The goal was always to apply this approach to solve major personal and social problems experienced by people (Skinner, 1953), and this early work by Fuller and Lindsley, as well as other earlier applied researchers such as Bijou and Ferster, set the stage for a functional analytic method that emphasized experimental control of behavior.

The term "functional analysis" started to operate as an umbrella term to encompass a much broader strategy of understanding functional interactions between environment and behavior at the level of the individual that was then generalized nomothetically via principles of behavior. This strategy included experimentation but also attempts to collapse consistent experimental results into established principles of learning and behavior, and once established, to extend these results theoretically in such a way that allows us to make pre-experimental inferences about complex forms of human behavior (i.e., the development of theories or laws). A notable example of that final stage occurred when Skinner (1957) described his verbal behavior theory as "a functional analysis of language," with virtually no research at the time supporting this extension.

ABA formed within this broader use of functional analysis. In what is regarded as the seminal article of ABA, the description of its seven defining dimensions by Baer et al. (1968), "functional analysis" is ubiquitous within each dimension. *Applied* refers to the application of functional analytic strategies to solve challenges related to human *behavior*. *Analysis* describes the strategy that necessitates a functional analysis of the on-going interaction between environment and behavior. Ensuring our technologies are *conceptually systematic* ensures that we are using established principles that extend from a functional analytic account. We must ensure interventions are *technological* so that we can isolate environment-behavior interactions and that manipulating the environment is *effective* in changing behavior (i.e., functional). And the final dimension, *generality*, ensures that the all-encompassing stream of functional interaction between environment and behavior is considered and that changes in behavior occur across contexts. This model essentially translates to the idea that behavior analysis is the application of functional analysis (broadly defined) to address behavior that matters to people.

That means that behavior analysis cannot be defined by a set of techniques, even field changing techniques like EFA. And although we have been successful so far in applying functional analytic strategies with children with autism, ABA is not bound to a single population or a small subset of behaviors. Confusion on this point not only fails to appreciate the history of the term functional analysis that we have briefly described here, but also fails to allow our field, behavior analytic practitioners, and clients to realize our fullest potential.

A Summary

ABA emerges from within an idiographic functional account of behavior, not a structural account of behavior. This distinction is not ABA-specific, rather, it is used to distinguish approaches within several scientific disciplines. The underlying philosophy of ABA is behavioristic but not in a traditional way, rather what is "radical" about radical behaviorism is that functional analytic concepts are applied to the scientist as well (Moore, 2007). That step opens the field to the analysis of private events but always as part of a functional and contextual approach (Zettle et al., 2016; Ivancic & Belisle, 2019). All forms of behavior can enter into behavior-behavior relations, but when they do, the analysis is always functional and contextual. This avoids the mentalistic error. ACT is especially focused on those functional contextual properties that determine how behavior-behavior relations work and specifically as applied to solving challenges of human behavior.

WHAT IS ACT FOR BEHAVIOR ANALYSTS?

ACT as an approach used by behavior analysts must not only consider functional analysis – it must be defined by it. Dixon et al. (2020) describe how each of the seven dimensions of what delineates applied behavior analysis as introduced by Baer, Wolf, and Risley appear within ACT-based interventions. In each dimensional area, ACT meets the requirements of a behavior analytic approach, which suggests that it should be practiced by behavior analysts. The range of applications of ACT does indeed extend beyond the boundaries of behavior analysis, however, some careful parameters need to be followed by those practicing ACT as behavior analysts.

First, there should be consideration as to the match between client and ACT. If the client in question fails to demonstrate a relational repertoire such that words or symbols have functions and such functions are in part derived, ACT may be too difficult for that person to comprehend. Given that ACT is a largely talk-based treatment, the person you talk to will in fact need to understand the words spoken. Additionally, since a fair amount of ACT is rooted in metaphor and experience, there will need to be some capacity to be guided experientially and to understand how a metaphor might be related to one's own life.

Second, the primary dependent measure of interest should remain constant prior to and during an ACT intervention. For behavior analysts, such a measure usually entails a measurable and countable verifiable manifestation of behavior. Caution should be taken when drifting towards more subjective indexes of treatment efficacy. For example, psychometric test score changes, while important within some domains of practice, should be viewed as supplemental rather than primary measures of interest. Of course, the self-report of subjective experience by a client is in fact behavior and may lend important information to covert private events for most practicing behavior analysts; again these are secondary to the objective behavioral outcomes that led to treatment in the first place.

Third, the clients, target behaviors, and settings need to fit the defined scope of practice of behavior analysts. This varies from region to region, but it is a mistake to think that simply because the intervention is ACT-consistent, these professional concerns do not apply. What is critical to note is that ACT is not an intervention in and of itself. There is no single formalized protocol called "ACT" that is applied to any and all challenges. Rather, ACT is an intervention framework that is broad in scope and highly variable in practice. When we understand the core principles underlying ACT-based interventions, we can be much more specific about what a treatment entails and remain well within the scope of what constitutes behavior analytic intervention. In fact, a lot of the tools already used by behavior analysts will apply here and can be augmented by considering core processes within the ACT treatment model.

Finally, should one accept ACT as being within the scope of practice of the field of ABA, individual behavior analysts need to be trained in ACT so as to stay within their scope of competence. Reading this book is one step. Seeking on-going training opportunities and supervision from more experienced behavior analysts on a case-by-case basis is another. This is not any different from any other behavior analytic intervention, and occasions to seek these opportunities are increasing exponentially in our field. This is an exciting time to be a behavior analyst, and it is worth taking a deep dive.

WHAT IS BEHAVIOR ANALYSIS FOR ACT?

Modern day behavior analysts grew up in the world of behavior analysis as a professional field, largely, although not exclusively, focused on people with developmental disabilities. ACT is of interest to BCBAs, in part because of what it can do, especially in combination with RFT, to expand the range of practice of behavior analysts. That increased range applies to work with people with developmental disabilities but also a wide range of other areas of human behavior.

But it is also worth considering what behavior analysis as a discipline and as an area of practice can do for ACT. We have just argued that ACT is behavior analytic, but the development of ACT as a behavior analysis program has additional steps that now should be taken. Some of these were begun in the ACT/RFT research program but have not been completed; others are steps that are possible now that were not possible 40 years ago.

Both ACT and RFT as programs of research and practice began in the early 1980s in a laboratory jointly run by a behaviorally oriented junior clinical psychologist and a full professor who was a basic behavior analyst. The clinical psychologist, Steven C. Hayes, is an author of this very book. At the time ACT and RFT were forming, he was an associate editor of the *Journal of Applied Behavior Analysis* (JABA) in the years from 1980 to 1983 and was a regular author in the *Journal of the Experimental Analysis of Behavior* (JEAB). Hayes was clearly a "behavior analyst" by any fair definition of the time.

The basic behavior analyst, Aaron J. Brownstein, does not appear on any major ACT or RFT writings because he died suddenly of a heart attack in 1986 at the age of 53, just as these articles were taking shape. At the time of his death, he was a member of the Board of Editors of *JEAB*, the President of the Southeastern Association for Behavior Analysis, and the editor-elect of the *Behavior Analyst*. Also, clearly a behavior analyst. Aaron was central in thinking through how behavior-behavior relations could be addressed non-mentalistically (Hayes & Brownstein, 1986) – a topic that we have covered extensively in this very chapter and that became centrally important once the implications of RFT began to become clear.

Steve moved to the University of Nevada as Director of Clinical Training soon after Aaron died, which accelerated the clinical application of ACT but slowed ACT as a form of behavior analysis more narrowly defined, especially as the field of behavior analysis itself began to narrow. You can still clearly see the behavior analytic focus in early ACT writings, however. For example, much as is being argued in the present chapter, Hayes and Hayes (1992) emphasized that social-verbal contexts exist that establish the linkage between private events and other behaviors, and that it was these contexts that are modified by ACT:

> Suppose an agoraphobic thinks "I am going to humiliate myself in this mall," then starts to feel panicky, and leaves the mall. A contextualistic behaviorist would not explain the panic or escape on the basis of the form of the thought per se, but on the contexts giving rise to the thought-emotion or thought-overt behavior relation. These contexts include a) those that give meaning to the content of the thought, or the *context of literal meaning*; b) those that establish the valence of humiliation, or the *context of evaluation*; c) those that allow the person to "explain" and "justify" behavior on the basis of the private events, or the *context of reason-giving*; and d) those that establish the goal of avoiding "undesirable" private events, or the *context of emotional and cognitive control*. Instead of trying to change the thought or the emotion, the therapist can change these contexts in an attempt to change the behavior-behavior relation itself.
>
> *(p. 242)*

Figure 1.4 compares a contextual approach to other approaches. Unlike a cognitive model in which thoughts directly impact behavior (or traditional behavioral models in which thoughts are viewed as an epiphenomena or are simply argued not to exist), a contextual behavioral model informed by RFT recognizes that private events can have a functional impact on other behavior, but that impact is itself regulated by context. Hayes and Hayes (1992) listed several such contexts in the quote above.

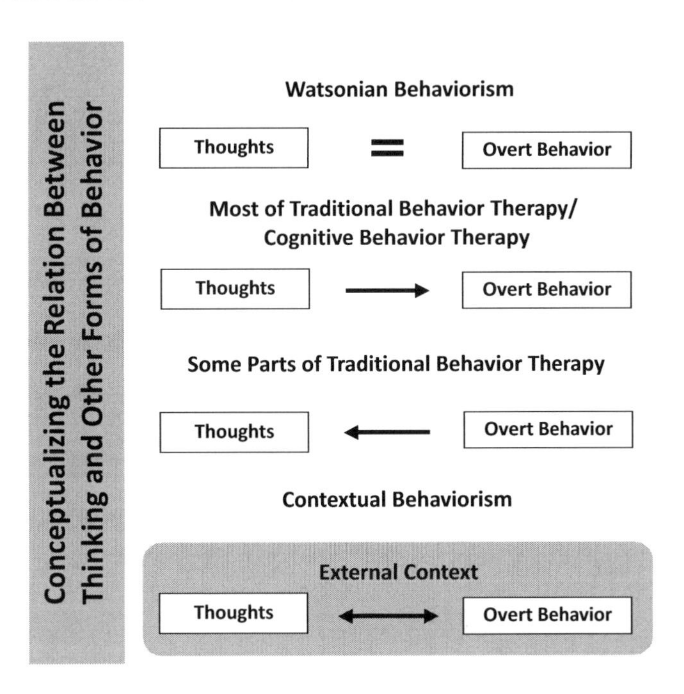

FIGURE 1.4 Comparing a contextual approach to other approaches.

Some of these have been widely studied since, but others have not, and the broader implications of this general approach have received only limited research attention. Behavior analysts are challenged by such questions, and their analytic approach is very much needed.

Take the example of reason giving. There is a long behavioral literature on say-do correspondence, and we know that when the social verbal community can monitor that correspondence, it has an impact on the likelihood of behavior. When we ask people "why did you do that?," they will likely provide an explanation for their behavior. Once that is said publicly, if people can monitor what then occurs, they can see if the person is being consistent and can provide consequences if they are not. That is why public knowledge of "cognitive" interventions is so impactful. If a child who is afraid of the dark is taught to say "I'm brave and can stay in the dark!" it has a major impact – unless that child is deceived into thinking that no one can ever know that they learned to do that. Then that same intervention has absolutely zero impact (Rosenfarb & Hayes, 1984). That same analysis applies to "reasons" – those verbal formulations of cause and effect that we all use to regulate social influence over our behavior.

Reason giving was the focus of the very earliest ACT studies (e.g., Zettle & Hayes, 1986). Measures were created of reason giving, such as one by the late Neil Jacobson and his students (Addis et al., 1995). Studies were done to see if the amount or type of reason given related to psychological problems and treatment. It did. Powerfully. For example, Addis and Jacobson (1996) found that reason giving was associated with worse outcomes for behavioral activation for depression.

But as ACT became more sustained by traditional clinical psychology, this promising start slowed down. A bit more attention was paid to the technology of ACT as a form of psychotherapy and the psychological processes familiar to clinicians that sustain its impact, and a bit less to the sociocultural contexts that were from the beginning as important or even more so. Perhaps that was necessary in the context of the time (e.g., emphasizing randomized controlled trials, since that was the only way initially to get applied methods taken seriously in a mainstream healthcare setting), but it left certain analytic tasks undone.

As behavior analysts come back into the fray, it is natural for these previous threads to be re-engaged. Where do self-rules come from and how do they operate? What are the social-verbal contexts that predict whether or not private events impact overt behavior? Why is reason giving so impactful? We need to know the answers to such questions, and behavior analysis can provide them.

We bring a broad background to this task. Mark R. Dixon attended graduate school at the University of Nevada during Hayes' tenure, and has had a 20-plus year career within mainstream behavior analysis as a BCBA-D, attempting to broaden the field's usage of ACT and address these very concepts. Jordan Belisle did his graduate training at Southern Illinois University in the world's first master's degree program in ABA. He worked under the advisement of Dixon, and continues to push forward an understanding of how language is best defined. The three of us thus represent three generations of academics linked to central topics and centers in the field of behavior analysis.

Another coming contribution is more procedural. Modern day behavior analysts are brilliant at turning principles into procedural specificity. Behavioral programming can matter, and it's worth noting how procedurally clear ACT-based work becomes in the hands of BCBAs. A book like Dixon's (the first author of this book) *ACT for Children with Autism and Emotional Challenges* (2014) is far more procedurally specific than classical ACT books written for a clinical psychology audience (e.g., Hayes et al., 1999). The *Accept. Identify. Move* (AIM) (Dixon & Paliliunas, 2018) curriculum by the same author expands this specificity with tiered lesson planning and values-based contingency management systems that integrate what we have learned about ACT-based approaches with what we already know about client-centered contingency management systems. We will include a number of examples in Part 3 of this book from both of these technologies.

A third area is behavioral assessment. Because of the focus on overt behavior, measures of psychological flexibility processes in that domain are far more likely to emerge from behavior analysts than from mainstream psychological laboratories. Idiographic measures uncontaminated by unwarranted psychometric assumptions are much more routine in behavior analysis, and the steps needed to measure context and overt behavior are more familiar to them. As idiographic analyses become idionomic (that is, as they generalize to nomothetic statements that help increase idiographic clarity), it is behavior analysts who will feel most at home. There is so much to unpack and to learn about when we start applying what has evolved in the field of ABA to those procedures and processes that are ACT consistent and already supported in the empirical literature.

Our point is simply this. Yes, ACT and RFT have a great deal to contribute to modern day applied behavior analysis, but the reverse is also true. This is a major reason that this book is even being written. We want behavior analysts to benefit from ACT and RFT, but they also have a major future role in developing these approaches.

2

A Brief History of the Science Underlying ACT

There are thousands of applied behavior analysts around the globe who face the unsettling reality that their training and the elegant simplicity in the behavioral approach sometimes fail to live up to expectations when applied to complex cases. Yet what really is "complex" about complex cases?

In our work with behavior analysts around the world, we have found that in most cases complexity devolves into trying to understand how direct programmed contingencies and verbally constructed contingencies involving private behavioral events can be combined into a functional analysis that leads to a coherent intervention linked to that functional analysis. Combining functional factors in this way is indeed more complex, but it stops behavior analysts for a reason that goes beyond complexity per se.

Most behavior analysts understand that private events, at least from the days of B. F. Skinner forward, are supposed to be valid behavioral targets, but they soon find out this dirty secret: direct contingency accounts alone do not provide adequate analytic tools to address them. Most behavior analysts understand that mentalism and dualism should be avoided, but there is an uncomfortable sense that addressing private events in any way *other* than direct contingency accounts alone is "mentalistic." It is the two horns of this dilemma that freeze behavior analysts in place. In the current environment, behavior analysts are often asked to address behavioral phenomena without behavior analytic tools that may be capable of providing a more adequate account of these very behavioral phenomena.

The sad result is likely to be one of four "solutions" to the dilemma. Each applied at scale represents a resignation and failure of our field to rise to the challenges that we set forth to solve when the field began.

Solution 1. Force direct contingency analyses on the situation, good fit or not, and then refuse to notice or admit that it is not working.

Solution 2. Decline to address the needs of clients when private behavioral events are involved, redirecting all such requests to following the traditional behavior management plan.

Solution 3. Refer out these cases to social workers, pharmacotherapists, or others who claim to know what to do about them, even if what they do is in no way behavioral.

Or *Solution 4.* Perhaps worst of all, revert to lay language and "wing it" in ways that are almost certain to make the very mentalistic error behavior analysts are taught to avoid.

DOI: 10.4324/9781003250371-3

All of these so-called solutions are common in applied behavior analytic practice, yet none are really solutions at all.

This happens not just with clients – it happens when staff or behavior analysts themselves need help. When behavior analysts feel stressed or worried, when they ruminate or struggle emotionally, they often try to muscle through with direct contingency methods alone, or they do nothing, or they seek professional help from anyone *but* a behavior analyst, or they apply mentalistic solutions on their own and try to hide it from their peers. The results are predictably poor. But can we deal with complexity without making this mentalistic error while remaining within the scope of ABA practice?

Private events – worry, rumination, emotional upset – are directly observable actions but to an audience of one. The mentalistic error is not one of addressing these events, it is in treating them as causes and ignoring the contextual events that have given them unhelpful functions as part of an overall behavioral system. That is why we covered these mistakes in thinking through behavior-behavior relations in the last chapter: they are ubiquitous. It's not because the targets are private: you could make that same error with overt behavior alone! Sometimes we even do that, such as when we ascribe leadership abilities to, say, high levels of academic achievement without analyzing if, how, and why they might be connected. Private events just make this error such an easy one to make that it has been tagged with the "mentalistic" label. Skinner called them "mental way stations," and despite what behavior analysts are commonly told almost as bedtime stories, his complaint was not that they do not exist! He did not want the battle to be fought there. His objection was that these were non-functional "causes" that, like all behaviors, could not be manipulated directly. Only contextual events can be manipulated like that, and as such, experimental analysis is the only way to test for prediction and influence. That is why he called the field of behavior analysis the "experimental analysis of behavior."

Here is how Skinner explained these ideas: "The objection to the inner workings of the mind is not that they are not open to inspection but that *they have stood in the way of the inspection of more important things*" (Skinner, 1974, p. 165, emphasis added), and "mentalism has obscured the environmental antecedents which would have led to a much more *effective* analysis" (Skinner, 1974, p. 165, emphasis added). Said in another way, mentalism is a pragmatic error, not a mistake about what is "really there."

Earlier we introduced how behavior-behavior relations can interact in really simple ways, but these relations must eventually make contact with the environment in ways that elicit or evoke relations and in ways that reinforce and strengthen their future occurrence. We will review this diagram in more detail later, but for now this basic idea can be summarized as behavior 1 and behavior 2 interacting together, each providing the contextual condition for the next, indicated by bidirectional arrows. Behavior 1 here represents relational behavior (this can be private but not always), and behavior 2 represents the overt behavior that eventually contacts the external environment. Linked behaviors are not new. Behavior analysts already work with linked behaviors when chaining a new skill, linking the various elements of a well-constructed task analysis. Why then shouldn't we assume that similar "links" operate in this same way?

This does not mean abandoning the antecedent-behavior-consequence model. Quite the opposite. Interacting streams of private and public behavior occur within an antecedent context that evokes these actions and may elicit physiological or reflexive responses. Moreover, consequences that occur contingently on the overt behavior may operate to strengthen or weaken not only the external action but also the public and private behaviors that co-occur with it. Think about a recent time when you solved a problem by "thinking it through." It worked, right? If so, you may be more likely to try to solve a similar problem in this same general way (reinforcement). When it has not worked, new strategies are employed in

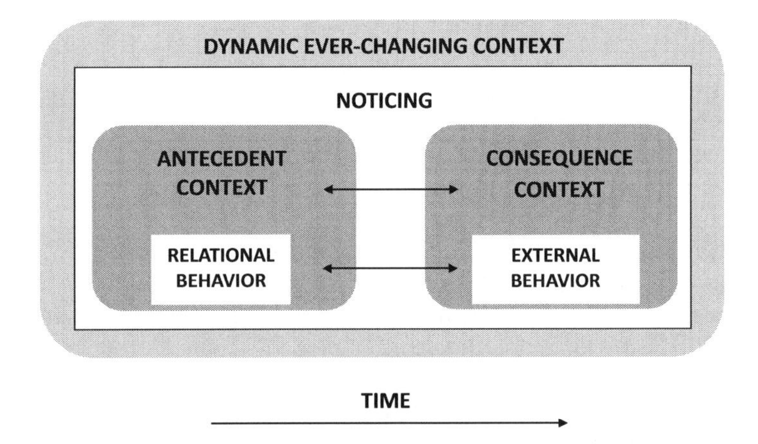

FIGURE 2.1 Dynamic ever-changing context.

the future (extinction induced variability). ACT challenges clients to notice these events (a behavior)! This too does not commit to the mentalistic error, because even the act of noticing is necessarily surrounded by a dynamic and ever-changing context of antecedent conditions and consequential functions extended over time (Figure 2.1).

Doing a fully adequate functional and contextual analysis when private events are involved is, however, challenging. We will argue in this book that Skinner himself got the details wrong because there were behavioral phenomena he did not know about. But the field has matured, and today these same complex cases are an opportunity to apply behavioral training and observational skills to the so-called inner world and to test out new behavioral ideas about how relational learning processes both uplift us and challenge us as people.

That is the approach we will try to train in this volume. We do not need to put aside any behavioral tools to do this. On the contrary, we need them all – but at a higher level of sophistication. Let's review the tools we will need, starting with the most obvious ones.

BEHAVIORAL PRINCIPLES AND A CONSERVATIVE APPROACH

Perhaps the most notable advantage behavior analysts have over others who seek to influence behavior is that all behavior analytic procedures return to a constrained and well-defined set of principles. For example, interventions to reduce self-injurious behavior (SIB) in children with autism, although varied in their topography, all generally assume that the behavior is maintained by positive or negative reinforcement. Operant extinction procedures for self-injury involve ensuring that what is reinforcing this undesirable behavior is no longer delivered contingently of the occurrence of the behavior. Differential reinforcement for SIB involves providing the functional reinforcer for another behavior or the omission of self-injury. Functional communication training seeks to build a new communicative response (likely, using positive reinforcement) that serves as an alternative behavior to SIB. In all of these examples, the behavior analyst is creating positive change by extending basic principles to a concrete behavioral phenomenon.

Extending from basic principles is an approach that is shared across all of the natural sciences (e.g., biology, chemistry). It is one of many consistencies between behavior analysis and other scientific disciplines. In all mature natural sciences, the goal is to apply principles in a highly *precise* way that does not distort their meaning, and to do so across a range of seemingly different situations (showing the *scope* of these principles). Furthermore, it is understood that basic principles should fit together across scientific levels of analysis such that, say, chemistry never violates principles of physics, showing the *depth* of these principles. When all three of these qualities are regularly present, a strong and progressive scientific program is being developed.

That is what we want in behavior analysis. We want principles that tell us how to manage behavior change, and to do so with precision, scope, and depth. When intervention options emerge that appear to open up new avenues of behavior change, it is important to seek a conceptual understanding of these methods and to make sure that basic principles are being applied without distortion, and that they truly apply across situations and levels of analysis. Such a conservative scientific stance identifies and builds on the benefits of analytic consistency, gradually validating the scope and depth of precisely applied principles. It is not often talked about this way but when a conservative approach is properly applied, it has another benefit: it is more obvious when *new* principles are needed. It is not helpful to allow basic principles to be distorted in order to maintain a superficial consistency across situations. That greatly slows scientific progress.

With any extensive and well-developed new technology comes new terms, but it is important not to conflate this with truly new behavioral processes. The latest smartphone appears on the surface vastly different from the flip-phones of yesterday – and is capable of doing more than we ever thought imaginable even ten years ago; however, at the heart are the same core design principles of electrical circuitry and computational programming. The same applies to behavior change technology.

This book is about acceptance and commitment therapy, or acceptance and commitment training. ACT extends from the same foundational principles of behavior as the technologies that applied behavior analysts are already accustomed to using, with one major exception: ACT embraces the existence of relational operants as a core explanation of human verbal behavior. That core conclusion from RFT is itself thundering into verbal training programs in ABA, and the Promoting Emergence of Advanced Knowledge (PEAK) system (Dixon, 2014, 2015, 2016) is a major reason why. Adding relational operant training to training in Skinner's verbal operants is now known to considerably speed up language acquisition and performance – a fact that is altering the practice of BCBAs worldwide (Dixon et al., 2017).

Relational operants are, we believe, now a well-established empirical fact in basic and applied behavior analysis. No new principles or needed to account for operants of this kind, since the idea of purely functional operants is as old as operant psychology itself and extends directly from Skinner's concept of operant conditioning as well as the functional views of many other behavior theorists such as Charles Catania, Alan Neuringer, Don Baer, and many others.

Conservative work in RFT has disentangled much of what is new about human verbal behavior and what is not. As an empirical fact, relational operants change how direct contingencies and stimulus pairings operate. For example, if a person learns in a matching to sample setting that "A is less than B and B is less than C" and B is then paired with shock, A will elicit less arousal and C will elicit more arousal than B (e.g., Dougher et al., 2007). Relational operants are "two-way streets" that alter the operant and classically conditioned stimulus functions of events based on their participation in derived stimulus relations. There is no name for such an effect. It is the impact of relational operants that requires new principles to describe their effects, not their existence per se.

When new principles are needed, we should add only what is needed to account for behavior without any distortion of existing behavioral principles. That is what has been done in ACT and RFT. The small adjustment of accounting for the impact of relational operants allows behavior analysts to open up the field – and consequentially their own practice – to solving behavior challenges that have been ignored within our discipline.

Consider the inactivity or lethargy associated with "depression." You do not need the syndromal label to think about these overt behaviors, and indeed there is an impressive history of behaviorists such as Charles Ferster (1973) or Peter Lewinsohn (1974) attempting to do so. The same with the avoidance of family and friends associated with social anxiety disorders. You do not need to treat psychiatric disorders to look at social avoidance. There is no reason for applied behavior analysts to shy away from addressing overeating that causes obesity and poor physical health; exercise to prevent heart disease; stopping smoking; improving social relationships and so on and so on.

All of these issues are behavioral problems that call out for behavioral solutions. All represent socially valid behavior change targets, yet behavior analysts are seldom sought to provide the solution. What ACT has done is to show how to proceed in such areas, using only behavioral principles as expanded by RFT and as nested within evolutionary science.

A growing research base on ACT, conducted inside and outside of behavioral journals, has supported this approach as a way to influence these behaviors and many others – typically with maintained outcomes when the intervention is withdrawn. There are now over 300 meta-analyses of ACT touching almost every area of behavior change (see bit.ly/ACTmetas); and over 900 randomized controlled trials (bit.ly/ACTRCTs), and thousands of open trials, single-case designs, and studies of processes of change (Hayes, 2019). These outcomes are achieved in ways that largely fit the model (Ren et al., 2019; Stockton et al., 2019), making it possible to construct broadly applicable change methods that extend from principles of behavior change. ACT fits the defining features of applied behavior analysis and thus should be thought of as a behavioral method that belongs in the behavior analytic tool kit (Dixon et al., 2020)

It arrives none too soon. Behavior analysts have often been ill-equipped and ill-prepared to implement intervention methods that address important areas of human functioning, especially when private events are involved. The result has been a field overly restricted to treating directly observable behavior with children severely impacted by autism or other language-related disabilities.

Learning ACT is not just about moving outside of autism service provision. The needs of traditional populations for BCBAs also require a larger set of methods. For persons with autism and typical range intelligence test scores, we see levels of anxiety, depressed mood, and suicidal thoughts or actions far exceeding that of their same-age peers (Dell'Osso et al., 2019; Segers & Rawana, 2014). Narrowly focused direct contingency technologies have also been less effective than is needed in addressing the chronic stress, worry, and self-doubt that comes with being a parent of a child, with or without a disability. Early research has established that ACT can be effective when embedded within parent training protocols to change the kinds of outcomes that BCBAs have historically avoided (Chua & Shorey, in press; Juvin et al., 2021). Learning to use ACT does not require a radical shift in our field or how we view it, but it will require a willingness to explore new ways to implement behavior analytic procedures and principles, and to consider how relational learning and derived stimulus relations interact with direct contingency learning processes that are far older on the evolutionary time scale.

Our goal in this book is thus to link ACT to well-established behavior analytic principles and processes and to help behavior analysts see how to include ACT in their practice. Accomplishing this aim can be helped by revisiting the core assumptions of radical behaviorism and how this extends directly from within an evolutionary account. Such a broad focus allows us to see overt behavior change in its larger context.

Interestingly, this does not require straying further from our roots. Rather, when we approach behavior in this way, we are much closer to the radical behavioral and biological/evolutionary assumptions that operated as the initial conditions of our field.

RADICAL BEHAVIORISM AND EXTENDING THE EVOLUTIONARY ACCOUNT

Radical behaviorism is a set of philosophical assumptions that underlies both the experimental analysis of behavior and ABA. The ACT community has slightly modified these assumptions under the banner of "functional contextualism." The changes are minor. They include adding the need for precision, scope, and depth of accounts as we have already emphasized in this book – clarifying what has always been the case within behavior analysis. The words "prediction and control" are changed to the clearer terms "prediction and influence" and are described as the goals of *our* science, rather than the goals of all science more generally, thus avoiding needless offense to scientists who may have different goals. According to a functional contextual or radical behavioral worldview, behavior can be understood functionally as the on-going interaction between behavior and environment. Psychological events are always the "acts-in-context" of whole organisms. Context refers to the history and current circumstances of the individual. This position is inherently monistic: although there are private events, there is no "mental world" outside of the natural world and reach of scientific inquiry.

At its heart, the radical (or functional contextual) wing of behaviorism represents an extension of pragmatism as an overarching approach to science. It has its roots in a philosophy of science extending from William James, John Dewey, and others, including John B. Watson. Pragmatism adopts an approach to science that seeks successful solutions to simple and complex problems. A "theory" is not considered adequate because of its complexity, elegance, or structure; rather, a good theory is one that works. This approach applies an evolutionary account to the behavior of scientists themselves – that is what is "radical" about it. It is "radical" because it is "to the root" not because it is extreme. Pragmatic theories are thus only ever provisionally "good" – they hope to be eventually replaced by newer and better ideas that either solve new problems or solve old problems more efficiently.

Dewey is one of the founding fathers of Western pragmatism, and Watson was his student early in his education and is considered the founding father of behaviorism as an approach to psychology. Watson was a behaviorist in a metaphysical sense (he rejected the idea of a mental life outside of the actions of organisms) and in a methodological sense in that he believed that a science of behavior must focus on behavior that can be directly observed. This represented a significant departure from an introspective psychology that was prominent at the time, focusing on consciousness and rationality instead of observing how people react to their world.

Watson's approach largely focused on reflex relations and emphasized respondent or "classical" conditioning as the primary behavior change process. While respondent conditioning still plays a considerable part in the experimental analysis of behavior and can explain part of why we react the way that we do to specific situations, Skinner directed the behavioral tradition more toward operant conditioning. Operant conditioning is a direct extension from Darwin's theory of natural selection. Whereas phenotypes are selected by survival, resulting in speciation, behavior is selected by its consequences, resulting in behavioral habits and repertoires. Reinforcement and punishment serve as selection mechanisms and establishing operations as a form of selection pressure – evolutionary processes on a shorter time scale. We now know this is not a metaphor because environment and behavior up- and down-regulate gene expression through epigenetic mechanisms. That was not known to Skinner, and evolutionists of the time often ridiculed Skinner's idea, but in hindsight he was far more right than he was wrong.

EVOLUTION AND THE FUNCTION OF BEHAVIOR

Behavior analysis is a field with its feet placed in two related disciplines: psychology and biology. Behavior analysts measure and analyze patterns in human behavior within a historical and situational context, but unlike many psychologists such situated actions are not studied as an internal manifestation of mental structures. Behavior analysts view humans as biophysical organisms that evolved from previous species but, unlike many biologists, view ontogenetic evolution as of equal importance to phylogenetic evolution and thus are resistant to structural accounts, as we covered in the last chapter.

Skinner was especially clear in fighting for the role of ontogenetic evolution as a legitimate part of the evolutionary sciences. The abstract of his 1981 article in *Science* on selection by consequences reads:

> Selection by consequences is a causal mode found only in living things, or in machines made by living things. It was first recognized in natural selection, but it also accounts for the shaping and maintenance of the behavior of the individual and the evolution of cultures. In all three of these fields, it replaces explanations based on the causal modes of classical mechanics. The replacement is strongly resisted. Natural selection has now made its case, but similar delays in recognizing the role of selection in the other fields could deprive us of valuable help in solving the problems which confront us.
>
> *(p. 501)*

Skinner was saying that genetic evolution, individual learning, and cultural change are all actions that must be explained not solely based on the physical make-up of the organism ("the causal modes of classical mechanics") but rather based on the role of variation and selection in the interaction between the organism and the environment spread across time. In the final sentence of his final paper, finished the very evening before he died, Skinner's (1990) last words were directed to the profound implications of evolutionary science for behavior analysis: "A better understanding of variation and selection will mean a more successful profession, but whether behavior analysis will be called psychology is a matter for the future to decide." (p. 1210).

In this book we take that last sentence seriously, and it is worth a brief restatement so that ACT and RFT can be seen as an attempt to elaborate the connection between behavioral science and evolution. It helps extend behavioral principles to ACT if we understand that Darwinian evolution depends on six basic features that can be summarized with the acronym "VRSCDL" (roughly pronounced "versatile"): *Variation and Retention of what is Selected in a Context at the right Dimension and Level.*

Variation and Selective Retention

A core of all evolutionary accounts is concern with variation and selective retention. Darwin knew nothing of genetics but realized that particular offspring vary in features that might produce differential rates of survival in given contexts, and if these were passed down by hereditary lines, that simple mechanism could be the origin of a species. For example, if severe drought meant that only birds with strong beaks could crack open a limited but available food source, such as dried seeds, these beak variants would be selected by differential survival rates and spread throughout the subsequent population. Mutations can increase the range of variants available. Most are relatively minor and many are disadvantageous, but some provide greater survival or mating potential. When members of the species with the mutation are more likely to survive and reproduce, they are more likely to transmit the mutation or variant to successive members who are in turn more likely to propagate the genetic information to successive generations. Through a combination of migration, environmental pressures, and chance, physical and behavioral variants (what biologists call "phenotypes") and even new species may emerge, providing a naturalistic explanation of life on earth and its enormous variety and complexity. Variation is initially blind, but regulation of variation itself can evolve – for example, bacteria that are deprived of a crucial nutrient immediately start varying at much higher rates in their reproduction (Hersh et al., 2004).

In behavior analysis, variation is also a given because it is the seed corn of selection. As a comedian once said, if you always do what you've always done, you'll always get what you've always got. As in biological evolution, variation can also initially be blind, but it can also be a side effect of behavioral principles, such as in the burst of variation that is produced by extinction, or when reinforcement is provided for behavioral variation itself (e.g., Neuringer, 2002), or when rules that restrict needed variability are undermined. Selection occurs when an aspect of survival or success is achieved in the interaction between the organism and the environment, altering the likelihood of variants reoccurring. In behavior analysis, reinforcement is an example. Retention occurs via such things as physical changes in the organism (e.g., in genetic evolution when DNA is passed on through reproduction and replication), which in behavior analysis may involve retention through behavioral habits and the strength of operant classes. What programs this whole process is the context within which behavior occurs. In natural selection, "selection pressures" determine life and death outcomes; in behavior analysis the internal and external environment are the contingencies that lead to the selective retention of action.

Context

"Context" is implicit in variation and selective retention, but it needs to be added explicitly if evolutionary principles are to be a guide to applied intervention. In biology, context determines the selection pressures that operate on variants. When a moth that stands out from its background is eaten by a bird, that is context for gradual changes in the coloration of moth species. The same applies to behavioral evolution within the life span, and an applied person thus needs to think about whether, say, behavioral changes produced by an applied program will be sustained by natural contingencies in the social environment faced by clients. Applied evolutionary science is a small and recent field, which is why behavior analysts are so much more used to thinking of how to change contextual events than biological evolutionists are. We *are* the field that has attempted to alter variation and selection by manipulating the context within which variation and selection occur. We have done so successfully in some applications, and that is nothing to scoff at. In the history of our species, the ability to alter our own context to select for and retain behaviors that are more advantageous to ourselves and to our species is a major leap forward, and we are the field that did it. But why stop at simplicity? There are so many challenges that we still need to solve.

Dimensions and Levels

Variations can succeed or fail at different levels of organizational complexity. A cancerous cell that can evade the immune system and succeed in unregulated growth can bring down a multicellular organism. A selfish and deceitful worker can get rich while causing a business to fail. Multilevel selection means that selection is occurring at multiple levels of organization simultaneously, and thus the behavior analyst may need to think at the level of an operant, a repertoire, or a culture practice all at the same time.

In addition, at any one level of organization there are multiple specific dimensions that may be involved. At the level of the biological organism, we may need to attend to organ systems, brain circuits, and genetics; at a psychological level we may need to distinguish contingency-shaped behavior or rule-governance, among other behavioral dimensions.

Darwin realized that variative and selective retention occurs simultaneously across multiple dimensions and levels, such as biology and culture. Skinner pointed to three areas of selection: genetics, behavior, and culture. Others have argued (e.g., Jablonka & Lamb, 2014) – and we agree – that relational learning establishes a new contingency stream that interacts with those three. It is important to note that all of these levels and dimensions are interacting. For example, operant learning processes have profoundly altered how genetic evolution works. By the Cambrian period (more than half a billion years ago) operant and classical conditioning allowed animals to seek out or construct specific niches based on reinforcement (e.g., an animal could seek out an environment with preferred food resources). This process was likely the source of the "Cambrian explosion," as operant behavior led to distinct selection pressures, which then resulted in the evolution of characteristic phenotypes (Ginsburg & Jablonka, 2010). For example, once generations of a particular breed of bird were digging in river mud to find edible crustaceans, the evolution of the scoop-shaped and filtering structures of the flamingoes' beak could occur due to variation and selection (Schneider, 2012). Operant learning thus served as a kind of "ladder of evolution" (Bateson, 2014), and far from behavior and learning being just the passive result of biological evolution, it has instead been the driver of it.

In many ways, that is also a core idea of behavior analysis: how to use behavioral principles to evolve on purpose, culturally at least and perhaps even biologically. It is the opening argument of Skinner's *Beyond Freedom and Dignity*. It is the core of his article "Why Are We Not Acting to Save the World?"

If we understand how contingencies of reinforcement and punishment and relational learning interact, we can help our clients "evolve on purpose" by developing repertoires that serve their long-term interests by addressing the complexity of human functioning. But evolution is always on-going, and here we begin to touch on what is different about ACT, behaviorally speaking.

RELATIONAL FRAME THEORY AND TRANSFORMATIONS OF STIMULUS FUNCTION

A challenge with the strategy of looking for behavior change principles in non-human animals to infer behavior change principles in humans is that species-specific phylogenic differences can be ignored in the account. Consider the situation where a person is put into a discrimination study involving magnetization, where they are required to engage in a response whenever the magnet is turned on and avoid the response when the magnet is turned off. We know that sharks can engage in discriminated responding in this arrangement (Klimley, 1993) because they rely on magnetization for navigation. Humans, however, simply lack the equipment – we did not evolve magnetoreceptors. No schedule of reinforcement will produce magnetic discrimination in a human because of our phylogenic history.

Evolutionary continuity is temporal and organizational: new likely contains old and complex contains simple. If the reverse was the case, evolution could not work, since biological evolution is a tree, not a ladder, and when we look across the tips of evolutionary branches we are looking both backward in time and forward in time – back to a common ancestor and forward to the present day. We do not know if something may be new that impacts the performance being studied when comparing two species, and if such things do exist we will not likely find them in relatively barren environments far from the evolutionary niches of particular species. That is one reason psychobiologists and ethologists tended to view Skinner so harshly as evolutionarily naïve.

He wasn't. One of his first published studies (Barnes & Skinner, 1930) was on tropism in ants. Skinner was not interested in non-human animals for their own sake – he studied rats and pigeons as a way of getting to principles that would be applicable to human complexity. Skinner knew full well that his strategy of seeking generally applicable principles with simple responses in relatively barren environments across species might fail. It was a strategic risk, but he argued that absorption into the commonsense features of human complexity was by far the greater danger. He gambled that if there indeed are learning processes that have been passed along for millions of years, his strategic approach would find them, but he never argued that they *must* exist, only that they *might* exist and, as his approach progressed, that they *do* exist.

It turns out that he was right. The principles of operant and classical conditioning apply to all organisms that have evolved since about 545 million years ago (Ginsburg & Jablonka, 2010). There were even earlier learning processes (e.g., habituation and sensitization), but it was operant and classical conditioning that really changed the pathway of evolution, since these processes meant that now organisms could seek out specific niches based on learning and thus alter selection pressures in a massive way.

When special abilities are noticed, it is common to start with the physical phenotype and then explain the behavior. For example, a cheetah's running speed will be used to explain its predation strategy, or a flamingo's odd beak will explain its feeding patterns, but that approach is usually a mistake. These physical features co-evolved with environment and behavior, which is better viewed as the driver of evolution. The reinforcing effect of small crustaceans caused many generations of flamingoes to be exposed to the selection processes that evolved their odd beak shape and structure (Schneider, 2012). As those physical forms occurred, other evolutionary steps were possible. The wings of the small dinosaurs that we now call birds likely evolved for temperature regulation, not flight.

The special cases of operant and classical conditioning, that have evolved over the more than half a billion years that these processes have been in place, also make that same point. Taste aversion – learning to avoid food that makes you sick even if sickness comes several hours later – is now almost universally treated as a special case of classical conditioning (Welzl et al., 2001). It is a temporally distorted form of course, but it is easy to imagine how this temporal distortion evolved. Suppose a food source that is in an animal's environment is poisonous. Suppose that on average it causes the animal to throw up 25 minutes later, and half of the animals eating it will die. Members of that species that could associate the taste of that food with a sickness that came 25 minutes later would avoid further exposure and be more likely to survive in that environment than an organism that could only associate the taste and the illness over, say, 15 minutes and thus might eat the same toxic food again. Since that 25-minute window is more like a distribution curve than an on-and-off switch, longer and longer temporal delays would naturally evolve as the relative degrees of food safety produced by classical conditioning take hold. There are neurobiological structures needed for specialized learning of this kind, but structures do not evolve in order to do things the organism is not doing. The long neck of a giraffe did not evolve in order to eat leaves high up in trees. Rather, individuals with slightly longer necks in an animal species that was eating leaves in trees were more likely to survive and reproduce, passing the physical trait along to offspring.

Consider the systems that we know support what you are doing right now: reading a book. You have a cerebral cortex with considerable surface area and a frontal and prefrontal cortex with exceptional complexity. We do not know exactly why these neurobiological features evolved in humans, but we do know that the frontal and prefrontal cortex (the "executive functioning" areas of the brain) have been neurologically linked to problem solving and to other actions that involve language. Cerebral cortical areas also participate in the complex cooperative social behaviors that we see in humans. Rats, pigeons, and sharks are unlikely to develop a social network of such a complexity – they simply lack the equipment. But it is also equally true that earlier levels of complex social and problem-solving behaviors may have been important enough to the social primates called hominins (that is, to humans and extinct human species) to have provided a selection pressure for the establishment of the neurobiological structures needed for such behavior as we see it today. We can consider this issue in a more sophisticated way once we drill a bit deeper into human language itself.

Ontogeny describes the changes that occur within the lifespan of the organism, and regardless of phylogenic affordances, behavior may still need to be shaped. The stories of feral children supported the important role of context in directing cognitive and social behaviors, such as John Liège in 1600s England who was lost by his parents in the woods. Reports of bizarre behavior resembling non-human animals surfaced, such as walking on all fours and strong foraging skills, and the boy demonstrated no discernable language or communication. Scientific interest in feral children increased in the 18th and 19th centuries. An example is "Peter the Wild Boy" who was also found in the wild and was subsequently raised by King George I of the English royalty. Like John, Peter showed incredibly adept survival skills like rummaging and foraging, but with significant language learning deficits. Cases such as these suggested that a complex brain is not enough to account for language and cognitive development – a social context immersed in language is needed to develop many of the skills that we all take for granted.

In the previous chapter we began to describe how Skinner provided a first behavioral model to account for the development of human language in *Verbal Behavior* (1957). This theoretical account was written without direct experimental work with human subjects and represented an extension of operant theory to account for language learning. His model emphasizes the role of direct reinforcement in language learning. For example, manding emerges when the speaker engages in a response specifying a reinforcer that is strengthened when the reinforcer is delivered by the listener. Tacting occurs when the speaker labels an object in the environment and receives generalized reinforcement from the listener. Applied research extending from this account followed targeting elementary verbal operants that were relatively simple, such as tacting, manding, echoics, and intraverbals, and this research was largely focused on interventions for individuals with disabilities, such as autism, that impact language learning.

This is not to say that Skinner claimed all verbal behavior was directly reinforced – he did not. But his account did not give us specific enough information to translate into a useable technology for behavior analysts. Research on traditional Skinnerian operants did not readily extend to complex forms of verbal behavior such as those involved in reasoning, thinking, humor, storytelling, perspective-taking, and so on, which left applied behavior analysts in a tough spot.

Murray Sidman (1971; Sidman & Tailby, 1982) cracked the code on a core feature of human functioning – the fact that derived relations can emerge without direct reinforcement of specific instances. He called what he found "stimulus equivalence."

Imagine that a person is taught that the word "dog" is spelled D-O-G and then reads that a D-O-G refers to a physical dog (four legs, furry, barks). That person will then be likely to also say "dog" when shown the text D-O-G and write the text D-O-G when shown a picture of a dog. This process is referred to as symmetry and represents the simplest form of a derived relation. Direct reinforcement with a specific word or object is not needed for most people to make this relation – it could easily be repeated with unfamiliar objects such as a metronome. Most people will also derive that the word "dog" refers to the physical dog and say "dog" when shown a picture of dog and asked, "what is this?" Sidman referred to these as transitive and equivalence relations respectively, where the derived relation and instance of verbal behavior emerges based on a shared relationship of these stimuli with a common stimulus (i.e., D-O-G). We could substitute any verbal, textual, or pictorial stimuli into this same basic arrangement and get the same outcome – as have been shown in literally hundreds of studies. A simple three-member equivalence class can readily be extended to several more members with each additional member exponentiating the number of relations that are derived.

Behavior analysts may be familiar with directly reinforced relations as identified by solid arrows in a basic three-image diagram (Figure 2.2): here "dog" (A) to D-O-G (B) (A–B) and D-O-G (B) to the physical dog (C) (B–C). Dashed arrows represent the derived relations (that emerge without need of direct reinforcement), including the symmetrical relations B–A and C–B in this case, as well as the transitive A–C relation and demonstrating equivalence with the bidirectional C–A relation. Together, these relations constitute an equivalence class and provide a first example of "Rel-B" expressed in the earlier figure. Rel-B stands for "Relational Behavior" and includes equivalence relations as a starting point.

Stimulus equivalence was a major leap in our understanding of human language and cognition – and it appears that Sidman may have arrived at a functional pattern of behavior that is uniquely or at least especially human. Despite repeated attempts to model transitive and equivalence relations in non-human animals, they have never been shown to engage in this pattern of behavior at the same complexity as humans. Half a century after it was first described, there are no generally accepted empirical demonstrations of stimulus equivalence in non-human animals. There are, however, good demonstrations of stimulus equivalence in human infants (Lipkens et al., 1993; Luciano et al., 2007).

Equivalence-based instruction is today an accepted part of the skill set for applied behavior analysts. While that is good, and stimulus equivalence is a great starting point, there are two major pieces of the puzzle left unsolved if we stop at stimulus equivalence.

First, stimulus equivalence is a finding but not an account. How did this ability evolve? What are the contextual conditions that are necessary for derived relational responding to emerge? Without an answer to these questions, we are left without a method to strengthen

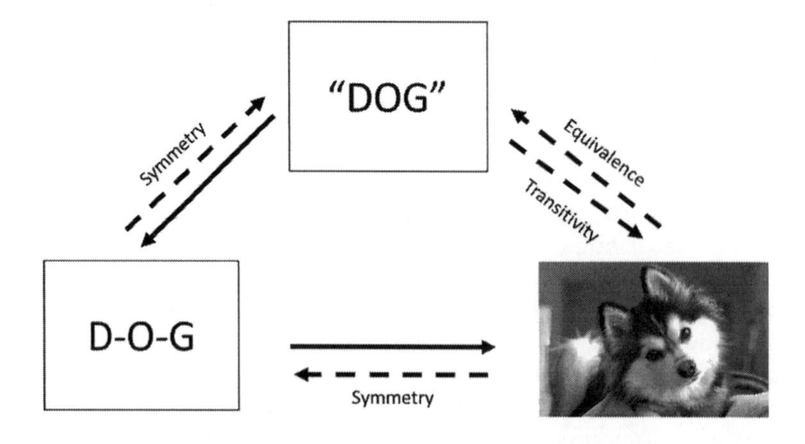

FIGURE 2.2 Stimulus equivalence diagram.

derived relational responding if it is absent, such as is the case for some individuals with severe disabilities. Metaphorically, we are in a similar situation as researchers on taste aversion before they understood that this was just a special case of classical conditioning. Once that was understood it was easier to modify it when need be (e.g., to avoid unwanted side effects of cancer treatment on food consumption by avoiding pairing with novel tastes).

Secondly, not all relations are "the same." A stimulus can be bigger or smaller than another stimulus, faster or slower, or can contain or be contained by other stimuli, just to name a few. As humans deal with more and more complex situations – those requiring abilities that lead to reasoning, thinking, humor, storytelling, perspective-taking and so on – it gets hard to imagine how to deal with these situations using only direct contingencies and equivalence alone. Try to ask a friend for help with your house and backyard while you are absent on a vacation, using only stimulus equivalence, and you will realize the problem. If derived relations are important in human behavior, how can we address these other kinds?

Those two limitations leave behavior analysts without a method for altering patterns of derived responding when these patterns lead people to suffer. RFT and its extension into ACT arguably solves both of these theoretical shortcomings.

How does derived relational responding emerge from a contextualist account? The answer RFT provides is highly compatible with Skinner's initial verbal behavior model and with the history of behavior analysis. We derive relations because we have a history of reinforcement for deriving relations as a generalized operant pattern of behavior. The idea that "___ is an operant" is the shortest and simplest of all possible behavioral theories, and it applies to RFT. The core of RFT is simply the claim that *relating is an operant*. That general claim translates in the case of stimulus equivalence to *equivalencing is an operant*. In the case of comparisons, it becomes *comparing is an operant*. And so on.

Consider something like generalized imitation, or the simple theoretical idea that *imitating is an operant*. At first, each instance of imitation likely requires direct reinforcement; however, after multiple exemplars are reinforced, a person can imitate essentially any movement or action that the person is capable of performing. The behavior becomes topographically boundless.

Figure 2.3 shows how this might occur in the context of developing relational verbal classes as a generalized operant. We do not simply derive relations because "doing so is rational"; rather, verbal relations influence changes in external behavior (Ext-B) that makes contact with contingencies of reinforcement. When we can derive information about the environment without being directly taught, more often than not, this allows us to contact reinforcement and to avoid punishment. Early in development, these initial instances of deriving relations are likely directly reinforced, either by solving simple problems or by social praise from family. As these examples of deriving relations add up, doing this can occur readily and lead to predictable changes in overt behavior and a generalized pattern of contacting reinforcement and avoiding punishment *by* deriving relations.

If this strategy is so effective, why does it appear that humans are the only animal on the planet capable of deriving immensely complex verbal relations? This is for the same reason that humans rarely adapt by pecking objects – chance variation and selection at the phylogenic level did not result in our having a triangular hardened bone at the end of our face (colloquially, a beak) that we can smash into things and maneuver in elegant and sophisticated ways. What the chance evolution of our species *did* accomplish is a deeply networked frontal and parietal cortical brain structure that appears to be where deriving may occur (e.g., Dickins et al., 2001; Schlund et al., 2007). That is not to say that we need to appeal to neural structures as an explanation any more than "having a beak and beaks peck" is a sufficient explanation. We seek a functional explanation, and functional explanations necessarily assume that operant responses are topographically boundless.

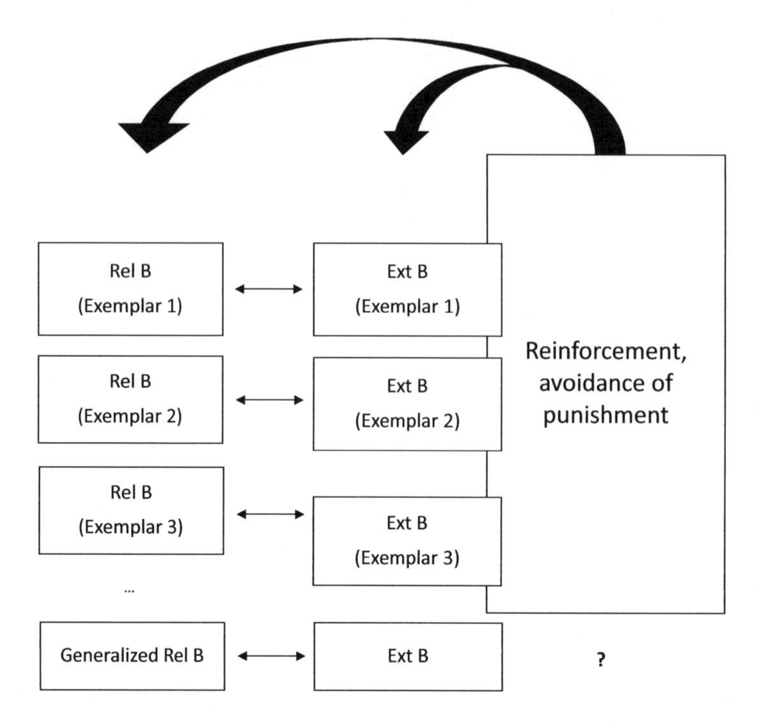

FIGURE 2.3 Developing relational verbal classes as a generalized operant.

The idea of topographical boundless operants can initially seem odd to behavior analysts, but really it shouldn't because an operant is a functional unit, not a topographical one. Operants can be of any size or shape that transition the world from one state of affairs to another. Skinner described seeing as an operant, or driving to the beach as an operant. Behavior analysts have trained porpoises to engage in novel tricks as an operant (Pryor et al., 1969) or to respond randomly on a keyboard as an operant (Neuringer, 1986). By definition, novel behavior or a random sequence cannot be defined as a topography.

There is no a priori reason that has ever been specified that would *prevent* derived relational responding from emerging in much the same way, and now, over several decades after this simple idea was presented at ABAI (Hayes & Brownstein, 1985), there are several hundred empirical studies that comport with the idea and none that contradict it. Whereas relatively simple instances of deriving relations or inference are reinforced at first, after multiple exemplars, deriving relations occurs readily within a wide range of stimulus arrangements – it becomes automatic. This likely account of early formation of derived relational responding fits with why, for example, feral children are unlikely to demonstrate this type of response: the environment necessarily supports its development.

RFT is notoriously said to be hard to understand, but that is because (a) language about language is hard and feels inherently abstract, (b) we need a handful of specialized terms to describe what a derived relation is and how it applies to a range of specific types of relation, and (c) relational operants operate on other behavioral processes. Hanging on to the core of the theory – relating is an operant – can anchor these discussions, especially for applied behavior analysts who are used to thinking of behavioral phenomena, such as imitation, in a more purely functional and behavioral way.

RFT deals with the issue of "sameness" by introducing contextual cues that specify the type of relationship between two stimuli. A can be "equal" to B, but A can also be "more than" B. And, if A is "more than" B and if B is "more than" C, we can also derive that A is "more than" C and C is "less than" A. Relational contextual cues can specify a variety of relations that have been modelled in the basic experimental research, such as frames based on coordination (sameness), distinction (difference), comparison (relative property), opposition (opposite), spatial (relative space), temporal (relative time), hierarchical (categories), and deictics (perspective taking). Once that is clear, the stimulus equivalence concepts of symmetry and transitivity have to be tweaked so they can apply to all such relations: symmetry is a specific case of *mutual entailment*, and transitivity/equivalence a special case of *combinatorial entailment*. These are said to be qualities of derived relational responding.

An example of a more elaborate set of relations than the equivalence class above is shown in Figure 2.4. First, we say that the spoken word dog and the textual word dog are mutually entailed. They refer to the same thing. However, what they refer to is not this singular image of a dog or even just dogs that look like this dog as might be inferred from the figure. Dog is a hierarchical term that contains a myriad of different dog breeds that contain more or less similar features (four legs, long nose, wagging tails). However, just because any and all of these animals can be referred to as "dogs," we cannot simply assume that they are all the same. As illustrated in this example, some dogs are *bigger* than other dogs, where "bigger" is the contextual cue that specifies the relation. We can derive therefore that some dogs are "smaller" than other dogs. Given knowledge of how two dogs are related to a third dog, we can make assumptions about the relationship between the two dogs, even if they have never been directly compared (combinatorial entailment). What this gives us is a much more complete and elaborate understanding of what a dog is and illustrates the importance of expanding the traditional equivalence account for a much more elaborate and accurate account of relational behavior (Rel-B).

Of course, the diagram shows images of dogs, and something like relative size can be inferred without the need for language per se. But this could be easily illustrated by using names of dogs, such as "Chihuahua" or "Mastiff." These names are not formally similar to the physical stimuli to which they refer. Yet given information that a chihuahua is smaller

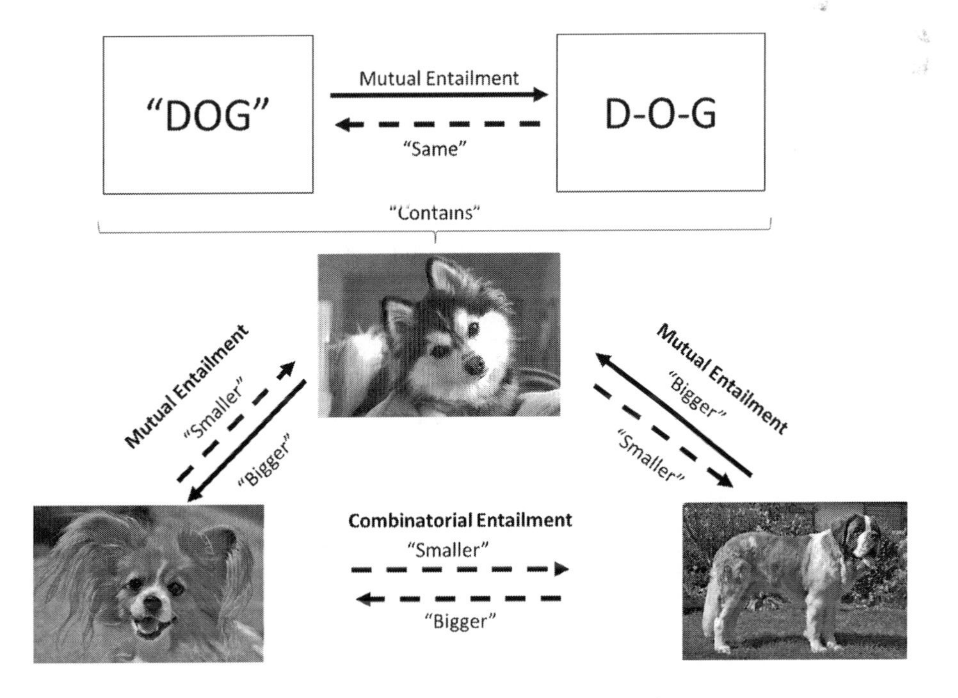

FIGURE 2.4 Relational contextual cues diagram.

than a husky and a mastiff is bigger than a husky, most people will derive that the chihuahua is also smaller than the mastiff and that the mastiff is larger than the chihuahua, even if they have never seen these dogs breeds before. Thus, once language enters into the equation, verbal relations can be entirely arbitrary.

Relational contextual cues can be applied in some instances based on social whim or convention. We can say that "mal" is the opposite of "good" in Spanish, or we could say that "gibbity" is the opposite of "good" in a language we made up. When relational operants can be brought to bear based on related events based on social whim or convention, derived relational responding becomes "arbitrarily applicable derived relational responding." That is such a mouthful that most RFT researchers just called it "AARR" or "AARRing" if they want to maintain its status as a gerund. As a class AARRing might include non-arbitrary instances (a mouse "is smaller than" an elephant), but the test of arbitrary applicability is that the same relational contextual cues be applied to any stimulus set (e.g., "a nickel is smaller than a dime" which is not true in a formal or topographical sense).

The last concept that we need to visit before progressing is something called the transformation of stimulus function. Transformations of stimulus function are central to understanding how relational frames could affect behavior that we are interested in influencing through behavioral intervention. To continue with the dog example above, imagine that a person is subsequently bitten by a dog. Because functions can be transformed based on verbal relations, we could anticipate that this same person may feel anxious when they hear the word "dog," such as being told "I have a pet dog and I would love for you to meet her," or when reading the word D-O-G in a book or magazine. We interact with words and symbols in the same way that we interact with stimuli that are physically present. These words and symbols can be externally present or, in the case of thinking, internally present, adding even greater complexity to how we interact with our own relational behavior.

The reason why we need to call this "transformation" is that the functions that are altered by relational framing are dependent on the specific underlying relational frame. If you were asked "what does an ice cream cone taste like" you might smile and point to a dish of pudding. If you were asked "what does the opposite of an ice cream cone taste like" you might grimace at the taste of dirt in your mouth and point to a bowl of dirt. The term "taste" is a context that selects the gustatory functions of ice cream cones (and not, say, what they look like), but the affectively positive taste of ice cream can be flipped into negative tastes by the underlying verbal relation. (You should only be so lucky that what occurs to you is dirt and not dog poop!)

Transformation of stimulus function is where we see the interplay between Rel-B and Ext-B, or relational behavior and observable behavior. In a strict ABC model, we might assume that people respond exclusively to antecedent stimuli that precede the response; however, RFT posits that the antecedent stimulus events interact with verbal relations that are entailed with the stimulus event, and it is this combined process that elicits or evokes the observable behavior that ultimately contacts contingencies of reinforcement or punishment.

We earlier gave an example of this phenomenon by describing a classical study done by the late former ABAI President, Mike Dougher (Dougher et al., 2007) which found that if a stimulus "B" elicited arousal due to pairing with shock, after learning that "A < B < C" people showed more arousal to C than to B, even though C had never been paired with shock, while A showed less arousal than B. This effect cannot be stimulus generalization – the stimuli involved had no formal similarity to B. It cannot be stimulus pairing – both A and C were paired with B an equal number of times. What is it then? We need a new term – it is a transformation of stimulus functions through derived relations.

These five features – mutual and combinatorial entailment, relational contextual control, transformation of stimulus functions, and functional contextual control – define relational framing. The simplest of behavioral theories, relating is an operant, becomes a bit complex only because precise behavioral definitions of derived relations are needed to study and apply such a theory. Applied behavior analysts are not usually surprised by that fact alone because they know it can be complex to deal with many operant targets in a precise way in behavioral programming, whether that target is imitation, aggression, or cooperation. RFT is hardly unique in that regard. The examples above represent relatively simple relational classes for illustrative purposes, but it is easy to conceive that relational behavior is vastly complex. We introduce these examples here to provide the necessary framework to start to unpack human behavior and to develop interventions capable of influencing it.

We do not know yet if relational framing can be trained in non-human animals. So far, the answer appears to be "only to a limited degree and with great difficulty." One sea lion named "Rio" did appear to show equivalence when equivalencing was trained as an operant (Schusterman & Kastak, 1993), but there were methodological problems, only one of three animals showed it, and it was very arduous and lengthy to do. Ron Schusterman changed the procedures he used in subsequent studies in ways that moved the test more toward a mere functional class (which however interesting is not controversial and is not the same thing as AARRing). It has never been fully and directly replicated, and both Rio and Dr. Schusterman have since passed away. A recent review of symmetry in non-human animals (Lionello-DeNolf, 2021) found that across the many attempts to show the phenomenon, about 30% of the animals *may* have shown it and, in accord with RFT, "studies that reported the strongest evidence for symmetry used successive matching-to-sample procedures that included training on both symbolic and identity relations" (p. 309). There were extensive procedural modifications, however, and these methodological changes are notorious for creating new ways for non-human animals to show actions that look the same but are functionally different from what is known with human studies. As we expand beyond equivalence, no rigorous experimental methods have yet been claimed to find relational framing across multiple forms of stimulus relations in non-human animals.

A full-length review of each of these frames and their relationship to ACT is outside of the ambit of this book, and we will only briefly touch on even more advanced models of relational behavior. But we do not want this section to close without mentioning that, just as is the case in something like taste aversion, when behavioral principles have species-specific applications, it is important to say why and to do so in ways that appeal to the evolutionary history of the species, not just the physiology of the organism. That has been done with relational operants (Hayes & Sanford, 2014).

The long and short of the argument is that multi-level selection gave an evolutionary advantage to hominins as tribal primates if they cooperated within their troops and bands. Perhaps as a result, normally developing human infants have some degree of non-verbal perspective-taking skills and both recognize and reward cooperation (for a review see Hayes & Sanford, 2014). Many animals show characteristic gestures or sounds to certain objects, and many also show characteristic responses as a listener to these gestures or sounds. What is missing is the coordination between these two repertoires in a way that could lead to robust forms of mutual entailment and thus to a verbal community.

Human infants will reach for and provide a toy to a stranger who enters and points to it, but will reach for that same object and try to put it away during "clean up time" when an adult who is helping to put away toys points to it (Liebal et al., 2009). If early humans could provide a specified object when a speaker emits a mand, that same kind of cooperative action would lead to social forms of "mutual entailment" that would give an advantage to human groups. As this social form was internalized, a gradual process of cultural, psychological, and neurophysiological development could make these useful actions more likely, evolving a verbal community (a key feature of Skinner's account that was itself never fully explained) and creating selection pressures for neurobiological changes that would further support these forms of relational behavior. Said more simply, instead of culture leading to cognition, cooperation came first.

THE ROLE OF PRIVATE EVENTS AND MOTIVATION

Private events include private stimulation (i.e., the environment within the skin) and private behaviors (e.g., thoughts) that are only immediately accessible to the person who is experiencing the event. It is likely true that non-human animals experience private events. For example, we can assume that dogs experience hunger pangs, feelings of coldness, and similar events – even if not in the same exact form as people.

Private events are exceedingly more complicated when it comes to humans. Humans engage in complex verbal behavior that forms their world into relational networks of incredible complexity. That complicates a functional analysis of behavior even before we get to the domination of human private events by derived relational responses. Skinner agreed that covert verbal behavior is part of the entire behavioral episode that behavior analysts seek to explain, but he did not realize that relational operants operate on other behavioral events.

Take for example attempting to use direct contingencies to predict whether or not a person shows up for their first blind date. It is their first date, so there is no known history of reinforcement or punishment. There may be a generalized history of reinforcement or punishment for interacting with strangers that influences the decision. However, the person also likely engages in a complex sequence of thinking that guides the decision. "Will he or she like me?" "Do I look my best right now?" "Am I ready for a relationship?" "Sally said he or she was nice, but Tom said he or she was mean, but I trust Sally more than Tom." The person observes the event as they think it through, but these data are unavailable to the behavior analyst. Using traditional data analytic strategies only, the behavior analyst is left only the option to record whether or not the date occurred. What is potentially even more problematic is that defeating ways of problem solving, like excessively negative self-evaluation, may participate in many more patterns of behavioral avoidance that are part of the same functional class, but appear entirely unrelated when we are left only to examine overt behavior processes.

We need a set of behavior change processes capable of addressing the role of events as they occur for people, and that leads to technologies that are effective ways of altering the function of those private events when people fail to contact the life that they value. These processes and procedures have to address well-established behavioral principles, including relational framing and the VRSCDL evolutionary processes of which behavioral selection is a part. We need assessment methods and intervention methods that make such a broader process-based functional analysis possible.

ACT, RFT, and the "psychological flexibility model" is the best developed behavior analytic approach that appears to be capable of achieving these ends. Showing how that is so and how to make use of that knowledge is what this book is about.

Many of the techniques that we discuss in this book will seem familiar to behavior analysts – and others will not. When procedures and processes appear to deviate from "treatment as usual," we will attempt to define and rationalize the procedures or processes from within a strictly behavior analytic framework based on direct contingency principles as augmented by RFT and nested underneath an extended evolutionary account. We ask only that readers approach this moment with a willingness to critically examine existing approaches and to entertain the possibility that these procedures and processes can produce a new path forward. This will not need to be done at the expense of the old path. It is still there.

The first step in this journey involves reconsidering behavioral flexibility from within an operant learning framework. We will examine adaptive responding and how relational learning may help explain what the literature suggests are effective ways of dealing with private events in a "psychological flexible" manner.

To that task we now turn.

3

Psychological Flexibility and the ACT-Based Approach

We can all look back at our lives to find moments when we needed to be more flexible. Perchance it was a period when something "had to give" following a period of immense struggle. Perhaps it was a period of trying to do the same thing over and over without forward movement or progress. Eventually you tried a new way of behaving – a new way of being.

It could well have been this flexibility that brought you to this point in your life here and now. You might have had to make bold decisions to pursue graduate school and a career. Or maybe it was ending a toxic relationship and moving on with your life. Or it was starting a new fitness routine and sticking with it.

Whatever the case, we all face moments in our lives where we can continue with old ways of being or doing – or explore new possibilities as they present themselves. Knowing when to stick with something and persist in the face of hardship and when to pivot towards new patterns of behavior is at the heart of psychological flexibility. And that quality of action is the target of all acceptance and commitment therapy (ACT) interventions.

Why are there now over 300 meta-analyses of ACT in almost every area of human imaginable? Why has the same model and basic approach been successful in treating a multitude of behavioral and psychological challenges such as depression (e.g., Bohlmeijer et al., 2015), anxiety (e.g., Arch et al., 2012), addiction (e.g., Bricker et al., 2020), or chronic pain (e.g., Wicksell et al., 2013), among other sources of human suffering? Why has that same model also extended to the construction of successful intimate relationships (Daks & Rogge, 2020), or high performance at work (Hayes et al., 2006), among many such positive aspirational areas?

We think it is because ACT is based on a functional and contextual understanding of human behavior that extends behavioral principles to derived relational responding and private events, and integrates itself within the broader world of evolutionary science. Behavior analysis was always designed with breadth in mind, but it needed a more adequate model of human language to address complex human behavior in a broad and flexible fashion. Relational frame theory (RFT) was necessary to move from models of behavior that apply to all animals to those that are designed around those behavior patterns that occur uniquely in humans. That is what the psychological flexibility model does. It's not a panacea, and it's not finished. Very likely, as with all scientific theories, it is wrong in areas we do not yet know about. But it has created undeniable progress in our field and in other fields that have adopted and adapted ACT-based strategies.

DOI: 10.4324/9781003250371-4

ACT does not assume that human struggles are symptoms of a hidden "disease" lurking somewhere in the soul, mind, or hidden in the synapses between brain cells. Rather those who implement ACT attempt to alter the *function* of psychological distress so that it can be used as a tool to guide effective action, and then puts these same skills to the broader task of building a life worth living. Self-management, or what Skinner referred to as "self-control" is central to ACT, where strategies are developed in such a way that people can implement them to operate on their own behavior. To develop a world around behavior that is ACT consistent to promote psychological flexibility.

To do this requires a radical assumption that may seem foreign to behavior analysts, and even more foreign to most other people as well. That is, aversive events are a completely normal part of being alive. How would life be different if people never evolved to feel pain or illness? Seriously, take a moment to think about that question. Think of the many ways that life would be radically changed. We would never avoid collisions or impacts that cause tissue damage. We would never avoid toxic chemicals that over time diminish the functioning of our organs and tissues. We would have a much more difficult time navigating our world without a built-in organic system that allows us to learn what to approach and what to avoid that evolved in all animal species.

The same is true of psychological pain. We are taught to integrate a variety of felt events (states of reinforcability, tendencies to respond, bodily sensations, external context, and so on) under emotional or dispositional labels. We use that ability to give directions to the social community, too. Without "anxiety" we would enter a situation that has previously been threatening with less readiness to respond effectively. Without sadness, we might be less vigilant about possible sources of loss or less oriented toward how important love is in our lives when unavoidable losses occur such as in the natural death of a loved one. Neurological research on human empathy suggests that we can literally feel the pain of others, and we have evolved a nervous system to help us do that (Iacoboni, 2009). Not only is the ability to feel pain and to perceive the pain of others necessary for our own survival, but in many ways the survival of our species as cooperative, language-ing organisms likely depended on it and still depends on it.

Without the capacity for physical and psychological distress, we would be much worse off and would die at a much younger age. And yet, many psychiatric, psychological, or sociological approaches are designed with the express purpose of minimizing or relieving psychological distress to the point that it can no longer serve a healthy function (Andrews et al., 2020). Much of this is the equivalent of trying to fix a car by disconnecting its warning lights. It should come as no surprise the United States is the most heavily medicated population on the planet – yet its members experience rates of depression, anxiety, and suicidality that are unparalleled in any other developed nation (Tikkanen et al., 2020). Hiding from or suppressing difficult private events is not a real solution. Our automatic problem-solving response, supported by the mainstream cultural response, is to grab for smaller, sooner reinforcers at the cost of larger, later ones.

Pain or distress plays a role in the three-term contingency that guides most existing behavior analytic intervention approaches. Consider the process of negative reinforcement. When a stimulus event is aversive, and when behavior effectively removes the aversive stimulus event, the behavior is likely to increase in probability or rate in the future. Even positive reinforcement functions can be interpreted through this same lens, such as when the acquisition of food removed hunger pangs, or the presentation of a blanket removes the feeling of coldness. We can distinguish these two processes primarily by the action implications for the analyst. If we dive deeply enough, it becomes difficult to tell whether putting the blanket on is negatively reinforced by the removal of cold or positively reinforced by the presentation of warmth.

But that very fact suggests that aversive events often play some role in action. Without the capacity to feel cold, the blanket has no purpose, just as without the capacity to sense food deprivation (to "feel hungry,") consuming food would have a less obvious purpose. Life is a constant ebb and flow of painful events and relieving painful events. That cycle is what fosters learning and adapting. Most behavior analysts already view behavior in this way.

We will need to extend this traditional account in at least two ways, however. First, aversive stimulus events are not always external but can be private and can be impacted by derived relational responding. Second, verbal rules can result in relatively "stuck" patterns of behavior that paradoxically result in an inability to escape pain due to a clash between direct contingencies and the contingencies established by an evolved form of behavioral regulation that may be 100 to 1,000 times more recent. Those features are arguably what elevate the universal dance of painful events and relieving painful events into human suffering: a chronic and unsuccessful struggle that leads to needless pain as current solutions repeatedly fail.

AVERSIVE STIMULUS EVENTS ARE OFTEN PRIVATE AND VERBAL

Aversive stimulation is often thought of as in external form, with events such as shock, physical punishment, removal of preferred items, or exposure to other kinds of physically stressful stimulation. In the history of behavior analysis, a variety of behavioral interventions have used aversive control to alter behavior and it is concerning that most of these interventions have been conducted using persons with minimal verbal repertoires, a fact that has long been criticized by leaders in the behavior analytic community (Sidman, 1989). In contrast, much of the work in the field of psychotherapy seems to focus on using verbal interventions to reduce aversive control. The reasons for this are many but part of it may be that as the primary cause of distress begins to become more abstract, we move further from the actual physical stimuli existing in our immediate environment. And there may be some merit in this.

We have previously noted that in 1938 Skinner his operant model may not apply fully to humans due to our unique capacity for language. Later, in 1957 in *Verbal Behavior*, Skinner attempted to update this statement by providing a purely operant account of human language and cognition. We speak because doing so has been reinforced by the verbal community that listens to what we say and has been trained to act accordingly. We think and problem solve because doing so allows us to contact greater reinforcement. As we move through childhood into adulthood, these abilities – speaking, thinking, problem-solving – strengthen and begin to take shape. The result is a speaking, thinking, and problem-solving person. We all speak, think, and problem-solve in different ways, but specific patterns of these types of behaviors are still operants like any other. We can still develop a functional analysis of this type of behavior that is so important to how we live and adapt in our lives. But what happens when the way that we speak, think, and solve problems actually leads us to experience more pain, not less? And what if the way we normally use these operants leads to pain becoming chronic? What if human suffering itself has to do with the way that we speak, think, and solve problems?

Symbolic language occurs when a person is responding in terms of words, rather than stimulus objects themselves, but in a mutual or bi-directional way. Symbolic language is necessarily referential. That is – symbols refer to stimulus objects and "carry back" (the etymological meaning of re-ferrying) some of their functions. Without this connection, we could not possibly respond to symbols, words, or thoughts in a functional way. Rule-governed behavior occurs when we respond based on verbal symbols that we have learned through the on-going interaction with our verbal community, rather than by interacting directly with external contingencies. "Do not touch the hot stove because it will burn" specifies a contingency. And we do not need to touch the stove, contact pain, in order to avoid it. Rather, "stove" refers to a specific kind of object. "Touch" refers to a specific kind of action or movement. "Burn" refers to an aversive private event. And "do not ... or else" specifies a negative reinforcement contingency where avoidance is achieved given the omission of the behavior and object relation.

We introduced stimulus equivalence and RFT in the previous chapter. In combination with Skinner's *Verbal Behavior*, these approaches give us a beginning way to understand how much of what we do actually has very little to do with direct contingencies – rather it is our response to our own verbal behavior about them. The need for RFT to account for this relationship can be seen in the example we have been using. "Do not ... or else" is not a simple equivalence class – it describes a temporal and contingent *relation*. See–touch–burn is not symmetrical in the same way that the elements in a physical "stove" equivalence class are. "Stove" implies a physical stove, but see–touch–burn does not imply burn–touch–see. With a very small additional step, it can do it in another way, however, and that is what is at the core of RFT: see *before* touch *before* burn does indeed imply burn *after* touch *after* see. Adding that, providing a classic behavior explanation (namely, that relational responding is operant behavior), is what RFT does.

And here we see a simple unit of problem-solving that could operate with overt behavior within a behavior-behavior relation. That is, if someone sees the hot stove and infers that touching the stove will result in hurt, and then infer that turning the stove off will result in the avoidance of hurt, then the link with the eventual overt behavior of turning off the stove becomes clear. In this case, taking a step back and thinking about the consequences of the stove being on, in the present moment, and making a choice about how to move forward is the target of intervention, instead of simply teaching a habitual or rote response of avoiding stoves. Both result in the same end result and the stove is avoided, but the former strategy is likely more generalizable to any number of situations and problems that life presents, without the need to directly train every single response topography.

The authors of this book are deeply interested in the study of RFT and together we have produced scores of scientific studies exploring this model of human language and cognition. The RFT community has produced several hundred more. RFT is *the* behavioral component that needs to be added to traditional behavioral principles to understand an ACT intervention approach. We need to understand how a person interacts with their world relationally through their verbal behavior – in ways that are spontaneous and even unpredictable at times. For review, the three major extensions are: (1) trained relations entail two-way and combined relations beyond those of equivalence, or sameness; (2) verbal relationships can transform the function of environmental stimuli producing extraordinary influence over behavior that we seek to influence; and (3) relating itself is operant behavior and becomes self-organized.

Let's tackle these in turn.

As in our point above, almost all complex sentences need more than equivalence to be understood because not all relations are the same or equivalent. For example, a young child is bitten by a dog named *Doug* and experiences fear and dread whenever he sees a dog, hears a dog, hears the word "dog," or even when he hears the name "Doug." Stimulus equivalence alone explains this (at least at the outcome level) as the aversive experiences of the dog and dog bite transfer to the other relations. Now what if the same child is told that his schoolteacher *Sally* is *meaner than* any dog he has ever met? It is not simply that the fear and dread will transfer to Sally, rather the function is transformed into something much larger. And because *Sally* is *contained in* the school, and other people like Sally attend or teach at the school, attending school can become an overwhelmingly anxious private experience that has no basis in any experience that took place at the school – the entire event is both private and verbal. That brings us to transformation of stimulus function as the second extension.

Consider another scenario where the child is told that a new friend is different from those mean children who used to tease and demean the child at the school or playground, or even is their "exact opposite." It is possible that this could reverse the avoidance functions and establish the new friend as a reinforcer. How does something that was a punisher (being around people) turn into a reinforcer (being around people) simply due to the introduction of a new verbal relation? These examples are again relatively simple, but this brings us to the third extension. Patterns of relational behavior can be viewed as a higher-order pattern of behavior that is self-organizing. Consider an adolescent who is diagnosed with a major depressive disorder and has a dense history of reinforcement for relating to the world verbally in negative and avoidant ways. "This will never work." "I am useless." "This is such a drag." Psychologists refer to this pattern as negative scanning. Precisely because this pattern of relating is so strong we can predict that the adolescent will relate to most new events in this same pattern – a pattern that becomes stuck and inflexible and leads to even greater suffering.

But why don't these problematic and defeating contingencies take root and reduce these patterns of relating? Superficially one might suppose that the missed opportunities for the young child avoiding school and schoolwork would negatively punish challenging avoidance relations. The adolescent missing out on life, friendship, dating, and other opportunities should in much the same way be enough to alter these relational frames.

This is the traditional question encompassed by the term "neurotic paradox" that behaviorists interested in clinical work pondered decades ago. Decades of research into such challenges show that these patterns often do not change. They become stuck and appear almost disconnected from the external contingencies – or the world – within which they occur.

In non-human animal models of aversive control, there is no benefit to "moving within" if the goal is prediction and influence with precision, scope, and depth. It is better to say that the animal eats because it is food deprived, rather than because it is hungry, or to say it avoids a shock, not pain. It is not because private events do not exist in non-human animals that we stay with what can be manipulated directly, but rather because an experimental analysis is not helped by noting that, say, food deprivation is an establishing operation that alters the reinforcing function of food AND there are likely felt private accompaniments to that effect.

With humans, it is more complex due to the transformation of stimulus functions that occur due to relational framing. Behavior-behavior relationships can be established in some contexts that require attention to private events or a full functional analysis is impossible. Relational framing allows the person to observe and describe private events, and the conditions that seem to produce them. As private events enter into relational networks they can participate in the regulation of overt behavior, and they enter the ability of people to regulate their social environment. A host offering a guest a piece of pie will likely be better able to provide reinforcers to her guests if she asks "are you hungry?" than if she asks "are you food deprived?" Even shortly after a huge Thanksgiving dinner a luscious pumpkin pie a la mode may evoke a "yes" to the first question whereas a blood sausage pie may evoke a "no" regardless of food deprivation. Even farther from direct contingencies, a polite guest appreciates how hard the host has worked; she may answer "of course I am!" and eat every bite – even if she is not particularly hungry – because she is saying "yes" to avoid feeling guilty later.

What causes these relationships between private events and overt behavior are the contextual cues regulating relational framing and those regulating a transformation of stimulus functions. External contingencies can be altered by private events because these events can engage in forms of rule generation and rule-following. No behavioral events are "causes" of other behaviors within the same individual in behavior analysis, but unlike non-human animals, the analysis of direct contingencies needs to be supplemented by an analysis of the indirect contingencies established by relational operants. These contingencies of meaning are as real, manipulable, and important as any contingency stream, but they have traditionally been missed in behavior analysis.

RULE-GOVERNED BEHAVIOR CAN PROLONG SUFFERING

A major imperfection in a generalized behavior theory was originally observed between humans and non-humans exposed to schedules of reinforcement. This was known from the early days of behavior analysis because the highly predictable schedule effects on responding demonstrated with non-human animals were often not seen when humans were exposed to the same schedules (e.g., Lippman & Meyer, 1967). Less dramatic differences were obtained when instructions were avoided (Weiner, 1970), and minimal differences were found when pre-verbal children were studied (Lowe et al., 1983), or those with significant language disabilities were examined (Orlando & Bijou, 1960).

Verbal rules can impact sensitivity to changing external contingencies – or the probability that a person will change their behavior when contingencies that once maintained it change. In a basic experimental arrangement to test for sensitivity to changing contingencies, the experimenter will establish some sort of response under a specific schedule of reinforcement. For example, Shimoff et al. (1981) compared shaped to instructed performance with interval and ratio schedules, each with a superimposed differential reinforcement of low rate (DRL) contingency. For both schedules when the DRL contingency was relaxed, the response rate increased for most subjects whose original behavior was shaped but not for those who were instructed.

A long string of experiments on rule-governed behavior ensued within behavior analysis, which continues to this day. We will return to this topic periodically in this book, but for now we need only note that study after study compared behavior under the control of verbal rules rather than that established by external contingencies – a distinction first made by Skinner (1969). The research on rule-governed behavior blossomed under the so-called "language hypothesis" (Lowe, 1979) – the idea that most differences between human and nonhuman performances could be traced to the effects of verbal events on human action (a book-length summary of that era can be found in Hayes, 1989). A lot was learned, but it turned out that a more sophisticated understanding of rule governance was needed to make full sense of the data.

It was shown that to a large degree schedule sensitivity could be predicted depending on the rules that the participants were given at the onset of the experiment, as they interacted with programmed contingencies. Across hundreds of studies, we can say that participants who were never given a rule and learned by direct experience instead usually demonstrated greater response flexibility when contingencies changed. Those who contacted contingencies through rules showed a more complex pattern. It depended on why and how well they were following the rule in the first place, what they learned while following the rule, whether the rule-giver could monitor compliance, whether the rule remained in place, and a long list of similar variables (Hayes, 1989).

From 35,000 feet what we see in these experiments is that behavioral flexibility may be inversely related to particular types of rule-governed behavior. When a client is suffering in their life (i.e., failing to obtain valued reinforcers), the inability to adapt may be the result of inaccurate or untested rules about external contingencies, and of the many ways rules alter the impact of the environment. Verbal rules establish new kinds of contingencies – what might be called contingencies of meaning. When behavioral rigidity and loss of valued reinforcement is resulting from verbal rules rather than direct experience with external contingencies, we refer to this as psychological rigidity, and ACT was developed as an intervention process to establish psychological flexibility as an alternative to getting stuck in maladaptive patterns of behavior.

ACT seeks to establish greater flexibility in responding by altering the function of relational framing in an adaptive and context-sensitive way. That often means reducing the influence of rules when those rules no longer contact chosen reinforcers. It can also mean, however, following verbal rules when that produces contact with chosen reinforcers. We can start by operationally defining what exactly is meant by behavioral flexibility and psychological flexibility as it participates in human suffering and human solutions.

THE NATURE OF PSYCHOLOGICAL FLEXIBILITY

Flexibility is defined in common language as the quality of easily bending – but not breaking. This definition appreciates the convergent higher-order behavior dimensions of resistance and non-resistance. For a physical object to be flexible, it must change or adapt when pressures are added but must be stable enough that the physical bonds are not compromised such that the object snaps. Behavior may be similar. We want behavior to change or adapt under new environmental pressures. We do not want behavior to become overly stereotypical – in part because there is then not enough healthy variability to adapt to changing contexts. However, we do not want behavior to adapt to such an extent that patterns become universally unstable and unpredictable from moment to moment. We do not want people to "snap." A definition of *psychological* flexibility must also appreciate how private events and rule-governed behavior may uniquely participate in the behavioral rigidity of humans as immensely complex, cognitive animals. Being flexible in the context of external contingencies may necessitate attending to private events occurring in the present moment and reducing the function of verbal rules that lead to inflexibility.

The earliest work on ACT talked about each of the issues in turn – such as the unhelpful dominance in some contexts of verbal rules in behavioral regulation (termed "cognitive fusion") or the at times unhelpful avoidance functions of private events (termed "experiential avoidance") – but there was no term for the overall model until the early 2000s, when "psychological flexibility" came into use.

The earliest definition of "psychological flexibility" was given by Hayes et al. (2004, p. 12–13) in the form of a question that also described its six features. It was deliberately worded in lay language terms because it was presented in a form of questions that one person might ask another who was struggling with a psychological issue. This is the "psychological flexibility question":

- given a distinction between you as a conscious human being and the psychological content that is being struggled with (*self as context*),
- are you willing to experience that content fully and without needless defense (*acceptance*),
- as it is and not as what it says it is (*defusion*), AND
- do what takes you in the direction (*committed action*)
- of your chosen values (*values*)
- at this time and in this situation (*contact with the present moment*)?

This was obviously not offered as a tight definition cast in behavior-analytic terms, but a great deal of behavioral research and analysis has focused on these six elements of psychological flexibility and how they interlock together. We will describe this work in Part 2 of the book.

The goal of psychological flexibility is to build a vast and contextually sensitive behavior repertoire that allows a person to contact reinforcers that truly matter to them, especially in the long run. Functionally speaking, all of the various elements of psychological flexibility are designed to create a topographically broad and adaptive operant class of maximizing valued reinforcement. Indeed, that could be taken as a functional definition of psychological flexibility. This runs in contrast to any strategy that attempts to build a small or narrow repertoire of behavior that leads to outcomes that people do not actually value.

As we will discuss throughout this book, this is a major departure from how much of the world (and, we argue, some behavior analysts) views behavior change. Undoubtedly, building simple behaviors that solve a narrow set of problems is much easier; however, it is not clear that it is more fruitful in the long run. It is our claim that broad and adaptive patterns of values seeking lead to transformations in the lives of clients that we serve – above and beyond simply altering the form or function of narrowly defined behavioral targets. That is an empirical claim and one that, we believe, the present data support.

ACT AS A STRATEGY TO PROMOTE GREATER PSYCHOLOGICAL FLEXIBILITY

Hopefully, at this point, we have done enough justice to this topic that readers are starting to notice how verbal relations can fall into stable (or, "stuck") patterns that support behavioral rigidity. This rigidity is different from the type of inflexibility that can be developed in no-human animal models through intermittent schedules or dense learning histories because a direct history of reinforcement and punishment is not needed. When relational verbal behavior is functionally involved in behavioral rigidity, we refer to this as psychological rigidity. Some behavior analysts may shy away from the term "psychological" due to negative verbal relations established in graduate school and supported by the contemporary behavior analytic verbal community. Admittedly a great deal of psychology is dualistic or mentalistic in the sense we described earlier in this volume but avoiding a word simply because of aversive functions is the same type of verbal rigidity that causes our clients to suffer – and we believe it causes our field to suffer as well.

We use "psychological" here simply to distinguish behavioral inflexibility that is under the functional control of some external history of reinforcement or punishment without the involvement of relational framing, and behaviorally rigidity that is due to verbal relations. This distinction is not superfluous – it is functionally important.

Consider an intervention to address self-injurious behavior that withholds attention when self-injury occurs. This might work – but only if the function is access to attention. If this is the wrong function, hundreds of experimental functional analysis studies suggest that the intervention will not work. Self-injury will persist. In exactly the same way, if challenging patterns of behavior are functionally maintained by one's own verbal behavior and our solution is to adapt the external contingencies surrounding the behavior – we may never actually deal with what is causing the person to suffer. It is true that a powerful enough external positive reinforcer or punisher may be sufficient to change behavior for a while, but once our contrived token system or other method is removed – if the verbal relations persist the behavior will likely resurge. By definition, inflexible behavior is resistant to change. However, if we can promote greater psychological flexibility by altering the function of maladaptive patterns of relational verbal behavior, we might have a chance to address behavior challenges once complex language shows up.

Psychological flexibility is the target of ACT interventions. An ACT intervention, at least as conducted by a behavior analyst, is not designed specifically to address typical clinical "disorders" such as "major depression" or "panic disorder." ACT, if done functionally, promotes psychological flexibility as a set of skills designed to lead to changes in overt behavioral targets.

The known breadth of targets is a bit stunning. If we consider only controlled single-case or group comparison designs, the list of ACT outcome studies exceeds 1,000 studies and would include all of these areas and many more: trichotillomania, managing diabetes, drug and alcohol addiction, panic disorder, depression, chronic pain, parenting, tinnitus, epileptic seizures, procrastination, professional sports, exercise, dieting, dealing with stroke, prejudice, stigma, suicidality, burnout, stress, excessive pornography use, weight loss, eating disorders, managing HIV, learning, health behaviors, relationship skills, health anxiety, obsessive-compulsive behavior, managing psychotic symptoms, asthma, smoking cessation, gambling, coming out, perpetrating, domestic violence, trauma, occupational stress, work performance, social cooperation, drug detoxification, teaching, training, communication, giving speeches, and leadership. Improving these outcomes is not the point, however, until we know what values-based reinforcers are for the person. For example, if ACT is being used with a person addicted to substances one of the first things likely to be said is "we are not here to make you stop using." If somehow really moving a person closer to the life that they value involves the use of addictive substances who are we to say they shouldn't use them? We are behavior analysts, not narcotics officers. Of course, the reality is that 99.9 % of the time the physiological and social effects of prolonged addictive substance use tend to move people further from their values, so reducing use becomes part of engaging more flexibly with the world. Further, if we can address the escape functions that come with language – and if substance use provides a means to escape aversive private events, such as difficult thoughts – then the need for cocaine, heroin, alcohol, or what have you may diminish as greater psychological flexibility is achieved. But the valued outcomes are up to the client, not us. We can choose not to work with someone if their goals create ethical or legal problems for us. If we as behavior analysts can become the experts in promoting psychological flexibility as a pattern of responding that can be used in combination with all other behavioral methods to pursue valued behavioral goals, this opens up our scope of practice beyond what we ever could have imagined.

COGNITIVE FUSION AND EXPERIENTIAL AVOIDANCE: A PATTERN OF SUFFERING

Fusion and experiential avoidance are very common in clients that behavior analysts work with using ACT. These two processes readily lead to choices that are dominated by smaller, sooner, negative, and often private reinforcers over larger, later, positive, and often abstract reinforcers but staying at that level of analysis quickly becomes cumbersome and it can scare away many people who are not used to "behavioralese." In addition, sometimes behavior analysts themselves need terms to orient them to broader sets of technical accounts.

When behavior analytic concepts and sets of functional analyses reach a certain level of complexity, middle-level terms can be helpful in summarizing them using singular terms that are understood and digestible for clients and that provide a shorthand for other behavior analysts.

This has long been common in applied behavior analysis. We may speak of "aggressive behavior" without having first to stop to say it involved potentially harmful physical contract, was schedule-induced, altered what functioned as sensory reinforcers, or had a history of secondary reinforcement, and so on. Yes, when we do a specific piece of research, we will need to specify how we are measuring "aggression" but that does not make "aggression" a technical behavioral term. A term like "schedule-induced aggression" is a technical behavioral account, but the overall term "aggression" is still helpful when it is not clear why it is occurring or when speaking to a teacher or others. Those many details will be explicated as needed in a specific instance or pattern of "aggressive behavior" as a summary abstraction from an on-going behavioral stream. The term "aggression" refers to the entire set of functional analyses. New ones may emerge; old ones may become more precise – but the overarching term is still helpful and even necessary when dealing with complex behavior.

The need for middle-level terms becomes all the more important, however, when dealing with verbal events involving relational learning. Relational framing can alter how direct contingencies work in a complex way. Detailed focus on the particular relational operants, their relational contexts, or the particular derived stimulus networks involved, and so on, can overwhelm sensitivity to the key operant classes involved. Having summary terms can help clients and behavior analysts alike have a language that supports understanding, communication, buy-in, and behavior change. Especially if major portions of the technical work have previously been done (e.g., previous functional analytic work has been successful) middle-level terms can be used without a major loss of precision. Two middle-level terms that are readily linked to our current knowledge of relational framing are cognitive fusion and experiential avoidance.

Cognitive fusion describes situations in which verbal relations and the transformation of stimulus functions they afford dominate over other sources of behavioral regulation in ways that produce ineffective or inflexible responding. Said in another way, cognitive fusion involves responding that is dominated by the functional altering impact of relational operants on antecedent external events rather than to external events as they otherwise exist.

We have already discussed schedule insensitivity as a common byproduct of rule-governed or verbally-governed behavior. Speaking as a behavior analyst it is not technically accurate to say that "cognitive fusion" *causes*, say, schedule insensitivity or troublesome changes in the stimulus control based on verbal relations. Rather, cognitive fusion is this very process expressed using a summative middle-level term. Relational operants and the transformation of stimulus functions they produce can evoke patterns of behavior that contribute to ineffectiveness, inflexibility, and suffering. Relational networks may inhibit effective contact with the environment due to inaccuracy, incompleteness, lack of testability, derived elicitation, undesirable motivative operations, induction of behavioral rigidity, and so on. These relations could participate in unhelpful forms of tracking, plying, or augmenting, and they alter the stimulus control of the present environment in an undesirable way, reducing the probability that a person will adjust their behavior even when doing so is necessary to achieve the desired outcome. "Cognitive fusion" describes that set of functional analyses.

Let's start with a very simple example.

Suppose a non-human animal ate a hamburger that was poisoned. No behavior analyst would be surprised to see that the animal would later avoid hamburgers for a long time, perhaps even from then on.

Now suppose a verbally abusive and highly critical father tells a teenage daughter "if you eat that hamburger your body will soon be disgusting, and no one will like you." Unlike the poison, this verbally described consequence does not need to be contacted directly for the hamburger to be revolting for a long time, perhaps even from then on. Indeed, the histories of persons with eating disorders are filled with such stories. The transformation of the stimulus functions is a technical name for what is going on as some of the properties of "disgusting" transfer to the hamburger and dominate over behavior related to eating and body. "Cognitive fusion" is a shorthand and summative middle-level term for such functional processes.

Experiential avoidance is a close pair of cognitive fusion and was one of the first parts of the psychological flexibility model that was explicated thoroughly (Hayes et al., 1996). It involves nothing more than behavior motivated by avoiding or escaping the form, frequency, or situational sensitivity of private events, even when doing so causes loss of valued reinforcers. You can see how cognitive fusion pairs readily with experiential avoidance. A relational network like "I am disgusting" can occasion intense private events such as self-loathing and shame. Trying to avoid such feelings even when, for example, it means life-threatening anorexia, is a form of experiential avoidance.

Often the details of a person's history are not known but terms like cognitive fusion and experiential avoidance, if they are not treated causally, can point to plausible places to look, based on a larger set of functional analyses conducted with others. The reason these patterns occur so commonly across people is because they flow so naturally from the clash between direct contingencies and relational framing. The details of each individual's history matter a great deal, but we know that virtually all verbally able people have times when they are cognitively fused or experientially avoidant because the behavioral processes involved are ubiquitous. They are virtually built into relational framing. So are their antidotes of cognitive and emotional flexibility – of defusion and acceptance in ACT lingo.

Suppose two clients have the thought "no one at the party will like me." For the first client, this thought is literal. They may have generated an entire narrative centered around their unlikability and inability to fit in. "The party will be better if I am not there" is supported by a broader relational network of "I am an unlikable and mean person." Thus, "no one at the party will like me" is not simply a fleeting thought that all of us have once in a while, rather to this client it appears a literal description of reality. This client avoids the party – and all of the positive reinforcers that may be there if he goes.

For the second client, this thought is not literal. Perhaps this thought is immediately followed by other verbal behavior such as "some people like me, and some people do not" or "everybody feels this way sometimes." This extended relational network may be supported by a broader relation of "I am willing to see how things go." Even without contradictory verbal statements perhaps a context may exist that diminishes harmful transformation of stimulus functions. Perhaps the thought "no one at the party will like me" is even followed by a smile because it is the constant refrain of a comedic character in that person's favorite TV show who always thinks that and then has a great time. Perhaps this second client has learned ways to contact such contexts deliberately. This client goes to the party and contacts the positive reinforcers, giving even less weight to their initial verbal behavior about the party.

Behavior analysts are already familiar with avoidance and escape functions as a form of negative reinforcement. What makes experiential avoidance powerful is the involvement of private events that have themselves become categorized verbally. What is being avoided are not external stimuli that can be readily removed. Through verbal relations themselves, aversive experiences can become internal and personal, difficult to observe publicly, and not easily altered (at least not directly) through intervention. For a verbally competent client who is avoiding parties and social gatherings, it may not be avoidance of the party per se that may be maintaining the behavior; rather, deciding to stay home may immediately remove thoughts about the party, thoughts about being unwelcomed or unwanted, feelings of anxiety that accompany those thoughts, and so on. This pattern is often maintained in part because it is dynamic in the sense that avoidance negatively reinforces thoughts such as "I cannot go today" or "maybe I will be ready to go to a party in a few weeks." Therefore, we would anticipate that as these verbal relations and their function-altering effects are strengthened, their content becomes increasingly fused or literalized, their evocative and eliciting impact on behavior is strengthened, and the challenge they present to flexible and effective behavior increases. Behavior becomes increasingly rigid and unchanging. The increasing impact of experiential avoidance is often paradoxical because attempts to alter the frequency or form of distressing thoughts or feelings can actually serve to increase their frequency or intensify over time (Wenzlaff & Wegner, 2000). Pursuing smaller-sooner-negative-private reinforcers amplifies motivative operations that evoke this pattern of behavior. A cycle of experiential avoidance can be very difficult to disrupt when challenges have persisted over an extended period of time.

In our experience, clients report that experiential avoidance is like plugging holes in a boat, yet somehow when one hole is plugged, two more emerge. That is because avoiding unpleasant private experiences fails to address what is causing the holes in the first place, and they inadvertently create more things to avoid – more holes in the boat. A rule like "avoid anxiety or else!" contains a verbal threat that will very likely elicit anxiety. Why would it not? "Or else" is in an equivalence class with a wide variety of aversive events or at least their verbal referents. But the freeze, fight, flee, or fail behavioral systems that are engaged by immanent aversive events can make effective action less likely or even impossible, further increasing the urgency of the "or else" message. Anxiety itself can become something to be anxious about.

Another paradox is that without better theoretical guidance we as behavior analysts may all too easily seek to alter the form or frequency of these private events so as to develop an effective intervention. After all, changing the form of difficult thoughts is just common sense, right? It may be but any behavior analyst knows that sometimes science sense and commonsense diverge. Without understanding extinction bursts, who but a behavior analyst could tell parents that a tantrum is a "good sign of progress" when a reinforcer is removed for harmful behavior? In a similar way, the core cognitive strategy of "detect, challenge, dispute, and change" in traditional cognitive behavior therapy (CBT; Beck, 1970) was highly logical and commonsense but it sometimes inadvertently led clients into suppressive strategies that *amplified* the harmful impact of troublesome thoughts. That is probably why meta-analyses showed that the cognitive elements of CBT were not reliably helpful (Longmore & Worrell, 2007) – the best CBT therapists used these methods in ways that did not run afoul of cognitive fusion and experiential avoidance but the weaker therapists often did not. Now that we know that cognitive reappraisal is more a matter of defusion and cognitive flexibility, it is a lot easier to give scientific guidance on how to use cognitive methods in CBT effectively.

This is why we dare not let applied behavior analysis continue to either ignore private events or to address them by seat-of-the-pants ideas. However logical it may seem, it typically does little good to focus on a private event in a subtractive or eliminative way because once learned, behavior can only be inhibited via extinction – it is never reduced to a zero probability. That is, it is never entirely subtracted or eliminated. If the very act of trying to eliminate or subtract is itself a context that increases the impact of one action on another, the analysis in effect is fighting at cross purposes – strengthening harmful impact in the fool's errand of eliminating mere occurrence.

OPERATIONALLY DEFINING VALUES AND AUGMENTING PSYCHOLOGICAL FLEXIBILITY

Cognitive fusion and experiential avoidance can result in patterns of behavior that appear stuck, but we have earlier argued that promoting psychological flexibility requires increasing pursuit of larger-later-positive-abstract reinforcers. That is the work of values and committed action in an ACT framework. By incorporating a conceptually systematic understanding of values and valued living, behavior analysts have much to add to any intervention model.

Values is another middle-level term. Wilson and Dufrene (2009, p. 66) defined values as, "freely chosen verbally constructed consequences of on-going, dynamic, evolving patterns of activity, which establish predominant reinforcers for that activity that are intrinsic in engagement in the valued behavioral pattern itself." This is a behaviorally sound definition and it is very close to what we have already laid out: larger-later-private-abstract reinforcers that can support psychological flexibility.

To connect these two ideas more explicitly. "Freely chosen" simply means that an appetitive choice is present between the values-consistent behavior and values-inconsistent behavior. We are not speaking of free will – we are saying that the choice is present and is situationally unconstrained. This is the same sense of "free" that behavior analysts are talking about with the term "free operant baselines" in studying, say, the matching law.

Choice behavior has long been the focus of behavior analysis and rightly so. Delay discounting. Concurrent chains. The matching law. All are domains of choice. Choices are context-dependent. In early animal research on addiction, a rat will consume less nicotine when the rat is exposed to an enriched environment compared to rats in a generic environment, activated through neurological changes in the rat's prefrontal cortex (Venebra-Muñoz et al., 2014). For humans, the context of choice includes "verbally constructed consequences" – abstracted and often private temporally extended reinforcers. A father wakes up at 5:00 am to take their child to hockey practice before school starts. What is the reinforcer for maintaining this choice, two days a week, for several months? Surely, there is little automatic reinforcement that comes with the sound of the 4:30 am alarm or stepping into a cold minivan while the rest of the block is asleep. Praise and positive social interaction may be a low-probability event given the other parents are just as tired and dreading the workday ahead. Perhaps the father really enjoys watching children skate in circles and shoot pucks into a net?

The reinforcement maintaining this is almost entirely private and verbal. "I want to be a good parent." "I really stepped up today." "Someday my kid will really appreciate this." Or even, "someday I will look back and really appreciate this." No matter the specific content of these private events, they are verbal and abstract reinforcers that specify a larger and longer-term outcome, and via a transformation of stimulus functions, they establish reinforcing functions intrinsic to these loving parental behaviors. These are what we mean by "contingencies of meaning" and "values" are a way of describing how relational operants interact with events to produce such reinforcers.

In later chapters, we discuss how to do an actual functional analysis of values, but for now our proof of concept can be expressed within a thought experiment. Imagine we did manipulate these variables. If the practice were moved to 8:00 am with no scheduling conflict, would the behavior still occur? If yes, we can infer the early morning is not a reinforcer. If the practice drills were altered from skating in circles and shooting pucks to focusing on some other skill sets, would the behavior still occur? If so, we can rule out watching the practice drills as a reinforcer. If other parents were not present or if the parents were to be separated at the practice, would the behavior still occur? Certainly, it would. Finally, if the father was convinced that doing this does not make him a good parent and that his child would likely grow to resent him for the early mornings, would the behavior maintain? If not, then we must assume that the function of this behavior lies in the verbal abstraction of larger-later reinforcers. Because the only way to change the behavior is either to remove this free choice (e.g., a change in schedule, promotion to a new hockey team, end of the season) or to change verbally abstracted reinforcers and the parents' private interactions with these early morning practices.

Lastly, values represent "dynamic, evolving patterns of activity, which establish predominant reinforcers for that activity that are intrinsic in engagement in the valued behavioral pattern itself." When the hockey season ends, the "good father" does not simply stop engaging in behavior that fits this verbal abstraction. Rather, different topographies of behavior fill the void in pursuit of this chosen value. Cooking dinner for the family when his partner arrives home from work. Helping his kids with their math homework so they can be successful in school. The topography changes. The function remains and it is intrinsic to the behavior itself – more akin to sensory reinforcement than to social praise.

Like all middle-level terms, the term "values" orients us to a set of functional analyses. These are always gradually improving as science advances – there is no full and final functional analysis of anything. In RFT terms, values serve an augmental function. Augmental rules are verbal stimuli (public or private) that augment (strengthen or support) the reinforcing value of external stimuli. For example, the TV commercial presents the phrase, "I bet you're hungry for a burger" along with the company logo. Those stimuli can serve a motivative function that elicits walking to a nearby restaurant that is open 24/7. The commercial is not an Sd – it cannot be because the burger is continuously available. It's a verbal establishing stimulus or motivative stimulus – an augmental.

When the alarm goes off, reinforcement is available for two concurrently available behaviors: hit the snooze button and go back to sleep or hit the cancel button and wake up. Option 1 offers more sleep and Option 2 likely leads to some experiences that you want to escape from (e.g., hockey practice, work, meetings) but also the abstracted positive meaning of "I'm being a good father." Larger-later-positive-abstract versus smaller-sooner-negative-private.

Note also that there is a hierarchical relation involved between the behavior of getting up and the value of being a good father that parallels the hierarchical relation between the actions of getting up and the person who is hitting the cancel button. "Being a good father" contains getting up; and noticing and supporting that pattern is an aspect of the person's repertoire. Some behavior analysts have argued persuasively that psychological flexibility cannot emerge until the person learns to frame their own behavior hierarchically with themselves and their own chosen values (Luciano, Törneke, & Ruiz, in press).

Arguably, life is a constant push-and-pull struggle between values-consistent and values-inconsistent choices. We just do not always think of them that way. We get stuck in "I will do this later," "I cannot do this," "there is something wrong with me." At the moment you are considering ACT or a similar strategy for a client, it is likely the case that rigid patterns of avoidance or escape from private experiences are occurring. Therefore, we need a way to begin the process of functionally assessing this struggle. We explore the idea of functional analysis more deeply in the next chapter.

4

Models of Psychological Flexibility

Up to this point we have presented acceptance and commitment therapy (ACT) in the abstract along with a brief history and a general orientation to psychological flexibility. What we have provided to this point is far from a technological account of ACT that can inform the development of effective behavior analytic interventions that can be used alongside existing behavioral technologies. That is what the rest of this book is about.

Attempting to do so is no small feat. There is no recipe book that can adequately address the very real challenges that consumers and clients will experience in their lives. There are no finite lists of ACT-based procedures that are deemed "behavior analytic" that we can pull from and plug into behavior intervention plans. ACT is not a one-size-fits-all intervention approach that can be applied for some fixed number of weeks to treat this or that clinical disorder. If it were, there would be no need to dig so deeply into the history and philosophy underlying ACT-based interventions or spend three chapters building an understanding of psychological flexibility as a broad target of behavior change.

This problem also shouldn't sound new or particularly nuanced to behavior analysts. The practice of behavior analysis, though deeply technological, has always been informed by behavior change principles along with empirically tested procedures in favor of scripted protocols applied broadly. Consider for example the process of treating self-injurious behavior (SIB). What we do not have is a 12-week self-injurious behavior (SIB) protocol that claims to work in 80% of cases to reduce or eliminate SIB. What we do have is an assessment framework, the experimental functional analysis, that assumes that most instances of SIB are maintained by one of four primary operant functions: escape, social reinforcement, tangible reinforcement, or automatic reinforcement. We apply an experimental design strategy called a multielement design to isolate the conditions in which the behavior is most likely to occur. And once we figure that out, we apply any number of strategies that directly address the identified function by reinforcing the omission of SIB or engaging in an alternative or incompatible behavior. Or we manipulate the antecedent conditions under which SIB is most likely to occur. Oftentimes, the most effective intervention utilizes a combination of these strategies that are tailored to the client and the context.

What is critical is that this experimental functional analysis intervention framework is built from a relatively simple model of behavior change. It assumes that behavior (B) occurs in an antecedent context (A) and is maintained by functional reinforces that are contingent on the behavior (C). This is the ABC model and is the foundation of contingency management and functional support strategies.

DOI: 10.4324/9781003250371-5

There are a number of such models used in ACT-based interventions. These models vary in their empirical support but nonetheless serve the critical function of guiding the intervention decisions of the behavior analyst by situating challenging behavior within a context. Moving from traditional ABC models to models that make room for private experiences and psychological flexibility as a higher-order behavior target will necessitate a scientific discussion of the role of models in science more broadly, before unpacking several models that can inform the development of ACT interventions.

A MODEL-DEPENDENT VIEW OF INTERVENTION

Hawking and Mlodinow (2010) in *The Grand Design* describe model-dependent realism as an approach to physical science that is deeply compatible with Skinner's radical behaviorism (Belisle, 2020). According to this approach, there is no "reality" that we can perceive independent of bias and interpretation. Science at best represents behavior that scientists engage in to solve challenges – and the quality of any given scientific theory or model is strictly a function of how well that theory or model allows for the solving of important problems. They give the example, "is light a particle or is light a wave?" Well, in some applications, treating light as a particle allows for greater prediction and the development of new technologies. In other applications, it is better to treat light as a wave. Light is therefore both a particle and a wave and neither a particle nor a wave, as inevitably both interpretations of light will arrive as obsolete as science progresses.

But wait, you may say. Surely, we evolved to be more and more in contact with the world *as it is*. Our visual system evolved to detect the different frequencies of visual light, for example, so obviously frequencies of light are *really there* even if we weren't sensing them.

Reality exists, yes. And yes, science and behavior analysis assume there are predictable and sometimes controllable relations among events – this is why it seeks to develop increasingly organized statements about those relations that allow our goals to be accomplished based on verifiable experience. But there is no reason to think our sensory systems detect reality directly or that our scientific rules correspond to a real world in any point-to-point way. Did you know in evolutionary computer simulations that allow the selection of successful working fictions instead of literal truth, the former often wins (Hoffman, 2019)? It is not so hard to see why if you think about it. That can easily happen if reality is darned complicated and our survival is fostered by simplification.

An analogy might help. Our sensory systems might be more like the operating system on your computer. It converts incredible strings of charges (we say they are strings of 1s and 0s, but that is just a metaphor) into, say, blue rectangular files on your screen that you dare not drag to images of trash cans or else they may be lost forever. We all know that computer files are not literally blue or rectangular. They do not really have a shape or color at all, and they do not reside inside a directory. And there is no actual trash can. We use a computer operating system because it helps us readily learn to operate the machine to achieve our goals. If, like the movie *The Matrix*, reality really is more like falling green letters, wouldn't it be better to let evolution create a simpler operating system, say one of colors, frequencies of light, and shapes, just as the programmer did for your computer with blue files and trash cans? After all, a workable fiction of say, visible light frequencies, might be far, far more readily adaptive than 1000100 101110110111101 00111 01001001011101101 111010 010111011011101011 101110110.

Evolution helps dial in effectiveness as measured by survival, but contrary to what most people believe, that need not be the same thing as literal truth. Not at all. We do not know when we see a poisonous snake that it literally has a particular size, shape, or color – and frankly we may not need to know that. What we *need* to know is that if we don't jump it could be lethal. Seeing it this way evolved to accomplish that end.

From a behavior analytic view, "science" simply represents the behavior of the scientist in generating or following rules inside a particular strategy called the scientific method. That pattern of verbal behavior can be highly adaptive (i.e., successful in solving behavioral challenges) or maladaptive (i.e., unsuccessful in solving behavioral challenges). Just like any rule-governed behavior, scientific verbal behavior can be inflexible when rules that were successful in one context fail to be so in a new context. The models or approaches we have used in behavioral science represent those rules. Rules operating as functional analytic strategies that have been immensely successful at solving some topographies of challenging behavior in individuals with disabilities, do not necessarily predict widescale success with other populations and challenges (Ivancic & Belisle, 2020).

This radically pragmatic idea about the relation of ontology (what exists) to epistemology (the process of knowing) is central to functional behavioral thinking. Skinner viewed scientific knowledge as

> a corpus of rules for effective action, and there is a special sense in which it could be "true" if it yields the most effective action possible... (A) proposition is "true" to the extent that with its help the listener responds effectively to the situation it describes.
>
> *(1974, p. 235)*

This profound and somewhat counterintuitive idea takes some getting used to. Note he does not say it is true because it describes the situation accurately. It's true because it helps us respond effectively. "Don't play with poisonous snakes." Got it. That is a good idea regardless of what snakes are "really" like.

Sometimes rules can be quite flexible. That is true for our clients, and it is true for us as providers. It depends on how we use models of behavior change. Approached in the right way, behavioral principles, RFT, and evolutionary principles give the scientist-practitioner the freedom to adapt and adjust their models of behavior change to fit the behavior, client, and context being presented.

The model most behavior analysts will be familiar with is a three-term or four-term contingency model. We will call this the A-B-C model. In the A-B-C model, the behavior analyst will employ any number of functional analytic strategies to isolate immediate antecedent (A) and consequence (C) variables that surround the behavior (B). By adjusting A and/or C variables, the behavior analyst hopes to bring about a change in B.

This model emphasizes external contingencies that are immediate, such as access to escape, attention, tangible items, or automatic reinforcers. As discussed, however, unique challenges arise when rule-governed behavior and verbal relations enter into the functional stream of behavior. The "A" variables may be very far in the past and continue to affect behavior by altering patterns of relational framing that "show up" at the moment that behavior is present. The "C" variables could also be delayed, probabilistic, abstract, or intrinsic. Often, they operate more as contingencies of meaning than as tangible outcomes.

Although ACT-consistent models assume that external functional interactions are present, these are not analyzed independently from analyzing the verbal relations and patterns that underscore maladaptive behavior. Of course, these verbal relations and patterns do not occur in a vacuum, they operate within a stream of As, Bs, and Cs. However, the key to developing a successful intervention necessitates a functional analysis of these verbal interactions and the rules that people follow that lead them to follow. In this chapter, we introduce the Hexaflex as a first organizing framework or model. Thinking about psychological flexibility consistent with the Hexaflex gives us a starting point to begin discussing ACT more pragmatically and to dig deeper into each of the core processes of this model. We will then discuss how this model is dissected or adapted in different ways to serve different purposes. What is most important here is that readers do not hold any model as absolute or "true." Rather, models are verbal stimuli that can help guide effective action for the behavior analyst as an applied scientist. By understanding the models more completely, behavior analysts can be more flexible and more effective in tailoring interventions to individual clients and their personal challenges and struggles.

INTRODUCING THE SIX CORE PROCESSES: ACT HEXAFLEX

A functional assessment model that has been a staple within ACT-based intervention is the ACT Hexaflex. This tool did not emerge until 2005 during a discussion on the ACBS listserv, 25 years after ACT development began, but it is so ubiquitous now that anyone interested in ACT will soon see hexagons everywhere – in the logos for ACT clinics, or on ACT book covers and so on. The term "Hexaflex" was initially just a fun tongue-in-cheek play on words, but it stuck immediately. A visual depiction of the model is provided below. The first is a model of psychological inflexibility. We believe (and several research studies now support this) that these six behaviors or operant classes are pervasive in the way that relational operants interact with direct contingencies to establish recalcitrant problems for people. When these operants are strong, they contribute to modes of responding that produce suffering far beyond what the environment itself might do unaided by poor forms of adjustment.

We unpack each of these six core processes in much more detail in Section 2 of the book where full-length chapters break down these processes' behavior analytically and extend the account to usable technologies for behavior analysts. For now, we introduce a foundational assumption of this model in Figure 4.1. What follows starts from the top of the hexagon and proceeds clockwise, one node for each semi-colon:

> We suffer the most when we ruminate on our past and fixate on our future instead of focusing on the present in a flexible, fluid, and voluntary way; when we fail to make contact with things in life that we value the most; when we act in ways that are impulsive or when we become inert and fail to construct broad habits of values-based action; when we get stuck trying fit with specific and narrow stories about who we are; when we allow our verbal rules about the world to dominate us needlessly; and when we attempt to escape, avoid, or cling to thoughts and feelings even when that harms values-based action.

These are the private contextual conditions within which suffering is most likely. If psychological flexibility is defined as a broad operant class of behaviors that maximize valued forms of reinforcement, we contact the fewest valued reinforcers when we get stuck in these modes of thinking. For this reason, this is called a model of psychological inflexibility.

As can be seen in the connecting lines, we also assume that each of these processes interacts and influences one another. This is not a "simple" model of isolated processes. When we ruminate on the past and fixate on the future, we may be less likely to contact our values. When we are fused to stories about ourselves (self as content) we may be more likely to make impulsive decisions that cohere with our self-concept and avoid situations that would otherwise allow us to contact things that we value. Our clients are no different. They suffer the most when these operants are strong and resistant. Our job is therefore to encourage and strengthen the opposite set of processes to support psychological flexibility.

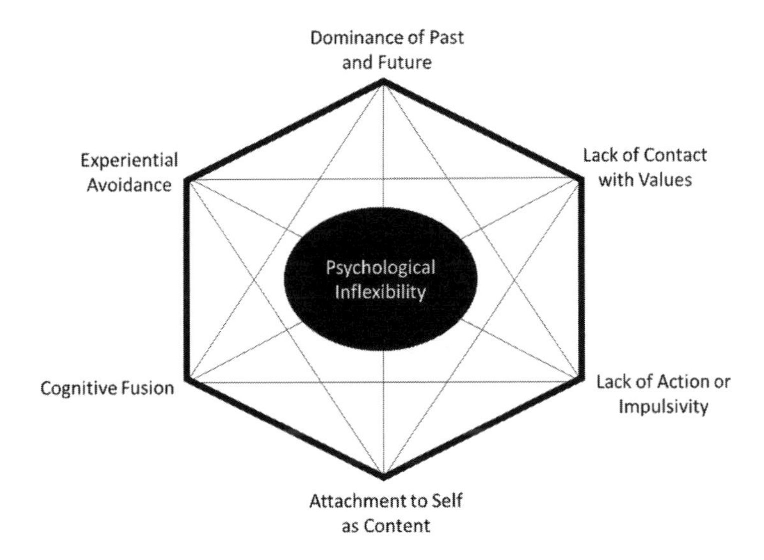

FIGURE 4.1 ACT Hexaflex diagram.

This same basic model can be flipped to provide positive process-based goals in each of the six areas. Again, starting from the top and proceeding in a clockwise fashion, we can promote psychological flexibility by strengthening present-moment awareness and attentional processes that are flexible, fluid, and voluntary; when we promote contact and clarity of chosen values – reinforcing qualities of being and doing that are intrinsic to behavior itself; we foster engagement in committed actions that are linked to larger and larger patterns of values-based behavior; we promote a perspective-taking sense of self that places life events into a hierarchical relation with the capacity to notice and observe one's own behavior (what Skinner called "seeing seeing" but from a locus or point of view); noticing the process of thinking in a defused or de-literalized way so as to diminish its unwelcome automatic dominance; and the acceptance or willingness to experience public and private experiences without unnecessary and unhelpful escape, avoidance, or attachment. The psychological flexibility model is shown in Figure 4.2.

These six behavioral processes are all middle-level terms that emerge from functional analyses of how relational operants bear on direct contingency control. In the three chapters so far, we have already begun to ease into them, and in the next section, we will take each in turn, breaking down the model in multiple different ways that can be adapted to meet the challenge at hand and to develop new strategies for functional assessment. Let's unpack each in more detail.

Present Moment Awareness

Behavior analysts are used to avoiding the concept of attention, and for good reason. Stimulus control is way of speaking about how the external environment impacts on action, and there is no increase in prediction and influence in the study of non-human animals that comes from "explaining" stimulus control by an action of the organism. The lighted key does not evoke pecking because the pigeon attends to it – it evolves pecking because of the history of reinforcement that establishes the stimulus control exerted by the lighted key.

Relational operants change this picture because these operants operate on other behavioral processes. The soles of your feet produce stimulation nearly continuously, but we rarely

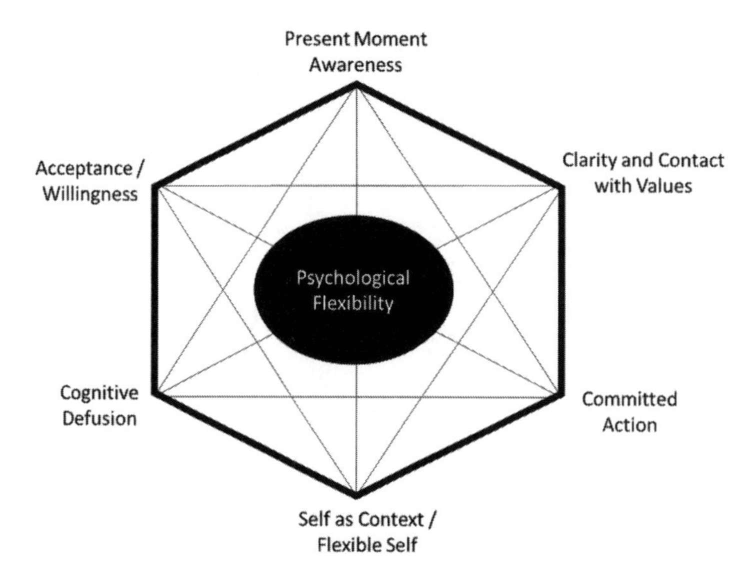

FIGURE 4.2 ACT Hexaflex diagram with positive process-based goals

notice these events. Suppose the ink on paper or the pixels on a screen of the sentence you are reading right now present relational events that suggest that you can attend to the feelings of the sole of your right foot and nothing else ... or the feelings of the sole of your left foot and nothing else ... or the feelings of the soles of both of your feet and nothing else. As these relational stimuli occur, the stimulus control exerted by your feet systematically changes due to relational operants that readily can augment or diminish stimulus control. Because of that fact, once relational framing exists it is useful to examine how verbal rule can augment or diminish stimulus control. "Attention" is the name for that domain of actions and it can be used in a flexible, fluid, and voluntary way to foster positive behavioral outcomes. That is done in the psychological flexibility model.

All behavior occurs in the context of internal and external events in the now. By learning to broaden or narrow, or to shift or persist in attentional focus a person can use second-order regulatory skills that systematically alter stimulus control – broadening, narrowing, shifting, or persisting as the task demands and present purposes require.

Many forms of "mindfulness" training can be understood in part in these terms, and in fact extended versions of the "soles of the feet" exercise you just did are known to be very helpful with regulating the impulsive or aggressive behavior of children with developmental disabilities (Singh et al., 2003).

Values

Strengthening clarity and contact with one's chosen values plays a centralized role within ACT. Why a person would seek to improve psychological flexibility through processes like present moment awareness or willingness to engage in committed action is to live a more values-consistent life. Clarifying what truly matters to a person is necessarily an exercise in strengthening or augmenting verbal relational behaviors that describe larger-later patterns of reinforcement. Values are not smaller-sooner rewards, such as a paycheck or negative reinforcers such as escape from uncomfortable thoughts or experiences; rather, values are broad hierarchical categories. Wilson and Murrell (2004, p. 135) pose the question, "In a world where you could choose to have your life be about something, what would you choose?" Behavior analytically, values can be interpreted as motivative augmental verbal stimuli that strengthen the reinforcing value of present moment reinforcers in accord with verbally constructed long-term consequences. A paycheck is reinforcing because it provides stability and safety. Time off is reinforcing because it allows for greater contact with family and friends and the opportunity to strengthen relationships. Once verbal behavior shows up, we no longer interact with consequential outcomes without evaluation, so we want to strengthen values-consistent evaluation of outcomes to direct behavior change processes.

Committed Action

Committed action describes patterns of behavior that allow a person to make greater contact with their chosen values. As noted by Dixon and Paliliunas (2020), "it is all too common for one to articulate what is important, valuable, or reinforcing but never to engage in behavior to alter the actual attainment of such preferred outcomes" (p. 24). There are numerous behavior change processes that behavior analysts are already familiar with that can strengthen the probability that clients will engage in committed action. Take something like shaping. We know it is unlikely that a person who values health and fitness will go directly from never jogging outdoors to jogging five miles, three times per week (even if they may fully intend to do so following values clarification). Establishing this intention could also result in injury or burnout – we want to establish commitment to patterns that are sustainable. By breaking down committed actions into smaller initial steps and building, we can achieve larger and larger patterns of behavior change. We will adopt a self-management or self-regulation approach to strengthening committed action that emphasizes working with the client to build routines, strategies, and targets that are likely to succeed within their life and context. This section will likely build on the many strategies that behavior analysts have already developed while integrating this process with the other core processes to promote psychological flexibility.

Acceptance/Willingness

Acceptance describes a willingness to experience potentially aversive events (or in some cases the possible loss of positive events), both private and public, that cannot be readily adapted or altered within the confines of one's present repertoire or context. Acceptance is not an end in itself; rather, promoting a willingness to experience uncomfortable or momentarily aversive events without avoidance can be necessary in pursuit of one's chosen values. Often time obtaining larger-later more abstract reinforcers consistent with identified values can require doing things that one might not normally do, delaying access to reinforcement, or losing out on smaller-sooner reinforcers that would otherwise be available. For the student with test anxiety, this could involve a willingness to enroll in classes and complete tests in order to qualify for a career that means much more than getting out of the test. For the person avoiding the social event, this could involve a willingness to feel uncomfortable at the start of the event, knowing that those thoughts will go away and leave only the positive social interactions that the person seeks. Defined in this way, acceptance represents another measurable dimension of behavior that, when targeted within ACT, can allow for even greater psychological flexibility. We emphasize the shaping of tolerance and augmenting values when promoting acceptance and willingness.

Cognitive Defusion

Cognitive defusion is one of the processes that is most linked to relational frame theory (RFT) as the basic model of human language and cognition and that separates ACT from cognitive therapy models such as cognitive behavior therapy (CBT). In traditional cognitive therapies, the goal is to alter the form or frequency of disordered modes of thinking (Luoma et al., 2010). As we have discussed, this way of thinking about thinking (metathinking) can be part of a larger pattern of verbal relational behavior that can promote experiential avoidance. Rather than altering the form or frequency of verbal relations, cognitive defusion strategies are designed to weaken the stimulus control of those verbal relations. Take as a simple example the college student who says, "I cannot enroll in the challenging mathematics class because I have test anxiety." The coordinated relation between "difficult college test" and "test anxiety" can lead to experiential avoidance that moves the student away from her values (i.e., psychological inflexibility). Instead of attempting to alter this verbal relation, we can attempt to alter its function such that the student may derive "I can enroll in the challenging mathematics class and have test anxiety." Anxiety is still present, the class is still challenging, but this relationship need not exert strong stimulus control over the choice to enroll in the class or not. By weakening or defusing relations that contribute to experiential avoidance, and by strengthening or augmental values and committed actions, we can build patterns of flexible adaptive responding.

Self-as-Context

Self-as-context is where ACT began (Hayes, 1984) in the realization that Skinner's "seeing seeing", which he used to explain self-awareness, had to occur from a consistent perspective or point of view of "I/here/now". This sense of perspective is linked to and hierarchically contains the content of self-awareness, but it is not defined by that content. You don't become a different person when you have an organ removed or buy a new car. The content change but the context of being aware, "I/here/now", does not.

Strengthening self-as-context necessarily requires weakening the rigid stimulus control of comparative verbal relations that we construct about ourselves, based on content. It is helpful to diminish the stimulus control exerted by stories that we tell about ourselves that often lead to experiential avoidance. Instead of seeking coherence between values and behavior (i.e., committed action), we may respond in certain ways to achieve coherence between a verbally conceptualized self and behavior (self as content). For example, a client may continue at a job that exacerbates physical injury because they want to "be tough" and they see themselves as "a provider." It could well be the case that the person values their family and the security afforded by their job, but fusion to this conceptualization of self may lead to avoidance of seeking other opportunities that confer access to the same reinforcers, but without the physical burdens and long-term damage that may limit achieving these values long term. Self-as-context requires relating to oneself flexibly and in context. One moment "tough," another "compassionate," but always "I." We will also discuss the idea of the transcendental self (i.e., I who transcends time and context) and emphasize promoting self-compassion within this core process.

REFRAMING AND INTEGRATING THE HEXAFLEX

The hexagon model of psychological flexibility can easily be organized into three higher-level dimensions: openness, centeredness, and engagement. Like the six core processes, these three pillars operate as middle-level terms that can make describing the objectives of ACT-based interventions clearer and can help connect intervention targets more with desired outcomes.

Open refers to the synthetic operation of acceptance and defusion that allow a person to more fully make contact with positive and negative experiences in their life. When harmful patterns of behavior become fixed and rigid, especially at the earliest stages of intervention, clients may not be open to the idea of change – or, clients are open to making small changes but seek to avoid any large or disruptive changes that may be necessary to achieve valued life changes. For example, a client may be experiencing toxic relationships with peers that support a myriad of harmful behavior topographies. When asked what they are looking to get out of their time with the behavior analyst, they report that they would like to "make some other friends who treat me well" and offer "hanging out with someone from work once a month" as a committed action. Although both of these small changes could participate in the process of change, these actions alone are not likely to lead to real long-lasting change. What may be necessary is revisiting entirely how they conceptualize friendship and the very real possibility that those toxic relationships may end. Moreover, the client may be extremely fearful of building pro-social friendships and relationships because they currently lack the skills necessary to be successful. Acceptance may involve promoting willingness to experience the pain of ending or distancing from friendships that are incompatible with life's larger valued reinforcers, and at the same time promoting willingness to experience the positive feelings that come with forging new friendships and relationships. Defusing from rules around not being "smart enough" or "attractive enough" or "funny enough" may be necessary to allow the client to be open to these new experiences without judgement or evaluation.

Centered refers to the clients' present capacity to notice the contingencies that operate on their behavior from a place of non-attachment and to adapt in turn. The metaphor of "being the still point in the turning world" may resonate with the pillar of centeredness. Present moment awareness is this active process of noticing private and public behavior as it ebbs and flows and noticing the antecedent and consequences that surround the behavior – to "notice" the world turning and to observe its direction. Self-as-context is involved in distancing from those content labels or evaluations that can alter one's experience of the present moment. Moreover, what someone notices and observes in the present moment can contradict conceptual labels of oneself. The critical feature of being centered is to notice these experiences without evaluation and attachment to the conceptualized self. Continuing with the same example, a client who is open to making large-scale changes in their life also needs to be centered to notice which relationships are compatible with the life they want to live and what relationships, as they presently exist, are incompatible. That is not to say that the solution is to exit those relationships that are not presently workable. At this stage of the ACT process, the most important action is simply to notice these events that will guide behavior in the next pillar.

Engaged refers to taking values-based actions. To make those small or larger scale life changes that are needed to live a more valued driven life. The first step is of course identifying exactly what those valued outcomes are. What ultimately is the client looking to achieve over the course of the ACT intervention? In our example, perhaps the client wants to have a more fulfilling career and to have relationships that feel supportive across multiple domains of their life. This is not the same as a goal because a "fulfilling career" and "supportive relationships" are aspirational and can never be completely obtained. Noticing these values does however provide a compass with which to evaluate outcomes that are being achieved in the present moment (i.e., is my career fulfilling and are my relationships supportive of my career and other areas of my life?). When the answer is negative, then committed action can support behavior that *is* supportive of this value. Yes, this could involve exiting relationships that do not fill this need. It could also mean having difficult conversations that are long overdue to effect changes in relationships that are stuck. Critically, engagement should be a highly variable and highly creative process of collaboratively developing solutions to achieve a more valued-driven life.

The pillars metaphor of these three dimensions (Figure 4.3) is appropriate because any two dimensions alone cannot sufficiently support meaningful and long-lasting behavior change. All three must be supported. Ensuring that clients are open is necessary to promote feelings of being. And ensuring clients are both open and centered is likely necessary to maximize engagement. There is no best way to approach this as a sequence, at least not that has been empirically isolated as a "best progression." There likely is no one-size-fits-all progression that will work in every case; rather, the behavior analyst should use a number of tools in their belt to tailor this intervention model to the needs of their client.

The open and centered pillars can be thought of as covering a domain of acceptance and mindfulness; the centered and engaged pillars as covering a domain of commitment and behavior change. The center pillar needs to be in both because it is always a person in a present moment responding.

All of these are behavioral processes, but some are more familiar to behavior analysts than others. Identifying valued reinforcers and identifying behaviors that contact those valued reinforcers is very much what behavior analysts already do. A critical nuance is an emphasis on self-management of committed actions and appreciating the role of verbal abstraction in the identification of valued sources of reinforcement. Moreover, "behavior change" can and will necessarily involve private behavior within the conceptualization of behavior change processes. All that said, creating goals and "committed action" and reinforcing follow-through of set goals is a core component of ACT and is necessary to produce behavior change.

Engaging in the present moment is also a behavioral process and choosing to set time aside for actions like meditating or observing mindfully can be committed actions in their own right. Accepting is also a behavior process, especially at the point where a person is tolerating immediate and potentially aversive sources of public and private stimulation in order to contact more fully chosen values.

On the other hand, processes like defusion and self-as-context may be less traditionally in the wheelhouse of behavior analytic interventions. As we will discuss in more detail

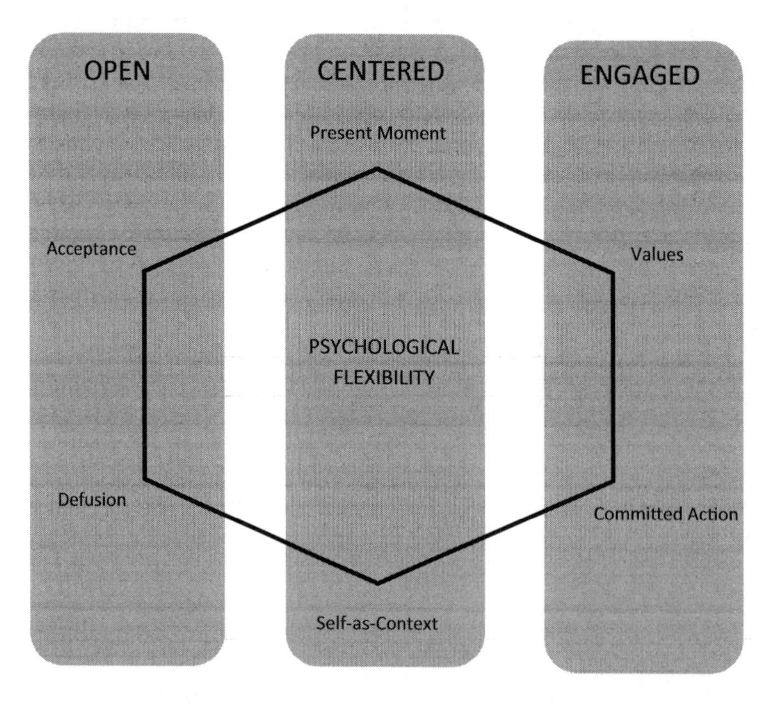

FIGURE 4.3 The three dimensions pillars

later, an acute understanding of RFT is likely needed to understand behaviors involved in cognitive fusion and conceptualization of oneself. In other fields of psychology, these processes are generally considered "cognitive" or causality if given to one's "mind." Hundreds of experimental studies now show that we can account for these complex patterns of psychological behavior in terms of patterns of relational framing that are the express target of self-as-context and defusion intervention components. Even still, the term "mindfulness targets" may resonate with non-behavior analytic communities and can successfully convey that these process of change targets are indirectly but necessarily linked to behavior change. Present moment awareness and acceptance are also part of this mindfulness half of the Hexaflex as both involve to a large extent private events. The act of noticing external and internal sources of stimulation is a private event. When we talk about acceptance, we are often referring to accepting aversive and appetitive experiences that occur privately. These processes are also closely linked to self-as-context and defusion that are necessary to promote acceptance and contact with the present moment. Therefore, these processes operate at the center of both behavior change and mindfulness and, for this reason, play a central role in behavior analytic applications of ACT within this model (Figure 4.4).

Without calling it out as such, Figure 2.1 from Chapter 2 showing behavior-behavior is an integrative model where we have attempted to embed adaptive behavior-behavior relations with the existing ABC framework that behavior analysts are accustomed to operating within. And for good reason. If psychological inflexibility occurs, it undoubtedly occurs in an antecedent context that includes discriminative stimuli and establishing operations that make psychological inflexibility (each of the six core processes) more likely to occur. Moreover, inflexibility is generally maintained by smaller-sooner-negative sources of reinforcement. Otherwise, why would it occur? In the same vein, to promote psychological flexibility, we likely need to arrange antecedent conditions that are likely to evoke behavior-behavior relations in each of the six core processes that are flexible and adaptive. We may also need to arrange or contrive temporary sources of smaller-sooner reinforcement to compete with naturally occurring avoidance contingencies to bridge the gap to when the client starts to contact larger-later valued sources of reinforcement.

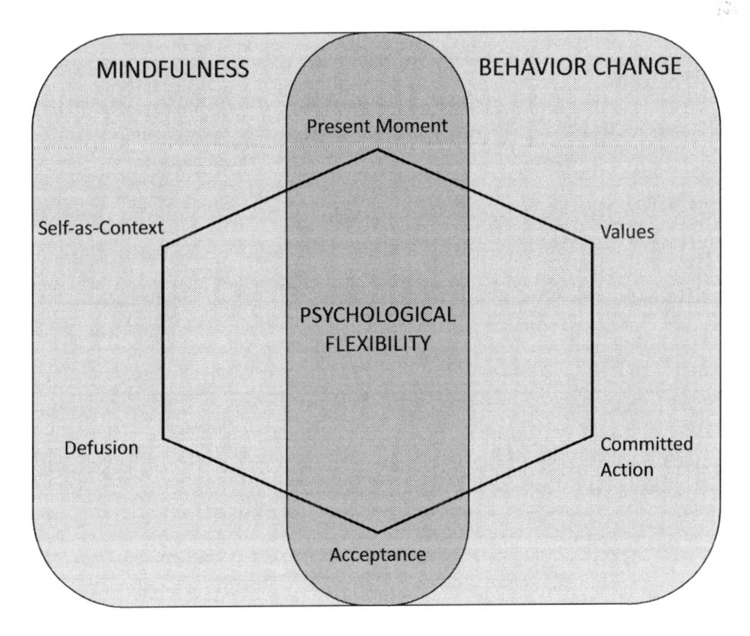

FIGURE 4.4 The Hexaflex.

From this conceptualization, some familiar behavior analytic assessment strategies may become readily apparent. For example, the traditional ABC narrative recording where practitioners record antecedents and consequences surrounding the occurrence of behavior could be adjusted to include self-monitoring where the client records the public and private antecedent conditions that occurred around the target behavior, such as choosing to binge drink for the client attempting to reduce alcohol intake. As well, the client can report the short-term and the long-term consequences of this behavior, both private and public. For example, they may have felt a temporary relief from stress from binge drinking but experienced self-loathing and a hangover the next day. This process can also help to identify more clearly target processes of change, such as defusing from the thoughts that operated as a motivating operation for binge drinking in the first place. Experimental analyses of antecedent and consequence conditions may also be possible given this model (Figure 4.5). For example, contriving antecedent conditions in a therapy session or using a speak-aloud procedure to determine which situations lead to behavior chains that ultimately lead to the target behavior. This same strategy could be used to determine the conditions under which the replacement (i.e., psychologically flexible) behaviors are most likely to occur.

We mentioned earlier that we would apply more advanced RFT frameworks where appropriate, and one framework that is made possible by this conceptualization is the hyperdimensional and multilevel model (HDML). Specifically, one assumption is that relational framing operates on behavior through the on-going process of relating (R) – orienting (O) – and evoking (E) that occurs within a motivational context (M) (Barnes-Holmes et al., 2021). This is referred to as the ROE-M. When dissecting behavior-behavior relations, behavior analysts may attempt to identify relational framing patterns (Rel-B) that operate within behavior-behavior relations. We will unpack this in more detail when discussing the six core processes. Because of transformation of stimulus function, relational behaviors likely play a role in determining which aspects of the environment we attend to or orient toward.

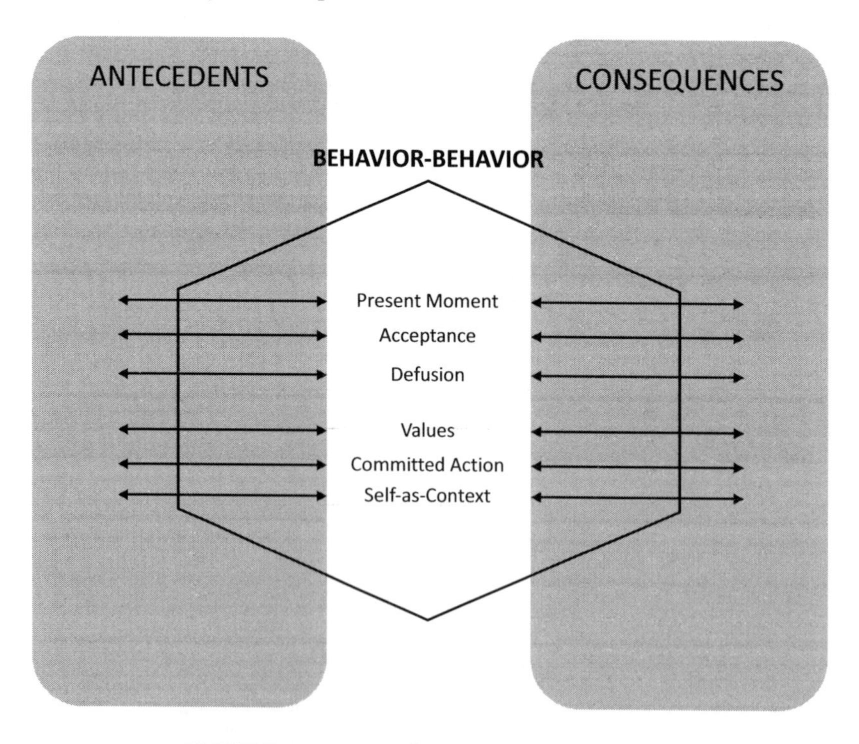

FIGURE 4.5 Antecedents and consequences.

This can be measured in a number of ways, such as by measuring actual attending behavior in a lab through eye gaze or by having clients recall situations, where what they "observed" may be far from the actual event that transpired (i.e., a function of fused relations rather than present moment awareness of the external environment). Finally, relational frames and orientation to stimuli in the environment can evoke behavior that is either maladaptive or adaptive – psychologically inflexible or psychologically flexible. Much research is still needed on the utility of ROE-M as a behavioral framework for complex processes within ACT, but such a model does have the potential to evaluate more molecular behavior-behavior and behavior-environment interactions that are targets of ACT-based interventions.

We can go even more molecular when evaluating patterns of relational framing, although even more empirical testing is needed in this arena. The Implicit Relational Assessment Procedure (IRAP) and the Functional Acquisition Speed Test (FAST) are both tools that are used to assess the differential relatedness of stimuli from within an RFT account. By comparing relative speeds of associational responses, these tests can give an estimate of the strength of relations that participate within behavior-behavior interactions. In our own work, relational density theory (RDT; Belisle & Dixon, 2020, 2021) takes a more molar approach by evaluating the interrelatedness and dimensionality of large and often complex relational networks. This is accomplished by concurrently evaluating the size and the strength of relational classes to generate predictions about relational behavior and transformations of stimulus function. Most critically, these extensions to the basic RFT account have the potential to inform each of the ACT models described above to support the development of new technologies to promote psychological flexibility.

Models interact. When we are on the right path, models also tend to converge and reach similar conclusions. These models are attempts at reframing and integrating ACT and the Hexaflex in ways that may have additional clinical utility. We now turn to discussing another model approach, the ACT Matrix, that can simplify ACT-based processes that can have utility in instances where simplification is necessary. This can occur when working with less experienced implementers, when operating at the level of organizations and systems, or when working self-management strategies into ACT-based interventions where the client will mediate much of the intervention (as is often the case). We will then turn to a more complex model that has the potential to integrate ACT more fully within contemporary advances in evolutionary science that is necessary to situate ACT, and potentially behavior analysis itself, within this larger evolutionary worldview.

THE ACT MATRIX: A SIMPLIFIED MODEL

The ACT Matrix (Polk & Schoendorff, 2014) provides a framework to start to interpret psychological flexibility as the on-going struggle between values-consistent and values-inconsistent behavior. It is a good starting point when learning ACT and is a first tool in the toolbelt of behavior analysts. In later chapters, we will expand upon this framework, but the usefulness of this tool will return as we visit specific challenges that behavior analysts may confront. We believe this is a tool that behavior analysts at this point in the book could start to experiment with themselves or with low-difficulty clients.

The Matrix seeks to evaluate behavior along two dimensions (Figure 4.6). We will start with the first dimension, which involves distinguishing between behaviors that are values-consistent and behaviors that are values-inconsistent. Actually, behavior analysts largely already use this model when defining accelerative or decelerative behavior change targets. That is, we want to decelerate maladaptive behavior and accelerate adaptive behavior. What you may not have considered is that writing a behavior plan is necessarily a values-centered endeavor because we select behavior targets based on specific values. We want to improve

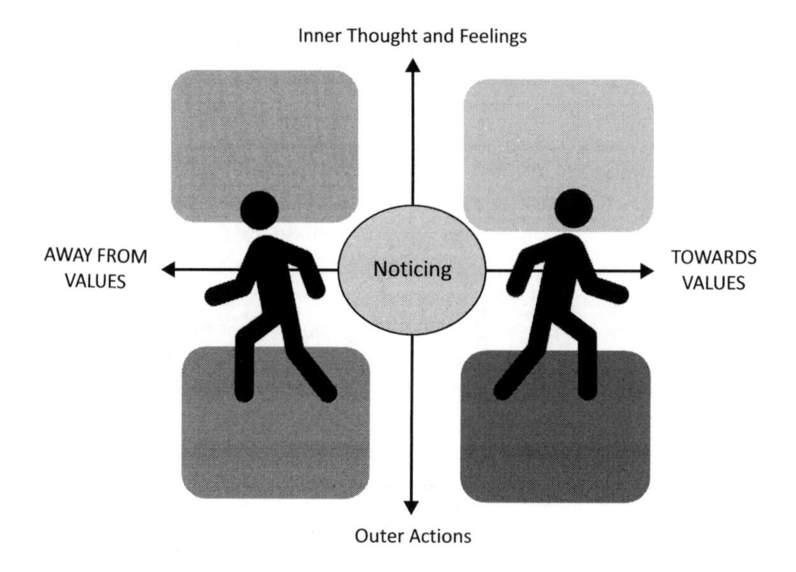

FIGURE 4.6 The ACT Matrix.

social skills to increase access to the community. We want to improve learning skills to improve performance in classrooms and other settings. This approach is consistent with the bottom half of the Matrix as we restrict our interventions to only those events that are publicly observable and accessible – the "hands and feet" of those we are working with. This strategy is not without merit, especially when working with individuals whose language is severely impacted such as those with severe forms of autism. By functionally evaluating external contextual conditions within which adaptive and maladaptive behavior occurs, we have been generally effective in developing behavior interventions. The risk is that if we restrict our work to only the bottom half of the matrix, we miss the private and abstracted functions that contribute to suffering once language shows up. If nothing else, the Matrix reminds us to consider these events when approaching functional assessment with clients.

The top half of the Matrix captures these private and abstracted functions that likely maintain "away moves" or can augment "toward moves." There are metaphorically in the person's "head and heart," and as private events, they are seen directly by an audience of one. Focusing on the top half is a starting point to functionally assess these events when we suspect private experience participates in inflexible patterns of behavior.

On the left, the client and analyst work together to identify the private aversive experiences (i.e., feelings or thoughts) that away moves allow them to escape or avoid. For example, making excuses not to go to the party allows the client to avoid anxiety about the party and thoughts such as "nobody likes me" or "they don't even want me here." On the right, the client and analyst work together to identify values that support or augment toward moves. Why do we want to increase or strengthen the identified behaviors in the first place? For this reason, although the Matrix provides an initial assessment, the process of completing the Matrix can also serve to augment values-consistent behavior by reorienting the client to *why* they want to focus on addressing or improving values-consistent behavior in the first place.

There are other versions of the Matrix but we have found that this one may be more usable by practitioners, especially when working with individuals most often served by behavior analysts. It simplifies the fairly abstract idea of private events to specifically focus on the things that clients think (head) and feel (heart) at the top and the common-sense idea that "outside" behavior may be guided by our "inside" experience. Therefore, you can start at the top-right of the Matrix and work your way around, following from lighter squares to darker squares, arriving at values-consistent behavior change targets. Like with the open-centered-engaged model, there is no true "correct" sequence, however, giving the behavior analyst a choice of how best to proceed given the flow of a session or based on other assessment data.

"Hands and feet" at the bottom also create a clear distinction for clients delineating covert experiences and overt behavior. For example, following an episode of challenging behavior, behavior analysts might ask a child "what happened?" Many readers will be all too familiar with the response "I got angry" or "I was really anxious." This version of the Matrix introduces the language necessary to then say, "That's what was happening in your head and heart, but what were you doing with your hands and feet?" Thus, the simple metaphor of the human body can serve as a verbal prompt for the child to attend to their actual behavior and have a real discussion about whether or not that behavior was in service of their chosen values, such as when asking the follow-up question, "did that move you toward or away from being a good friend?" and "when your head and your heart feel angry, what can you do with your hands and feet that would support being a good friend?"

These are honest and open conversations that occur without judgement to support psychological flexibility. Over time the verbal prompts are faded to foster independent problem-solving around the child's own public and private experiences.

The ACT Matrix is a relatively simple intervention model. In theory, any number of visual or verbal models could be constructed to support or augment psychological flexibility. The Matrix could be reconfigured as a seesaw where external forces push a person up or down, and a reaction is needed in order to move back to a state of equilibrium – consistent with values. Or the Matrix could be designed as a staircase or ladder, in which a person steps up towards values or steps down away from such values. As readers work through this chapter and the chapters that follow, adjustments to intervention models to fit within sometimes immensely complex contexts is the rule rather than the exception. These models are just tools. Keep this in mind as we visit the most complex model here: the extended evolutionary meta-model (EEMM). Our goal is to provide readers with the verbal behavior and tools necessary to successfully implement ACT-based assessments and interventions across a variety of contexts without being bound by any one single strategy. ACT is not a simple set of techniques; it is an entire approach centering around a singular pattern of behaving that research from our labs and others has supported is critical – psychological flexibility.

SYNTHESIZING THE HEXAFLEX WITH EVOLUTIONARY SCIENCE (EEMM): AN EXPANDED MODEL

The psychological flexibility model may appear initially strange to behavior analysts, but before diving into the details of the six processes in the next section of the book it is worth linking them to core behavioral ideas in a way that makes more obvious how they can lead to new forms of functional analysis. Only two additional points are needed to make the transition.

1. Behavior analysts are evolutionists.
2. Relational operants break up the behavioral stream in ways that require a multidimensional approach.

The first point should not be hard for behavior analysts because this point is richly embedded in the history of the field. In the abstract of his influential article "Selection by Consequences," Skinner framed behavior analysis as a part of evolutionary science:

> Selection by consequences is a causal mode found only in living things or in machines made by living things. It was first recognized in natural selection, but it also accounts for the shaping and maintenance of the behavior of the individual and evolution of cultures. In all three of these fields, it replaces explanations based on the causal modes of classical mechanics. The replacement is strongly resisted. Natural selection has now made its case, but similar delays in recognizing the role of selection in the other fields could deprive us of valuable help in solving the problems that confront us.
>
> *(1981, p. 501)*

Skinner's point is that function is not determined by proximal structural mechanisms ("the causal modes of classical mechanics") except as determined by processes of variation and selective retention at different scales of organization:

> human behavior is the joint product of (i) the contingencies of survival responsible for the natural selection of the species and (ii) the contingencies of reinforcement responsible for the repertoires acquired by its members, including (iii) the special contingencies maintained by an evolved social environment.
>
> *(1981, p. 502)*

We earlier summarized evolutionary thinking with the acronym VRSCDL (pronounced "versatile"): **V**ariation and **R**etention of what is **S**elected in **C**ontext at the right **D**imension and **L**evel. All behavior analytic concepts fit within this system. Successive approximation and shaping, for example, are selection and retention strategies that are built atop natural behavioral variation. Discrimination training brings behavioral variation and selective retention under contextual control. Motivative operations and reinforcement are selective processes. Extinction removes selective benefits but also leads to variation from which new responses can emerge. Response repetition and the construction of larger behavioral patterns or habits are retention strategies, and so on.

Skinner spoke in the quotes above about evolutionary processes at three levels of organization (biophysiological, psychological, and sociocultural). We know these levels interact. For example, variation and selective retention at the psychological or behavioral level alter epigenetic systems at the biophysiological level: a few weeks of meditation practice will reliably turn on or off nearly 7% of the human genome primarily through methylation of the gene systems involved in a stress response, such that particular areas of DNA can no longer be transcribed by RNA systems (Dusek et al., 2008).

What about behavioral or psychological dimensions?

This is where the second big idea comes in: relational operants break up the behavioral stream in ways that require a multidimensional approach.

It is obvious that evolution is dimensional when speaking of sociocultural or biophysiological levels. For example, everyone agrees that not only are genetic systems being selected based on their impact on survival, so too are epigenetic mechanisms.

At the behavioral or psychological level behaviorists are more cautious. There is good reason: you are far less likely to make the "mentalistic error" if all behavior is called "behavior." Even then the error can be made, however, as we pointed out in an earlier chapter. Furthermore, the problem with leaving all private events in an undifferentiated pile (notice we are not yet even saying "private behaviors" or "private antecedents" – we are using the vague terms "events" to cover it all) is that the specific ways that relational operants operate can then be glossed over.

Take emotional and dispositional terms. Skinner (1989, p. 13) noted that "words referring to feelings and states of mind were first used to describe behavior or the situations in which behavior occurred. When concurrent bodily states began to be noticed and talked about, the same words were used to describe them." In this very sensible behavioral approach, emotional terms evolved culturally based on public accompaniments that allowed people to refer to certain private events so as to control their social environment. For example, telling people you were "inclined to go" built on a felt sense of re-enforceability and response probability. It used the physical metaphor of an inclined plane because there was no other ready way to speak of private events. Saying you "wanted" something told the verbal community what you were missing. This is the etymology of "want" – we still use it that way in sentences like "for want of food he died." Again the overt event of missing something was used as a metaphor for an emotion.

This is good so far as it goes, but as people developed an entire vocabulary of emotional and dispositional terms it seems natural that they would use these terms to explain their own behavior. The terms would move from ways to influence others into verbal reasons to be believed or followed. "Why did you eat all the dessert!?" you'd be asked as a small child. Initially you might foolishly say "just cuz" and suffer the consequences but soon you'd be saying "because I was soooo hungry, Mama" and maybe you'd be cut some slack. Ever so gradually moments like this partitioned "feelings" and "thoughts" away from other kinds of behavior.

The psychological flexibility model has six processes (values, committed action, acceptance, defusion, self, the now), but another way to think of it is that it orients practitioners to six common socially-supported dimensions of behavior, with and the dominant functional and non-functional aspects within each. These are motivational events (values vs. short term reinforcers), overt behavioral events (committed action vs. impulsivity, procrastination, or avoidant persistence), affect (acceptance vs. experiential avoidance or attachment), cognition (ways of speaking about defusion vs. fusion with private verbal rules), self (self-as-context vs. entanglement with the conceptualized self), and attention (flexible attention to the now vs. entanglement with the past and future).

These are all forms of behavior. They are all contextually and historically situated actions. Nevertheless, relational operants have partitioned the behavioral stream via our own cultural history, and there is a benefit that derives from recognizing those divisions if we are careful not to ontologize them. Even young children are asked about motivative operations ("what do you want to eat, Johnny?"), affect ("how are you feeling?"), cognition ("what do you think you should do to solve that problem?), and so on. Every parent and every teacher will do the same to every child. It would be rude and foolish to visit a country and loudly declare "I will never learn nor use your language!" Why should behavior analysts take pride in doing such a thing to the mainstream culture? Using these terms and also knowing how to think of them in a technical way, if we are wise and careful, allows us to "have our cake and eat it too." Thus, while at one level it is all behavior, we recognize that relational framing interacts with the behavioral stream to create useful dimensions of action for various social and behavioral purposes.

If you put these two ideas together you arrive at a model of how to think of human functioning in a behaviorally sensible extension of evolutionary thinking called the "extended evolutionary meta-model" or EEMM (Hayes et al., 2020). The EEMM is shown in Figure 4.7.

Variation in this context refers to the ways in which psychological adjustments differ in their topographical and functional properties, while selection refers to consequences that tend to increase or decrease a particular psychological or behavioral variant. Context refers to the historical and situational features that determine whether a given variant will be

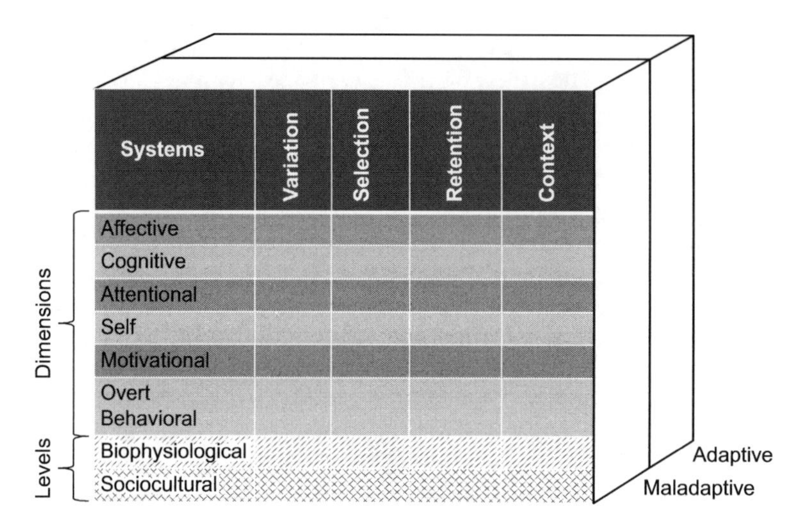

FIGURE 4.7 Extended evolutionary meta-model (copyright Steven C. Hayes and Stefan G. Hofmann; used with permission).

selected. Retention refers to the likelihood of a variant being maintained in a person's repertoire, phenotype, or culture.

In a series of articles (Hayes et al., 2019, 2020; Hofmann & Hayes, 2019), and books (Hayes & Hofmann, 2018; Hofmann & Hayes, 2020) the EEMM has been linked to process-based therapy (PBT; Hayes & Hofmann, 2017) and the psychological flexibility model. The processes of change in the psychological flexibility model are "theory-based, dynamic, progressive, contextually bound, modifiable, and multilevel changes that occur in empirically established sequences oriented toward desirable outcomes" (Hofmann & Hayes, 2018, p. 38). They are (Hayes et al., 2020):

- *theory-based*, because they are associated with a clear statement of relations among events and lead to testable predictions and methods of influence;
- *dynamic*, because processes may involve feedback loops and non-linear changes;
- *progressive*, because they may need to be arranged in an order to reach the treatment goal;
- *contextually bound and modifiable* to focus on their implications for practical changes and intervention kernels within reach of practitioners; and
- *multilevel*, because some processes supersede or are nested within others.

The psychological flexibility model can readily be fit into an extended evolutionary meta-model. The six core flexibility processes are shown in Table 4.1, and their corresponding inflexible versions are shown in Table 4.2 (taken from Hayes et al., 2020). As can be seen, the six processes typically presented in the "ACT Hexaflex" are here arranged in the corresponding psychological dimensions of the psychological EEMM. We will unpack these figures more fully in the following chapters but for now only a few points need to be made.

Healthy variation is not unlimited or chaotic – it is linked to context and purpose. Conversely, selective retention generally reduces variability, but if these aspects of evolving systems are properly context-sensitive, that reduction in variability fosters adaptation. Indeed, in some circumstances, healthy variability can itself be selected as retained such as when artists learn how to be consistently innovative and creative. Adaptation includes biological health and social functioning (the levels of analysis in which psychological events are nested) but it is also measured against chosen values and other underlying motivational operations.

TABLE 4.1

	Adaptive				
		Healthy *Variation*	Selection *Criteria*	*Retention*	*Context*
Psychological dimensions	**Cognition**	Defusion and cognitive flexibility	Functional coherence	Broaden and build using practice, and integration into larger habit patterns	Use conscious attention to maintain balance and effectiveness
	Affect	Acceptance and emotional openness	Feeling fully		
	Self	Perspective-taking, sense of self	Belonging and connection		Key strength of these processes
	Attention	Flexible, fluid, and voluntary attention to the now inside and out	Voluntary orientation		
	Motivation	Values	Meaning by choice	Key strength of these processes	Use conscious attention to maintain balance and effectiveness
	Overt Behavior	Committed action	Competence		

TABLE 4.2

	Maladaptive				
		Rigidity or Unhealthy Variation	*Selection Criteria*	*Retention*	*Context*
Psychological dimensions	**Cognition**	Fusion	Being right: Literal coherence	Broaden and build using practice, and integration into larger negative habit patterns	Attend to threats but otherwise show limited context sensitivity
	Affect	Experiential avoidance	Feeling "good" leading to a "happy numb"		
	Self	Conceptualized Self	Belonging through conceptualized specialness		
	Attention	Rigid attention to past or future	Involuntary orientation		
	Motivation	Self-gratification or external "success"	Meaning by imposition		
	Overt Behavior	Impulsivity, inaction, or avoidant persistence	Short-term behavioral gains at the cost of long-term competence		

(© Steven C. Hayes and Stefan G. Hofmann. Used with permission).

While variation and selective retention in context are relevant to all six flexibility processes, it is worth noting that self and attentional processes are especially key to the person's overall context sensitivity (because these involve consciously contacting the internal and external environment), motivation and overt behavioral processes are especially key to the person's ability to select and retain gains because what is not used as part of actual behavior is likely to be lost, and acceptance and defusion processes are especially key to the person's ability to vary actions in a healthy way between of the repertoire narrowing impact of fused rules and avoided or clung to private events.

In a more focused sense, people have certain basic motivative operations beyond mere health and survival (Deci & Ryan, 2000). These are satisfied over the longer term by adaptive psychological flexibility processes and are hindered by maladaptive processes (Hayes, 2019). Thus, the psychological flexibility model links to research on the importance of belonging, feeling, competence, and so on in motivative operations. The EEMM is not a blank slate.

For example, in phylogenetic time scales the need for cooperation and empathic connection in humans as social primates is plausibly related to a wide variety of human behavioral and physical phenotypic features (Tomasello et al., 2007). Relational frame theorists have argued that perspective-taking, joint attention, social referencing, and similar skills established the conditions for the acquired bidirectionality of stimulus equivalence and other relational operants (Hayes & Sanford, 2014). In the EEMM this idea is represented by the idea that perspective-taking is selected in part by belonging and connection. In a similar way, all six of the flexibility processes are linked to characteristic motivative operations that are broadly applicable to human evolution (Hayes, 2019).

APPROACHING THESE MODELS FUNCTIONALLY

All of this is in some sense arbitrary. Right side up, upside down, hexagonal, square, circular, or see-saw ... it doesn't matter. These "models" are just verbal devices used to solve problems.

You can adapt these models. Create your own models. What is critical is that we remember to always remain empirical in the testing of approaches grounded in models. No model is universally superior but we can identify the contexts within which various models are functional. All of these models become applicable only when derived relational responding reaches a certain level of sophistication.

This approach can be highly technical and we often use middle-level terms to orient us to sets of functional analyses. Often, they also help us link to the verbal behavior of other communities – other disciplines, the mainstream culture, clients, or their families or caregivers. Using what works should not be done in a sloppy way – indeed it requires more sophistication, not less, to use multiple language systems for different purposes while avoiding confusion. The rigid alternative (only talking behavioralese) has at times threatened the very existence of our field, and certainly has limited its growth.

In many forms of research and practice, it is the technical account that is more important for innovation within our field. That account is not easy because relational operants, while incredibly simple to describe behaviorally ("relating is an operant"), can be challenging to work with because they interact with other contingency streams that are several hundred to a thousand times older. Some of what seems initially strange to behavior analysts about the psychological flexibility model has evolved over decades to focus on how these behavioral systems interact. Thus, we ask for the readers' openness – but we do not ask for abandonment of skepticism. As we dive into the account of the flexibility processes all we need is this simple attitude: let's see!

PART 2

Approaching ACT Processes Functionally and Analytically

5

Present Moment

Drive past any suburban shopping center in the United States, and the odds are pretty good you will encounter a yoga studio and mindfulness center. Once an idea foreign to western culture, "mindfulness" has come to take center stage during the past decade and is an idea that is growing in popular culture and in the media. In 2014, Time Magazine published an issue titled "The Mindful Revolution: The Science of Finding Focus in a Stressed Out, Multi-Tasking Culture." Although mindfulness as a solution to the stress and chaos of life is a nuanced concept in western culture, mindfulness practice has played a central role in eastern cultures and religious practice – notably, Buddhism and Hinduism. Contemplative practice more generally is part of every major religion.

The basic tenet of mindfulness is that we suffer because our minds tell us that we want what we do not have, or we have what we do not want, or we have what we want and must cling to it. Our thoughts are consumed by ruminating on events that happened in the past and being anxious about events that may transpire in the future. We are driven by avoidance and attachment. We are rarely focused on events as they are occurring here and now, right here in front of us.

The whole concept of "mind" has been immensely problematic within behavioral science because it is given ontological and causal status. Behavior analysis has found notable success by avoiding mentalism. The error is fostered by assuming that non-physical entities like a mind or a spirit control behavior, but as we have argued, it occurs when any behavior-behavior relation is given causal status.

But we need not approach so-called "mental" events in a literally dualistic way and we need not approach the functional relation between behavioral events in a decontextualized way. The mentalistic error cannot be eliminated by vocabulary and no word is inherently mentalistic. Our goal is to move our science and practice closer to the core assumptions of radical behaviorism and its offshoot, functional contextualism. If this mindfulness revolution is real, can it be understood behavior analytically? Is there any utility in doing so?

A very brief review of what we've covered in the first four chapters of this book seems helpful here. The core philosophical commitment within these forms of behaviorism is that of *pragmatism*. Pragmatism is a realist position, but it holds that there is no fundamental truth or reality out there to be discovered that is alone and cut off from our interactions with the world; rather, our sensory systems and our behavior itself, including our ideas as scientists, are true only insofar as they allow us to behave more effectively within what Skinner called "the one world."

DOI: 10.4324/9781003250371-7

Mentalism is not based on the dictionary definitions of words – its cost comes from allowing a focus on the pragmatic impact of contingencies to slip away from view. Skinner objected to the concept of mind purely on pragmatic grounds. Here are two classic quotes we've already used: "The objection to the inner workings of the mind is not that they are not open to inspection but that they have stood in the way of the inspection of more important things" (Skinner, 1974, p. 165), and "mentalism has obscured the environmental antecedents which would have led to a much more effective analysis" (Skinner, 1974, p. 165). What a strange and beautifully consistent set of objections! He did not say, as many less careful behavior analysts would, "there is no freakin' mind!" That would move him over to a non-pragmatic truth argument and he knows not to do that. As a pragmatist, he instead notes that the concept has gotten in the way of what we can do as behaviorists: predict and influence behavior with precision, scope, and depth.

As we have increased our ability to do that based on relational framing principles, however, many of the phenomena that were only covered by literally mentalistic terms can now be addressed using direct and indirect contingency analyses.

And as that has happened sometimes it is easier for us to communicate with the world and our clients using more common-sense language about thought, emotion, mind, and so on but to do it in ways that do not impute cause and never make the mentalistic error. If we are careful, well-trained behavior analysts with the needed conceptual skills need not mind "mind." The issue is not the *literal* truth of words like "mind" (or any other word for that matter) it is how they alter our interaction with the world.

A bit of responsible cognitive flexibility helps us understand what others are talking about in their scientific research programs. Many different psychotherapies exist to treat clinical disorders, and some of them (cognitive behavior therapy for example) do a relatively good job of it. Unlike acceptance and commitment herapy (ACT), they have not been developed or analyzed using behavioral and evolutionary principles as expanded by relational frame theory (RFT). Nevertheless, it is worth considering the features of relatively successful forms of psychotherapy that talk in other terms to begin to subject their ideas and data to a behavioral analysis using our conceptual tools. That is, collaborative opportunities abound when (and only when) we are able to operate with our own rules more effectively, as ACT challenges us to do.

One common feature of many of the psychotherapies that are effective is the inclusion of interventions designed to teach the attentional flexibility needed to experience events as they occur in the present moment without needless domination by the conceptualized past or future. Mindfulness is the most common word for these skills. How to understand and establish those skills is the topic of this chapter. Ironically, much like Skinner's earliest conceptualizations, the word "mind" is never used when talking technically and is only introduced as a middle-level term to convey meaning to clients. We have to use words that clients understand or that have pre-established meaning, lest our approaches become more about training a new vernacular than actually solving the problem at hand. RFT describes why this is the case. "Mind" is already entailed with specific behavior patterns – and it is these behavior patterns that we want to build and support.

There is a large body of work in support of these methods. According to a meta-analysis published by Goldberg et al. (2018), mindfulness interventions across 142 non-overlapping samples containing just over 12,000 participants have been shown to be superior to no treatment and active controls. Evidence is mounting that training and practice in flexible attention to the present moment can influence a wide variety of important behaviors. Therefore, it is up to us to understand what exactly is happening as a behavioral process during mindfulness practice if we hope to develop conceptually systematic technologies to influence complex patterns of behavior.

BASIC BEHAVIOR CHANGE PROCESSES: STIMULUS CONTROL AND THE CHALLENGE OF BEHAVIOR-BEHAVIOR RELATIONS

Stimulus control occurs when stimuli come to evoke operant behaviors due to a previous history of differential reinforcement. S+ stimuli (also termed discriminative stimuli) are those that signal the differential availability of reinforcement for engaging in a specific response (i.e., the response has been reinforced in the past in the presence of S+). S- stimuli (also termed S-deltas) are those that signal the differential non-availability of reinforcement for engaging in a specific response (i.e., the behavior has not been reinforced in the past in the presence of S-).

The term *differential* is important for our purposes because in many ways even simple discriminated stimulus control is relational as we have already defined it – but in a non-arbitrary sense. To use an animal model for illustration, imagine two levers are present in an operant chamber wherein a rat can freely suppress either of the two levers. The first lever is green (LG) and the second is red (LR), and the location of LG and LR are randomized in each session. LG operates on a fixed ratio (FR) 5 schedule (S+) and LR (S-) never provides the reinforcer (EXT). Given this arrangement, we would anticipate almost exclusive allocation to LG (S+) over LR (S-), which would provide an experimental demonstration of stimulus control. Now, what would happen if LG was held at FR5 but LR was adjusted to a continuous schedule of reinforcement (CRF)? Even though no change was made to the LG schedule, we would expect almost exclusive allocation to LR.

This basic paradigm has largely been at the core of applied behavior analysis (ABA) treatments addressing challenging behavior. The first step is to identify the stimulus conditions that are most likely to evoke or that presently control the challenging behavior (S+). Next, define an alternative replacement behavior. Then, manipulate the reinforcement schedule so that the same stimulus conditions serve as an S- for the challenging behavior (EXT, or hold present rate constant), and as an S+ for the replacement behavior. These procedures are considered differential reinforcement procedures and are relational intervention procedures, manipulating immediate environmental stimulus conditions to obtain stimulus control over challenging and replacement behavior. That is, the schedules for both are controlled by the schedule of reinforcement relative to the other.

However, verbal relational behavior is immensely more complicated than this simple model as we illustrated when describing RFT. For example, imagine you were the rat in the operant chamber, but instead of a green and red lever, you were presented with a Donald Trump lever (DTL) and a red lever (RL). And let's assume that the schedules on both levers are held equal at FR5. Which lever do you allocate most of your responding to?

The standard matching law equation would predict roughly equal allocation to both levers. However, some readers of this text might be huge Donald Trump fans and therefore may allocate most of their responding toward DTL. DTL would therefore operate as an S+ not because of differential availability of reinforcement (schedules are equal), but rather because a verbal relational history with Donald Trump makes the DTL lever more preferred. Some of the reinforcing functions of "Donald Trump" transfer not only to the lever but likely to the reinforcers dispensed by it. The stimulus *function* of the lever has been *transformed*.

Other readers of this text may strongly dislike Donald Trump. Such readers may therefore avoid DTL, representing a transfer of the S- function. Transformations of this kind play a major role in human behavior due to relational operants. The basic phenomenon was shown early in the RFT research program (see Dymond & Barnes, 1995; some of this early work is summarized in Chapter 3 of Hayes et al., 2001) but it has also been shown now in applied behavior analysis. For example, Dixon and colleagues have demonstrated this phenomenon empirically with recreational gamblers (e.g., Zlomke & Dixon, 2006). In the basic arrangement, the gamblers are given access to concurrently available slot machines that differ only in color (e.g., LG and LR), holding the win rate constant across the machines. Participants then select one color (G) when shown stimuli that are "more" (e.g., first place, ace of spades) and the other (R) when shown stimuli that are "less" (e.g., last place). After this relational training, most gamblers will allocate greater responding to LG over LR, even though the payout is equal.

Phenomena of this kind may be observed in the context of what we would traditionally refer to as escape-maintained work refusal in children. Consider a child who is typically developing or has a milder disability, who puts his head down every time his teacher presents a math worksheet. The results of an experimental functional analysis may well reveal that this behavior is maintained by escape from demands, and at some level this may be accurate. However, why do the math worksheets carry an aversive function in the first place? Surely, the child's behavior of completing math worksheets has not been punished historically; rather, completing math worksheets only stands to receive reinforcers upon completion.

To understand the escape-maintained refusal more completely, we must consider the verbal relations that are evoked by the worksheet. One important example is the private verbal events (i.e., "thoughts") focused on the past or future may emerge as dominant features of the entire episode. These could include such verbal formulations as "I failed at this last time" or "I've always been bad at math compared to others," or more future-oriented verbal constructions such as "I'll never get this right" or even "I am too stupid to do this." The stimulus control exerted by the room may change as a result: the child may begin to scan the room for indications that others think he is stupid; or for possible sources of escape (e.g., the presence of a drinking fountain, pencil sharpener, or door to a restroom). Increased contact with these contextual events may then lead to distracting behavior as stimulus control broadens or narrows based on the verbal functions of the worksheet. Refusing to complete the worksheet allows the child to escape not just the task, but also the aversive functions that are established by these verbal relations regarding the worksheet. Although a traditional approach such as not allowing the child to escape the task until its completion could address this single topography, it fails to address the verbal repertoire and its impact on stimulus control. Because it is not addressed those behavioral processes may remain in place to create problems down the road.

Another example may be seen within a very common phobia – flying. Note, a *phobia* is considered an irrational fear of an object or event. The word "irrational" refers to the likelihood that the fear is unlikely grounded in direct external experience. Roughly 15% of Americans report a fear of flying, yet almost 0% have ever been involved in a plane crash. However, "airplane" may be verbally related to "dangerous," "heights," "crash," and "death," all of which carry avoidance and escape functions. It may be related to "trapped" or "humiliation" if the person fears that she will throw up or "lose it" and demand that the plane land. The impact of these verbal events may then focus on signs that the flight attendants may sense danger, on slight bumps or flection of the wings, on engine noise that sounds unusual, on possible tension in the captain's voice, on physiological arousal, on impending nausea, on subtle urges to get up and run or shout, or on visualizations of one's obituary, and so on and one.

These examples illustrate the potential complexity of stimulus control in verbal humans due to the transformation of stimulus functions through coordinated networks. Humans do not just interact with stimulus events due to their physical presence or absence or their direct history, either operant or classical. Verbal events can readily emerge that override stimulus control linked to the actual contingencies that are present.

INTERNAL AND EXTERNAL STIMULUS CONTROL

Skinner (1945) opened up behavior analysis to the study of private events: those that only the person themself experiences. Traditional approaches in ABA have largely ignored private events because they feel that direct contingencies tell us all we need to know about how and why private events exist or operate. The single biggest implication of RFT for behavior analysis is that this idea is false. The example we are looking at in this chapter is that of stimulus control. Once arbitrarily applicable verbal relations show up, stimulus control (both in an operant and classically conditioned sense) is not only exerted by objects and events in the immediate external environment based on their predictive relationship to other things (unconditioned stimuli in case of classical conditioning; response-consequence contingencies in the case of operant conditioning), but also by the verbal relations that influence these various forms of stimulus control.

Consider a series of experiments conducted by former Association for Behavior Analysis International (ABAI) President Mike Dougher and his colleagues about how verbal relations may influence internal experiences without direct exposure to aversive stimuli. In one study (Augustson et al., 2000; see also Markham et al., 2002), researchers presented an unfamiliar compound stimulus (CS1) prior to delivering a small cutaneous shock to consenting participants. Similar to the earliest research on respondent conditioning in animal models (e.g., Pavlov and salivation in dogs), CS1 became a conditioned compound stimulus eliciting momentary elevations in skin conductance. The compound stimuli remained the same, but the eliciting function has been transformed (S1 elicits elevated heart rate). Next, the researchers established verbal relations with new compound stimuli containing the CS1 images (CS2 and CS3), creating new coordinated verbal classes with CS1: (CS1 = CS2 = CS3). Importantly, after this class was established, the researchers observed that participants also showed elevated skin conductance when shown CS2 and CS3, and not when shown other compound stimuli, even though these stimuli were never paired with shock.

As RFT research has shown, however, not all verbal relations are frames of coordination or sameness, and for that reason even the powerful derived relation of stimulus equivalence cannot fully account for the influence of behavior-behavior relations by relational responding. Additional studies by Dougher and colleagues have shown that eliciting and evocative functions can also transform the function of stimuli through comparative relations with predictable and surprising outcomes (Dougher et al., 1994).

In one such study, a group of participants was trained to respond to a cue to mean "greater than" when two arbitrary items were compared (you already have such training with the cue ">" so we will use that here). Participants were then trained to pick an arbitrary stimulus (we will call it S2) given the presence of another such stimulus (S1) and to pick a third stimulus (S3) given S2. Said in more a common-sense way, they learn the network S1 > S2 > S3. The second group did not learn that network. Everyone then had S2 repeatedly paired with shock until they showed arousal when S3 appeared. The question is this: what did participants do when S3 and S1 appeared? Everyone showed much less arousal to S3 (after all it was an entirely different stimulus for those who did not learn the network S1 > S2 > S3, so stimulus generalization was minimal, and for those who did learn that network S3 is less than S2). When S1 was presented it was different. Those who had not learned the relational network showed minimal arousal, but for those who had, they showed more arousal to S1 than to S2, despite the lack of ever having been shocked in the presence of S1! Stated in words, if S1 was bigger than S2, and S2 predicted shock, S1 might predict a whopper of a shock.

Other studies have tested these transformations of function with other relational frame families such as opposition (e.g., Dymond et al., 2007) and other responses such as arousal function (Roche et al., 2000) and implicit and explicit measures of fear and happiness (Perez et al., 2020). If effects like these were due entirely due to training, they could be contained. The problem is that the relational control exerted by training with comparative framing (that is, the control exerted by ">") is just an example of a vast number of similar processes that are occurring all the time in human behavior. Once established, the impact of relational operants can be extremely indirect. Go back to the child refusing to complete math worksheets and you can see why. Even though the math worksheets may have never been directly paired with aversive or punitive environmental stimuli, and the child may never, ever have been told "you are stupid at math," a very indirect aspect of history (such as having been teased by peers about being in a special ed class years ago) might occasion private relational responses that construct relations among these events. The student may emit a relational response such as "I am stupid" merely by the sight of a worksheet due to aspects of history one could never trace down nor fully control.

Refusing to do the work, therefore, may be effective in avoiding some of the impacts of these thoughts and the aversive internal conditions these elicit, negatively reinforcing the refusal behavior. The worksheet still exerts stimulus control on the response, but the function is deeply intertwined with the child's own verbal relations surrounding not just the direct event, but any event that occasions a relational context.

Given the range and subtlety of relational cues, how can this negative behavior-behavior relation that emerges as a worksheet is distributed (worksheet evokes "I am too stupid to do this" which alters math involvement and performance and leads to escape or avoidance) be managed?

If the behavior analyst concludes "the cause of the avoidance of math is the thought I'm stupid at math" the mentalistic error is made. The thought, the avoidance, and their relationship are *all* "caused" by history and circumstances and thus no behavior – private or public – should be viewed as a "cause" within the same person as measured against the goals of behavior analysis (prediction and influence of behavior with precision, scope, and depth). They are all caused by the manipulable context. That is why we can construct intervention methods for this problem – and it is why ACT works. True, we may not be able to alter the history and current circumstance that together gave rise to the thought in the first place (in part because it is too subtle and multifaceted) – but we can change the context that produced an impact of one behavior (a "thought" or relational response) on another (avoidance).

There are several psychological flexibility processes that could help in that regard. We could diminish the transformation of stimulus functions exerted by the thought – methods we will explore in the chapter on defusion; we could reduce the aversive qualities of the resulting arousal itself thereby reducing the motivation for avoidance – methods we will explore in the chapter on acceptance; we could diminishing the dominance of a verbally conceptualized self that resides within the "I am stupid" network – methods we will explore in the chapter on the self; we could focus on what qualities the student wants to reflect in behavior and building habits around that – methods we will explore in the chapters on values and committed action. In this chapter, we will focus on another approach: methods that alter stimulus control so as to augment healthy contingency sensitivity in the here and now.

All six of these methods work by changing the context that supports an unhelpful behavior-behavior relation. The contingencies that sustain these contextual interventions are the larger later reinforcers that follow from adaptive behavior, rather than the smaller soon reinforcers that come from maladaptive behavior. For that to work, ultimately all of the flexibility processes need to be combined into greater psychological flexibility.

ALTERING STIMULUS CONTROL: PRESENT-MOMENT AWARENESS AND ATTENTIONAL FLEXIBILITY

Mindfulness, meditation, and intentionally interacting with the present moment are not something discovered by behavior analysts; rather these represent concepts that have played a prominent role in the mystical wing of wisdom and religious traditions generally. Some specific terms are associated with specific religious or cultural traditions, so it is important not to think of the analyses such as those inside ACT as being the same as these concepts in a religious context. Instead, scientifically, we need to be clear about what we mean. Scientists are only just beginning to understand the considerable impact that present-moment awareness processes, by whatever name, can have on stress reduction and physical and mental health (Grossman et al., 2004), and even genetic expression (e.g., Dada et al., 2018). In behavior analysis, we are beginning to see how these processes can impact observable, measurable behavior.

Research by Nirbay Singh, a doctoral-level Board Certified Behavior Analyst (BCBA-D) and the editor of the journal *Mindfulness*, provides a concrete example. In concert with Bob Wahler and other behavioral researchers, he developed a novel mindfulness practice intended initially for use for the control of aggression in persons with developmental disabilities (Singh et al., 2003). In this exercise, people are taught to focus on the soles of their feet when anger arises. In the initial study, evaluated in a single case design, dramatic reductions in aggression immediately followed. This has since been replicated numerous times, and in other populations, such as in persons diagnosed with severe mental illness (Singh et al., 2007). Furthermore, when *staff* who are caring for individuals with developmental disabilities are given similar mindfulness training, their use of physical restraints fell to near zero while their clients showed far fewer incidents of aggression (Singh, 2011).

Before moving ahead in the chapter, let's pause for just a few minutes to explore a particular form of the "soles of the feet" exercise personally, so you can get a sense of it. That will help create an experiential foundation for you before we discuss a few issues of assessment and intervention in this area. Please actually do the exercise – do not just read it.

- If you are standing, stand in a natural stance, with the soles of your feet on the floor; if you are sitting, sit comfortably with the soles of your feet flat on the floor.
- Breathe naturally and do nothing.
- Think back to an incident that made you very angry. Allow your feelings and thoughts to flow naturally, without restriction.
- Now, shift all your attention to the sole of your left foot.
- Notice how it feels, the shape it has, where there is pressure or heat. See if you can do so without moving or changing anything.
- After a minute or two, shift all your attention to the sole of your *right* foot.
- Notice how it feels, the shape it has, where there is pressure or heat. See if you can do so without moving or changing anything
- After a minute or two expand your focus to the soles of *both* of your feet at once. Do not shift your attention back and forth; rather, expand your focus to both simultaneously. You have to let some of the stimulus details dim to do this – sort of like how you can expand the beam of a flashlight but each part of what is seen now has a softer light.
- Notice how the soles of both of your feet feel, the shape they have, and where there is pressure or heat. See if you can do so without moving or changing anything.
- Continue for a minute or so more and as you do all of this notice that those angry thoughts can still be there but you need not let them be the focus of your attention.

When done with children with disabilities the exercise is even simpler (we will describe that at the end of the chapter), but this gives us a concrete experience to refer to in trying to understand how attention to the present moment might work.

Mindfulness training of this kind can be seen as an attempt to untangle the complex interplay between external stimuli and verbal relational behavior by augmenting stimulus control of events and reinforcement schedules occurring here and now, and selectively diminishing unnecessary control by private events. Singh et al. (2009) speculate on this process in their analysis of why mindfulness training in staff could have resulted in dramatic behavioral improvements in their clients with developmental disabilities:

> It enables staff to disengage themselves from a premature cognitive commitment to pre-empt or control the behaviour of the individuals, based on history. Staff can observe without judgment [and thus] to see positive possibilities where none or only negative possibilities, were envisioned previously. This enables staff to break the cycle of negative staff-individual interactions, thereby enabling more positive outcomes to arise.
>
> *(p. 198)*

Augmenting stimulus control of relevant features of the environment is something that most behavior analysts will be already familiar with. In traditional approaches to discrete trial training, correct emission of given verbal behavior is reinforced under specific stimulus conditions (e.g., say "dog" in the presence of a picture of a dog). Naturalistic environmental training attempts to achieve the same outcome as specific stimulus events occur naturally by prompting and reinforcing the desired behavior. Behavioral skills training goes a step further by incorporating instructions, modeling, rehearsal, and feedback, all of which are used to ensure that a target behavior readily occurs within the context of specified environmental conditions. In all cases, the goal is to narrow or restrict stimulus control to only the most relevant features of the environment in order to alter the function of immediate external stimulus objects.

Selectively diminishing stimulus control is also a common idea in behavior analysis. Habituation is a primitive behavioral process that antedates the evolution of operant learning and involves a reduction in the salience of stimulus events following their repeated presentation. Operant extinction reduces the discriminative control exerted by previously effective SDs when reinforcers are no longer made available on a contingent basis in their presence. Thus, both augmenting and diminishing stimulus control is an everyday idea for behavior analysts. Mindfulness training can be viewed simply as a special case of this more general process. What is different is the use of relational operants to establish a more general skill. Our goal in present-moment awareness is to teach a general behavioral skill of broadening or narrowing, shifting or retaining stimulus control in the present moment.

Take the soles of the feet exercise as an example. Suppose when anger arises, a child is taught to focus on the soles of her feet. As a behavioral skill, this is a deliberate verbally governed augmentation of a continuously available but normally weak source of stimulus control: the stimulation provided by one's feet. A verbally described discriminative stimulus is specified (namely to do this when one feels angry in the interest of avoiding aggression), but having an alternative response simultaneously diminishes its role as an eliciting stimulus or as a discriminative stimulus for sequences of behavior that could lead to aggression such as verbally or physically challenging whoever is making one angry.

This is training in shifting or broadening sources of stimulus control. As mindfulness training continues and other methods are used, the child or staff member learns to engage in forms of observing that shift, continue, broaden, or narrow sources of stimulus control. That behavior itself can then come under more and more refined operant control.

Readers with experience in mindfulness methods can quickly supply examples. Sitting and following the breath, and then noticing when the breath is no longer the focus and bringing it back into view, is a classic example. Focusing on just one instrument when listening to a piece of music, and then shifting to another instrument is a fun and useful training process in "meta-cognitive therapy" that is easy to use with children. Body scans that require noticing physical sensations in one part of the body and then another is a common and easy place to being; focused attentional methods such as looking at a spot on the wall or another. Literally hundreds of exercises have been developed that are easy to deploy.

The usual name for this process of focusing, wandering, and refocusing is "attentional control" though the gerund form is equally appropriate: attending. As with all free operants, a level of skill can be sought for attending that is flexible, fluid, and voluntary (in the non-mentalistic sense of "voluntary" meaning fully under operant control). As attentional skills are acquired such that contact with the present moment is more flexible, fluid, and voluntary, the client is becoming more "mindful."

There is little or no need to invoke attention when dealing with non-human animals. Just as discriminative control in non-human animals does not mean that this result is due to "discrimination" as an act, we would normally not say that the strength of stimulus control is "due to attention." The reason we need to begin to examine such processes as behavior analysts is that relational operants operate on other behavior and on other behavioral processes. In Mike Dougher's previously described study with shock, a history with a comparative relational cue evoked a relational response that led to more of a "conditioned emotional response" with a previously neutral event than with a trained conditioned stimulus (CS) due to the participation of the neutral stimulus and CS in a comparative relational frame. This behavior-behavior relation (comparing and the transformation of stimulus functions that results) can itself come under operant control.

The exact same analysis applies to mindfulness. Given training in mindfulness methods, we can present cues that evoke that training. As a result, alternative means of augmenting or diminishing, broadening or narrowing of stimulus control can be made available when needed.

Traditionally in ABA altering stimulus control has been achieved by making specific stimuli more salient. For example, a behavior analyst may add a color picture card to the environment to signal that reinforcement is available. These antecedent control strategies will be effective however only if the person makes contact with these events occurring here and now. Said simply the person needs to see the card. When relational operants interfere with being present, actual contingencies like that can be accidentally diminished.

One way to augment present-moment awareness is to verbally prompt the client to attend to specific stimuli. For example, "what do you notice on this paper," or "name five things that you see in the room." This approach requires the client to interact with events occurring in the present, rather than interacting with events happening at another time, place, or to other people. This strategy, like naturalistic environmental training, can be useful when present-moment awareness is desired within specific target contexts, perhaps as identified as part of a full functional assessment of behavior.

We can also augment immediate internal stimulus control by prompting clients to interact with their own private events. Private sensations function as stimuli, and those stimuli serve to elicit or evoke many behaviors that behavior analysts may seek to influence. For example, the woman who avoids flying is also very likely to avoid internal stress responses. In fact, she very likely interacts with those internal stress responses by thinking "this is too much to handle," or "I cannot do this." Because this verbal interaction with private experience is inevitably negatively reinforced through escape or avoidance, this interaction becomes increasingly more likely in the future. The behavior analyst may therefore ask her to notice how her body feels when she looks at a picture of the airplane. Greater augmentation can be achieved through a full body scan … or through progressive body relaxation strategies in which the person is prompted to notice individual parts of her body and to focus on letting go of needless muscular tension as a strategy to reduce the internal stress responses elicited by the airplane ride. By attending to immediate external and internal stimulus events, behavior analysts may be successful in weakening the stimulus control of verbal relations that historically controlled the behavior of interest.

In traditional discrete trial training, time is set aside each day to focus on strengthening operant behaviors. Meditation training sessions can serve a similar function if we consider flexible attention to the present moment to be a generalized higher-order operant.

These embedded approaches can also be conceptualized as setting events, or experiences at one point in time, that influence the probability or form of behavior at another point in time. When developing a regular meditation or mindfulness program, the goal is to alter the probability of behavior throughout that day and through consistent practice, to become more aware of the external contingencies that operate on behavior. That is, if we can strengthen "noticing" or "attending" at Time 1, we can observe a change in behavior at Time 2. This is testable when we measure behavior change directly and embed opportunities for mindfulness systematically into the context (e.g., twice per day for a total duration of 20 minutes per day). Daily "accept, identify,move" (AIM) lessons are one such example of embedding this training as a setting event, where one lesson per week is dedicated to promoting present-moment awareness.

DEPENDENT VARIABLES FOR INTERVENTION: ATTENTIONAL FLEXIBILITY

Detecting the skill of attending to what is present in a flexible, fluid, and voluntary fashion control can be accomplished in a variety of ways. When stimuli are present in the environment and detectable by the observer, informal observations of eye contact, body orientation, and physical engagement are possible. It is not difficult to notice when clients are noticing, and any good behavior analyst has likely developed some skills of that kind.

In structured laboratory or applied training tasks these discriminations can be made vastly more precise. Attending responses can be assessed through signal detection tasks, the impact of distraction, or the sensitivity of these to verbal control. More advanced technologies also allow for eye-gaze tracking that can provide a direct measure of the total time a person's eyes are oriented toward a specific task. This technology could be pivotal in tracking, for example, engagement in academic tasks by tracking how much a person actually is attending to the task and providing an opportunity to shape present-moment awareness. Neurobiological measures (e.g., high-density evoked potential measurement) can assess the breadth and flexibility of stimulus control.

Behavior analysts are used to dealing with problems of rigidity in this area when working with children with developmental disabilities due to their long and extensive interest in stimulus over-selectivity in individuals with autistic spectrum disorders or learning disabilities – but it has long been known that over-selectivity is not exclusive to those groups.

Direct observation data may be obtainable in many ways. We do this regularly with people when we believe they are not paying enough attention to us, such as by asking "what did I just say to you?" or by examining where they are oriented (e.g., are they even looking at the stimulus object right in front of them?). An easy way to directly measure if a person was attending to relevant features of the present environment is to momentarily remove the stimulus and ask, "what did you see?" or "did you notice *X*?" A correct response in this arrangement requires that the participant was aware of the stimulus objects that were immediately present, allowing for a measure of percent accuracy. Complex stimuli can be used to both train and test attentional flexibility, such as listening to music while focusing only on one instrument at a time – and then asking for the notes being played by that instrument to be produced orally.

Although a person can orient sense organs toward an object and not attend to it, measuring the duration of this behavior can provide an estimate of present-moment awareness under the assumption that if a person is not sensing a stimulus object, it is therefore unlikely that they are attending to it. Strategies such as momentary time sampling or interval recording are already in the arsenal of behavior analysts and could serve as appropriate tools to capture present-moment engagement in this way.

Less direct measurement tools for assessing attention to the present moment range from unstructured interviews, questionnaires, self-monitoring procedures, and direct observation methods. Unstructured interviews can include open-ended questions that attempt to ascertain the verbal relations that accompany specific stimulus events. For example, "When *X* situation occurs, what things come to mind?" By asking this question and recording the client's responses, behavior analysts may then assess if the response contains allusion to events in the present moment (e.g., "descriptions of *X*"), coordinated verbal relations with appetitive functions (e.g., "I hate *X*"), or deictic relations of there-then-them (e.g., "It makes me think of how everyone else has *Y* but I am stuck with *X*"). In something like the ACT Matrix, barriers to present-moment awareness are expressed in the "away-private" quadrant as these thoughts and emotional responses may clarify specific rules that compete against valued reinforcers expressed in the "toward-private" quadrant.

Additional probing can be achieved by introducing relevant contextual cues into the interview, such as "what does *X* feel like?", "how does *X* relate to your future?", or "how does *X* relate to your past?" The first question assesses for coordinated relations that carry aversive or appetitive eliciting or evocative functions. The second and third questions probe for events that are deictically related in the past or future. Barnes-Holmes et al. (2018) describe conducting a verbal functional analysis along with case examples where words with potential aversive or appetitive functions are presented by the behavior analyst, for example, the word "shame," and the defensive or avoidance behaviors of the client are monitored. This approach is analogous to an experimental functional analysis where different stimulus conditions are presented, however, in this arrangement the stimuli are verbal stimuli to probe for this verbal relational history that may contribute to challenging behavior.

Self-reports may take the form of general questioning by the clinician such as "when you didn't line up with the rest of your class, what was your mind doing?", or a similar question framed at the age and functioning level of the client. More explicit metrics might include a client's self-monitoring of their own "presence" in the environment at set intervals. This can occur in something like the ACT Matrix, or it can be embedded in regular conversation. Either way, regularly discussing what clients are noticing can not only provide meaningful data but can also operate as part of an intervention much like a self-monitoring program where tracking of one's own data can itself lead to a level of behavior change.

Standardized questionnaires can further streamline the unstructured interview process and afford the advantage of psychometric evaluation. That is, how do people typically respond to the same set of questions? What response patterns are most predictive of people living the life that they value? Questionnaires of this sort are already used in behavior analysis to ascertain the function of challenging behavior when interviewing caregivers. For example, "Questions About Behavior Function" (QABF) is a 21-item assessment that isolates the function of challenging behavior in terms of five function categories: attention, escape, tangible, physical, and non-social. Because all caregivers are presented with the same list of questions, the validity, reliability, and predictability of all questions and results of this questionnaire can be ascertained using statistical approaches that are becoming more common within ABA. Results support the early construct validity of the QABF with children with disabilities (REF) and correspondence with experimental functional analysis results (Matson et al., 2012).

One similar questionnaire designed to measure present-moment awareness specifically with children is the Child and Adolescent Mindfulness Measure (CAMM). The CAMM provides an estimate of mindfulness for youth over the age of nine years and contains ten items related to mindful awareness. Because the measure is relatively short, it may be useful for repeated measurement within a repeated measures design, although more research is needed regarding the sensitivity of the measure to capturing contextual shifts in present-moment awareness.

Present-moment awareness is also one component of the "Children's Psychological Flexibility Questionnaire" (CPFQ) which is the primary assessment used in the AIM curriculum. This 24-item assessment contains four items related to present-moment awareness and can provide a comparison against other core processes. There is also a caregiver version and a self-assessment version. More research is needed on this specific measure at the population level as well as its utility at the level of a single subject.

For adults, the "Mindfulness Attention Awareness Scale" (MAAS) may be especially applicable because it divides present-moment awareness into attention and awareness subscales. Attention refers to responding to immediate external stimulus events, whereas awareness includes simultaneous stimulus control and noticing internal and external stimuli.

Another very common tool is the "Five Facet Mindfulness Questionnaire" (FFMQ). The five factors contained within the questionnaire include: acting with awareness, describing, non-judging, non-reactivity, and observing. Evidence supports the factor structure of the FFMQ (e.g., Christopher et al., 2012) supporting the FFMQ as a self-report measure to capture changes in this ACT process. Several other measures are also available emerging from several fields interested in measuring mindfulness, and we encourage readers to explore these tools as they become available, evaluate the existing psychometric support, and match the assessment to the client's behavior and the context of behavioral intervention.

The above questionnaires are not exhaustive, and they measure many more processes than attentional control. We generally need to conduct more research on the contextual sensitivity of all measures. We describe them here mostly to give readers a feel for available options that can inform an indirect measurement of mindfulness.

We previously mentioned self-monitoring that is already a staple in ABA interventions and is often used as a concurrent outcome measure as well as an intervention in its own right.

Self-monitoring may be especially applicable in mindfulness interventions because it requires the client to notice themselves being present. This is referred to as meta-awareness (Epstein et al., 2008) or being aware of one's own awareness. The challenge is, of course, defining an objective observable unit of "mindfulness" to be measured and the specific behavior should be defined by the behavior analyst and client to ensure behavioral targets are meaningful.

One example involves having clients record the time spent meditating each day. Meditating generally occurs as a discrete activity with a clear starting and ending point, and duration can be captured using any device that contains a timer. If, however, the target is to increase the number of "mindful moments" throughout the day, which could take the form of intentional noticing for at least 15 seconds, then self-monitoring would involve the client keeping a tally on a readily accessible device immediately following each mindful moment. Both examples detail the necessity of self-monitoring within ACT interventions because the behavior analyst is rarely if ever going to be present when the behavior occurs (e.g., meditation) or the behavior is a private internal event unobservable to the behavior analyst (e.g., mindful minutes). We cannot stress enough, however, the importance of developing self-monitoring targets and operational definitions individually and based on the presenting needs of the client in context.

Talk-aloud measures (which were first used in psychology by John B. Watson) can be used to assess the presence of on-going private verbal events that may interact with contextual events. Although it is difficult to use, "silent dog" controls (Hayes, 1986) can be used to be more certain that ongoing verbalization of private events reflects what is present.

The absence of disengagement may be a converse metric of present-moment awareness, whereby the clinician can simply indicate the ceasing of non-engagement with environmental stimuli. Here simple frequency counts, intervals of engagement/disengagement, or momentary time samples are acceptable metrics to use. These sorts of measures also contain limitations, as it is not purely causal that given engagement with an object that a client may not concurrently be psychologically disengaged from the process. Our overt observations are helpful yet must be held with caution given the multiple processes of psychological interaction that may be possible.

ATTENTIONAL TRAINING AS AN INDEPENDENT VARIABLE

It is important to note here that, when treating present-moment awareness and attentional control as a process variable, there must be other socially relevant target behaviors that we are measuring to determine the efficacy of our interventions. For example, if a child is behaving aggressively at school, it is not enough to show that the child is engaging more in the present moment, but are we also seeing a decrease in aggressive behavior? For a man who is avoidant of social situations even though he values friendship, are we seeing an increase in social interactions? In behavior analysis, we are already very aware of how to capture these behaviors using a variety of data collection methods and training present-moment awareness should best be seen as a means for achieving these ends. The previously noted data on reduction of overtly measured aggressive responding following souls of the feet training provide an example.

Another example is provided by Twohig et al. (2006) who evaluated a series of ACT-consistent strategies to reduce chronic skin picking. Although the intervention targeted ACT processes including present-moment awareness, the success of the intervention package necessitated a change in the actual target behavior – skin picking, as a specific and measurable behavioral outcome. By tracking skin picking or any other behavior within a single-case experimental design, behavior analysts can evaluate the efficacy of their intervention package that includes strengthening present-moment awareness. If the intervention is efficacious, supports can be faded, success generalized, and eventually services discontinued to extended in less restrictive settings. If the intervention is not efficacious, behavior analysts can evaluate process measures to determine if present-moment awareness is being successfully strengthened, and if not, adaptations made to the intervention package to improve the treatment outcome. If present-moment awareness is improving but the challenging behavior persists, the challenge may not be occurring due to a deficit in present-moment awareness, rather other processes and factors must be considered to develop a truly efficacious strategy for any given client.

When we say we want to augment present-moment awareness in the moment, what we mean is that we want to strengthen the probability that a person attends to present-moment events when it matters the most. It is neither practical nor functional to be in the present moment all the time. Planning for a trip or self-reflecting on something that happened in the past necessitates deictic relating of events happening there and then rather than events happening here and now. On the other hand, there are moments when being aware of what is happening in the present can help to obtain valued reinforcers.

Take a professional golfer for example. Months of planning, scouting the greens, and developing mathematical models have led to a successful outing. Winning the tournament comes down to one final putt. Will they make the shot?

In that moment, it is critical for the golfer to let go of all of the planning and modeling that got them to this moment. It is just as critical to let go of the private thoughts and emotions that show up. Anxiety about missing the shot. Excitement about the parties and social reinforcers if he doesn't mess up this shot that he has practiced thousands of times. It is critical that the golfer notices the present-moment contingencies. The bumps in the road on the way to the hole. The distance to guide the strength of the shot. Where their feet are lined up and the angle of the putter. One moment. Here. Now.

Bernier et al. (2009) evaluated the impact of mindfulness and acceptance training with seven elite young golfers. The mindfulness training incorporated strategies from mindfulness-based cognitive behavior therapy as well as acceptance and commitment training techniques developed by Hayes and Strosahl (2004). Results showed that the golfers that practiced mindfulness and attended the training sessions improved their national ranking, compared to only two golfers in the control group. Similar results have been reported with elite swimmers (Bernier et al., 2009), free throws in basketball (Gooding et al., 2009), and increases in resilience in college baseball players (Vidic & Cherup, 2022).

Sports performance represents only one potential application of behavior analysis; however, most behavior analysts are tasked with influencing the behavior of clients where mindfulness-based strategies could play a central role. Let us consider how completing the mathematics worksheet for the child with autism engaging in self-defeating statements is similar to the professional athlete. The child wants to do well – yearns for it – and may have identified feeling smart and capable as something they value. Yet, when the worksheet shows up, the negative self-statements and feelings of anxiety and fear show up as well. The problem is not the worksheet, it is the behavior-behavior relations occasioned by the worksheet. We can practice present-moment awareness before completing the worksheet to augment attention functions, such as noticing three objects in the room or focusing on breathing or the soles of the feet. By engaging in this initial behavior of attending to the present moment, the functional control of negative self-talk is diminished. What remains is a worksheet – entirely within the skillset of the client – and the opportunity to complete the worksheet to move towards the abstract value of feeling smart and feeling able.

At first, the behavior analyst might prompt attending to this present-moment event; however, like any behavior, when prompts are faded, do we see the behavior occurring anyways? If the strategy is successful and allows the student to contact valued reinforcers, we should see the behavior maintain and strengthen even in the absence of the prompted intervention, where we might instead seek to measure generalization to other distressing situations in the client's life. Or the formation of intentional attending to the present moment as a generalized operant behavior-behavior strategy.

Getting started using present-moment awareness can take many forms. Basic techniques might include simply asking staff or clients to pause for a moment, notice the stimuli and environment around them, and actively attend to a specific external stimulus (object in room; sound; taste), or internal states (breath; weight of arms on lap; heartbeat).

ANTECEDENT AND CONSEQUENCE STRATEGIES TO PROMOTE PRESENT-MOMENT AWARENESS

We can also take what we know from the ABC model (or, A B-B C if we consider the behavior-behavior relations and want to make this more salient) to add some more behavioral flair and to augment present-moment awareness. If we developed a strong operational definition of present-moment awareness for a client and an appropriate measurement strategy, what could an experimental functional analysis (EFA) of this behavior look like? First, to measure the behavior, we could use a self-monitoring scale where the client indicates where their thoughts and feelings are currently like the scale below:

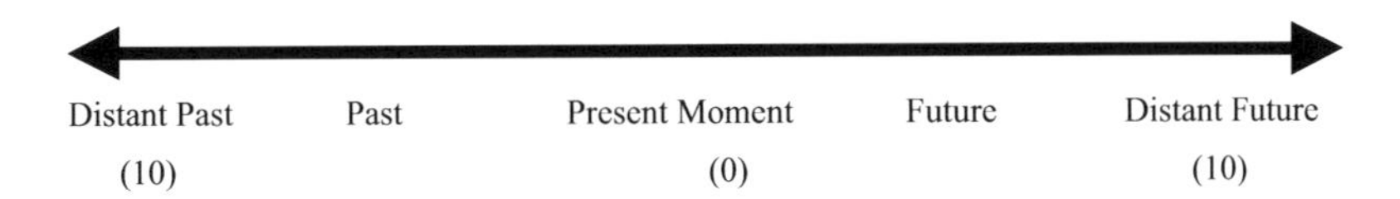

Notice our scoring system where the self-reported value represents absolute deviation from present-moment awareness. Our experimental question then becomes, "under what conditions is contact with the present moment most likely to occur?" For example, for a client with high rates of work refusal and indirect evidence that they are ruminating on how they will fail at the task, we might expect scores close to 10 when work is presented. Whereas, when the same client is engaging in a preferred task with which they are highly engaged, scores closer to 0 would occur. Our engaged condition is much like the control condition in the EFA, and we would expect greater values in the context within which present moment is least likely to occur. And if we also observe elevated rates of problem behavior in these or similar contexts, this may provide even more evidence of a behavior-behavior relation.

What then can we do with this information? Well, if we know that the client is not in the present moment under specific environmental conditions, then we also know that we can adjust or alter these conditions systematically. For example, we could take any of the present-moment awareness strategies described above such as noticing five things in the room or taking a series of deep breaths immediately before the presentation of work and then evaluating how this affects the work and present-moment awareness relationship. We might introduce environmental supports like headphones or the opportunity to work separately from others as a self-management strategy with on-going evaluation of present-moment awareness. In this way, we can measure present-moment awareness as a process variable en route to the successful intervention.

The ACT Matrix can also be used as either a setting event or antecedent-based strategy to promote present-moment awareness. A key feature of the Matrix is the on-going process of noticing. Noticing thoughts, feelings, and behaviors that show up that detract from one's chosen values. Noticing what those values are in the moments before identifying committed action as another way forward. That is why "noticing" is indicated in the center of the matrix. In this case, we are not asking the client to notice five things in the room or to attend to their breathing; rather, we are asking the client to notice the real contingencies that are operating on their own behavior, here and now. Behavior analysts may be especially well situated for determining when the best moments are to introduce the Matrix throughout the day to encourage this kind of noticing in those situations where present-moment awareness is the least likely to occur.

Consequences or schedules of reinforcement matter too, but not in a way that we are necessarily used to. The purpose of present-moment awareness is to bring people in closer contact with external contingencies. Therefore, it is very necessary to ensure that the external contingencies really do support the behavior that is the target of the intervention. For example, if a child really does value attention and social connectedness, and if the only way to obtain this is through what we have labeled "challenging behavior," then awareness of this contingency is not going to reduce the challenging behavior – it is in their best interest in some sense to continue it. We also need to make sure that opportunities for social connectedness are available when those committed actions occur. That "values" (intrinsic and far-reaching sources of reinforcement) are always available. On the other hand, valued reinforcers can be and often are delayed and that may require supplementing present-moment awareness with contrived reinforcers in the meantime while building this skill and delay tolerance. This is perfectly okay and can take the form of catching people in the present moment and reinforcing this, or by having people self-report times when they were in the present moment and making the link between this behavior and the values that they were able to contact more fully. Again, what is important is that these contrivances are faded so that the real and naturally occurring sources of valued reinforcement can take center stage and maintain the momentum built throughout the intervention.

THE PROCESS OF MINDFULNESS AND ATTENTION

Behavior analysts may not be used to thinking in terms of process variables that alter the context of behavior-behavior relations because so many of the key process variables we focus on are restricted to direct environmental contingencies. When behavior-behavior relations are at issue, however, it's important to track processes of change within the person across time and to see if intervention-based manipulations of the contexts that support a given behavior-behavior-relation actually alter them. For example, suppose mindfulness or attentional training is used to augment the ease of retaining a focus on current task demands without distraction, and the ultimate overt behavior being changed is academic learning. If the training produces better learning, but does not reduce distractibility, or it changes distractibility but fails to show that it is functionally related to the academic changes found, then there is no support for the claim that "mindfulness" or "attention" thought of as a process (at least as operationalized in the process measure) is functionally important.

Healthy contact with the present moment is a key feature of the psychological flexibility model. The reason it is hard, however, is due to other processes. Key among these are the repertoire-narrowing effects of a lack of emotional or cognitive flexibility. We turn to these in the next two chapters.

6

Acceptance

A way of thinking that is deeply ingrained in Westernized cultures is that we need to feel good – all of the time – no matter our experiences in the present or in the past. If we do not feel good in the moment, there is something inherently wrong with us that must be corrected before we can move forward in any meaningful way. Not only is there something that must be broken and therefore fixed, but we are *entitled* to feeling good. It simply is not fair that *they* (friend, family, boss, deity) made me feel upset, anxious, or depressed. And if *I* cannot solve it quickly, my life will inevitably fall apart.

How interwoven is this Westernized idea of "feel goodism" in our daily lives? Consider that the first thing people often say to one another is "how is it going?", to which the culturally appropriate reply is "it is going good," or simply "good." It is considered culturally taboo to say that things are going terribly and that our lives constantly feel like we are in a free fall. One could simply evaluate their social media to obtain a ready sample of feel goodism. Beautifully altered photos of people "living their best life." Who has not felt that their own life simply is not living up to the experiences of their friends on the other end of the screen? Yet, if we all feel that way, how accurate is this doctored reality?

And it runs deeper. It is downright unattractive to be seen feeling mad, sad, anxious, or depressed. That person who admitted that their day is going terribly is more likely to be avoided in future encounters. The teenager who posts on social media about their emotional struggles can be flagged and sent to seek counseling to fix those feelings so that things can simply return to normal. An existence free from struggle – an existence free from pain – is held up as "normal" or at least highly desirable even though any healthy human life includes the death of friends or family, rejections, illness, failures, and the like.

Feel goodism is even ingrained in our human service institutions. In many areas, the *Diagnostic and Statistical Manual of Mental Disorders* (DSM; APA, 2013) is predicated on this very notion, where identifiable patterns of negative feelings or affect beyond a certain threshold are considered disordered. People can be prescribed psychotropic medications – anti-anxiety agents, anti-depressants, antipsychotics, mood stabilizers, stimulants, and so on – for even routine emotional pain. Thirteen percent of the United States population over 12 used anti-depressants during 2014, a 65% increase from 15 years earlier; and a quarter of those now on anti-depressants have used them for a decade or more (Pratt et al., 2017). In the ten-year period from 1998 to 2007, people using psychosocial methods alone to address mental health issues fell nearly 50%, and by 2007 only 1 in 10 people with mental health problems addressed them that way. Using psychotherapy *and* medications also fell about 30%. Meanwhile, 60% of people use nothing but medications – up a third in ten years

DOI: 10.4324/9781003250371-8

(Olfson & Marcus, 2010). Meanwhile, in the United States, approximately one in five adults has a diagnosed mental disorder and this number continues to rise (Kessler et al., 2007).

What are the cultural contingencies that maintain this? Many of them appear to be built into human language itself.

Say the word "pain" to someone and they immediately think of how unpleasant these physical feelings called "pain" can be. But a moment's reflection shows that they help us avoid damage to our bodies – much as a warning signal in a car might help avoid collisions. Feeling guide action. Touch a hot stove and remove your hand. Get a stomachache from overeating and eat more moderately next time.

If we think about it, we know we need pain like that and especially we need the *capacity* to feel pain. The total absence of pain is hardly an attractive situation. Congenital insensitivity to pain and anhidrosis (CIPA) is a rare medical condition that inhibits people from feeling any pain. One of the reasons CIPA is so rare is that few people with the condition reach adulthood –they experience far more injuries such as bruises and broken bones (Shin et al., 2016).

Nevertheless, if we can avoid pain, or escape, or at least dampen it down, all the better. Right? Verbal problem solving alone leads us to this conclusion, but scientifically speaking, often the answer is "no," because the effort is ineffective and the costs of avoiding, escaping, or dampening down are simply too high.

In chronic pain, for example, often the physical pain will not just "go away" and indeed focusing attention on that outcome and seeking to produce it (through opiate use; doctor shopping; risky operations; and so on) is part of why chronic pain is so disruptive to a high quality of life. But an even more readily accessible example of the problem that sits inside this commonsense understanding comes when we focus on psychological pain, especially the kind that is linked to historically produced private events such as the emotions, thoughts, or memories produced by abuse, betrayal, failure, harsh judgment, and the like. Should we say "if we can avoid it, escape it, or at least dampen it down, all the better" in that area as well?

In many, many examples of behavioral pathology, the individual has implicitly answered "yes" to that question and gone on to experience the terrible consequences such an answer often produces. Experiential avoidance is one of the most dominant, toxic, and repertoire-narrowing forms of coping known to behavioral science. "Experiential avoidance" describes an attempt to diminish the form, frequency, or situational sensitivity of private events even when doing so causes behavioral harm. It is a form of affective rigidity that is as common as human problems themselves. When the client is first asked why they are seeking treatment in the first place, responses such as "to feel less stressed," "to not feel depressed anymore," or "to feel less anxious" are by far the most common answers. That very formulation of one's life situation in terms of feelings that are evaluated and targeted for change is but a hair's breadth away from trying to diminish the form, frequency, or situational sensitivity of private events – even when doing so causes behavioral harm.

Stress, depressed mood, and anxiety are signals of past and present situations. Many of the immediate attempts to diminish them can carry risks of amplifying them. Attempts to diminish or subtract them (or to lock so-called "positive" feelings into place – an issue we will address later) diminish their usefulness, much as turning off warning lights in a car would produce short-term gains at the cost of long-term pains.

Take alcohol abuse as an example. It is very easy to fall into the trap of "drinking to cope" and even convince oneself that binge drinking serves a greater purpose. A client might report, "I cannot imagine how bad things would be if I couldn't drink." And of course, this has some basis: alcohol tends to inhibit activity in the executive functioning areas of the brain that are involved in problem-solving and decision-making. It dampens down sympathetic arousal, alleviating anxiety. But the problems are still there when the alcohol wears off and done repetitively it begins to produce long-term problems of its own.

Drinking may temporarily avoid unwanted experiences but it does little to correct the present situation or the nature of past events. Engaging in this strategy regularly might lead to a loss of friends, family, or even one's own children; it might lead to a loss of work, health, or a sense of meaning. In other words, the causes of psychological pain grow. When the solution is to drink again, a self-amplifying loop – a contingency trap – may emerge to exact a higher and higher cost.

This diagram here shows that although an experience like anxiety can lead to avoidance and temporary relief, the result is that the conditions under which anxiety occurs can worsen, leading to even more anxiety and even greater patterns of experiential avoidance. Moreover, as we avoid these feelings, we may become intolerant of those feelings, thus even minor inconveniences can evoke strong patterns of avoidance. Harris (2019) provided the acronym DOTS to describe ways that people avoid, usually by distracting oneself by doing something less productive or values aligned, opting out of events, thinking or attempts at thought correcting through excessive rumination, or engaging in self-harming behavior including substance abuse or other strategies (Figure 6.1).

Replace "alcohol" with any number of ways that we experientially avoid such as overuse of drugs, excessive working, social withdrawal, gambling, suppressing thoughts, refusing to acknowledge feelings we do not like, and so on, and it is clear that while the topographies might vary hugely it is the shared function that is at the root of the problem. Trying to feel GOOD can lead to *more* difficult feelings and to a life that is not in touch with what history and circumstance can teach as behavioral guides.

The forms of avoidance we have discussed so far are not that different functionally speaking from a common experience that clients with autism may experience around building meaningful friendships. Here, the client is faced with a choice. On the one hand, showing up to an ambiguous social situation with differences that impact neurotypical social processes can lead to painful moments and social rejection. On the other hand, retreating from social interaction to avoid the anxiety that comes with social punishers they may have experienced in the past is painful in a different way that does not hold our hope of growth and change.

Learning how to have friends might depend on a willingness to "engage anyway," even with the anxiety, fears, and neurological differences that are uniquely theirs. Rates of anxiety are far more common in autistic populations (van Steensel et al., 2011), and rates of suicidality range all the way up to 42% (Hannon & Taylor, 2013). There are good reasons to believe that experiential avoidance is a core barrier to change in those statistics.

Experiential avoidance can fail for several reasons (Hayes et al., 1999). First, attempting to control the form or frequency of unwanted private events can lead directly to the unwanted events because of a clash between behavior guided by verbal rules and common-sense contingencies. For example, when research participants are asked to suppress

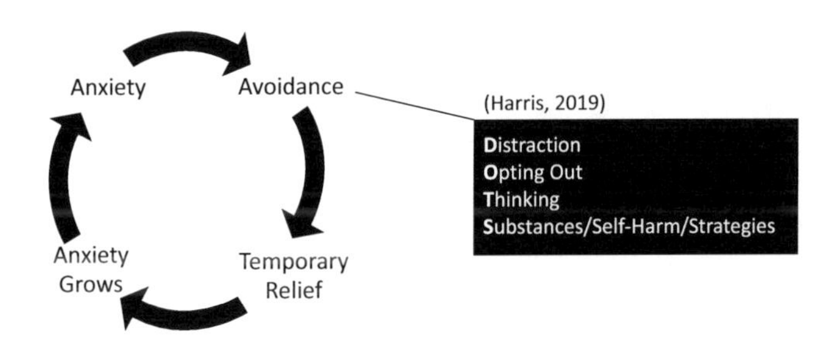

FIGURE 6.1 DOTS Diagram.

a thought, researchers paradoxically observe an increase in the thought or feeling after a short period of suppression (Wenzlaff & Wagner, 2000). To demonstrate, try to avoid thinking about a purple elephant for the next minute. Whereas you may have never thought of a purple elephant before – now it is very hard to stop thinking about it. You can do it for a while, by distraction and the like but as soon as you check to see if it has worked, it hasn't. The reason is simple: the rule "avoid thinking of _____" contains a verbal stimulus that produces those thinking reactions once the target is specified verbally.

Second, contingencies that can be harmful exist in the external environment, where attempts to suppress thoughts and feelings could fail to notice those contingencies. Those actual contingencies may then produce what a person is trying to avoid. For example, a person in an abusive relationship may try to avoid the emotional pain of that abuse and end up staying in the relationship where further abuse is likely.

Third, although we *can* sometimes avoid or suppress unwanted experiences, doing so can come at a considerable behavior cost. Take for example a client experiencing severe social anxiety. The person could simply avoid all social events. Doing so might work in the short term to reduce anxious feelings; however, the costs are considerable. On top of never contacting those meaningful relationships that they yearn for, the person will contact awkward situations of declining all social invitations, missing out on opportunities for professional growth that are socially mediated, or limiting experiences with loved ones because they can never go anywhere social together.

Fourth, if the external event literally cannot be changed avoidance may prevent useful actions that might help deal with the situation. For the person experiencing grief and refusing to accept the loss of a loved one, no amount of experiential avoidance will bring that person back. Going through a grieving process, acknowledging the contribution the deceased person made to one's life, going through their papers or settling their financial affairs, and so on may all be made impossible by a refusal to grieve in a more open way.

Finally, efforts to change may actually be contradictory to the target of change. Peace of mind is an example – it describes a condition of openness to what is and what comes next, but effortfully trying to produce such a state is not peaceful. A feeling of confidence is another example. Taking steps to get rid of a lack of confidence suggests that there is something about you that must change, now, which is not a self-confident action. Many avoidant actions are like this – stop worrying or else; until you learn to feel good about yourself, you will always be messed up; if they see who you are they will not like you so you need to fake it until you make it; you need to plan how to be more spontaneous; you need to figure out how to get out of your head. In all these cases rules point to behaviors that cannot be rule-governed in that way and still function properly.

Acceptance and willingness represent the opposite processes of experiential avoidance. If we hope to undo a densely established and culturally embedded pattern of experiential avoidance for ourselves and for our clients, we must focus on willingness and acceptance as the alternative way forward – a first step in getting unstuck.

Luoma et al. (2007) define acceptance and willingness as "being open to one's whole experience while also actively and intentionally choosing to move in a valued direction" (p. 24). Other texts make a distinction between acceptance and willingness as two separate but related processes. For example, Hayes, Strosahl, and Wilson (2011) define behavioral willingness as "the voluntary and values-based choice to enable and sustain contact with private experiences or the events that will likely occasion them"; and psychological acceptance as "the adoption of an intentionally open, receptive, flexible, and nonjudgmental posture with respect to moment-to-moment experience" (p. 77).

If we are to draw a distinction, then willingness represents immediately observable behavior that can lead to greater contact with valued reinforcers in the short term. For example, the person abusing alcohol is willing to watch a sporting event that evening without consuming alcohol, or an autistic person may be willing to approach a new person at lunch – and both of these actions are in the service of larger-later values (sobriety and building meaningful relationships). Willingness is a first step but does not necessarily require acceptance. The person abusing alcohol is willing to not drink while engaging in something else that is distracting. The autistic person is willing to white-knuckle it and push through the aversive experience of approaching another person, but this does little to address the functional processes that give rise to their anxious experience in the first place. Whereas both of these solutions probably represent strong behavior change targets in the short term, these small and superficial changes must be the start of the journey – not the end of it.

Acceptance could therefore represent a broader repertoire of experiencing and learning from aversive and appetitive private and public events in ways that help establish effective repertoires of values-based action. Defined that way, acceptance necessitates observing and noticing public and private contingencies as well as actions that are needed to directly address the causes of one's suffering and to passionately approach their values. Acceptance is not surrender, it is a first and necessary step toward changing what truly matters. In line with its etymology (it comes from Latin for "to receive" as if to receive a gift) acceptance allow us to receive the gift of our own history.

Consider a secularized version of the serenity prayer written by theologian Reinhold Niebuhr that gained popularity in the 1940s:

I choose to practice grace to accept with serenity
the things that cannot be changed,
Courage to change the things
which should be changed,
and the Wisdom to distinguish
the one from the other.

"I choose…" represents the on-going behavioral processes that are engrained within acceptance and willingness and "…to practice" captures engaging in acceptance across multiple exemplars as a broader repertoire or pattern of behavior is what we are trying to foster in acceptance and commitment herapy (ACT)-based approaches. The remainder speaks to accepting what cannot be changed *and* being willing to change (really change) parts of life that are not coherent with what someone values. When we are open to experiences – we can use how we feel as a guide to direct us towards what really matters.

Suppose a person abusing alcohol has recently lost their job and their social circle is shrinking each day – drinking provides an immediate escape. Although they may be willing not to drink for a night or two, they may not be willing to face directly that their life is falling apart around them. Willingness of that kind may be necessary to foster acceptance. If they can accept that they cannot have both alcohol as an emotional crutch *and* have a meaningful job and build back old relationships and foster new ones, what remains is a dichotomous choice between staying stuck and moving forward.

Acceptance viewed in this way is more of an all-or-none process as it relates to experiential avoidance – you cannot do both, they are incompatible. And if we can foster acceptance, at least momentarily, this can be our springboard to utilizing strategies from the other five core processes of the ACT Hexaflex to help achieve the valued outcome of returning to work and building relationships.

Similarly, for the person avoiding social interactions with others, willingness to interact alone does not change the fact that the person feels lonely and feels unacceptable as themselves – a view that might have only been strengthened by therapeutic approaches aimed at changing who they are. Acceptance in this case could take the form of accepting one's differences and all of the aversive private experiences that entails in order to foster meaningful friendships and being accepted for who they are once again. A "I am different and that is okay" beyond just the words spoken is a springboard to opening up the other core processes to more deeply exploring those differences, their functions, and learning to explore their world with curiosity as someone who is neurodivergent. What they may find is that people are even more willing to accept their differences when they themselves are more willing to embrace those differences from the outset.

We have mostly talked about accepting aversive private and public experiences, but what about appetitive experiences? The word "accept" is used in many different ways in our language and includes things like "accepting a gift." When we look at acceptance as a broad behavioral process that is more like "accepting the gift" of one's history in the service of effective action, we need to promote accepting and embracing aversive experiences *and* appetitive experiences, even with the knowledge that affective experiences ebb and flow. Doing so is part of living life more completely, and in this way, acceptance is a necessary process to not only move towards one's values – but to feel the positive emotions that come when contacting those values without needless defense and without needless clinging.

Accepting a gift is always easier said than done. Who has not had the thought, "I don't deserve this" or "this is way too much" after receiving a really good gift? This experience is not restricted to receiving presents as gifts but appears in many situations throughout life. The person who is avoidant of romantic relationships could experience these exact thoughts, and those thoughts are occasioned by happy moments in a relationship that quickly turn to dread and to avoidance. People know that positive experiences will fade, and people are relevantly averse to loss versus gain (Tversky & Kahneman, 1992). The new pet that brings you joy will age and eventually will die. The romantic relationship will end someday one way or another – at least in a physical sense. Joy can thus signal the end of joy and an avoidant person may conclude that it is easier simply never to feel joy at all. Avoiding joy confers all of the same limitations as avoiding aversive experiences – it is a high-cost process that can easily become rigid. Therefore, part of the ACT process must involve encouraging acceptance of all experiences, and the ebb and flow of experience, in the service of valued living.

That also means that acceptance in ACT necessitates a degree of non-attachment. Embracing something fully necessitates a willingness to let it go. All experiences, positive or negative, are necessarily fleeting and momentary – to be followed by new experiences. When we cling to past experiences, positive or negative, we are not open to experiencing new experiences that could be just around the corner. The recovering substance user looking for a new job during recovery risks rejection and being turned down and must be open to experiencing rejection with the knowledge that rejection is temporary. Moreover, once that new job is secured, there is a chance that they are fired, or the company is downsized – the positive experiences are temporary too. But the skills learned and the successes in the job can lead to new opportunities when looking for the next position. This ebb and flow of experience and acceptance of all of it is what we need to foster as behavior analysts – and doing so is an immensely powerful technology.

Before moving ahead into an analysis of affective openness, let's pause for just a few minutes to explore an exercise personally, so you can get a sense of it before we discuss why it might work. Please actually do the exercise – do not just read it.

Saying Yes

- Sit in a quiet place and spend a few moments focusing on the soles of your feet, using the methods we explored in the last chapter.

- Allow your eyes to move about the space you are in. Focus on one object (do not pick a human being to focus on). As you notice it, find something in it that is flawed – something you do not like. Perhaps it's too old, or not in fashion. Perhaps it's dirty or takes up too much space. Find something and look at the object from the point of view of "no, I don't want you here."
- After two or three objects have been looked at that way, attend to the next object in a different way. Observe it, mentally describe it, and appreciate it. See if you can welcome its properties, much as you might when seeing an old friend. If it's old, notice and appreciate it with that quality. Say "yes" to the object, exactly as it is.
- After a minute or so, allow your awareness to move through your body. Do the same thing in the same order and see what happens. Initially with each sensation that appears, notice it and observe it in the context of "no." No – I don't want you. No – go away.
- After two or three sensations have been looked at that way, attend to the next sensation in a different way. Observe it, mentally describe it, and appreciate it. See if you can welcome its properties, ask it to say "hello." Notice where the feeling begins and ends; notice its qualities. Say "yes" to the feeling, exactly as it is.
- Allow your attention to move around the space you are in once again and when you come back into a normal state of awareness spend a few minutes writing freely on what you noticed about this experience and the differences between these ways of approaching your context with the external and internal world.

BASIC BEHAVIOR CHANGE PROCESSES: EXPERIENCING IN THE SERVICE OF VALUED LIVING

Understanding acceptance and affective openness generally in terms of basic behavioral processes starts with unpacking basic research on conditioned and unconditioned avoidance responses. Avoidance in an animal model could be shown when the animal is placed in a chamber with a shock grid and a lever. The shock grid will activate unless the rat suppressed the lever at a scheduled rate or duration. Therefore, we would expect an increase in response rate or duration in order to avoid the electric shock. Escape in this same animal model occurs when the level press terminates an already existing shock. Again, successive exposures to the aversive event yield quicker rates of responding to escape such contingencies.

Avoidance can be established in a number of ways that include conditioning aversive motivating operations through pairing (surrogate, CMO-S) or signaling (reflexive, CMO-R). A CMO-S is established when a neutral stimulus is paired with the unconditioned aversive stimulus and the functions transfer. For example, in forward conditioning, if a tone is presented prior to the electric shock, then the tone will obtain the aversive functions of the shock, and the rat may come to press the lever in order to avoid hearing the tone that was previously paired with shock. This pairing process involves respondent conditioning processes that interact with the operant pressing of the lever. A CMO-R involves a stimulus that signals the onset of an unconditioned aversive stimulus contingent on the omission of behavior. For example, the tone is followed by a shock within ten seconds if the rat does not suppress the lever. In this case, we would expect an increase in lever pressing in the presence of the tone.

Is avoidance just a temporally extended escape function? Possibly, when we take into account private experiences. Consider a situation similar to the rat and the signal tone where you receive an email from your boss. The "timer" has begun. An email back will avoid a punisher in the form of a reprimand or a passive-aggressive email seeking your response.

But for people this is not so simple, as feelings of anxiety inevitably emerge but may dissipate once the response email is sent. You are off the hook for now. In this way, the aversive event is avoided, but the current private experience of feeling anxious is escaped until the next email is received. This escape contingency can be a powerful reinforcer producing high rates of behavior – and your boss knows it!

For humans, relational framing makes experiential avoidance even more pervasive. We already gave basic experimental examples showing that respondent and operant functions can be transformed in terms of relational frames. When words or thoughts carry that aversive function, the avoidance and escape contingency is necessarily present. For example, the thought, "I am so stupid" will lead to an elevation in negative emotional arousal, and any behavior that terminates these aversive feelings will be negatively reinforced. By definition, we can therefore assume that experientially avoidant behaviors will only strengthen as we indulge the smaller-sooner negative reinforcement contingencies – or what we refer to as psychological inflexibility. It is precisely because of the negative reinforcement contingency that these patterns of behavior can become stuck and resistant to change.

Escaping is also much harder because of relational framing. Consider that almost any stimulus can be related to another stimulus across some dimension. How is a penguin like a hotdog? They are both smooth. How is orange juice different from the sun? One is hot and the other is cold. What this means is that relational networks that carry aversive functions may become even larger and more elaborate, such that almost any stimulus that a person contacts in the environment can evoke a stream of aversive thoughts and emotions initiating the escape contingency that we have described above. In this way, escape and avoidance can become more intense, more frequent, and possibly even more resistant as language evolves around the emotional problem at hand.

We can create a behavioral model of avoidance with non-human animals easily enough once we ignore the participation of relational framing. We can do it with "willingness" as well. In one arrangement, a rat could be placed in an apparatus where receiving the reinforcer necessitates experiencing a small shock (e.g., Hayes et al., 1979 did this using a "nose poke" apparatus placed in front of the food cup). The more the rat is deprived of food, the more likely it is to tolerate the shock in order to access a food reinforcer (Hayes et al., 1979). If we wanted to shape greater tolerance to the shock stimulus, we could gradually increase the magnitude or duration of the shock commensurate with increases in the amount of the reinforcer or the degree of food deprivation.

This shaping process is not dissimilar to tolerance training used already in behavior analysis and other forms of behavior therapy to promote willingness and engagement. Generally, the client is exposed to more and more difficult tasks in order to shape willingness. Willingness to engage in a work task provides another example, where schedules of reinforcement are quite dense at the onset of training, such as a break every five questions answered on a work task. As the student accomplishes this successfully and shows a greater willingness to complete the tasks, the number of questions is gradually increased toward a terminal threshold.

These two examples also illustrate why a behavioral model of willingness is necessary but not sufficient to develop a comprehensive strategy to address acceptance. For the client undergoing exposure therapy, we may diminish the arousal response, but this is not the same thing as fostering a willingness to experience the arousal response and behave in terms of one's values even when anxiety shows up. For the student learning to complete more work, this again is not the same as teaching the student to identify what really matters and to complete tasks that may seem insurmountable in the moment because doing so is necessary to achieve the life that they want to live. A behavioral sensible model of acceptance must encompass a broad range of approaches instead of avoidance behavior across contexts that cannot be accounted for simply by exposure alone, and it needs to do a good job of anticipating the role of relational framing.

In acceptance training, we want to reduce the evocative and abative functions of negative emotional arousal as an MO. That is, instead of simply diminishing the MO, we want to change what patterns of behavior the MO evokes or abates. For clients experiencing high levels of experiential avoidance, the MO generated by aversive situations or private experiences will evoke stable patterns of avoidance responding such as self-distraction or self-medicating. Instead, in ACT, we want this same MO to abate stuck and rigid patterns of escape and instead evoke variability in pursuit of valued reinforcers. Acceptance of that kind thus necessarily operates within a framework of values as this helps specify what the alternative behavior is that we want to augment or strengthen in moments of struggle.

For the person abusing substances, for example, we might present stimuli that bring their value of being a good parent and spouse into the moment where experiential avoidance is most likely to occur. By doing so, we hope to strengthen or augment reinforcers available to foster willingness and acceptance as alternative patterns of behavior under the same MO conditions. If we are successful across multiple exemplars of distressful events, a generalized operant pattern of willingness and acceptance may emerge, fostering long-term impactful change.

ACCEPTING POSITIVE EXPERIENCES AS WELL AS NEGATIVE EXPERIENCES: A BEHAVIORAL MODEL OF NON-ATTACHMENT

Affective openness and flexibility need to include a behavioral model of excessive clinging to positive experiences as well. Take, for example, the leaning of positive reinforcement schedules. If in an animal operant chamber one establishes effective behavior (e.g., a bar press) to access small amounts of food and then the amount of the reinforcer is very, very gradually reduced, the organism can be trapped in a schedule that ultimately will require more caloric energy expended to achieve a tiny edible reinforcer than the energy supplied by access to the edible. Said more simply, the animal will work itself to death in the pursuit of gradually diminishing positive reinforcement.

Some positive reinforcers diminish naturally. Addictive drugs may be powerfully appetitive, but opponent physiological processes settle in re-establish homeostasis. As that happens what used to produce euphoria eventually produces only feelings of normality

Although applause, Instagram likes, or lengthening one's vita look quite different from bits of food, these positive events can produce the same kind of "working oneself to death" behavioral patterns in some conditions. Attachment to verbally abstracted reinforcers can diminish relative to one's baseline due to the operation of hierarchical framing for example. Your 100th publication will on average produce less emotional uplift than your tenth publication, and ten "likes" will be more uplifting when you have only 100 in total than when you have 1000 because one is a "small part of" and one is a "big part of." These kinds of reinforcers can easily lead to "workaholism" in its various forms.

For emotions to be useful sources of behavioral regulation they have to vary – they have to come and go. But trying to prevent that in the case of appetitive consequences itself produces emotional responses and these often diminish the very emotions the person is trying to cling to. We all have friends who "always keep smiling" regardless of what is happening. The effort to do that as naturally sad or worrisome things happen is neither itself happy nor attractive to others. Over time people will avoid being in the presence of "forced sunshine faces," and that means forced happiness can soon lead to some degree of loneliness and social abandonment. This explains some of the ways that attachment to more verbally produced "euphoria" can go awry in the repertoire narrowing patterns reflected in narcissism, greed, thrill-seeking, or simply "don't worry, be happy."

Measures of emotional attachment are now appearing (e.g., Sahdra et al., 2010). In confirmation of the analysis above, experiential attachment appears to be about as much of a negative, repertoire-narrowing process as experiential avoidance (e.g., Sahdra et al., 2015).

People do not necessarily ask for help when they are attached as often as when they're avoidant because our culture often actively supports and helps maintain workaholic and power-seeking behaviors and other forms of attachment. It is worth noticing that there is far more interest currently in issues of "mindfulness" than there is in "attachment" even though in wisdom traditions both are targets of change. In terms of human difficulty, behavioral rigidity can emerge from either source. The solution in either case is to help establish more emotional and experiential openness. Acceptance of the ebb and flow of private events and the willingness to seek out situations that may lead to that in the service of values-based behavior is relevant to both positive and negative behavioral motivation.

DEPENDENT VARIABLES FOR INTERVENTION: AFFECTIVE FLEXIBILITY

Measuring willingness and acceptance can be accomplished to some degree by measuring different forms of avoidance because these two processes are somewhat interrelated and incompatible. You cannot both accept and avoid the same thing at the same moment. A concern with avoidance is compatible with a behavior analyst's use of ACT principles both because avoidance is a familiar concept and because many clients are referred for services because of behavior that is experientially avoidant if the client has developed language to that level of sophistication. Therefore, reducing the experientially avoidant behavior is a common and socially valid target for behavior change.

Take for example the person with social anxiety who is looking to increase their social engagement. We know that current levels of social engagement are low, and our assessments have identified that they are avoiding social events because of the aversive private experiences that show up whenever they are around people. Moreover, canceling social plans immediately relieves their experienced anxiety in the moment because they no longer need to fixate on the pending social event. The most direct measure will simply be to observe the frequency and/or duration of attending key social events as something that the behavior analyst seeks to increase and to measure how frequently the person backs out of social opportunities as a behavior that the behavior analyst seeks to decrease.

This same basic strategy can be used for an adolescent with aggressive behavior who avoids completion of work tasks and all of the aversive private verbal behavior that shows up when the work task is presented. Acceptance in this case could involve either completing the work or walking away from the task momentarily and engaging in mindful breathing before reinitiating the task (i.e., accepting that the work cannot be completed now, but can be completed once I am in contact with the present moment). All of this assumes that the learner sees the link between the work and their values, showing just how connected these processes truly are. In any case, we can track work completion as the percentage of work tasks completed or we can measure how often they engage in mindful breathing and successfully re-engage the task. We might also expect a decrease in the experientially avoidant behavior (i.e., aggression).

Like with present-moment awareness, observing external behavior is a good starting point and is likely necessary at some level for behavior analysts implementing ACT-based intervention. However, direct observation may not be sufficient alone. Moreover, when we only evaluate momentary changes in public behavior, we might miss more extended and elaborate changes in acceptance as a generalized pattern of operant behavior. As a supplement to these over-behavioral assessments, self-report instruments can be used as corollary measures or in pre-post evaluations to capture broader changes in acceptance. For example, participants who score high on measures of experiential avoidance tend to perform worse in a variety of basic laboratory tasks that measure tolerance as well as how aversive events impact performance. Zettle (2005) showed that scores on the "Acceptance and Action Questionnaire – II" (AAQ-2), a self-report measure of experiential avoidance, were predictive of how long people are willing to keep their hand in cold water (i.e., to tolerate discomfort). In another experiment, participants who reported high levels of experiential avoidance and were placed in an experimental task that simulated being drunk reported greater discomfort and were less able to complete a perceptual motor task (Zettle et al., 2007).

Beyond simply providing a direct behavior to observe, these contrived laboratory experiments can allow for an analysis of contextual factors that might influence tolerance and performance. For example, Feldner et al. (2003) compared an acceptance protocol to a thought suppression protocol during a carbon-dioxide-enriched air challenge. Participants who demonstrated high levels of experiential avoidance at the onset of the study showed even greater anxiety and emotional discomfort when given the through-suppression protocol, whereas the acceptance protocol appeared to reduce experiences of anxiety and emotional discomfort.

This same basic strategy of comparing acceptance to suppression has been replicated with similar results across a wide variety of other tasks, such as emotional processing on cardiovascular habituation or emotional responses while watching films for individuals with depression. These basic laboratory experiments provide empirical support for the view that the relational patterns altered in an acceptance strategy can effectively change momentary behavior.

High correlations between measures of experiential avoidance and actual behavior in each of these tolerance tasks suggest that willingness to experience aversive events could represent a generalized pattern of behavior. These types of tasks could therefore be used at the beginning and end of ACT-based interventions as a corollary measure to behavior change to see if the process of acceptance and willingness may have participated in a change in overt patterns of avoidance. A simple example is asking a person to sit in a comfortable chair and then to hold their breath as long as possible. Simply timing the length of breath holding has been shown to move with ACT interventions and to predict long term follow-up outcomes (Jeffcoat & Hayes, 2012).

Because researchers have developed so many versions of this same general task, it is also possible to use multiple tasks to test for generalization of acceptance skills. For example, if a person is taught to mindfully interact with the cold-water task and results suggest that this increases tolerance of the task, what happens when they are exposed to the enriched air challenge? Generalization could occur if they use this same general strategy, and we see an increase in willingness across both of the tasks.

These types of tasks are also somewhat limited. Over the short term at least, overt distress tolerance skills can occur using suppressive means of dealing with private events so without augmentation they may not capture the more complete model of acceptance that we described above. Second, acceptance is necessarily connected to one's values – artificial demands to maintain contact with cold water or some other physiologically aversive stimulus may not properly assess the capacity for valued living. Finally, capturing single units of behavior in a confined context is fine, but we also need ways to measure more fully the process of acceptance as a generalized operant.

One approach is to fit assessment tasks to the individual client. For a client who is unwilling to accept aversive thoughts about their body, we could use talk-aloud procedures (Hayes et al., 1998) or physiological measures while viewing altered bodily pictures to assess how private experiences are being addressed across a range of bodily stimuli. Implicit relational assessment procedures, such as what the Implicit Relational Assessment Procedure (IRAP) provide, are another example of means of verbal assessment.

We can also capture broader patterns of experiential avoidance using self-report tools such as the AAQ-2. The AAQ-2 can be completed quickly because the assessment contains only ten items that are presented on a seven-point Likert scale. The items test for experiential avoidance using questions such as, "I'm afraid of my feelings" or "emotions cause problems in my life," where higher scores provide evidence of experiential avoidance. This measure has achieved strong internal consistency and has been used as an outcome measure in multiple research studies on ACT. Moreover, the results from the AAQ-2 are highly correlated with the direct assessment strategies that we describe above, further supporting use of this tool to specifically measure acceptance and experiential avoidance.

Several other tools also contain subtests for acceptance within a broader assessment of psychological flexibility. For example, the "Comprehensive Assessment of Acceptance and Commitment Therapy" process (CompACT) is a 23-item measure of psychological flexibility. The CompACT contains three major subscales: Openness to Experience (OE), Behavioral Awareness (BA), and Valued Action (VA). The first subscale contains items directly related to acceptance and willingness as a broader construct, with questions such as "I try to stay busy to keep thoughts or feelings from coming."

Beyond these measures that are often used as pre-post outcomes, or dependent variables, continuous data collection of acceptance and willingness could be achieved through ecological momentary assessment (EMA) and experience sampling methods., and this applies to each of the ACT processes. EMA can be done with pen-and-paper or using a smartphone app. Behaviorally focused items are essentially a form of self-monitoring.

An example is the "Process-Based Assessment Tool" (PBAT), a set of psychological flexibility-focused items that are taken using this temporal density assessment, such as measures of processes and outcomes two to three times a day for a month. Examples of two affect-focused items from the PBAT are "in the last few hours I did not find an appropriate outlet for my emotions" or "in the last few hours I was able to experience a range of emotions appropriate to the moment." Idiographic research shows that such items are quite likely to relate to common clinical outcomes as they occur in real-time (Sanford et al., under submission)

ACCEPTANCE AND WILLINGNESS TRAINING AS INDEPENDENT VARIABLES

Acceptance training plays a central role in overcoming experiential avoidance, which is needed to not only move towards one's values but to experience that behavioral journey more fully. To some degree, promoting greater willingness can be accomplished simply through exposure. The question is, why.

Being exposed to a stimulus repeatedly can reduce response-eliciting functions. That could happen in part through a process called habituation which antedates even operant and classical conditioning in the evolutionary time scale and is simply the reduction of response due to repeated stimulus presentations. Exposure could also reduce learned eliciting functions that may have been acquired through classical conditioning and its stimulus-stimulus pairings. Finally, exposure in an operant sense might involve the repeated presentation of previously repertoire-narrowing events in contexts that establish greater response flexibility and new learning in their presence.

Exposure is at the core of many classic behavioral methods, including the easiest methods of behavior therapy such as systematic desensitization. At the time it was developed it was argued to be a form of counterconditioning based on "reciprocal inhibition." A list of distressing events was organized from the most distressing (i.e., touching a strongly feared object) to the least distressing (e.g., looking at a picture of the feared stimulus from far away). After training in deep muscle relaxation the analyst and the client then repeatedly presented the least fearful item on the list (in imagination or in actuality) while remaining totally relaxed until the event felt easily tolerable (using a subjective unit-of-distress scale or "SUDS" – a 1 to 100 rating scale of distress to track the client's reaction), at which point exposure moved on to the next item.

In its heyday desensitization was the most studied behavioral method in the world but the simple models of why it worked quickly fell apart. For example, it did not really matter whether the hierarchy of stimulus presentation was followed from the least to the most or the most to the least (e.g., Krapfl & Nawas, 1970).

The more operantly sensible idea that exposure allows new forms of learning to occur is gradually gaining ascendence in the exposure literature (e.g., Craske et al., 2012). In this more "constructional" approach, previous fear conditioning is undermined by adding new learning linked to the feared event or situation. For example, exposure methods may reduce rigid avoidance or attentional patterns and build patterns of observing, describing, noticing, appreciating, and the like instead.

This shifts the focus from fear reduction to an issue of repertoire expansion. In a sense instead of subjective units of distress, a more telling measure would be subjective units of willingness where 100 is totally willing to be present and feel while exploring new behaviors and 1 is totally unwilling to do so. Here a hierarchy might make sense, not because of counterconditioning but because of new behaviors and best learning in a step-by-step fashion. Perhaps the client is totally willing to look at a picture of a distressing event from a distance while eating ice cream, or (in some modern forms of desensitization) tapping their leg or moving their eyes.

That approach can readily be expanded to internal, private events. Traditional systematic desensitization might not detect that the person is escaping thoughts or suppressing feelings, but from an acceptance and willingness perspective it is not hard to add instruction for the person to notice and say aloud what their body feels like, or to label and describe what emotions are showing up.

When that approach has been tried in exposure work, the results have been highly supportive. Merely putting feelings into words (what is called "affect labeling") significantly increases the impact of exposure (Kircanski et al., 2012).

You can understand this from the psychological flexibility model.

A present moment focus instead changes the relationship of the person to their own experiences. We all have the option to instead observe those negative thoughts and emotions as they arrive. To feel them and to hear them non-judgmentally. These are strongly repertoire steps that alter the functions of fear but add to the functions of the moment, much as adding water to a glass of saltwater makes it much less salty but not by removing a single grain of salt.

If we can train clients to be more willing to accept and learn from thoughts and emotions as they show up, they will inevitably observe and notice that the thoughts are temporary and fleeting, there are many healthy response options when they appear, and perhaps even that these experiences contain worthwhile information about one's history and the current situation. These actions change the context in which the original stimulus occurs. It is still present, but loses much of its repertoire narrowing power, as the behavior analyst encourages the client to go deeper and deeper into noticing their own private behavior. A context is created that undermines unhealthy behavior-behavior relations.

We can also promote acceptance by introducing stimuli that operate as augmental rules that strengthen the probability that the client will choose acceptance over avoidance in the moment. For children or persons with developmental disabilities, this could take the form of presenting "acceptance" as a choice prior to engaging in a task that they may have historically avoided. For example, by placing accept or avoid on a card and establishing a history of reinforcement for choosing "accept" and completing the task to obtain the valued reinforcer. This requires also honoring the choice to avoid, analyzing the factors that participate in this choice, and adapting those factors throughout acceptance training. Ultimately, we want to strengthen acceptance as a general pattern of behavior and can do so by reinforcing the choice to accept.

For adults with high-level verbal abilities, this could take the form of writing one's values on a post-it note and placing the post-it note near where they typically make the decision to avoid. For example, a person who avoids distressing thoughts by overeating might place a post-it with their values on the refrigerator so that their values can augment the probability that they will accept and experience their thoughts fully and curiously, instead of eating to avoid as they have done in the past. In both examples, it is imperative that these contrived supports operate within a broader training structure and are faded as mastery is achieved. Ultimately, we want acceptance to occur without prompts and as a generalized pattern of behavior, which can be achieved only when the client is left alone in their world, external reinforcers have been removed, and what remains is the choice to approach or avoid the life that they value.

We can also embed acceptance training through experiential exercises that increase in complexity over time. For example, in a group, we could promote a sense of shared humanity (a target in self-compassion training) by encouraging each person to write their fear on the post-it note, then walk around with it in the group. To maintain greater confidentiality, we could have clients submit the post-it notes, shuffle them up, and give one to each person to illustrate that we all carry "stuff," but it is our relationship with our stuff that matters. For children, we could also illustrate the importance of training and approaching new things by having them write with their non-dominant hand and allowing them to notice that their writing improves with practice. Acceptance is no different.

More ACT-based behavior analytic curriculums are rapidly becoming available, such as the "Accept. Identify. Move." (AIM) curriculum (Dixon & Paliliunas, 2018) that describe these activities in detail for behavior analysts to embed in existing behavior plans. That is one reason this book is written more as a general guide – so that readers can see how the many available resources fit together within a behavior analytic approach. Because the six psychological flexibility processes all fit together and interrelate, however, it takes time and practice to see how to move ahead with any particular target problem.

ANTECEDENT AND CONSEQUENCE STRATEGIES TO PROMOTE WILLINGNESS AND ACCEPTANCE

Acceptance as a behavior can be measured in a number of ways that we described above, but to set the scene let's imagine that data are being collected using an app-based EMA system, where the client is asked to manually record their reactions when in situation *X* that has been identified as a situation where avoidance has been historically likely. For example, presenting in front of a class for a classroom teacher. Using a tool like the ACT Matrix, they identified that they are likely to engage in simply reading directly from their prepared materials or generating "busy work" for the class to engage in. When they are at their best, they are presenting information dynamically and feel a sense of connection with the students in the class, and instructional tasks are provided only as needed to supplement learning with moment-to-moment sensitivity for how the students are feeling (engaged, bored, etc.). The class begins – the teacher reacts. What we might then ask the teacher to record are (1) the class content; (2) a rating of their anxiety and urge to avoid on a scale ranging from 0 to 100; and (3) a rating of their avoidance ranging from completely avoidant, 0 (reading directly from the slides and avoiding any direct and meaningful interaction) to willingly engaged, 100.

By simply making this choice evident, we might get some of the way. Indeed, "noticing" itself can be part of an intervention and this data collection strategy encourages noticing. In the data, what we are looking for is a greater engagement score (3) even when anxiety and the urge to avoid are high (2). Because of gradual exposure, we may also notice the urge to avoid diminishes slightly over time as engagement increases, representing a change in the CMO.

But what else could we do to expedite this process even further?

Some antecedent and setting event strategies that center around present-moment awareness could provide a solution that alters the MO (2) and thus affects the behavioral outcome (3). As a setting event, when the teacher engages in meditation each morning immediately before class, the urge to escape may lessen. As an antecedent strategy, the teacher may engage in the "noticing five things" exercise immediately before the lesson. By collecting data on both the affective MO and the outcome response, we can isolate where precisely we are being successful within this behavior stream.

If we have evidence that the greatest source of momentary distress operates as a function of their own thoughts, defusion exercises that we review in the next chapter could also operate here to interact with the content in new ways. In this case, we may not see a change in the affective MO (2) but may observe a change in the response nonetheless (3). Something similar may occur when presenting values-consistent stimuli. For example, the teacher values feelings of connectedness, so having her complete the values-to-committed action section of the ACT Matrix immediately before teaching the class could also alter the probability of the desired response pattern even though the affective MO remains.

Combining Acceptance with Present Moment Awareness

At this point, you are probably starting to notice the lines between present-moment awareness and acceptance are becoming blurry. In behavior analysis, we are used to clean distinctions between terms that guide practice. However, even with something as simple as distinguishing between antecedents and consequences. Overconsumption of a reinforcer (i.e., satiation) operates as an antecedent that suppresses immediate rates of behavior. Small access to a reinforcer can evoke high rates of behavior to contact more of the reinforcer (i.e., induction). It does not take long before even this simple distinction becomes obscured.

That is not to say these distinctions are not useful – they are because they allow us to work with people's environments to influence behavior. Without distinctions, we would not have intervention models. Up to this point, we have reviewed deeply two of the core processes of the Hexaflex model.

Present-moment awareness and acceptance are deeply intertwined. Each process is needed to accomplish more fully the other. Often taking the charge to practice mindfulness occurs when noticing *something* is not working – something *feels* wrong. Perhaps too much stress is beginning to take its toll emotionally, physically, and socially. Those dreams that seemed just around the corner are starting to slip away.

Willingness also shows up repeatedly throughout present-moment training because being in the present moment is often more difficult than being psychologically somewhere else. There is a reason that we spend so much time fixating on the past a ruminating on the future. When we attend to the present moment, including present thoughts and emotional experiences, often times those thoughts and emotional experiences are painful. Interacting with those experiences requires a willingness to sit with the pleasurable and the painful moments, and accept that doing so is necessary to move forward.

Present-moment awareness is also the primary strategy used to foster acceptance. Acceptance is all about taking in the good and the bad more fully and more completely. This first involves being present and attending to external and internal experiences without judgement or evaluation. Only by noticing these events can they operate as stimuli to influence behavior change.

When we are in the present moment fully, we can also go deeper into noticing and contact even more levels of stimulus control. For example, in the moment you might notice that you are feeling angry. What does feeling angry feel like? Where in your body do you feel angry? Is there something past these physical sensations that participate in feeling angry? Does it have a smell? Does it have a taste? When we start to explore "angry" with genuine curiosity, we become the observer of our own anger – and this changes how anger functionally operates within a stream of behavior by entirely disrupting what would typically come next – fighting, fleeing, freezing, or more broadly – experientially avoiding.

A lot can be accomplished with these two processes alone and we will even further build our model with each new process, highlighting their on-going interaction in promoting greater psychological flexibility.

7

Defusion

Imagine a young CEO who is about to attend her first major corporate meeting, with major implications for her and her company. She feels anxious about the meeting (aversive private experience) and does not think she is good enough to succeed (increasing feelings of anxiety through transformation of stimulus function). Suddenly, she starts feeling ill. She thinks, "I am feeling too sick to go to the meeting," and her heart rate decelerates, and feelings of anxiety immediately dissipate. "Someone else can take the meeting, it is really not a big deal." Anxiety subsides even more, and the meeting is missed. "Wow, I really do feel better, and I am glad I took the time to take care of myself, I really was quite ill." Guilt and other feelings that might accompany a missed opportunity are avoided. Not only is missing other meetings reinforced, but this way of thinking about meetings is also reinforced. And it might not stop at meetings but might be generalized to other anxiety-provoking events and patterns of experiential avoidance. Suddenly, she finds herself not only avoiding her career but also her friends and to some extent forming deep and intimate relationships with her family. Her psychiatrist recently diagnosed her with a generalized anxiety disorder.

These tricks of the mind were emphasized in early cognitive behavioral therapy (CBT) approaches that sought to remedy cognitive distortions such as mind reading, black-or-white thinking, or personalization. The basic idea was that if we could alter the content of one's thoughts then we could change their behavior. And this approach has worked to a point, including in the treatment of anxiety disorders like that experienced by the young CEO.

More recent research has shown us that simply altering the content of one's thoughts is easier said than done. Deliberate attempts to control thinking content can become perilously close to thought suppression. Research on thought suppression has shown that attempting to alter the form or frequency of thoughts can actually be counterproductive, leading to an increase in the very content that people try to avoid (Wang et al., 2020). Not only is the mind quite tricky, but the mind also fights back. For metaphorical purposes, attempting to control the mind directly is like feeding a monster – attending too closely to the behavior-behavior relation only strengthens it. Recall that we must attend to stimulus events to respond to them, and this is precisely why present moment is a critical process. When our attention drifts elsewhere to primarily focus on thoughts and feelings that are the source of struggle, we can become consumed and controlled by them.

Cognitive defusion offers an alternative way forward. Instead of trying to alter the form or frequency of unwanted thoughts (i.e., the behavior-behavior relation), we want to alter

DOI: 10.4324/9781003250371-9

their function on behavior. If we can do so successfully, then new behavior will contact alternative streams of reinforcement (ideally, valued reinforcement) and strengthen schedule sensitivity and psychological flexibility. Let's unpack what this can look like in practice.

Think of an unpleasant thought that you experience. This requires present-moment awareness and willingness to sit with this thought. It may be a fear or worry you frequently encounter, or the common thought of "I'm not good enough." Now, instead of trying to think of reasons why the thought is not true (thought suppression), try singing the thought as if it were the "happy birthday" song. What happens to the thought? The content remains the same, but what happens to its effect on behavior? When we have done this exercise in workshops or with clients, we typically observe laughter and a sense of joy that comes from the activity – as if the weight has been lifted from the thought.

We did not change the thought at all, at least not the content or the literal words, but by changing how we interact with the thought, we change the behavior that the thought evokes. That is, we changed the "context of literal meaning" which changed the function of the thought as it occurs within a behavior-behavior relation. Research has shown that defusion is often more successful than cognitive restructuring in influencing things like smoking (Hooper et al., 2018) or food cravings (Hooper et al., 2012) as well as other common experiences. For this reason, defusion plays a central role in acceptance and commitment treatment (ACT)-based interventions and does not require changing our minds, but changing our interaction with our minds. This distinction is critical in understanding how ACT differs from more traditional CBT-based approaches and opens the door for behavior analysts to help a client work with their mind instead of against it.

BASIC BEHAVIOR CHANGE PROCESSES: DEFUSION AND RELATIONAL RESISTANCE

Defusion is all about diminishing stimulus control exerted by patterns of verbal relating. In other words, your thoughts have less power over your actions. And in doing so, defusion strengthens control exerted by direct experience. Perhaps more than any other process, there is a direct link between defusion and relational frame theory (RFT). Imagine a simple experiment where given stimulus A, a person is trained to pick stimulus B, and given B, to pick stimulus C. The result would be a combinatorially entailed A=C and C=A relation. If we then pair A with an aversive stimulus such as shock, we can expect physiological arousal functions such as increased skin conductance when a person is exposed to C via a transformation of stimulus functions. But how can we undo such a relation so that it no longer transforms the function?

Once a relation has been established, it cannot simply be erased. For instance, putting the A=C and C=A relation under extinction conditions does not work, because it is a derived relation, and thus was never reinforced directly in the first place. And punishing the A=C and C=A relational response doesn't work either, because it would likely transfer the aversive functions of the punisher to the A and C stimuli, potentially furthering our problem. We observe this clinically when the client beats themselves up verbally for saying or thinking the wrong thing. Now instead of simply thinking the unwanted thought, it is coupled with "I am doing this poorly" or "I am so stupid" or "why am I like this?."

We might say that the A=C and C=A relation is fused. In therapy, cognitive fusion occurs when thoughts are held to be literally true – or believing that A indeed is equal to C, or whatever the relational structure of the potentially harmful thought (e.g., A is more than C, A is worse than C) – and when the resulting transformation of stimulus function is excessive or context insensitive.

"Fusion" as we describe it here could therefore be synonymous with "resistance" as a property of relational strength and functional impact. A relational class is fused when its two key properties according to relational frame theory (relational derivation and stimulus functions that are transformed by relational derivation), are resistant to change.

Behavioral researchers have done a good deal of work modeling the resistance of behaviors in basic laboratory arrangements, often using rats as experimental subjects, often under the label of "behavioral momentum theory" (BMT; Nevin, 1992). BMT can trace its lineage all the way back to Thorndike (1911) but has been extended to applied behavior analysis (ABA) extensively (e.g., Critchfield & Reed, 2009). Resistance can be modeled quantitatively in the lab as: $\Delta B = \text{-x} / \text{m}$. Delta always means change, so ΔB is an estimated change in behavior. According to BMT, a change in behavior is a function of a disruptor (e.g., extinction, punishment) over the mass or resistance of the behavior. The less a behavior changes when a disruptor is applied, the more resistant the behavior is to change. Resistance research has regularly been conducted with people with disabilities in clinical settings in relation to challenging behavior (e.g., Parry-Cruwys et al., 2011).

Early in 2020, we attempted to extend the account to complex relational behavior in relational density theory (RDT). The idea here is that if relational behavior is behavior like any other, then we should be able to model the resistance of relational classes to disruptors. The details of the model are beyond this book, and research is underway to work out the specifics of how complex relational behavior operates. The initial focus has been on relational derivation, and the early evidence on RDT suggests that relational classes that contain multiple relations that are strongly held are also more resistant to change. This is not altogether negative. For example, when learning a new academic concept, it is important that well-established facts are generally resistant to misinformation that fails to cohere with what you are learning. However, when those relational classes carry psychological negative functions relative to other behavior (such as experiential avoidance, as we covered in the last chapter), cognitive fusion facilitates very resistant patterns of psychological inflexibility.

For example, consider the simple thought "I am so stupid" as presented in Figure 7.1. On the right, "I" is related to "stupid" in a frame of coordination. These are strongly linked, which we can represent by the fact that the events are close together in space. "I" is also related to "failing a class," which supports the relation "I am so stupid." This is how we are used to interacting with rule-governed behavior – relatively simple rules with clear links and a simple logic. These relations might be easily overcome with something like examining

HIGH MASS/RESISTANCE	LOW MASS/RESISTANCE
"There is no hope"	
"Failing my marriage" "My kids don't want me around"	
"Failing a class"	"Failing a class"
"I" "STUPID"	
"Failing another class"	"I" "STUPID"
"Not respected at work"	
"Everything comes so easy to other people"	

FIGURE 7.1 Relational density theory diagram.

the evidence for the thought, such as "well, have you ever passed any classes?" or "is this class really something you have put all of your time into?" These verbal relations are much less likely to lead people to suffer, and sometimes simple corrective verbal relations of this kind can work reasonably well.

But consider the left half of the figure. Here "I" and "stupid" are still related and are the same distance apart. What is different is the sheer number of relations that operate within this same space, related to both "I" and "stupid" in different ways, potentially adding even greater resistance to this way of thinking. Not only is the person on the right failing their class, but thoughts of failing the class may occasion thoughts about their marriage falling apart and their belief that their children don't want them around. On the other side, they also think about a second class that they are failing, they do not feel respected at work and feel that everything comes so easily to other people. It is not hard to see how all of this may be related to their thought that "there is no hope."

This kind of "dug in" psychological suffering may be far harder to change.

Let's try to examine the evidence again to convince the person on the left that they are not stupid. "But you have passed other classes before…" "*Yes, but I am failing two classes now and it is just getting more difficult…*" "Maybe the classes are getting harder, but it will just take more work…" "*Both classes are coming so easily to everyone else, and I don't have the time to commit like they do because my marriage is already falling apart, and I spend all of my time at work trying to support my kids…*" And so on. Every point of counterevidence you could make feeds into some other supporting relation, strengthening the network even more and demanding more and more of the person's time and attention.

The pattern on the left is far more fused than the right and any negative psychological functions that are made more likely by these verbal relations are also much harder to change. Here we see the futility of thought suppression, cognitive reorganization, positive self-statement, affirmations, and all of the other traditional armamentarium of cognitive intervention – there aren't just one or two weak verbal relations that we are contending with, but rather there is an entire ecosystem of relations that support an experiential avoidance function and that are likely to be inadvertently strengthened by common sense cognitive interventions.

Understanding this problem is key to understanding why defusion exercises are a necessary alternative. For our deepest challenges, restructuring this space may be insurmountably difficult. And even if we are successful, the cognitive approaches require on-going maintenance to prevent falling back into old patterns. Worse in some way, some cognitive techniques may be more likely to work at lower levels of difficulty, drawing people into a kind of behavioral trap. That is not just a theoretical possibility. Positive affirmations like "I'm a good person!," for example, have been shown to be helpful provided you don't really need them (Wood et al., 2009). What kind of help is that?

We already introduced singing the thought as a birthday song as an example of a defusion exercise. Below we talk about a number of different strategies that accomplish this same general goal of transforming the function of literalized content. When we sing happy birthday, we are bringing contextual cues into the situation that can alter the avoidance functions of the thought.

For most, birthdays are largely positive experiences, and the song is generally paired with desserts, birthday presents, and being surrounded by family and friends. In addition, if the intervention is well timed the irony of singing something aversive as a birthday song can be very funny ("irony" is itself a kind of relational incompatibility). Furthermore, singing requires deliberate amplification and elaboration of verbal material. All of these relations and functions are incompatible with the avoidance functions of the thought, providing a new context that undermines a negative behavior-behavior relation.

Now, the point of this simple exercise is *not* to change these relations, and a birthday song not going to remove the very real challenges that the person on the left is experiencing in their life. But if a song can undermine the verbal spiral that inevitably leads to "there is no hope," then that time and energy can be spent accepting these events as they are today and engaging in committed action toward improving these events tomorrow. The way "out" is to engage in meaningful external behavior that progresses towards one's values, and not continuing to dwell within about how life could be better *if only* everything was perfect today. Because what if "if only" never comes?

TRANSLATIONAL RESEARCH ON DEFUSION: A GROWING EXPERIMENTAL BASE

We have some evidence of this weakening of verbal stimulus control in a series of research studies on gambling. In one study, we created verbal stimulus control over slot machine gambling by pairing the colors associated with slot machines with "more" or "less" gambling stimuli (Zlomke & Dixon, 2006). The idea was that if gambling was under verbal relational control, then participants would show a bias for the slot machine that was the same color as "more." In fact, this did occur, and we have replicated this general finding in other casino games (e.g., roulette, Dixon et al., 2017) and in the context of promoting pro-climate purchasing to combat climate change (Matthews et al., under review).

These studies suggest that we can create fused rules that people will follow above and beyond the direct contingencies that they experience. Moreover, as summarized by Belisle and Dixon (2020a) and later shown experimentally (Belisle & Dixon, 2020b; Belisle & Clayton, 2021), the stronger relations are at one time, the more resistant those same relations will be to change when competing information is introduced that could lead to alternative rules. Moreover, old relational patterns may support the emergence of new relations that cohere with existing rules. This means that when thoughts are fused, similar other thoughts are likely to emerge, generating even greater resistance to the problem.

Belisle et al. (2019) demonstrated how defusion may be a potential solution. In their study, they replicated the slot machine bias, where one group of participants was more likely to choose a red slot machine after receiving relational training. However, a second group completed a series of defusion activities immediately after receiving the relational training. The defusion activities involved identifying positive and negative things that are red and black, things that are both red and black, and repeating red-black-red-black as fast as possible for two minutes. The point was to blur the lines between red and black, and to reduce the functions of both colors. As a result, the participants in the defusion group not only showed less bias towards the red machine but actually showed greater schedule sensitivity.

We highlight this work not because it is our own, but because it shows the interplay between fusion and defusion – and how it might influence a person's behavior. Other experiments have shown this same pattern with other behavioral outcomes and varying defusion exercises. For example, Moffit et al. (2012) conducted a randomized control trial comparison of cognitive defusion and cognitive restructuring on cravings for chocolate. In their study, all participants were given a bag of chocolates to carry around with them for one week, and uneaten chocolates were returned at the end of the study. Results showed that the odds of abstaining from consuming the chocolate were more than three times higher for the defusion group than the restructuring group.

In another study, Mandavia et al. (2015) compared two defusion and two thought suppression approaches on decentering and reducing believability of negative body image thoughts. The defusion exercises either included a rapid vocalization component where participants stated the thought repeatedly and rapidly or did not include this component. The results showed that the inclusion of this component led to the greatest decentering of the thoughts and reduction in believability compared to the other conditions – and both defusion conditions were more impactful than the cognitive restructuring conditions as well as a control group.

Although these examples represent behavior that may be experienced by clients with addictions, food cravings, or negative body images, there is also emerging research showing how effective defusion exercises can be with individuals with autism. Eilers and Hayes (2015) evaluated the influence of a 30-second defusion exercise that involved young children with autism saying rigid and restricted rules in a silly voice. Then, they exposed the children to situations that historically evoked high rates of challenging behavior. Results showed immediate suppression in rates of challenging behavior following the defusion exercises across each of the three child participants, demonstrating precisely how something like cognitive defusion could be used within a treatment plan.

RELATIONAL FRAMES INTERACT IN COMPLEX WAYS

Part of the therapeutic process is about changing relational frames of relational frames – or the way we interact with our own verbal behavior. The scenario below shows how relational framing may play a critical role in the defusion process. This is an example of a young Autistic adult who is unable to approach men to initiate conversations that could potentially lead to a romantic relationship. They are fused to the thought that people find them weird and that nobody would want to date them, let alone talk to them. Like with acceptance, this process begins with an acknowledgment of the situation, that approaching someone is uncomfortable, and thinking about it might occasion thoughts of inadequacy and bring up densely established relations or rules about being weird or different.

However, moving forward *with* these thoughts is better than getting stuck and ruminating on the thoughts, but may require defusing the thoughts in order to get unstuck. In this case, holding those thoughts loosely and choosing to practice one of many possible defusion exercises before approaching the person. Part of this process may involve interacting with the deictic frames of "I am weird" contextually (i.e., self-as-context) and with self-compassion for the experience that these thoughts are difficult for any person, but that being oneself is necessary to fully and completely experience the relationship that they desire. Finally, all of this also requires accepting that approaching a new person may succeed or may fail, but in either outcome, approaching the person is in line with a broader value of pursuing genuine romantic relationships, without sacrificing those things that make them unique.

A more traditional cognitive approach would involve attempting to examine the evidence for this thought, "does everyone in your life avoid you?" "Is being weird such a bad thing?" These might even be things we have said to clients – and doing so might be helpful at some level. Defusion, however, offers a different way forward and a strategy that can generalize to other thoughts throughout their life, regardless of the content. It is not hard to imagine this same process applied to enrolling in a challenging college course or applying for a new job. Or, in an entirely different context, choosing whether or not to become a parent as a person with autism.

This approach is also far different from the social skills training approaches that we have traditionally adopted in behavior analysis. Sure, certain behaviors may improve the probability of successful interactions, but if those behaviors do not cohere with how the person behaves as a function of their own extended learning history, relationships may fail simply because the learned social skills only go so far. This is often referred to as "masking" by the autistic community as an attempt to temporarily behave in different ways than one normally behaves – defusion and other approaches within ACT offer an alternative to masking as a way to pursue life's reinforcers.

Fusion and defusion are difficult concepts to grasp, and we are learning more seemingly every day. It is for this reason that we recommend all behavior analysts who implement ACT-based approaches become versed in RFT. Doing so will be critical to conducting defusion functionally beyond simple exercises, to really dissect the relational frames that participate in behavior and weaken their control.

INDEPENDENT AND DEPENDENT VARIABLES FOR INTERVENTION

When we think about measurement in the context of cognitive fusion and defusion, we must determine (1) "what fused ways of thinking contribute to the challenge at hand?" and (2) "how fused are those thoughts?"

Answering the first question requires listening without judgement to the stories, explanations, and reasons that clients provide in discussing their challenges. In an ACT-based approach, these verbal narratives may be part of complex behavior-behavior relations that we attempt to weaken with defusion interventions.

Open-ended questions can allow for an analysis of the content of these fused relations. For example, the question "when you think about your struggle, what thoughts immediately come to mind?" can evoke descriptions of verbal behavior that the client has noticed in the context of their struggle. Because of relational frames, orienting the client to their struggle may evoke the same verbal behavior that occurs when the struggle is occurring. Let's use the example from earlier of the client pursuing romantic relationships. "When you struggle to approach people that you might be romantically interested in, what comes to your mind in that moment?" The client may respond with, "I cannot possibly approach them because I don't know what to say and they will think I am super creepy for even trying to talk to them." At this point, we are already starting to see some of the relations that may be participating in our client's experiential avoidance.

We can dig even deeper with probing questions within the conversation, such as by validating the initial statement and asking for even more detail. We might say, "It must be hard when that thought shows up, what are some other thoughts that you have around approaching others, for example at a coffee shop or at the bar?" To that they may reply, "I have autism and that makes me different. Most people don't understand what it's like and this makes it so hard for me to make friends. They think I am strange, and they don't get me. And I don't even know what to say to them." By probing deeper, more potential verbal relations are uncovered. In this case, fused rules related to being creepy, unwanted, different, and their diagnosis of autism may all participate in avoidance of talking to others in settings, where doing so is completely appropriate.

If you think of using a tool like the ACT Matrix, discovering the content of fused verbal relations is embedded in the process. That is, the content is contained in the bottom-left of the matrix (private experiences that move us away from our values), and the process of doing the matrix is designed to bring awareness to the relationship between these private experiences and the behaviors that constitute experiential avoidance.

These strategies are really a form of qualitative analysis that involves collecting as much open-ended self-report information as possible and looking for consistent themes. When similar patterns are evident across multiple challenges in a person's life, this may indicate highly fused relations that should be targeted within intervention. A qualitative analysis may be sufficient to answer our first question, "what fused ways of thinking contribute to the challenge at hand?" However, this does little to help answer our second question, "how fused are those thoughts?."

We need a way to attach a number to "cognitive fusion" to allow for a quantitative analysis of fusion as a process in order to evaluate the efficacy of defusion interventions in experimental analyses. Only then can we truly analyze something like fusion and defusion scientifically.

Fusion and Defusion as Dependent Variables

A considerable amount of research in basic experimental RFT labs is presently attempted to determine how verbal events are related to other verbal events, how strong are the transformations of stimulus function, and how resistant are those relations to change. All of this is in the service of quantifying "fusion" and "defusion" as dependent variables and predictor variables within ACT.

Some of this work extends from the idea that every relational response is related to every other relational response in some way. For example, if you were asked "how are a pig and a lettuce plant related?" you could generate a response. Doing so might take a few seconds, but any number of responses is possible. "Pigs don't like lettuce." "If I eat enough lettuce I won't feel like such a pig." Now, what if you were instead asked, "how are a pig and bacon related?" This response comes much easier and quicker. "Bacon comes from a pig." Therefore, we might conclude that "bacon" and "pig" are *more* related than "lettuce" and "pig."

This idea of differential relatedness led to the idea of differential arbitrarily applicable relational responding effects (DAARRE; Finn et al., 2018) that underlie technologies such as the Implicit Relational Assessment Procedure (IRAP). In the IRAP, participants are presented with a sample stimulus and comparison stimuli and must generate a predetermined response that is consistent with a contextual cue. The idea is that when the contextual cue linking the stimuli is consistent with the learning history of the participant, they will generate the response more rapidly. This then provides a variable (*D*-IRAP score) that describes the differential relatedness of stimulus comparisons introduced throughout the procedure.

The IRAP is an important development when examining fusion as a dependent variable that we may want to influence with defusion exercises because stronger relations may be considered more "fused" (i.e., having a more extended and elaborate learning history). Early research showed that the IRAP was able to detect relational biases including racial bias, gender bias, and political affiliation, and could even be used to predict clinical outcomes like depression and anxiety. This supports the role of cognitive fusion as a process variable that could influence other behaviors that we care about in behavior analysis.

Moreover, engaging in defusion exercises appears to influence scores achieved on the IRAP. For example, Ritzert et al. (2015) evaluated the relationship between spiders and fear in a non-clinical sample, and their results showed that the defusion intervention led to a decrease in fear as measured in the IRAP compared to thought suppression and a control condition. In another study, Ferroni-Bast et al. (2019) created an IRAP designed to detect perceived failure following an insoluble task. Participants were then exposed to a defusion audio recording or a control recording. The results however failed to support a change in IRAP scores in either of the two groups. Despite differential findings, these studies and others support the use of the IRAP as a corollary outcome measure that may be useful when evaluating the effectiveness of defusion or comprehensive ACT-based strategies; however, we caution readers against using the IRAP for functional assessment purposes at this time but strongly encourage more research in this area.

DAARRE-based models are one way to evaluate verbal relations, and more research is needed to link these scores to the broader construct of cognitive fusion. Fortunately, fusion and defusion are assessed as competing processes within a number of self-report measures. An entire assessment called the Cognitive Fusion Questionnaire (CFQ;) is the most widely used measure of cognitive fusion (Donati et al., 2021). The CFQ-7 contains seven items directly related to cognitive fusion and are assessed on a seven-point Likert scale. Additionally, the assessment has a strong internal validity and has been translated into multiple languages. Comparisons with self-report assessments of such things as depression or life satisfaction, and the assessment of other ACT-processes support the utility of the CFQ-7.

Measures of fusion may also be present within other assessments of ACT-based interventions. We have already discussed the Acceptance and Action Questionnaire – II (AAQ-II) as a measure of acceptance and action, and inside it, the client is asked to rate different statements on a scale from "never true" to "always true." At some level, this very scale asks how far the client takes the statements literally. In other words, high scores on the AAQ-II may be indicative of cognitive fusion. And we already know that high scores on the AAQ-II (i.e., fusion to rules that exhibit low levels of acceptance and action) predict negative outcomes that behavior analysis is designed to treat or prevent.

Other self-report tools provide items specifically designed to assess cognitive fusion. For example, in the CompACT, ten items are dedicated to assessing openness to experience. These include statements such as "I go out of my way to avoid situations that might bring difficult thoughts, feelings, or sensations," "thoughts are just thoughts – they do not control what I do," and "I can take thoughts and feelings as they come, without attempting to avoid or control them." Within each of these questions, it is easy to see how practicing cognitive defusion could play a key role in promoting openness to experience as one part of psychological flexibility. The Child Psychological Flexibility Questionnaire (CPFQ)-Child Report also contains items specifically related to cognitive defusion, such as "If I think something, that doesn't mean it is true" and "my thoughts don't make me do what I do," which could provide some insight into present levels of cognitive fusion. All of these measures could be used along with self-monitoring of the frequency of fused thoughts to accompany an analysis of the changes in target behaviors.

Defusion Interventions as Independent Variables

A good starting point to evaluate cognitive fusion quantitatively could be to measure the degree in which people become desensitized to the direct outcomes of their choices as a byproduct of rigidly adhering to fused rules. Recall that the biggest challenge surrounding rule-governed behavior is that rigidly following rules can diminish a person's ability to contact and react appropriately to contingencies which can lead to being stuck in unworkable behaviors. Experimentally, we could test any number of defusion exercises by generating rules that align with (or diverge) from programmed contingencies within a contrived task and evaluate if the exercise produces greater control of the contingencies of the task when compared to the rule.

In practice, we already do this with defusion exercises. For example, if we are trying to increase the behavior of approaching others like in the above example, we could compare the rate and duration of social exchanges through self-monitoring in the presence or absence of the defusion exercise. Doing so could show functional control of the defusion exercise over approach as part of a behavior-behavior relation. This analytic approach could be used with any overt behavior if becoming less fused-like leads the client to engage in values-guided behavior. This general strategy could also be used to compare defusion exercises to other processes such as present-moment awareness, where defusion represents interacting with verbal stimuli in a functionally different way, and present moment involves attending more directly to present internal and external stimuli. For each specific client, we can determine which strategy works better to produce the desired change in behavior.

There is an emerging body of research showing that practicing defusion can lead to changes in other behaviors that we may be interested in as behavior analysts. For example, practicing defusion can diminish emotional arousal as a response to distressing thoughts. Again, consider that the purpose of defusion is to weaken the effect of a person's thoughts on their behavior. Pilecki and McKay (2012) evaluated this by showing participants videos designed to elicit feelings of sadness, fear, or disgust, and then had participants complete the Stroop task that involves attending to competing stimuli (i.e., words and colors). Their results showed that, although participants rated their emotional responses as comparable with or without the defusion exercises, they were better able to perform on the Stroop task following defusion compared to thought suppression exercises or a control condition. For adults with autism, Maisel et al. (2019) a brief five-minute cognitive defusion technique could momentarily reduce the believability and discomfort of distressing thoughts experienced by autistic participants.

In the above, the defusion exercises are introduced as an independent variable and the target behavior change as the dependent outcome. When considering defusion exercises as potential independent variables within a broader ACT-based treatment approach, there are a number of ways to go about developing the exercises. Assaz et al. (2018) provide some general categories that defusion exercises tend to fall into that can help delineate between certain exercises as dependent variables.

First, several exercises involve playing with words, such as saying the word over and over again (word repetition), singing the word or thought as a song, spelling the thought backwards, or saying the thought in a silly voice. The first strategy, word repetition, provides a good example. It may temporarily weaken stimulus control in the moment through habituation and by reducing the relational and functional contextual cues that rely on word order and grammar to establish the impact of verbal events. Even though the effect is temporary, the lesson provided by a dramatic reduction in the meaning and impact of words may be quite long-lasting.

A second category includes disrupting the thought-action stream. For example, the therapist and client may go for a walk and take turns being the person behaving (e.g., walking around the building) and "the mind" (e.g., evaluating and judging everything the person does). Another example could involve shooting a basketball into a net while the other person tries to distract the shooter by saying evaluative statements of past and present events. A third might be to walk around the room while saying aloud "I can't walk around this room." These exercises are designed to experientially simulate engaging in behavior even though thoughts and feelings are present. In these cases, the goal is to reinforce successfully completing the tasks even with "the mind" present.

A third category involves observing and identifying relational responses as they occur in the moment and creating distance by adding qualifiers, such as "I am having the thought that..." From an RFT perspective, adding this statement can help to take the content of the thought less literally. For example, the thought "I am not interesting, and nobody wants me around" is functionally different from "I am having the thought that I am not interesting, and nobody wants me around." Another common example involves visualizing thoughts and leaves on a tree and psychologically watching the leaves fall from the tree into a stream and be carried away into the distance. In these examples, we are recontextualizing thoughts as something that is spatial distant instead of literal.

By understanding defusion exercises in this way, we can manipulate various aspects of defusion within a broader approach to intervention and program evaluation. First, we could do something resembling a dosage analysis by setting targets for engaging in defusion exercises. For example, we might set a goal to practice ten defusion exercises over the course of a week. At first, these exercises may be prompted by the therapist, but over time, the prompting may fade to transfer stimulus control from the therapist to the external situations that lead to unwanted thoughts and emotional experiences. In other words, the client gets put in charge of engaging in defusion practices.

Similarly, within a broader ACT curriculum such as Accept, Identify, Move (AIM) (Dixon & Paliliunas, 2018), we can also vary the percentage of daily lessons that focus on defusion compared to the other processes within ACT. This may be especially important when measures indicate that cognitive fusion plays a centralized role in the challenges that clients experience. Behavior analysts might also use single-subject experimental design strategies to compare defusion exercises or broader defusion training programs. Do these strategies work differently for different clients, or are they best used together within a larger training package? Answering these questions and others as they relate to cognitive defusion is entirely within the wheelhouse of behavior analysts. What we do know is that training defusion as a broad class of behaviors may be necessary to allow clients to contact the present moment with acceptance and willingness, showing just how interconnected the ACT processes really are.

ANTECEDENT AND CONSEQUENCE STRATEGIES TO PROMOTE DEFUSION

We have largely talked about defusion *as* a form of antecedent intervention. Where behavior analysts may be especially valuable is in identifying those moments where something like defusion could be most useful. For example, using a time-based scatterplot, the behavior analyst may notice that challenging behavior arises most often during lunchtime, and the consequence is the opportunity to avoid peers. The same person expresses feeling connected to their peers as a held value. If we know this is when and where challenges show up and we have evidence that rigid rules play a part, then immediately prior to this moment could be a good place and time to engage in any number of defusion exercises before approaching the moment.

In many ways, defusion exercises operate as that alternative adaptive behavior. You can *either* avoid this situation *or* interact with the thought differently. You choose. When we think of defusion in this way, then how can we make the latter choice even more likely? A simple solution is to prompt defusion in the moment. "Hey, let's both sing a really hard thought we're having right now like the Addams Family song." Another way to augment defusion would be to take permanent products from earlier defusion exercises, like drawing the thought as a goofy-looking monster and putting that monster immediately into the context.

The bottom line is that defusion can be comical and people are very hesitant to engage in these things publicly. We all share an unfortunate history of being ridiculed and mocked when we act out of normal. Isn't that a shame? Consequences like social praise can offset this history and build trust that can be shaped while practicing defusion. Even more broadly, creating a culture within the workplace where it is okay to act silly and to express one's thoughts and feelings in this way, and to socially reinforce or reward creative expression of this kind becomes the new normal. Fostering a culture of defusion.

COMBINING DEFUSION WITH PRESENT-MOMENT AWARENESS AND ACCEPTANCE

Defusion supports the other processes that we have reviewed to this point – present-moment awareness and acceptance. Present-moment awareness might be easy when the present moment is not that bad. But what when the present moment reality sucks to be in. The person with the gambling problem may notice that their marriage is falling apart because of their addiction. Contacting these very real contingencies is made even worse when language evaluating the contingencies starts to show up, such as "my life will be ruined if she leaves me," or even, "their lives would be better if I wasn't around anymore." These are rules that specify contingencies that are likely highly fused and, if taken literally, will lead to dire outcomes. The least of which is returning to the casino again to escape the thoughts when the present moment is too much to handle.

But what if we can defuse these thoughts using some of the strategies that we have discussed to this point? The man still has a gambling problem. His wife may still leave him, whether or not he sorts out the problem. She might try to take the kids from him. All of this is true and neither he nor the behavior analyst has any control over this contingency. It simply is. But if we can weaken the thoughts surrounding this event at the moment when he most often chooses to go to the casino, we create a space for him to choose another way forward. "I am having the thought that my wife is going to leave me, and __________." The "and" box might include "I can still show up to my kid's soccer game," or "I can still be there for dinner tonight with her." Again, she still might leave him. His kids may still resent him for the pain he caused. But here, now, in this moment, he can choose to live in accordance with his values and to be the person he wants to be.

Doing this requires acceptance that the contingencies are out of his control – and for the behavior analyst, the uncomfortable reality is that most of the contingencies that affect our clients are out of our control. Sure, it would be great if we could get the wife to sign a contingency contract that says she'll stay married to him if he does not gamble. But we have no way to control if she keeps her promise, nor should we want to. What we can do is encourage acceptance and willingness to show up to the present-moment disaster that gambling has caused with clarity and focus. To defuse from the literality of one's evaluations of the event and to choose a better way forward.

Many behavior analysts work with people with disabilities, but this same way of thinking about the challenges our clients face still fits. In the present moment, our clients *have* a disability that impacts their life (that is the definition of a disability). That disability does not go away when they successfully contact the present moment. Real contingencies that exist in a world made by people without disabilities for people without disabilities do create contingencies that are wildly disadvantageous to our clients. And as much as we might want to change these realities in our society (and should advocate for such), our role with the clients is to help them move towards that which they value anyways. "I am having the thought that because I am autistic nobody wants to talk to me, and ______________."

The "and" box might include "I can approach him because I want to see where this leads," or "I can apply for that job and see if they call me back." People might not respond well every time. Social differences are part of the world of people with autism spectrum disorder (ASD). But that doesn't mean we cannot encourage our clients to try – and to try again, and again. And defusion will help to promote the acceptance and present-moment awareness that is needed to do so.

8

Values

Values are *the* central concept of acceptance and commitment therapy (ACT) that tie together the other core processes by giving them a purpose. Why do we want to be in the present moment? To move closer to what we value. Why should we accept the easy things and the hard things that show up in our lives? Because doing so allows us to do what is important to us in life. Why should we engage in defusion exercises when thoughts become stuck? Because when we do, it is easier to engage in what matters most to us.

If psychological flexibility processes are all centered on creating a topographically broad and adaptive operant class of maximizing valued reinforcement (as we argued in an earlier chapter) then the whole point of engaging in any behaviors that we train in ACT is to maximize our ability to act consistent with our chosen values. To make greater contact with the things in life that matter.

We have discussed values throughout this book because discussion of any topic grounded in models of psychological flexibility must begin and end with values. What readers may not know is that this core process of values is actually deeply embedded within our science itself. It is a concept that is truly all-encompassing.

Values are the reason why we engage in science in the first place, and they are at the heart of the form of pragmatism that is applied within radical and contextual forms of behaviorism. The big idea is that the purpose of science is to solve important problems. A good scientific theory differs from a poor scientific theory primarily because the former can solve problems more effectively and efficiently than the latter. To these earlier philosophers, science was simply a behavior that some members of society engaged in to solve problems more effectively. By understanding the aerodynamics of lift and drag, we are able to achieve flight, and today fly from country to country and continent to continent. Technological advances in computer sciences have brought about today's smartphones and the internet, allowing us to access anyone anywhere in the entire world.

Pragmatism is the scientific philosophy that puts "successful working" first. But notice that we did not say that psychological flexibility is about maximizing *any* reinforcer – a good criminal can do that – rather it's about maximizing *valued* reinforcers and thus in a special sense psychological flexibility depends on values.

That is certainly true of the people served by science. The global community as a whole values the ability to interact with friends and family. We value easy access to information. We value the ability to communicate over long distances personally and professionally, and to take advantage of the health and safety that are afforded by scientific advances. We value justice and kindness. These are generally shared prosocial values of members of human

DOI: 10.4324/9781003250371-10

society for evolutionarily sensible reasons – and these shared values are examples of what maintains scientific progress.

It thus should come as no surprise that behavior analysis itself is grounded in scientific pragmatism. We engage in science to help us learn how to change behavior using principles that are precise and broad in scope, and that allows us as a human society to achieve valued outcomes. For Skinner, this meant knowing how to rearrange our world to select socially important behaviors to society, exemplified in his fictional work *Walden Two* (1948). For the practicing behavior analyst, this means rearranging our client's environment, and the way they interact with it, to help them to achieve their personal values, dreams, and ambitions. And in so doing, moving closer to our own value of influencing meaningful change in the lives of people that we serve.

The relationship between behavior analysis and values because more explicit as an applied wing evolved. Here is how Baer et al. (1968) put it in their foundational article on applied behavior analysis, in discussing what the word "applied" even meant:

> The label "applied" is not determined by the research procedures used but by the interest which society shows in the problems being studied. In behavioral application, the behavior, stimuli, and/or organism under study are chosen because of their importance to man and society, rather than their importance to theory.
>
> *(p. 92)*

The important segment here is "importance to man and society". It means that what we value defines what our field is attempting to achieve in society and in our work with clients.

The importance of values is further captured in behavior analysts by its emphasis on producing socially valid behavior change. We say that behavior change is socially valid when the change leads to a marked improvement in the lives of clients, caregivers, and stakeholders. "Improvement" is a relative idea that requires clarity about what matters to the consumers, that is, we cannot say something "improved" unless we have a targeted direction or goal that we are moving towards. We want a child to headbang less (valuing safety). We want another child to interact more socially with others (valuing relationships). We emphasize this point in *Research Methods for the Practicing Behavior Analyst* (Belisle et al., 2021) when discussing targets for behavior change, where we want to increase behavior towards chosen values and reduce behavior away from chosen values.

But *whose* values are we most concerned with as the field exists today?

Although perhaps not intentional by Baer, Wolf, and Risley, their quote above places emphasis on the importance to "man" (a collective term at the time for people) and "society," rather than the importance of behavior change to the individual whose behavior is actually being changed. In a follow-up paper speaking specifically to social validity, Wolf (1978) outlined the following criteria:

(1) Are the specific behavioral goals really what society wants?
(2) Do the participants, caregivers, and other consumers consider the treatment procedures acceptable?
(3) Are consumers satisfied with the results?

(p. 207)

Here again, the values of the society are emphasized – with "acceptability" and "satisfaction" at the level of the clients and consumers as secondary considerations. Putting the needs of society ahead of the needs of the individual cannot be the case in behavior analytic practice as it exists today. Rather, ACT-based approaches challenge us to put the values of clients and consumers at the forefront of not only our targeted outcomes but within our procedures used to achieve said outcomes.

This point is so important that it bears mentioning again. Putting the values of clients and consumers first in the field of behavior analysis is not optional. Behavior analysis as a field is responsible for helping people to achieve their values through intentional behavior change. We are not the only ones... but need to affirm that clearly. The Task Force on the strategies and tactics of contextual behavioral science put it this way: "research needs to be explicit about its prosocial purpose and to seek scientific knowledge that fosters social justice." (Hayes et al., 2021, p. 180). Adopting this stance is not only ACT-consistent, but it is pragmatic in the deepest sense of using science to help people move towards valued reinforcers.

When we have been at our best as a field, we have influenced change in ways that matter most to our clients and their families. The experimental functional analysis is one example that we have already discussed. This was an immensely important discovery because it allowed clients to achieve greater independence in living *and* it created alternative strategies to the overuse of punishment – something that in historical terms human society is gradually moving away from in all facets of life.

When we have been at our worst, our targets for behavior change had little if anything to do with the values of those we serve – or worse, were in direct contradiction with those values. Most behavior analysts will be familiar with some of the controversies surrounding the use of ABA technologies within the autistic community. Some of this comes from the use of punishers, such as electric shock, which has gained attention all the way to the United Nations Human Rights office (www.ohchr.org/). Living in a world free of corporal punishment is clearly something valued by many members of this community.

Perhaps less obvious are interventions that target behavior change targets such as eye contact or social normalization that clients themselves may not have identified as highly valued. "Normalization" at any level likely misses the point once we start building interventions around personal values. Unfortunately, services are often provided based on the *Diagnostic and Statistical Manual of Mental Disorders, Fifth Edition* (DSM-V) diagnoses that are predicated on "deviation from normal" as the target of behavior change. We can do better as a field, and as practitioners, when we lead with the personal values of our clients and consumers.

In intervention, this will largely take the form of helping clients to identify what they truly value in their lives (not just what society tells them to value) and to identify targets for behavior change and environmental factors to influence behavior in the desired direction. This chapter will visit this emerging science of values and valuing from a behavior analytic perspective.

BASIC BEHAVIOR CHANGE PROCESSES: AUGMENTAL REINFORCING FUNCTIONS

As noted by Skinner (1971, p. 103) offered a description of values as "the discrimination between a thing and its reinforcing effect, suggesting that "a science of values" is one that examines the history of an individual and their current context to determine what behaviors are likely to occasion reinforcement." This description acknowledges that the effectiveness of a reinforcer does not simply depend on its physical properties, but that other factors may influence how reinforcing something is to a person – and that what is rewarding for one person may not be rewarding to another person.

In order for you to get a better understanding of what it means to work with values within behavior analysis informed by an ACT/relational frame theory (RFT) perspective, it's important that you have access to your own. Connecting with our deepest values serves as a profound motivative operation In the following exercise, you are asked to pick a guide or hero, someone we look up to in a given area. Doing so will help you to tap into a deeper "whole person" sense of what you want to reflect in your actions: in doing so you are implicitly revealing your values. Here's how you do it:

- Focus on a domain where you want to act with more of a values-based set of reinforcers.
- If you were to pick a guide or hero for you in this area – someone who could support and empower you in some important way – who would it be?
- Allow your thinking to range freely and pick anyone who lifts you up and empowers you as a guide and example in this area.
- Picture that person and their face in front of you. Take a little time to do it.
- What does this face represent to you? What strengths or qualities? Allow memories or images to build out this appreciation. Allow yourself to be touched by it. Consider the possibility that these qualities you appreciate are ones you would like to manifest in some way with your life's moments.
- Now go behind the eyes of your guide face and look back at your face. Take your time to picture what he or she would see. What research or strength does your guide see in you? What if you knew what more you yearned for?
- Now come back behind your eyes now and look again at the face of the guide. Again, take your time. Consider this question and gently allow an answer to form: if this person were actually to give you guidance, what would it be? Whatever shows up, take time to hear it and appreciate it.
- Now metaphorically bring your guide "back inside you" since after all that is where this began, and this face came from your imagination. What positive guidance were you given? How does it land with you? Is there wisdom in this advice? Can you do what was recommended? Is this indeed something you yearn for?
- Finally, get out a blank piece of paper and write freely for two to three minutes about what you noticed or learned doing this exercise.

Within ACT, we are specifically interested in how verbal relationships may influence the reinforcing functions of stimulus events beyond their physical representations.

Human values are based on all of our experience, but they are owned when they are *verbally constructed*, meaning relational frames interact in complex ways that result in strengthening or weakening of the effectiveness of a reinforcer through transformations of stimulus function. Values are also *global* in that they do not describe terminal events or outcomes (e.g., I value winning this chess game), but represent broader abstract categories of reinforcement (e.g., to relate to others socially) that can be instantiated but not consumed fully. As noted by Luoma et al. (2017), values are often stated as qualities of on-going action, such as "to raise one's child kindly and attentively" (p. 200). Finally, it is also important that values are *freely chosen*, in the same sense that Skinner meant the term "free" meaning in the absence of aversive control. A free operant, as we say. When something is truly valued, it should exhibit reinforcing properties that are intrinsic to behavior – intrinsic qualities of being and doing. So much of the ACT process involves working with clients to really sense, own, and define what they value – here and now – beyond what society tells them they should value.

An RFT account of values that satisfies each of these criteria is provided by Plumb et al. (2009). According to these authors, values operate as motivative rules that emerge primarily through hierarchical relational frames. Recall that in hierarchical frames, multiple stimulus relations are contained within the same general category. For example, someone who values reading, writing, and producing research may also value engaging in scholarship. Another person who values dating their spouse and playing with their children may also value building meaningful relationships with their family. This model is shown in Figure 8.1 adapted from Paliliunas (2021).

Through transformations of stimulus function, "value" transfers from lower-level hierarchical stimulus events (e.g., playing with one's children) to the categorical value descriptor (e.g., building meaningful relationships with family), and vice versa. For example, if the same person is told that exercising is part of building meaningful relationships with family by prolonging a healthy-active life, it is possible that these reinforcing functions transfer from family to events associated with exercising, competing with the potentially high response cost of exercising. This is especially true at the beginning stages of a new fitness schedule, which often comes with experiencing pain and fatigue.

Some values are *more* important than other values. For example, protecting one's family from harm or hardship might be more valuable than building social relationships with peers. Therefore, given the choice between showing up to work on time in order to live in a safe neighborhood or showing up late to be with friends, when values are considered, we might expect a person to choose the former over the latter.

Although we can live better when we follow our values, we often neglect them. Values choices are not some internal thing that sits inside of us and constantly influences our behavior. We make many decisions each and every day without ever considering our values. Valuing is a behavior and it is only when we engage with what matters, that valuing can have the desired influence over other of our actions. For this reason, ACT-based interventions constantly redirect clients to connect their values. We all do this naturally – we just don't specifically not the process. We put pictures of our loved ones on our own desk; we wear rings as symbols of values-based commitments; we write down meaningful quotes and hang them on the wall. With a little thought, it is easy for behavior analysts to create strategies that make connections with values choices more available in the environment where committed action can occur.

We tend to fail to live in accordance with our values when values are unclear, or when we "go through the motion" of noting values that do not truly represent what matters most to us. The motivative operations engaged by the values-based transformations of stimulus function cannot work if the work is not done to connect verbally with appetitive qualities of

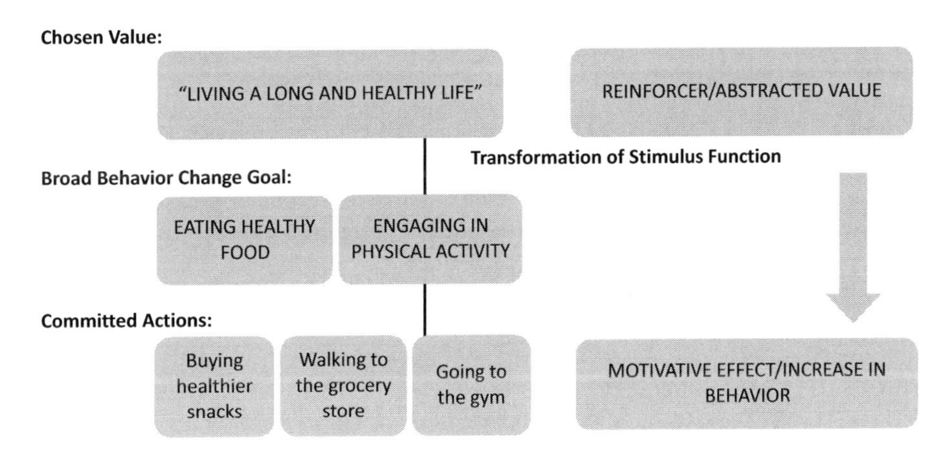

FIGURE 8.1 RFT Diagram

behavior. Moreover, values can and often do conflict with our other interests. For instance, when you wish to maintain a healthy diet, but also crave fatty fast food. For this reason, simply *identifying* values as a kind of intellectual exercise is not enough. We need to rely on the other ACT processes covered so far, present-moment awareness, acceptance, and defusion, to weaken the reinforcing value of these smaller-sooner negative reinforcers and allow for values to maximally influence desired behavior change.

Distinguishing between values and goals is also important. Values are motivative verbal stimuli that increase the reinforcing functions of the intrinsic qualities of actions. Goals, on the other hand, are rule statements that specify an external consequence that can be obtained, consumed, or finished. Ideally, goals link to one's values. For example, if someone values serving others by being a stronger and more flexible behavior analyst, a goal may be to read this book. Stated another way, "if I read this book carefully from start to finish, I will move towards being a stronger and more flexible behavior analyst than I am currently." In this way, goals can operate as an antecedent verbal stimulus that evokes action – and we encourage goal setting throughout ACT-based interventions. A goal becomes a committed action when the goal directly aligns with one's chosen values, which we discuss in much more detail in the chapter on committed action. But once the goal is reached – for example, this book is read – there are still other things to do to become a stronger and more flexible behavior analyst. Values are present from the moment they are affirmed but they are never fully consumed or finished. We do realize however that a value for a five-year-old child may be much different than a 50-year-old adult. Here the child may have a much greater blur between the concepts of values and goals. For they may value extra candy, video games, or free time. Values and goals will start to separate for such children, as there becomes an increased awareness of the social contingencies and participation within a verbally mediated world.

INTERACTION OF RELATIONAL FRAMES

The above provides an initial breakdown of how values may operate, but as noted by Biglan and Barnes-Holmes (2015), additional relational frames are highly related to this core process. Temporal relations likely play an important role when clarifying one's values. For example, by comparing my life here and now to how I would like to live my life in the future (i.e., what I want my life to be about), values can be made clear. This temporal-deictic framing can be seen in the "attending your own funeral" metaphor, where the therapist asks the client, "if you were able to attend your own funeral, what would you like for people to say about you?" Oftentimes this metaphor elucidates a stark contrast to how the person is living their life here and now, and how they would like to be remembered by others, where the latter is more representative of their values. Then, committed actions can revolve around behaving in a values-consistent way here and now to achieve the way they want people to think of them today and in the future.

Causal frames also play an important role in connecting values to committed action. For example, "in order to be a good spouse I must…" represents a conditional statement of "in order to achieve Y" (valued outcome), "I must do X" (committed action). Behavior analysts will be already familiar with the use of causal/conditional relational frames, albeit in a much simpler form. One common way to implement this principle with clients involves making statements like "first this, then this." For example, "first two math questions, then take a break."

Relational frames are also a crucial part of clinical conversations that involve values. This can be seen in the context of a parent of a young adult woman with an intellectual disability, and their value of fostering their daughter's independence and autonomy. In this case, the parent has to decide whether to advocate for their child to remain living with them in their home or for her to live in a supported living apartment with personnel.

Here again, we see the juxtaposition of a choice that may appear easier (the daughter staying in the home) and is even consistent with something both the parent and the daughter value (time together). By digging deeper into relations around their values, however, independence and autonomy may show to be valued higher by both the parent and their daughter. When discussing values, hierarchical relations are central because this choice is only one of many that the parent and their daughter will experience together, as she explores adulthood and begins to clarify her own values. This decision represents one in an entire way of being – being independent – that we can help foster through an ACT-based approach. Deictic relations also remind us that the values we hold here and now can be different from the values we had at another time in another context, and that our values may be different from those of others. In this case, it appears to be important to this family that support staff also value the daughter's autonomy, so they too take part in creating a context that supports her independence.

When we treat values as separate categories, we often fail to do justice to our heart's deepest needs and wishes. Think of a person who has just experienced a first heart attack, but who refuses to make the necessary changes to their lifestyle, because they feel their high work, high stress, low self-care way of being is necessary to support their family and their loved ones. This way of living is clearly not working to their benefit, and they would be well-advised to merge these values systems to promote healthy and active living.

The more a person's values are interrelated, the more resistant these values are to external disruption. To continue with the example above, if we can help the client to make connections between their health, their family, and their job, we might be able to construct a strong enough relational network that can compete with the stressful day at work or the argument with their spouse that would otherwise diminish their healthy choices.

We all know a person who has been able to achieve lasting behavior change – and this change is supported by multiple values. For this reason, we believe this is an area ripe for behavioral research that could allow for an even deeper understanding of how values operate.

INDEPENDENT AND DEPENDENT VARIABLES FOR INTERVENTION

So much of our applied science in behavior analysis has explored ways to measure the value of reinforcers. A lot of this work can translate measuring values as dependent variables within behavioral intervention. Preference assessments provide an apt comparison. In a standard preference assessment, a child is presented with concurrently available choices and selects among them. The objects that are most frequently selected and engaged with are assumed to operate with greater reinforcing value – or at the very least – are preferred.

Values often represent competing choices. Should I go to the gym or take the afternoon to relax? In other words, do I value my health or my leisure more in this moment? It is likely that what we value may ebb and flow from one moment to another, which is why it's important to frequently monitor one's values throughout behavioral intervention.

When we have gathered sufficient data across multiple comparisons, we may start to see patterns emerge. For example, what if we added "family" and "time spent at the casino" as two choices in our arrangement? And let's say we ran this like a preference assessment where the value that is selected first is removed from the array, then the second value is removed, then the third, generating a values hierarchy in the moment. In this case, depending on the values system of the client, we might see "family" as almost always arriving as the highest-rated item, and "time spent at the casino" as the lowest-rated item. Leisure and fitness bounce back and forth between the three to four slots.

Consider a person who is living in line with their values and is presented with those same four options: family, leisure, fitness, and gambling (which isn't really a value but is something that some might identify as highly valued). And let's assume that they rank these items in this order. If we were to then track how much time they spend engaging in each of these areas, the time distribution would likely resemble our values ranking: family > leisure > fitness > gambling. Conversely, we can apply the same strategy to a person with a gambling disorder. The person may rank the values in the same way, but gambling is what they find themselves spending the most time doing and thinking about. In this case, there is non-coherence between what they value and what they do. That degree of deviation between values and time spent may highlight the severity of emphasis needing to be placed on value-adherence treatment.

Valued Living as a Dependent Variable

When we talk about valued living, we can start by attempting to operationalize what precisely it means to live a life consistent with one's values. Blackledge and Barnes-Holmes (2009) give the following definition of valued living:

> "ways of responding that give increased access to relatively stable, long-term sources of positive non-verbal and verbal reinforcement."
>
> *(p. 42)*

Viewed in this way, there are a number of options available to behavior analysts to measure valued living as a dependent variable.

Perhaps the closest standardized assessment to this process is provided in the *Valued Living Questionnaire* (VLQ). The VLQ is a relatively straightforward assessment. The first step requires clients to rate the importance of each of ten valued domains using a Likert style scale. The domains include family relations, marriage and intimate relationships, parenting, friendship and social relationships, employment, education and training, recreation, spirituality, citizenship and community life, and physical well-being. Although the Likert scale is a subjective measure and "value" may differ across individuals, the point is to obtain a measure of relative importance of each item at the level of the individual. The second step requires clients to rate how consistently they are living within each of the valued domains. Then, importance and value are multiplied to arrive at a composite score representing the importance and consistency of valued living. Research on the psychometric properties of the assessment supports the internal consistency and test-retest reliability of the measure (Wilson et al., 2010) as well as comparisons across populations (Vanbuskirk et al., 2012).

A similar questionnaire that is specifically designed to measure the consistency between values importance and values consistency is the *Valuing Questionnaire* (VQ). The questionnaire was developed to be brief enough and sensitive enough to capture changes in valued living from week to week when used frequently as a self-report measure. The Valuing Questionnaire does not delineate values into specific domains that may be somewhat arbitrary and subjective. Instead, the questionnaire treats values broadly by asking questions such as, "I spent a lot of time thinking about the past or future, rather than being engaged in activities that mattered to me." Some items are framed positively (progress) and others negatively (obstruction). This measure has since been adapted to multiple languages and tested across several populations that are served using ACT-based approaches. A major strength of this assessment is the ability to identify potential barriers to valued living. You can also calculate importance-consistency discrepancy to detect areas of inconsistent valued living using the VLQ by subtracting consistency from importance (Miller et al., 2016).

Another way to measure values is the Values Bull's Eye developed by Lundgren et al. (2012). To complete the Bull's Eye, the client is given a target with seven concentric circles that is divided into four life domains. The client then denotes four valued living domains in each quadrant, then indicates how successful they have been in terms of living that value recently. Their response is quantified such that responses closest to the bull's eye are scored a "7" and responses closest to the outer circle are scored a "1." High values attainment occurs when the four domains are closest to the bull's eye, suggesting that the client is "on target" with their values. The speed at which this can be completed could provide an avenue for embedding values-based measurement within single-subject experimental designs or tracking values attainments across time with clients.

Values card-sorts can be done using pictures or objects as a kind of preference assessment. Implicit measures such as the Implicit Relational Assessment Procedure (IRAP) can avoid excessive audience influence over values statements.

In our experience, each of these tools can be used within an ecological momentary assessment (EMA) for continuous measurement of values throughout baseline and intervention. In this way, if specific items appear to be endorsed as an area in need of intervention, these questions could be presented randomly or event-based through any of the EMA strategies that we have reviewed to this point.

Tracking values-consistent behavior is not difficult to do which is why it's so important to assess and evaluate a client's values at the onset of any intervention. *If* we are successful in working with our clients, *then* the ultimate measure of values-behavior coherence will be if our target behaviors increase in frequency (and value-incoherent behaviors decrease). That is, we live a more valued life when we behave more in terms of what we value than what we do not value. For this reason, all of the existing behavioral measures that we have grown accustomed to (e.g., rate, duration, latency) are the purest form of measuring values achievement when our target behaviors reflect our client's values.

Establishing these targets of behavior change could be accomplished by first asking the client to identify what they value, and second, to identify actions that move them towards these values (as well as actions that move them away). In tracking behavior, these "towards moves" may operate as accelerative targets (things we want to increase), and "away moves" may operate as decelerative targets (things we want to decrease). In this way, the personal values of our clients are part of the treatment planning process.

Values Clarification and Presentation as an Independent Variable

It is crucial that clients are clear about what they value throughout the intervention process. Therefore, values clarification can operate as a predictor or independent variable that behavior analysts may wish to target. Behavior analysts must be able to answer two questions when it comes to values clarification. First, is a lack of clear personal values leading to greater psychological flexibility (predictor)? Second, if values are not clear, focused, and personal, can we intervene to help clients clarify their values in the service of valued living? If a client does not know what they personally value, there isn't a compass to guide any of the ACT-based strategies that we have discussed so far. And without values clarification, we risk setting arbitrary behavior change goals that may or may not actually lead to the client living a better life.

When working to clarify values, one important dimension of values to focus on is vitality. Vitality can be defined as feeling strong physical or intellectual vigor. As described by Blackledge and Barnes-Holmes (2009), we can assume this to mean that a sense of vitality occurs when a way of living produces strong, positive emotions. If we accept that "valued living" means a person is contacting reinforcers in their life that they value the most, then it follows that values are accompanied by a sense of vitality. They are functionally linked behavioral processes.

For this reason, gauging a client's sense of vitality around valued outcomes can help to guide values clarification exercises. For example, imagine working with a young adult with autism who expresses valuing friendship. Without digging any deeper, a logical next step would be to teach social skills that maximize access to friendship. But what happens if we dig a little deeper focusing on vitality? Imagine you ask the client to imagine what friendship looks like to them, what would they say? Because of social conditioning and training, you might expect them to repeat back the scripted steps of being a good friend and describe very contrived neurotypical activities that they might engage in, such as going to a sports event or entertaining guests in their home.

Next, you ask, "when you think about doing this, how does this make you feel inside?" The client responds honestly, "it makes me feel anxious and bored." That is not vitality. You might then ask, "well, what would hanging out with a friend look like to you that would bring *you* an intense feeling of fun and enjoyment?" Their response to this question is critical within a values clarification exercise because it will help guide the behavior target in a way that promotes valued living and, consequently, feelings of vitality for them. Their response may not be typical. The result may be a smaller array of people who share those interests. But, if they are successful with the help of a behavior analyst in contacting friends with shared values and interests, what they achieve is friendship in a way that matters to them, without needing to act like someone else whose preferences and hobbies are fundamentally different from their own. They can be themselves *and* foster meaningful friendships.

When values are clear, we should also observe changes in valued living as a dependent variable along with changes in the target behavior. In the example above, we would expect an increase in social interaction of the young adult, not because of any contrived source of reinforcement, but rather because what they are engaging in is valuable to them – above and beyond anything we could contrive in a traditional behavior plan.

We do not always consider our values when making decisions, and this is especially true when behavior is inflexible and leads us in directions that are opposite of what we value. When examining "values" as an independent variable, we have to consider the context of verbal behavior about values. How often are we discussing values with our clients? Are we embedding stimuli in the environment that are designed to reorient our clients towards their personal values?

Discussions around values or values-based activities can occur at regular intervals – adjusted to the most appropriate frequency for each client. We do not want to spend all day talking about our values because doing so leaves little time for actually pursuing them. Is revisiting values at a specific time each month sufficient within a broader behavior plan? Do we need to intentionally engage in values-based activities once per week? For some clients, it might be necessary to revisit values once per day or even multiple times per day. The frequency of values-based discussions or exercises will also influence how you go about developing a protocol centered around values. For example, revisiting values once per month can probably be accomplished with a relatively consistent structure, such as the ACT Matrix. However, doing this every single day could become tedious and yield diminishing returns.

Instead, attending to one's values daily could incorporate daily activities. These procedures could also be combined, such as completing values-based activities once per week and revisiting values more directly using the matrix once per month. The critical feature is that behavior analysts are explicit about what they are doing to support values so that their approach is technological and easily replicated.

We can also put reminders of personal values directly into a person's environment. For example, one strategy to improve healthy eating could be to strategically place values statements related to healthy eating throughout the house – such as on the inside of cupboards or fridges. The basic idea is that when the behavior of going to grab that midnight snack is most probable, consideration of values is brought into that moment. This strategy will not work every single time. Setting events like a stressful day at work or food deprivation (or, more commonly, nutrient deprivation) will be more present some days than others. Nonetheless, we might expect that this simple intervention reduces the likelihood of a person grabbing a late-night snack.

Ghezzi et al. (2020) demonstrated this basic effect in a simulated work task where participants were required to compete with other participants in a pay-for-performance work arrangement. Results showed that the motivative statements were effective in temporarily improving cooperation under the same competitive contingencies. Moreover, the more people interact with these values, there may be an even greater potential for behavior change through transformation of stimulus function.

Eating healthy and arbitrary work tasks are good illustrative examples. We have used this strategy frequently with clients that we work with. It starts by considering the moments when challenging behavior is most likely to occur. This can be obtained through direct observation and ABC analyses. For example, when a middle school child with a disability engages in high rates of aggression prior to a specific class in order to escape the class. In this case, we might embed a brief review of values immediately before the class and set a reasonable goal to build on (i.e., committed action). This could take the form of reminding the client of their value, such as by saying, "Earlier today you told me that you really value being engaged at school and with people in your class. You also said it makes you feel upset when you try to hurt others and you feel proud whenever you can make it through a class. *Today*, how long are you willing to be in the class before having time to work independently?" Notice the emphasis on the client and their ability to self-regulate and work towards their values. First, the values are theirs – chosen by them – and clarified along with the behavior analyst earlier in the day

In that moment, consideration of values is brought to the present moment when problem behavior (maintained through negative reinforcement) is most likely. Second, the client is given the freedom to choose their own committed action based on where they are that day and given an alternative choice (work independently). The client might choose five minutes. They may choose 15 minutes. What is important is that they were able to contact their value of being engaged with the class and peers and could choose their threshold. This also provides data for the behavior analyst to review and consider that is much safer than aggression in order to search for patterns that predict the client choosing shorter or longer durations. This is a radically different way to think of addressing escape-maintained behavior compared to more traditional escape extinction strategies.

Like with values clarification, embedding values discussions into the environment will vary considerably from person to person and must match the individual, their values, and their challenges. However, these strategies provide a method for behavior analysts to utilize values-based strategies technologically within behavior plans across a variety of populations and challenges.

ANTECEDENT AND CONSEQUENCE STRATEGIES TO PROMOTE VALUES AUGMENTATION

Within the ABC model, values not only describe reinforcement, but they also augment reinforcement. Small momentary reinforcers like the feeling of sweat and pain during a workout are given meaning when one considers their larger abstract value of health and wellness, transforming what might operate as a punisher into a reinforcer. For the new parent, tending to a fussy child is given meaning when considering who that child may grow to become – a healthy, happy, and well-adjusted adult. Behavior analysts are especially well equipped to identify moment-to-moment reinforcers and to ensure that indicators of progress are present to bridge the gap between right now and eventual valued outcomes.

A values-based token economy system may therefore not rely solely on contrived backup reinforcers but rather may involve a symbol or representation of a valued outcome and the movement of tokens following committed actions that move towards this outcome.

Alcoholics Anonymous (AA) is a program for those recovering from alcoholism and has had mixed success at sustaining absence from drinking. A potentially salient feature of these programs is the use of colored chips that represent the number of days sober. A first chip, the 24-hour chip, represents the initial decision to live a sober life. Chips are accumulated as days pass. These chips are not exchanged for anything. They exist simply as a signal representing movement towards a valued outcome.

Could we adjust this framework when working with clients to signal moment-to-moment movement towards valued outcomes? This could take the form of a visual schedule where the client marks when milestones are achieved, like days not aggressing towards caregivers or staff. For people in a committed relationship that is struggling, the number of days engaging in productive and supportive conversation instead of blowing up and letting conversations derail. In some ways, these exchanges can serve as a social medium to indicate and celebrate progress. We are social creatures, and we crave social forms of reinforcement that can come with indicators of successful achievement. Unfortunately, "successful achievement" is too often defined by the values of others, where ACT challenges us to develop these strategies that we know can work but in the locus of chosen personal values.

The defusion exercises provide a ready-made antecedent intervention strategy that can be embedded at the moments where experiential avoidance or challenging behavior is the most likely and when one suspects that cognitive fusion plays a central role. To create distance between one's thoughts and feelings prior to the moment of interaction with the stressful event may be enough to encourage success. Shaping should also play a central role too. Do not attempt to utilize defusion in a low-controlled and highly evocative context right away. Start in a controlled environment with a challenge that the client views as workable to build momentum. As they contact success, consider introducing more difficult situations and allowing less environmental control.

It is also important to consider the content being targeted through defusion. Metaphors are important because they work with concepts without needing to move too quickly into dealing with potentially traumatic private experiences. When first learning to defuse, and when first learning to implement defusion-based programming, it is important to stay at this level of metaphor or more benign thoughts and feelings. ACT has been used successfully in working with trauma, such as in the treatment of post-traumatic stress disorder (PTSD) experienced by military veterans, and we believe behavior analysts can play an important part in an interdisciplinary team in that regard, but it is important to always stay within one's scope of competence and to work interdisciplinarity as the populations and challenges we are being tasked with change as they inevitably will.

COMBINING VALUES WITH PRESENT-MOMENT AWARENESS, ACCEPTANCE, AND DEFUSION

Other flexibility processes – present-moment awareness, acceptance, defusion – need to be put in the service of our client's chosen values. Ultimately, each of these processes is a means to one singular end – living a valued life. Consider how values could increase the likelihood that clients engage in each of the three processes.

Present-moment awareness is an active process that requires response effort and can compete with other activities for time – and most of those activities serve immediate negative reinforcing functions, like answering that pressing email or preparing for an important meeting. Values therefore serve to increase both the automatic reinforcing functions of engaging in the present moment as well as the reinforcers that become available through present-moment awareness. As we discussed, one common way to improve present-moment awareness is through daily meditation and sticking to a routine (e.g., meditating every morning before breakfast). However, this might also be challenging to stick to, especially when setting events like stress and sleep deprivation increase motivation to stay in bed instead of engaging in meditation. It can be very easy for the train to fall off the tracks. One simple intervention could be to put a banner up in your bedroom that contains stimuli related to the value underlying meditation. Doing so could serve to augment the reinforcing functions around the act of meditating in the morning and help to foster the meditative practice.

Another example could occur when a client is hesitant to engage in present-moment awareness exercises as an alternative to engaging in challenging behavior. Consider that at the point of developing a behavior plan, it is likely that the challenging behavior has a dense history of reinforcement, whereas engaging in present-moment awareness is less established in their repertoire. In this case, revisiting values as the reason to engage in the present-moment exercise could be effective by not only augmenting the physical sensations that accompany present-moment awareness, but also the reinforcing value of the improved outcomes that come with not engaging in the challenging behavior. In this case, the two strategies are deeply interconnected.

The same strategy necessarily applies to acceptance. Why should clients accept potentially unpleasant experiences? Values *are* the reason for acceptance. Acceptance occurs when doing something that might be difficult is necessary to experience a more valued life. In each of our practices, it is very rare that acceptance-based exercises occur without an explicit discussion of values surrounding acceptance. For the person with a social phobia being asked to interact with people, they are choosing to do so *because* of their value of being part of a social community. Or because they see the relationship between engaging with others socially and other outcomes that they value, like better relations at work.

The more we are able to bring an intentional discussion about values into opportunities to practice acceptance, the more likely acceptance processes are to effectively change behavior. Moreover, *if* the outcome of acceptance is truly something that the person values, the experiences that they previously avoided may come to obtain reinforcing functions in their own right. In this way, acceptance is a temporary process when values are considered, because the transfer of reinforcing functions may mean that "accepting" is no longer a necessary part of the behavior-behavior sequence. The person comes to enjoy the event or similar events in their own right.

We all have had this experience on the first day of class as a child. The first day is always the most stressful. It may have been several months since we have seen our friends and we know the schoolwork is only going to get harder. The first day requires a great deal of acceptance, and in our practice with young clients, a lot of discussion is centered around values and prompts to remain in the present moment. But as the year goes on, from week to week, habituation occurs and positive reinforcers such as friends and relationships, and perhaps even the content of the schoolwork, show up. Eventually, the act of going to school becomes less hard, prompts to be in the present moment less necessary, and "acceptance" quickly becomes excitement for what can be experienced that next day.

The interaction between defusion and values offers considerable opportunities for behavioral researchers. *Both* of these processes are about rules and how we work with them. In the case of defusion, we seek to weaken the power of rules that maintain psychological inflexibility. In the case of values, we seek to strengthen the power of rules that maintain psychological flexibility.

The role of relational frames is most evident within these two processes. Not only that, but the things that we know can lead to fusion, such as being surrounded by fused rules about how the world works and being presented with those rules in moments when challenges are likely to arise, are also the strategies we use to support consideration of personal values. By embedding them throughout the environment and bringing values-based stimuli into the moments when challenges are most likely to occur. Because these processes appear to be so deeply related through human language, we might anticipate that defusing problematic thoughts could open the door to considering one's values. Strengthening values-orienting behavior could reduce the frequency of thoughts that we would otherwise address through defusion.

Moreover, because values *are* verbal, it is easy to see how values held too tightly could be workable in some contexts and self-defeating in others. For example, someone might indicate that they value "work-life balance," which is not altogether problematic. However, if this value leads to the person continuously missing deadlines or failing to act as a coherent part of a team, the result won't be balanced but rather will be a failure to progress professionally, which could negatively impact both work and life. Both may be balanced but balanced with little value or feelings of vitality.

Therefore, when values-based rules start to be applied inflexibly, defusion exercises may be effective to reduce the control that the rule may serve. In this example, the exercise involves the analyst asking, "yes, and…": "I value work-life balance…" "… and I value feeling productive in my work…" "… and I value the chance to travel and experience life with my family…" … and so on. In so doing, the analyst is helping the client to clarify their value further and introducing greater contextual sensitivity to the rule. The result may well be greater work-life balance, but in a way that is functional and flexible.

It should come as no surprise that values are so deeply related to the processes we have visited so far. Values underlie *everything* in the ACT model. They are the reason a model exists in the first place. Not only that, but values are the centering principle of any pragmatic science and are necessary for our field to progress forward. When we lead with values in the moment, and as an overarching guiding principle for our field, we are most likely to affect the changes that we value. And more importantly, that our clients value.

9

Committed Action

Clarifying what matters most to you can inevitably lead to feelings of panic and defeat. Why am I not living the life I want? How can I possibly achieve the quality of life that I know I deserve? In the literature, we see feelings of value achievement initially go down, as clients notice that their lives as they are living them are not consistent with their deepest held values. Only when we choose the path of working towards the things in life that we value instead of working to avoid the things in life that we fear, do feelings of value achievement go up again. Taking the steps to broaden and build habits of values-based action is called committed action, and it is the process that links instances of values work to actual changes in living that persist across time and situations. When committed action skills strengthen, we see overall improvements in valued living and quality of life.

Let's break down "committed action." *Action* simply refers to behavior: the measurable and observable interaction of an organism with its environment. Our lives are defined by nearly infinite actions occurring at multiple levels and multiple scales, from setting an alarm to making breakfast to all of the things that we do at work and at home. Not all actions are in the service of chosen values, and in the case of clients seeking acceptance and commitment therapy (ACT)-based treatment, many actions may actually be a disservice to chosen values. Values give directionality to actions. Actions that are motivated and reinforced by chosen qualities of being and doing are "values-based," and when steps are taken to increase the frequency of values-based action we call the resulting actions *committed actions*. These actions have the special quality of giving our lives meaning and producing feelings of vitality.

The *New Oxford American Dictionary* defines "committed" as: "feeling dedication and loyalty to a cause, activity, or job; wholeheartedly dedicated." When someone is committed, they are working towards a valued end. This is important because values are larger-later-abstract reinforcers that are often competing with smaller-sooner-negative reinforcers that maintain psychological inflexibility. Commitment requires foregoing short-term gratification while knowing that remaining committed will produce longer-term outcomes that are much more meaningful. "Wholeheartedly" matches the value portion of ACT models as well.

Whereas *values* are motivative operations that give us a reason to engage in ACT processes, patterns of committed action give us a way to increase their life centrality. This process is directly linked to principles of behavior change that behavior analysts are already deeply familiar with, since habits of action that build over time are the focus of all constructive behavioral work. If we can identify the behaviors necessary for values to flourish, the next question necessarily becomes, "how can we arrange an environment that supports committed action?"

DOI: 10.4324/9781003250371-11

Skinner talked a great deal about self-control from "Science and Human Behavior" forward. For Skinner, self-control did not mean an internal act of the will but rather intentionally making changes to the environment that supports desired behavior changes. Take for example the person who is trying to eat healthier and has noticed that snacking on potato chips at night is a barrier to achieving their value of health. A self-control strategy might be to avoid buying unhealthy snacks at the grocery store and to prepare healthier alternatives that are available at night.

Behaviorally speaking, the stress of the day and a history of snacking produce establishing operations and habits of action that lead to consuming snacks at night before bed. That motivation and habit is less strong during grocery shopping, especially if the person avoids shopping while hungry or tired. Preparing healthy snacks beforehand (e.g., slicing up a few apples and storing a handful of slices in plastic bags placed in the refrigerator) might set up an environment in which doing the right thing is easier than alternatives. Deliberately not buying unhealthy snacks at the grocery store is a form of rule-governed behavior that several hours later means that accessing unhealthy food might require a late-night drive to the corner store. If a few fresh apple slices are in hands reach in the refrigerator, doing the wrong thing will take much more effort than choosing an immediately available healthy food. Eventually, eating a healthy snack before bed (or not snacking at all) is more likely to strengthen.

If living a healthy life is a value, this is a good example of a committed action. Foregoing unhealthy snacks at the grocery store and preparing healthy snacks for the week represent committed actions that support the chosen value of living a healthier life.

We can also measure both the process of change (values-based habits of actions) and the outcome (unhealthy food consumption) through analyses of grocery purchases, monitoring of food preparation, and monitoring of unhealthy snacking throughout the day. If an ACT-based intervention targeting those processes was effective at achieving a values outcome, then we would be able to say that intervention was successful.

There are elements of committed action that go beyond Skinner's analysis of self-control. Luoma et al. (2010) note that "commitment involves both persistence and change – whichever is called for to live in alignment with one's values in specific contexts. Commitment also includes engaging in a range of behaviors… [that] often requires being flexible" (p. 239).

Committed action cannot become rigid and prescriptive, which is a real risk that behavior analysts need to be aware of, especially when ways we are used to thinking about behavior change strategies can itself become rigid and prescriptive. In ACT, avoiding this is critical because engaging in rigid ways that have been unyielding to suffering is precisely why the behavioral challenge has emerged in the first place.

We cannot just replace one rigid rule with another. When rigid responding is part of the problem, promoting flexibility in responding must be part of the solution.

Consider parents with a young child with autism who engages in frequent tantrums which have led this family to avoid going out in public. Shopping, dining, and social engagements are all largely non-starters for this family because of the risk of public outbursts. But this is no life to live. Avoiding public places was an adaptation that worked for a time, but as feelings of restriction and isolation increase it is no longer workable. Furthermore, as the child gets older, simply avoiding others will be a major barrier to their autonomy and personal growth. This interacting behavior system of the child and their parents is rigid and stuck. Their day-to-day life is invariable. Invariability was once the solution – but it cannot continue to be the solution.

We want to work with the parents to commit to small solutions and build on these commitments as they achieve success with new patterns of behavior. Moreover, part of the process will involve identifying actions that are attainable, flexible, and values-oriented.

One week might involve doing a home routine that is *different* from the scripted routine of cooking dinner while the child plays on their tablet. The next week might involve driving past a park or stopping in the parking lot and enjoying a preferred takeout meal together. Ultimately, we want to work up to going shopping or going to a restaurant.

This should not be something as rigid as a typical objective of, "mother and child will go to restaurant X every Friday evening." This is too narrow and can quickly become another rigid pattern. The activity needs to be variable (restaurant, park, zoo, store, family, and friends); the time needs to be variable (morning, afternoon, evening, with and without excessive planning); and the day needs to be variable. The value of experiencing life together as a family is achieved when there is enough flexibility in accomplishing that value that a broad repertoire of committed actions is available in most situations. At that point, we can say these choices are "free choices" in Skinner's sense of freedom – namely without needless aversive control.

We also know that it is not enough to achieve behavior change and to just hope that broad ad flexible behavioral patterns will emerge. The reality is that the same environmental events that maintained rigidity in the past can quickly become present again. In what has been termed the VRSCDL model, we need to promote variability *and* retention so there is a kind of dialectic balance of healthy variable and healthy maintenance of established patterns. The commitment is to a larger ongoing pattern of creative broad and flexible patterns of values-based behavior. As that happens, naturally occurring reinforcers become more available for this family. When they do go out, that event is *less* about engaging in the action while doing everything possible to avoid a meltdown, and *more* about enjoying and experiencing everything that is now available to enjoy and to enjoy together.

Committing to change is easy. Staying committed to change is hard and requires a willingness to experience the thoughts and feelings that show up when we engage in committed action. A willingness to experience the discomfort that comes when old patterns are disrupted. Thus, all of the other psychological flexibility processes are needed for committed action as a process to be maintained. This process involved committing to change and recommitting to change when things happen in life that knock us into old habits. There is dense scientific literature that tells us how to support behavior change – a lot of which comes from within our own science of behavior analysis. This chapter will explore the science of behavior change in the context of committed action with a focus on self-control, willingness, and psychological flexibility.

BASIC BEHAVIOR CHANGE PROCESSES: OPERANT VARIABILITY AND INDUCING CHANGE

Behavioral variability represents another higher-order dimension of behavior (i.e., behavior pattern; Neuringer, 2012) that is useful when unpacking behavior change processes underlying committed action. Research with animals such as pigeons (Page & Neuringer, 1985) and with humans (Neuringer, 1986) has established that variability in behavior can be described as an operant. As noted by Neuringer (2012), basic experimental studies have established that variability and invariability can come under control. For example, if variability (i.e., engaging in responses that differ from other responses) is reinforced in the presence of a green light, and rigid responding is reinforced in the presence of a red light, we might anticipate that presenting a green light will induce variability whereas the red light will induce relatively rigid ways of responding.

This is a contrived example, but each of us has observed this in our own behavior at one time or another. Consider that college class where you felt free to be creative and to make mistakes. In short – to be variable. Now think of a different class with another professor where there was only one single correct answer. You might have felt restricted and that efforts to think outside of the box could result in punishment. What you might not have known is that features of that context – the professor, the classroom, the instructional topic, or even the time of day, all likely evoked or diminished variable and creative behavior.

We also know that variability is susceptible to schedules of reinforcement. A classic example is something called the lag schedule. In a lag schedule, a behavior is reinforced when (and only when) the behavior is different from the previous emitted behavior.

What these experiments show us is that we can foster variable and creative behavior when the environment supports it, and *that* is exactly what we are trying to do when developing committed actions. At the moment when a client is seeking services, behavior likely lacks variability and is maintained by short-term gratification that strengthens rigidity and punishes variation. When variation is punished to the point of inaction, we call it process-learned helplessness (Seligman, 1972). For clients, this could take the form of making excuses or lying to avoid uncomfortable situations or contexts. Although the excuse-making or lying may vary from situation to situation, the act of avoiding itself is invariable.

Variability is a necessary first step to selection and ultimately retention. If we continue doing the same thing day after day, there is no way to contact positive sources of reinforcement that could select behavior that is more in line with one's chosen values. When we talk about committed action, we are talking about deliberately becoming the type of person we want to be. And it starts by coming up with actions that are *different* from what we have tried before. Those actions may move us towards our values. Those actions might fail. And when they do fail, we gain new information to develop new commitments that are more likely to succeed. Naturalistic sources of reinforcement and punishment take effect, and as long as clients notice those reinforcers and punishers, and are willing to accept that engaging in committed action will not always yield immediate rewards, then those real-world reinforcers can begin to select those actions that lead to valued outcomes.

Evoking variability is *the* primary goal of some ACT-based interventions – a good example is when fostering creative hopelessness. The process of creative hopelessness involves (1) building awareness of experiential avoidance, (2) examining the workability of attempts to control or suppress behavior, (3) capturing that experience through metaphor (Luoma et al., 2010), and then (4) increasing experiential contact with the lean or absent reinforcers (number "2" on this list) that emerge from step 1 on this list as a massive motivative operation designed to lead to *something* different that is more likely to deliver valued reinforcers long term.

We know that experiential avoidance does not take on a singular form. Much like psychological flexibility, experiential avoidance is boundless and pervasive. The first step in creative hopelessness involves noticing the specific patterns of experiential avoidance that participate in the challenge that brought the client to the behavior analyst in the first place. We might well assume that these patterns have not been workable, either for the individual or for their family and caregivers, or else they would not be seeking support. But it is critical that the client explores this themselves. What are the long-term outcomes of this pattern of avoidance? What personal costs are there in relation to chosen values? Here, we are helping clients notice that their way of behaving cannot continue long term, and the time to change – to behave variably – is now.

Metaphors can help transition from feelings of hopelessness (I am not doing enough) to behavior that is self-validating (i.e., carries approach functions). Several apt metaphors are available. For example, struggle can often feel like being on a hamster wheel that goes nowhere. How would it feel to simply step off? When you do, you might start to notice all of the exciting places to explore around the cage. The wheel was like a monster at your party that you've spent hours trying to keep out of the house. What if we let the monster in?

The purpose of these metaphors is simply to create a context that supports values-focused variability. Because when behavior is variable, it is likely to contact new reinforcers (and punishers) and new streams of behavior are selected.

MAINTAINING BEHAVIOR CHANGE OVER TIME AND COMBATING RESURGENCE, RENEWAL, AND REINSTATEMENT

It is important to remember that "flexibility" is both bending *and* not breaking. When behavior patterns are not workable, it is important to be variable. On the other hand, when behavior patterns are starting to contact valued reinforcement, it is equally important to persist. This is the inherent balance between variation on the one hand and selective retention on the other.

Clients will experience roadblocks throughout the treatment process. Negative reinforcers that had previously maintained old behavior patterns are still available even as new patterns are established. Moreover, reinforcement rarely operates on a continuous schedule – and long periods of time of days or weeks may pass without external reinforcement for staying on track and investing in new behavior patterns. Ironically, we know from the client's problems themselves that persisting is in the person's repertoire: after all, most clients have been persisting in behavior that produces suffering for years. The good news inside that painful news is that persistence per se is not impossible, rather the issue is now how can we help clients persist in new and more healthy patterns of action when the initial excitement or momentum has worn out?

ACT contains some ideas about that.

First, there are the motivative functions of values. Small events like a casual conversation with a coworker might not be highly valuable in their own right. But for the person working through social anxiety, knowing that the casual conversation is in the service of a much larger value of building meaningful friendships can increase the central importance of that small conversation (and the probability of having similar conversations in the future). Maintaining committed action likely requires on-going discussion of values and frequently relating daily events back to their importance in fostering valued outcomes.

Second, we can learn a great deal from a growing body of research on behavioral resurgence and how to deal with it when it occurs (Sweeney & Shahan, 2013). Resurgence applies when a person faces punishment or extinction for a newly established behavior and returns to a previously established but subsequently extinguished behavior. This behavioral process has been observed in animal models and with humans (Kestner & Peterson, 2017) and in derived relational responses as well as directly shaped behavior (Wilson & Hayes, 1996).

Consider the situation where you have recently started to trust people more in relationships. But then, a person violates your trust, and you feel hurt. Because of your previous history of not trusting people, and your current experience of being punished for trusting again, it is only logical to cut off trust entirely. This is resurgence in real time. However, a return to baseline performance is not what we need in this situation. We need to trust and trust again because only by persisting can we achieve that meaningful trusting relationship that we value.

One way to combat resurgence is to develop broader skill repertoires as replacement behavior. Rather than simply teaching one replacement behavior, behavior analysts can establish multiple replacement behaviors. In so doing, different behaviors that serve the same valued function can be acted out prior to relapsing. Within ACT, we can do this by fostering broad and creative solutions to problems that are in the service of chosen values. For example, for a client trying to live a healthier life, it means finding multiple forms of exercise that they find enjoyable and working with the client to build their exercise around more and more sources of reinforcement (e.g., joining exercise groups, tracking progress). By doing so, even if the client experiences a setback, like chiggers on a hike, the result is not a complete abandonment of exercise, but perhaps only a temporary abandonment of hiking as only one specific form of exercise.

Combating resurgence is going to play a large role when using ACT approaches to foster greater social engagement with children with autism. Autism and social skill deficits go hand in hand. Neurotypical children do not always respond in the most appropriate way to the social behaviors of neurodivergent clients, which might deviate from what neurotypical kids are used to. For them, it makes sense to avoid uncertainty. Of course, we want to build a more accepting world and we should try to, but that does not change the fact that children on the spectrum might experience setbacks as they approach social situations. Here again, we need to focus on augmenting situations by frequently revisiting values and fostering a broad and flexible repertoire that provides creative and variable solutions to contacting social reinforcers. Perhaps approaching these kids in the sandbox went poorly, but we do not need to abandon friends altogether. Instead, we might alter our approach, or find a new sandbox altogether with new people and shared interests. In other words, the focus should be on *functional* persistence. People need both persistence in approaching valued living, and healthy variability in how they achieve it.

We know that resurgence is not the only pathway to relapse, however. Reinstatement is when a reinforcer for unwanted behavior reoccurs independent of deliberate action, thus evoking old patterns of behavior. This process is easily evoked in the lab by simply delivering the reinforcer on a variable time schedule. In real life, this same basic sequence can occur for a number of reasons. If a friend bails on social plans it may free up the evening to stay in bed even if a socially withdrawn person is trying to avoid staying in bed. A social outing with colleagues that was supposed to be light and casual may end up at the local bar where binge drinking is being reinforced and encouraged as in the past when a person had a substance use problem. We cannot just avoid all such situations – it's just not realistic. Instead, when reinstatement is a risk, we need to rely on the other ACT processes we have discussed so far and to groove habits of values-based action that include such scenarios. By expecting the unexpected and leaning more heavily on present-moment awareness, acceptance, defusion, and values relapse can be prevented in moments of reinstatement.

Most of the methods of "relapse prevention" developed by the late Alan Marlatt and colleagues can easily be crafted for this specific goal (e.g., Chawla et al., 2010). One potentially useful strategy from that approach that is highly ACT-consistent involves "surfing the urge" (Bowen & Marlatt, 2009). When reinforcers show up, so too can the urge to behave in ways that access them. Surfing the urge is a mindfulness technique that involves noticing the urge and, instead of fighting to get rid of it, simply observing the urge increase in intensity and slowly decrease in intensity. Rather than feeding the urge, people are taught to simply notice its rise and fall. Research has shown that this simple technique can be effective in reducing smoking relapse in college students (Bowen & Marlatt, 2009) and even aggression in autistic adolescents (Singh et al., 2019).

Another relapse process is renewal, in which the context shifts in some notable way and behavior returns to old patterns. When we start to build momentum in ACT, that behavior change is occurring in a specific context. But what happens when life pivots again? The only thing we can be certain of in our future is that it will be different from our present. One way to combat renewal is to focus on committed actions that bring about changes in the environment that can exert control over behavior. Skinner referred to this as self-control (intentionally changing the environment to change behavior). For example, a committed action may be to create a space at home that is only used for practicing meditation. The committed action creates an environment that is constant in an ever-changing world. Regardless of what is happening at work or in one's relationship, this meditation space is present. Then the context in which that environment is accessed, and systematically and deliberately altered – such as mediating when hungry or fed; happy or sad; all alone or when people are in the house; before or after exercise; and so on.

Another example to avoid relapse could involve selecting social media sites that allow for greater contact with social communities that have similar values. Many behavior analysts already do this by joining communities that foster more progressive and person-centered forms of behavior analysis. This allows for greater availability of social reinforcers and can influence other changes in one's career that can bring about more valued reinforcement in that life domain. In this case, seeking out and joining social communities with shared interests and values can be a committed action that protects against renewal. The community is always around in the background and, even if one or two communities disappear, a flexible and variable social community can help resolve this potential barrier.

Finally, as behavior analysts we must accept that relapse is going to happen and we need to cast intervention methods in ways that foster healthy persistence even so. Adjusting to relapse is necessarily part of a process of success. What we want to reinforce is the process of committing and recommitting, over and over, as long as it takes – that is what committed action in the ACT model is all about. "Commitment" means seeking a pattern that gradually becomes larger and larger – sometimes by including a deep dive into the contextual causes of the behavioral relapse. Resurgence? Reinstatement? Or, renewal? If we can pinpoint the environmental change that produces relapsed behavior, then new committed actions can be developed that specifically target that event. Perhaps we did not anticipate that an old friend would show up with all of their experiential avoidance functions. Knowing that this can occur and in valuing that friendship, how can we adjust our environment and behavior to both hang out with our old friend and continue down the path toward a more valued life?

This process needs to be creative and collaborative, with the client playing an active role in the development of solutions. Ultimately, maintaining behavior change after the termination of behavior therapy is the goal of any intervention. Clients need to be able to pivot and adjust, to be variable and persistent, without your help. Research suggests that is a feature of ACT-based interventions that leads to superior long-term outcomes. For example, in most smoking cessation programs, a relapse mid-treatment reliably predicts long-term treatment failure, while in ACT-based smoking cessation programs often mid-stream slips later become quits (e.g., Gifford et al., 2011; Luoma et al., 2012).

SCIENCE OF VALUES-BASED GOAL SETTING FROM WITHIN A BEHAVIOR ANALYTIC FRAMEWORK

A major component of ACT-based intervention, or really any behavior-analytic intervention, is goal setting. Insurance authorizations contain lists of goals and objectives. IEPs contain lists of goals and objectives. Goal setting is not only pervasive in behavior analysis but also foundational in almost all applied disciplines.

Inherently, goal setting is a self-control strategy that leverages what Skinner called rule-governed behavior. We have already talked about the role of rule-governed behavior in maintaining psychological suffering, but we can also use rules to help ensure our own success. Stating a goal is essentially stating a contingency between the goal and an assumed or stated outcome of the goal. "I will read two chapters of this book this week" is a goal with an assumed outcome – and if you are saying it right now it may be with the assumed outcome of learning ACT processes more completely so as to be more helpful to clients. "I will play with my child more this week" is a goal – perhaps with the assumed outcome of achieving a greater connection with your child or perhaps with the hope that your child falls asleep more quickly in the evenings after vigorous play.

What makes this common behavior method of goal-setting ACT consistent are the intended outcomes. In ACT, goal setting is important to the degree that goals link directly or indirectly to chosen values. In ACT, goal setting should specify how actions will instantiate and build greater contact with valued reinforcers – including those that are intrinsic to the behavior itself.

The origins of the SMART acronym for goal setting are not entirely clear (Lawlor & Hornyak, 2012), but this framework is commonplace across industries and serves as a good reminder for behavior analysts about how to create potentially useful goals. When setting goals, we want to ensure that they are specific, measurable, attainable, relevant, and time-bound. What exactly are we setting out to achieve? How will we know that we have achieved it? Is the goal something that we can obtain with our current skill set? How does the goal relate to one's chosen values? And when do we expect the goal to be accomplished? If we can answer each of these questions in the affirmative, then goals can serve an important function when fostering committed action – once they are vitalized as values-based.

Behavior science can also contribute greatly to how we understand attainability within the SMART model. We know that what may not be attainable today can be attainable tomorrow through the learning process of shaping. Shaping refers to the differential reinforcement of successive approximations of behavior. We can incorporate shaping into goal setting by meeting clients where they are at and being conscientious of not pushing too hard too early. What are they willing to do *today* in the service of their chosen values? When struggle is deeply ingrained, we often cannot think small enough. For some clients, simply sitting in their seat for five minutes may be a massive commitment. For others, simply saying hello to someone in the hallway is a major feat. Or maybe avoiding drug use for half a day is a major milestone. It is critical to accept and reinforce these approximations in order to build momentum at the earliest stages of treatment. Behavior analysts are also familiar with taking small steps at first and building to major leaps later as behavior change accelerates. We want to take advantage of this in our goal-setting as well.

The importance of values work to goal setting has been studied empirically and the outcomes are fairly clear. ACT-based training in how to create clarity regarding values adds significantly added to the behavioral impact of goal-setting (e.g., Chase et al., 2013). There should be no surprise in this since values consistency from an ACT perspective is a powerful motivating operation. Adding values to more traditional behaviorally based self-control development strategies holds great promise. Here methods such as self-monitoring, feedback, and goal setting could all be overlayed with an eye toward values.

Guiding committed action is an art that is mastered with practice and with deep consideration of behavior change principles. Coaching clients through committed action takes patience and will require self-observation and reflection on the part of the behavior analyst. Sometimes clients will move slower than we would like. Other times they move faster than we feel comfortable with. But as long as we are flexible and encourage our clients to be flexible, committed action is perhaps the most powerful tool in the belt of behavior analysts who utilize ACT-based approaches.

INDEPENDENT AND DEPENDENT VARIABLES FOR INTERVENTION

In order to measure committed action, behavior analysts simply need to measure behavior in all of the usual ways. Belisle et al. (2021) summarize the process for selecting a valid and reliable measurement system. First, we need to operationally define the "action" that we are looking to increase within committed action. Operational definitions should be clear and objective so that two independent raters could agree on what a unit of the behavior looks like. For example, if a person is looking to leave their house more often, what constitutes leaving the house? Is stepping into the front yard enough, or do they need to travel at least one block away from the house? There is no right answer to this question, and it depends on the client and the targeted behavior change.

Committed actions are also accelerative or constructive. This means that we are always looking to *increase* their occurrence. This distinction appreciates that reducing unwanted behavior is always an active process. To illustrate, we can reframe "not smoking for one week" as "going one full week without smoking." In the former, it is the omission of the behavior, whereas in the latter, it is engaging in all of the ACT strategies learned to that point in time to accomplish the goal of not smoking for one full week. The distinction is subtle – but important.

We also want to be clear about the dimension of behavior that we are looking to measure (and therefore, to accelerate). Rate measures how often the behavior occurs, whereas duration measures how long a behavior occurs. Selecting the right dimension is crucial. For example, someone might only leave their house once during the day, but they were out for several hours. In this case, duration is likely the more important dimension to capture, rather than simply the number of times a person left the house. Latency measures the time between the onset of a stimulus event and the onset of a behavior. How long does it take for a social interaction opportunity to present itself and for the client to actively engage in the social interaction? In this case, a reduction in latency is evidence that interacting socially is strengthening and avoidance is weakening. Because "commitment" shows up especially in behavioral resilience and persistence, it is important to assess not just gross rates of behavior when assessing response strength but also the latency to re-emergence of desired behavior when it is disrupted and the persistence of behavior in different situations and motivational conditions.

All of this above is likely just a thumbnail review for most readers, but there are specific considerations that should be made within the context of ACT-based interventions. Whereas we are used to thinking of behavior change as the primary target in behavioral interventions, we also want to see that the key processes of change are involved in committed action. It does not serve people to establish habits that are experientially avoidant, fused, out of touch with the present context, and that are not values-based. Said in another way, we need to measure behavior functionally, not just topographically. Stepping beyond measuring only behavioral topographies that are directly observed to capturing more data linked to the functional process of committed action, could have important and beneficial implications for how we (and others) view our field.

Committed Action as a Dependent Variable

Directly observing behavior change can be accomplished in some settings, such as in therapy centers, residential facilities, or in schools. When this option is available, all of the tools that applied behavior analysis have developed already to observe and record behavior should be the first order of business. When continuous recording of behavior is not an option, time sampling methods like partial or whole interval can also be considered. Although less accurate compared to measures like rate or duration, time sampling data can be easier to collect and to train non-behaviorally trained members of the community (e.g., teachers or paraprofessionals) to collect. The time sampling methods involve segmenting the observational period into prescribed intervals and recording if the behavior occurred during the interval (either for the whole interval or only for part of it).

Direct observation data might not be the most appropriate or available in every instance. These times include when the agency does not have the personnel to directly observe behavior, when the data of interest is a private event, when self-observation is a component of the intervention, or when directly observing behavior violates the privacy of the client receiving the therapy. For clients who are likely to be served using ACT-based approaches, these situations are more likely than in many other behavior analytic applications. Let's consider each in turn.

First, agencies may not be built to directly observe behavior. We have been privileged as a field because places where behavior analysts work very frequently have staff members who are available and trained to collect direct observation data; however, one of the biggest advantages of integrating ACT concepts into the tool belt of behavior analysts is to expand behavioral technologies into new domains. Consider applying ACT within an industrial setting to improve workplace culture and production centered around shared values. It is unlikely that anyone in a supervisory position is around at all times – and even if they are, they are likely performing their own managerial tasks. Although the company may choose to employ a behavior analyst to focus on improving workplace culture and employee performance, the additional resources needed to directly observe behavior change can be prohibitive. Instead, productivity can be measured in terms of permanent products, or the rate at which the employees produce as an aggregate following the development of an agency-wide ACT intervention. This same challenge could be generalized to working with staff in a traditional applied behavior analysis (ABA) setting, like therapeutic interventions for children with autism. Staff members are available to observe the behavior of the children receiving service, but not to observe the therapists. Here again, permanent product data such as the number of trial blocks recorded could provide an alternative.

Second, the data that is being collected may be a private event. Although most committed actions are directly observable, this is not always the case. Take for example steps taken to improve self-compassion and greater emotional openness, and clients are being asked to pause and to observe and label how their body feels when difficult emotions arise. It is difficult to monitor such behavior without self-report. In a therapeutically appropriate situation, an ACT trainer could coach an effective tacting repertoire focused on emotions and their bodily accompaniments, but as these methods are used in vivo we may have to rely on self-monitoring data, where the person records when emotions arose and what bodily sensations they produced. Steps may need to be taken to ensure that self-monitoring data are reported accurately and to minimize social desirability bias, such as encouraging the client to take such measures using talk-aloud methods that avoid self-editing (Hayes, 1986; Hayes et al., 1998).

Finally, observing everything a client does is simply not a luxury afforded in most settings. Imagine following a parent or a client experiencing depression around all day simply to record if they engaged in mindful breathing that day. Not only would this be incredibly disruptive to the effectiveness of the behavior plan, but they would probably report you for stalking them. People enjoy their privacy – and they have a right to it. Our answer to this "problem" (which is not really a problem at all) in the field cannot be to only operate in settings where privacy is not afforded. Instead, we need to become comfortable with permanent product data, self-report data, and the use of other technologies to track behavior in the real world.

One way to accomplish this is the use of ecological momentary assessment data (EMA). EMA data collection systems often use a smartphone app that allows participants to record their behavior. This can occur at fixed times throughout the day, randomly throughout the day, or clients can choose when and where to enter the data. In doing so, EMA offers an alternative to many of the self-report data systems we have described so far by allowing for the collection of continuous behavior change data and by analyzing changes based on within-person idiographic variability. Measures are being created specifically for these purposes within the ACT community (e.g., Ciarrochi, Sahdra, Hofmann, & Hayes, in press), using new forms of statistical analysis that fit with the idiographic focus of behavior analysis (e.g., Sanford et al., in press).

Overall estimates of committed action are also included in some standard psychometrically validated self-report measures. A strength of these measures is that they link directly to values. For example, both the VLQ and the VQ that we have described in earlier chapters measure the degree to which clients believe their current behaviors are aligned with their chosen values. These measures can therefore provide strong experimental evidence that an ACT-based intervention is effective in promoting greater engagement in committed action.

Committed Action as an Independent Variable

In all of the previous chapters, we have emphasized that *values-based behavior change* is the primary goal of ACT-based interventions. This means that changing behavior for the sake of changing behavior is not enough. When viewing committed action as a process variable, we need to always ask how engaging in the committed action is likely to change the lives of our clients for the better, as defined by their values. Will this action foster better relationships with their family if that is of importance? Will it allow them to be more able to contribute to their own well-being?

Activities and exercises that center around committing to values-centered action should produce changes in other outcome measures that we are interested in. There is a vast literature on ACT interventions showing that they lead to reductions in feelings of depression, anxiety, and hopelessness. In clients with disabilities such as autism, we might expect when clients engage in more committed action, that feelings of self-efficacy and self-worth may improve. These outcomes are not substituting for overt behavior change but they also should not be ignored.

ANTECEDENT AND CONSEQUENCE STRATEGIES TO PROMOTE COMMITTED ACTION

As with the other ACT processes, time and place are incredibly important. A defining feature of behavior analysis has always been to go where the behavior is occurring, instead of arranging a contrived time and place that is convenient to the therapist during prescribed office hours or by appointment. So, when is goal setting best situated for the greatest chance of achieving behavior change?

As a setting event, the setting of committed actions can occur as regular practice at the beginning of the day to set the occasion for productivity. This is a self-management strategy whereby a verbal stimulus, often in a listed form but not necessarily, is created to then guide behavior throughout the day. To-do lists or a daily calendar can easily become in the service of things that are not freely chosen values – like working to meet the exclusive demands of others or the demands of a conceptualized self. To link this more closely to values, stimuli that augment values functions can be put immediately into this context. For example, by starting the week by writing one or two values that will operate as a central theme throughout that week and can be seen when setting committed actions. In this way, values can ebb and flow flexibly with collective motivating operations in effect at that time, like when yearning for greater connectedness with family one week and feeling the urge to be creative the next week. All of these are self-management strategies that are well within the wheelhouse of behavior analysts to not only utilize, but to optimize.

Setting committed actions can also be used to transition from one segment of the day to the next. In fact, segmenting the day in and of itself is a self-management strategy that like chaining breaks the larger task of an entire day into smaller and more manageable chunks. For example, for a client who is struggling in math class with productivity and elevated rates of challenging behavior, setting committed actions immediately prior to the math class related to both behavior and performance could augment the probability of success. For the client who experiences immense anxiety at home following long and challenging days at school or at work, concluding the school or workday by setting committed actions for the next day could disrupt the need for verbal and private self-scrolling of to-do lists that have previously served the function of "not forgetting anything important."

A challenge with committed actions may be that the stimulus, either written or verbally stated, may not be present in those moments where committed action may be the least likely to occur. In this case, behavior analysts might consider ways to bring those commitments to the psychological present. For example, by establishing a verbal relation between the goal and a symbol and ensuring that the symbol is present immediately before the low-probability event. This can also be accomplished as a conversational stimulus. For example, the behavior analyst might say, "Now I know that this is something that is very hard for you *and* we are working to accept that! Remember that you committed to ______________. Do you still feel like you can honor that commitment?" Framed in this way, the verbal stimulus is made immediately present and the question honors the reality that motivating operations that may have been present at the time of making the commitment may no longer be the same. The client has a choice to honor the commitment or to step back, to recommit, and to try again another time. When that other time comes, the other ACT processes that we have reviewed so far may help to strengthen the probability of honoring the commitment as a series of available self-management strategies. And in this way, honoring the commitment is a choice that the client is making, and it is their success to own.

Reinforcers can also be used to even further strengthen the probability of engaging in the committed action and this can be accomplished as a collaborative process. Why not make the client an active member of building the contingency management system? This could start by having the client identify commitments that are easy and commitments that are hard, and awarding different point values for each that are exchanged for backup reinforcers. Ultimately valued sources of reinforcement will be what maintain (or fail to maintain) longer-lasting behavior change, but creating point-based games or incentives around performance can help bridge the gap between what is hard now and what will be contacted later.

COMBINING COMMITTED ACTION WITH PRESENT-MOMENT AWARENESS, ACCEPTANCE, DEFUSION, AND VALUES

Behavior change is necessary to alter our experiences with our world. Committing to such change is hard. Each of the six core processes of ACT plays a role in allowing committed action to occur.

Present-moment awareness allows a person to experience the real-life present-moment contingencies surrounding their behavior. Present-moment awareness is necessary to contact those valued reinforcers that show up during committed action, and to notice their absence when behavior is not values-based.

Engaging in committed action can be uncomfortable and, when behavior is not well practiced, may only produce small reinforcers. Acceptance is necessary to push through these earliest stages of committed action in order to contact reinforcement. Moreover, acceptance is also necessary to willingly experience the positive feelings and changes that come with committed action knowing that positive experiences themselves will come and go.

When thoughts show up that foster experiential avoidance instead of committed action, defusion exercises can weaken their momentary control and open up the window to engage in committed action.

Ultimately, committed action is only "committed" when a clear link exists between the action and a person's chosen values. Moreover, engaging in committed action is made more likely by presenting values as motivative stimuli that are likely to evoke action. Values can also be an effective guide to developing committed action goals, such as when using a tool like the ACT Matrix that makes the link between values and action explicit.

Engaging in the six core processes can also be in and of themselves committed actions. Committing to a meditation routine to foster present-moment awareness is a committed action. Committing to doing and experiencing something uncomfortable that is part of a values life journey is a committed action. Committed to defusion exercises even when they seem goofy and only tangentially connected to the problem at hand because they loosen unhelpful forms of relational stimulus control is a committed action. Committing to the on-going discussion with friends, family, and loved ones about what really matters the most to you as an individual and to the group of people you find yourself around the most is a committed action.

All of this takes commitment. The process of going through an ACT intervention is at its core all about the deliberate evolution of a human life by broadening repertoires to allow for greater variability as well as persistence. If we can commit to each of these processes and act to change our lives, the vast literature on ACT suggests that change is just around the corner.

10

Self-as-Context

It is a uniquely problem to question ourselves and to ask who or what we are meant to be. Our pets never worry about such things. They don't fret about how others perceive them, or if they are living up to their own standards. Only humans do this. We work extra hours to please our bosses and to feel like a "productive employee" or a "hard worker." And we go the extra mile to be a "good parent" and a "good spouse." But what happens when we fail to live up to these expectations? Self-criticism starts to emerge, and with it the temptation to distract or distance ourselves from thoughts of inadequacy or low self-worth. This could be direct, as in putting in an effort to satisfy whatever version of ourselves we are attempting to construct. Or it can take the form of engaging in behavior that moves us away from what we truly value. In either case, experiential avoidance and living up to conceptualizations of oneself that we construct are deeply interwoven processes.

These conceptualizations can also be negatively framed. "I am a criminal and will always be a criminal"; "all of my family are criminals"; "alcoholism runs in my family." These types of rules may foster a sense of inevitability. Who "I am" causes me to suffer and it must be that way! We see these rules show up in work with children in low socioeconomic communities with high rates of crime and in children with a history of delinquency. We also see this in work with children with autism who may internalize negative relations about the disorder. "What is wrong with me?"; "My autism causes me to lash out"; "I cannot have friends because of my autism." Autism becomes the core component in a personal narrative that necessitates suffering and limited opportunities.

Sometimes these conceptualized labels also provide an escape. For the child who believes incarceration is an inevitable part of growing up, this rule may provide a reason to skip class or experiment with drugs or alcohol at an early age because there is nothing to lose – the outcome has already been decided. For the child with autism, there is no reason to try to approach others to develop meaningful relationships or to put in the extra work to understand concepts presented in their classes – "their autism" is going to hold them back anyways. That is simply just who they *are* – or at least, who they have the thought that they are.

We all carry these labels. Depressed. Anxious. Hyperactive. Inattentive. Too smart. Not smart enough. This should come as no surprise given our entire model and approach to psychological intervention has historically been about sorting people into categories. Sit in any class on abnormal psychology, and you will find this nomothetic approach on center stage. If you fit into (insert box), then you will experience "negative outcomes later in life." The psychology of individual differences has been at this game for a long time.

DOI: 10.4324/9781003250371-12

But this top-down normative approach cannot predict any clear outcome for individuals because there is no behavioral process being described. There is no consideration of the dynamic and ever-changing context within which behaviors occur being detailed. A science of average – a science of the so-called "normal" and fusion of oneself to categories or normal and not normal – does not apply to the individual person, even probabilistically. Behavior analysts have long taken that position from Murray Sidman's classic text on tactics of scientific research (1960) but it's only within the last two decades that mainstream psychology has become awakened to the mathematical facts that make this a certainty.

It is only recently that the strategy we most need to follow has a fully applicable name. We used the word *idionomic* in Chapter 1. It probably slipped by you, but it is based on such a cool and established scientific fact that it is worth bit of explication. "Normal" refers to where you fall as compared to others (think bell curves or standard deviations). We all are socialized to believe that these comparisons predict trajectories within people. For example, we likely would readily accept the idea that a person with this IQ score will likely succeed in school or a person with that personality type will fail at this job. This view is so common in psychology, it is hard to avoid.

The reason it is false is that it could only be true if differences *between* people can reliably predict trajectories *within* people.

They can't.

That idea is radical in psychology, but stated in another form, it is actually old hat in the field of physics. For nearly 100 years (based on an accepted mathematical proof of what is called the ergodic theorem; see Birkhoff, 1931) physicists have known that a model using average states of the system can't predict the actions over time of the elements of the system unless those elements show (a) no trends over time and (b) all elements respond to events in exactly the same way. If those two conditions apply, the elements are said to be "ergodic" and then, yes, normative statistics at a given point in time predict trajectories of the individual elements over time. There are indeed ergodic phenomena like that in nature (a few noble gasses for example) but human behavior is not one of them. We do not treat frozen clones. Human behavior changes, violating condition (a), and it does so in ways that are idiographic – unique to the particular person – violating condition (b).

From the beginning behavior analysis was built in a different and quite unique way. What "behavioral principles" describe is how contingencies contacting the individual's behavior change behavioral trajectories, seen against the variability of behavior within that person over time. These are then generalized to nomothetic principles across people or other organisms (e.g., principles such as "reinforcement") if and only if these principles help us understand individuals better. That's what "idionomic" concepts are like: they start with highly precise descriptions of idiographic patterns, which are then scaled to nomothetic generalizations that can be applied across organisms can that help us understand and model the individual better.

Idionomic concepts are quite rare in most of psychology. They are the meat and potatoes of behavior analysis.

When we think about this in terms of grouped averages, the conclusion seems logical. Most people will win more than they lose. But because of natural variability in systems, this outcome will rarely if ever occur for an individual over multiple occurrences across time. Since one of the authors of this book teaches at the University of Nevada, Reno (SCH), he is glad most gamblers do not understand the ergodic error or his salary might not get paid!

Within our culture, we have a mismatch between how we talk and think about behavior and how behavior actually works – including our own behavior. This "average" approach to understanding our own behavior is consistent with what we can call a conceptualized self. I am like this. I am like that. It's a normative, decontextualized way of thinking. It can readily foster psychological inflexibility because it is focused on comparisons between people rather than the variability that occurs within people.

Take the "big five" theory of personality. Suppose I've bought into the normative idea that some people are introverts, and some are extroverts. If you look *between* people the same personality types keep being found (that's why they are called the "big five"). You would think that meant if you assess the same person over and over, some people would behave consistently within themselves (e.g., they would behave as introverts almost always) or at least the variability across situations for most people would show five different styles. But that is not what happens! When it was tested no one fit the "big five" perspective over time (Molenaar & Campbell, 2009). Instead, so-called introverts were extroverts in a variety of situations; or entirely idiographic patterns emerged (e.g., a given person might have eight different ways of interacting, not five). The big five personality dimensions were abstractions that did not describe actual people. And yet, how many people might've spent their lives living inside a story that they are "extroverts" or what have you. And what patterns of invariability do these nomothetic descriptors serve to augment?

The conceptualized self is like an ill-fitting suit that culture makes for you. These concepts are put atop people – they were not built idiographically. That is especially why they hurt, and our clients have often lived inside them even when these labels are stigmatizing and unfair.

There is another sense of what "self" even is, however, and when this other sense of self is trained it helps people free themselves from harsh judgmental categories.

This other sense can be illustrated using a house as a metaphor. The *contents* of our lives are like the objects in the house. When we start to define the house by these objects, we miss out on so much of life as it is lived. Content changes. Old stuff is replaced by new stuff. Families move in and families move out. The house contains these changes but cannot be entirely defined in terms of them.

People are like that. Thoughts, emotions, reactions, and behavioral propensities are ever-changing. As whole people, we notice or observe these psychological events, and our lives contain them. The house includes furniture, and yet it is also distinct from the furniture; it is not fully defined by the furniture.

In one sense the house is distinct from the furniture. In another sense, the house includes or contains the furniture. In no sense is the house fully defined by the furniture. Metaphorically that is what people do to themselves when they define themselves in terms of self-judgments and comparisons to others. The conceptualized self often takes the form such statements (e.g., "I am ______________" or "I must ______________") such as "I am a hard-working employee" or "I'm dumb."

Conceptualizing oneself in these ways can foster unhealthy inflexibility when what is needed is outside the rule-based view of self.

In acceptance and commitment therapy (ACT), the power that thoughts, emotions, reactions, and behavioral propensities have over behavior is greatly reduced when the individual is able to view themselves as more than self-concepts describing various content elements, especially in comparison to others (e.g., I'm not smart; I'm unlovable; I'm mean; I'm an introvert; and so on). The way that can be done is to notice that we also have a perspective – "I, here, now am having the thought that I'm not smart." From that perspective or point of view a thought like "I'm not smart" is in me, or known by me, but it does not fully define me. ACT and relational frame theory (RFT) researchers call this sense of self by the term "self-as-context" or the "perspective-taking sense of self."

Perspective-taking skills are hard to notice. You've probably had the experience of being in a conversation with someone and then suddenly having a sense that you are noticing that conversation almost as if you're off to the side looking back at it. If you look at your perspective, your perspective needs to change, sort of the way two mirrors when they're held up close to each other can sometimes produce reflections that echo back and forth into a continuous series of images. The sense is a bit spooky.

The self-reflective nature of perspective-taking leads to metaphors being used frequently when helping clients to explore self-as-context. We just did that when we were talking about a house with furniture in it. Self-as-context is the "I" in the content statements of "I am _______," or "I must __________." Whereas the specific content of these statements is ever-changing, the perspective of the whole person called "I" is in a sense constant, and by a process of elimination, that sense can be discovered. This happens in verbal training when children report what happened to them and they learn through trial and error to report from a consistent perspective or point of view. In a sense, they learn that "I" means to report from "here, now." When asked "what did you have for breakfast?" at first they might say what their sister had for breakfast, but they soon learn that "I" means "from this perspective or point of view."

Promoting self-as-context as a repertoire is especially important when rigidly adhering to a conceptualized version of oneself is inconsistent with one's chosen values. The adolescent with autism who struggles with the diagnostic label around "autism," may benefit from reconceptualizing autism in a way that is more flexible and dynamic. Sometimes interpreting events from the lens of "autism" can be empowering, like in some of the advances made within the neurodiversity movement. In other contexts, a person benefits by defusing this label and simply interacting with events as "I am" (a person with many labels; with many features; I contain a history of events). A sense of transcendence across time and place begins to emerge as a result.

This sense of transcendence begins to emerge for most children in preschool (McHugh & Stewart, 2012). Children in preschool can answer questions about their past and about their future while appreciating that there is a constant perspective across those experiences that in some sense is "me." This change in a sense of self corresponds with major shifts in human language and cognition that take place during this time. Children younger than four years show grammar and syntactic structures that largely resemble their parents and grandparents. However, around the age of four, children begin to show grammar and syntactic structures that are truly uniquely their own.

Undoubtedly, these complex patterns of behavior are highly influenced by interactions with other members of the community. The multiplicity of derived relational processes creates a system that is vastly complex and variable. In the context of that complexity, we see the emergence of a psychological individual. It is critically important that we can shape perceptions of self that are flexible and adaptive, giving clients the tools, they need to achieve the lives they value. Doing so requires a deeper dive into behavioral processes underlying self-as-context.

DEICTIC RELATIONAL RESPONDING AND HIERARCHICAL CLASSES

Evaluations of self-as-context likely begin when the child first learns to name and categorize objects because even the mutual roles of speaker and listener involve perspective. Bidirectional naming or equivalence classes are necessary to establish verbal behavior about environmental stimuli.

Verbal labels are evoked by shared content or characteristics through stimulus abstraction. Consider how we learn to identify the color red. If a child is shown a red ball and is reinforced for uttering the word "red," we might expect that the child can also point to the red ball when they hear the word "red." Without additional examples, however, we do not know if the speaker or listener responses are controlled by the redness of the object or the ball-ness of the object. Abstracting the color red (abstracted tact extension) likely requires multiple examples using many different red objects like a red block, red train, red shoes, among other objects, in order for the color and no other features to provoke the right response. Thus, "red" is the shared content controlling both the speaker and listener response.

Although colors are relatively simple naming responses, we can assume that the same process is involved when children learn to abstract other characteristics, such as "nice" and "mean." Even though specific instances of niceness and meanness are infinite, they share common properties that once established can control identification or categorization of people or events. For example, children start to identify some children as "friends" and other children as "enemies" around the age of four, corresponding with the explosion of language that happens at this age (Liberman & Shaw, 2019; Oldenburg et al., 2018). Naming and categorizing are part of what it means to be human.

Oftentimes these labels can carry approach or avoidance functions. For example, a child might define a friend as someone who is nice to them, plays with them during recess, and works with them on classwork. When they observe these actions taking place, they may be more likely to identify the other child as "friend" and to approach them in shared social situations. Conversely, when they observe someone being mean to them, avoiding them at recess, and choosing to work with other people in class, they may not label them as "friend" and instead avoid them in shared social situations.

Not all children will necessarily frame friendship in this same way. Relational framing is a highly individualized process that requires an idiographic approach to appreciate its complexity. For example, another child may have learned that friends are people who *look like* them, sharing either their gender, race, or economic status. Another child may believe friends are people who *do things for them*. These different patterns could promote healthy or unhealthy relationships that persist in different forms into adolescence and adulthood.

This same general framework likely holds true for any other example, such as being a good student, a good parent, a good employee, and so on. What is often missed is that labeling oneself as a good friend or a bad friend requires understanding the difference between "I" and "you." Social comparisons of self versus others are occurring constantly. "I am a good friend and they are a bad friend." "I am a hard-working employee because others do not work as hard as I do and deserve less recognition than I do." It is because of these social comparisons that we are able to understand ourselves. Someone can only be a "good parent" if other people are average or bad parents. Someone can only be a hard worker if other people are lazy. Someone can only be autistic if other people are neurotypical or neurodivergent in different ways.

These "I versus you" comparisons are necessarily part of both perspective-taking and the conceptualized self. Critical functional differences appear when deictic relations of here-versus-there and now-versus-then enter into the analysis. This insight helps us see how we can begin to strengthen and train self-as-context when it is weak or absent.

Conceptualizing oneself based on content can readily ride roughshod over context. For example, the statement "I am stupid" is normally not constrained to a single place or context and does not reference a specific point in time. We can easily add time as a first context when we modify the statement to "sometimes I feel stupid," or "I feel stupid in this moment." It is worth noting that this statement may seem somewhat similar to the defusion exercise of saying, "I am having the thought that..." which serves to "deliteralize" judgmental statements. Localizing self-evaluations in time can reduce the unnecessary transformation of stimulus functions such as allowing "stupid" to become part of a self-story that persists across time.

Here-versus-there relations can further contain a self-concept to a specific context or location. For example, consider the statements "I feel stupid in my statistics class" or "sometimes I feel really stupid when I talk to that person." By understanding that perspective-taking involves frames of time, place, and person, when we add deictic information, we restrict the transformation of stimulus function to a temporal and situational context to a degree, avoiding the formation of a broadly framed conceptualized self that is based on feelings of inadequacy.

Simply noticing and describing the contexts within which a thought or feeling shows up can be critically important in its own right in fostering a broader sense of self and other flexibility processes. For example, if someone notices that they "feel stupid" in a specific class, committed action can lead to greater feelings of competence in that area without needing to entirely reconceptualize oneself. Feeling more confident in a statistics class can simply be about spending more time studying statistics.

Perspective-taking is verbally fostered by deictic relational responding (I-versus-you, here-versus-there, and now-versus-then). Consider how important this form of deictic relational responding is when working with children with autism who already show diminished perspective-taking skills beyond an intellectual disability (Cardillo et al., 2020; Pearson et al., 2013). Deictic relational responding is known to play a role in the theory of mind development with implications for children with autism spectrum disorder (ASD; Weil et al., 2011).

A special consideration with this population is that earlier learners may still be working on the development of a conceptualized self. It is important not to fully disrupt that process when working with this population. While the data are still early, self-as-context should likely only be a focus when self-as-content has started to emerge and shown to participate in a client's psychological inflexibility. When introducing self-as-context, Autistic clients may also struggle with some of the metaphors that center around the use of deictic relational frames. Therefore, additional steps may be required to better illustrate and explain these concepts, or to seed them into other forms of verbal training as we have been describing.

Hierarchical frames are also heavily involved in self-as-content and self-as-context verbal processes, allowing for conceptualizations of one's experience. Thinking of ourselves using hierarchical categories is a normal part of the psychological development of children. First, children learn to distinguish from adults as they differ in size and shape. Furthermore, learning to classify oneself as a child among other children, and later as a "small kid" or a "big kid." We have also historically categorized ourselves along the gender binaries of "boy" and "girl," although this too may be less prevalent in Autistic communities and increasingly less prevalent in society more broadly (Cooper et al., 2016; Hyde et al., 2019). Later conceptualizations of self can emerge along any number of dimensions, based on things like race, religion, sexual identity, politics, height, or weight. These self-categorizations can also transform stimulus functions, such as by avoiding others who fit into an opposite categorization. When fused, categories can influence the way we think, reason, and problem-solve. For example, identifying with a specific political party might shape the way that we view issues of social importance (Slothus, 2010).

As this applies to "self-as-context" it means that our various skills and experiences can be framed as parts of us that are included or contained by verbal awareness (like that house with furniture). Research has shown that the hierarchical relation with "I" fosters greater psychological flexibility.

When held too tightly, exclusive identification with hierarchical categories can restrict the social communities with whom we interact. For example, someone of a specific faith may only interact with other members of that shared faith about issues related to spirituality. The risk in this is that we create echo chambers with only a very narrow range of rules to select from. Other ways of thinking or alternative rules that could be more adaptive in another context may never even be contacted and therefore have no chance to influence behavior. Again, conceptualizing oneself along these dimensions in a flexible way can be incredibly adaptive, especially when doing so clearly aligns with freely chosen values. However, when self-conceptualization competes with freely chosen values, or when values are never freely chosen at all (i.e., values simply cohere with expectations of the conceptualized group), promoting processes consistent with self-as-context may be specifically advantageous.

Moving beyond simple perspective-taking skills to experiencing oneself in a transcendent sense involves frames of distinction. At the level of experience, we can distinguish between that which is observed and the one doing the observing. Skinner appealed to the importance of not just seeing but also seeing that you see as a source of self-knowledge and self-control. What ACT added (Hayes, 1984) is that there is a next step: seeing that you see from a consistent perspective or point of view. You observe yourself observing.

Building on that we can shift our perspective. That enables us to distinguish between "I" as an active observer here and now and "I" as an observer in the past and in the future, while also appreciating elements of sameness or consistency in this experience. This can be illustrated when a client is asked to imagine their earliest memory as a young child. To observe how their thoughts and feelings in that moment may be different from how they are feeling today. A version of experience less impacted by the dense verbal relations and rules that have developed since that moment in childhood. In this moment it is important to also experience the constancy in that experience – that the child is still present and still experiencing here and now. In this way, promoting awareness of the transcendental represents an ongoing competition between sameness and difference.

That same flexibility of perspective-taking allows children to understand and use social stories, or for people to learn to put themselves in other's shoes and feel empathy. Thus, perspective-taking is a key skill that is part of human socialization.

CORE BELIEFS AND RELATIONAL DYNAMICS

Just as a conceptualized self involves fusion with self-judgment, there are clear similarities between the process of defusion and promoting self-as-context. Defusion involves weakening the behavioral impact of rules that are no longer workable, whereas self-as-context emphasizes weakening those content rules that are directly related to self. Understanding differences in the strength of rules about oneself and relational coherence could be useful in even further understanding this process behavior analytically. Relational density theory assumes that the strength of verbal rules is not all equal. Some rules are stronger than others. Rules may cohere with or interact with other rules producing even greater resistance or strength. If true, then we might assume that there are some self-rules that will be easier to contextualize than others.

Rules that may be highly resistant to change are those that participate in other rules. For example, the rules "do not have sex before marriage" and "I must go to church every Sunday" are both centered around rules of religious virtue. Right and wrong as prescribed by a specific verbal community with traceable roots to Westernized religions. The core belief in this case is that religious adherence is virtuous, and this likely ties into rules about what it means to be a good family member, partner, friend, or member of other communities. A rule like, "I feel guilt" can be easily contextualized as "I feel guilt right now because of this event, but guilt doesn't define me." Rules regarding what it means to be moral or virtuous, however, can be less easy to contextualize.

We can imagine core beliefs visually consistent with the diagram in Figure 10.1, where each point in the geometric space represents a rule, and the closer the proximity of each point, the more the rules cohere with or support adjacent rules. For example, Rule A is likely highly resistant to change because Rule A exists in close proximity to other rules, each with its own history of reinforcement. To contextualize Rule A would require contextualizing related rules B and C as well, which might not be workable, at least not early in the application of self-as-context intervention. On the other hand, Rule L exists further away from other rules. This rule may not cohere as strongly with other rules, and therefore contextualizing this rule could be much more easily accomplished. One of the advantages of using metaphors to illustrate concepts like self-as-context is that rules regarding metaphors do not operate with this same elaborate and extended history and are likely quite distant from core beliefs.

For example, an undergraduate college student is thinking about leaving their home for the first time to go to graduate school. Core beliefs around what it means to be a good family member and to achieve feelings of connectedness are centered around ideas related to spatial proximity to family. That is, to "be closer" means to actually be physically closer. It is easy to see how this rule can become unworkable as the student restricts where they might go to graduate school to only those schools that are in the same city or state. Moreover, upon graduation, this same rule could restrict where the student chooses to pursue a career or to further their education. The chess metaphor challenges the student to consider a chess game where the pieces are the content items (i.e., self-as-content) and the chess board is the context within which the pieces move and change and interchange (i.e., self-as-context). The pieces move around, but the essence of the game remains the same regardless of the spatial position of the pieces at any given time.

When asked to relate this back to this experience, the client may notice that being physically close is *one* way to be close to family. That is one arrangement within which feelings of closeness and connectedness have occurred in the past. But it is not the only way that this value can be achieved now or in the future. Someone can live three blocks away and still can feel very far, whereas someone else can live three states away and feel very close, which adds another contextual dimension. What is more important than being physically close is maintaining that emotional and psychological connection that defines their family, and committing to maintaining and building that relational closeness even if doing so creates physical distance.

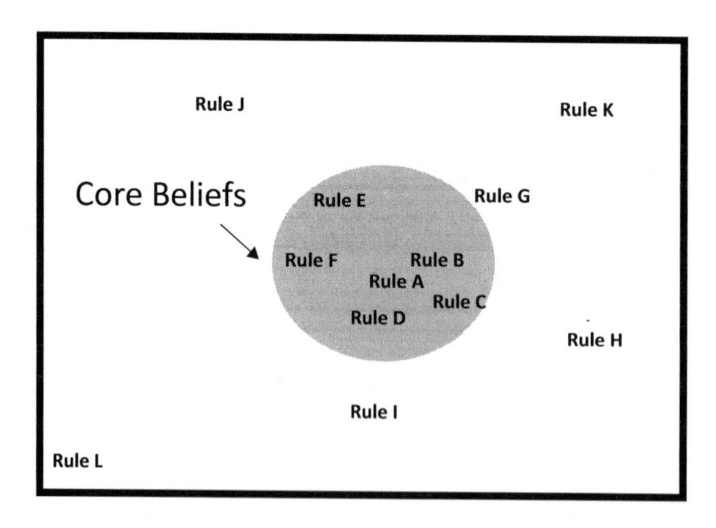

FIGURE 10.1 Core beliefs diagram.

What may be critical when viewing self-rules in this way is that self-conceptualization *can* center around one's chosen values. "I am someone who cares deeply about feeling connected to my family." "I am someone who values advocating for my disability community." Part of values clarification is the identification of core values that can operate as rules that augment committed action. We can therefore recenter content that may be values-inconsistent (e.g., "I must stay close to home") around chosen values (e.g., "I value being connected to family") that may influence decisions of people to support multiple values (i.e., "I can feel close and connected to family while pursuing the career of my dreams").

Self-concept is also closely related to self-identity, such as gender identity, sexual orientation, and other ways in which people identify themselves and their social groups. Again, the critical feature is that one's chosen identity is, in fact, *chosen*. Much like other core beliefs, one's identity is often assigned, such as by assigning gender at birth or assuming straightness within a heteronormative society. When this assigned identity aligns with a person's lived experience and real (not just perceived) valued reinforcers, then identities can be socially helpful. Conversely, when assigned identities fail to align with lived experience and valued reinforcers, such as when one's sexual orientation does not align with a heteronormative view of relationships and intercourse, then we arrive at much the same problem as when core beliefs fail to support personal values. By encouraging exploration of one's identity we are promoting self-as-context, or a flexible view of self that is guided by careful examination of valued reinforcement. In the field of behavior analysis, non-traditional self-identification occurs at higher rates in autistic communities (Cooper et al., 2018; Davies et al., 2021), and self-exploration is something that can and should be supported within ACT-based interventions when inflexible self-identification or rigid attempts to act in ways that are "socially normal" are causing suffering for clients (e.g., Singh et al., 2020; Yadavaia & Hayes, 2012).

Regardless of the content, when we view self-concept as a dense and elaborate network of relational frames that include deictic, hierarchical, and distinction relations, "context" takes on a clear target for intervention. Simply, can we bring context-sensitivity into one's view of themselves? Answering this question is necessary when assessing self-as-context as a dependent process variable within behavioral intervention.

SELF-AS-CONTEXT AS A DEPENDENT VARIABLE

Self-as-context is not only one of the more difficult processes to operationalize (hence the heavy use of metaphors), but it may be one of the more difficult processes to measure. Qualitative measures of verbal statements made by clients could provide a fairly accurate direct measure. For example, self-as-content statements would include "I" rule statements used in conversation, such as "I am __________," or "I must __________." This strategy could also be successful in isolating the specific content that the client is fused to that participates in their psychological inflexibility.

Conversely, the use of qualifying language, especially when that language contains cue words associated with here-there and now-then could indicate self-as-context statements or rules, such as "sometimes I…" or "I feel like ____________ in this context." These strategies are not perfect and probably should not be the targeted outcome of intervention. However, information gained from informally interviewing clients and qualitatively analyzing their responses could provide specific information.

Other more standardized measures also exist to evaluate self-as-context. In addition to the measures that we have already discussed that encompass multiple ACT-related processes, the "Self-As-Context Scale" (SACS; Zettle et al., 2018) provides a brief ten-item inventory of self-related processes. Early psychometric evaluation of the SACS identifies two patterns of behavior: centering and transcending. Centering items are those that are related to acting calmly in response to aversive events. Transcending items measure invariant perspective-taking, which is characteristic of the observing self. Scores on the SACS correlate with measures of psychological flexibility, and the inventory seems especially sensitive to transcendental processes. Items include statements like, "Even though there have been many changes in my life, I'm aware of a part of me that has witnessed it all." Participants then rate the item on a seven-point Likert scale ranging from Strongly Agree to Strongly Disagree. In this way, the degree to which the self-rule coheres with a person's experience can be estimated quickly and can serve as a corollary measure within ACT-based interventions that specifically target self-as-context.

Another measure is the "Self Experiences Questionnaire" (SEQ) which has been primarily evaluated in the context of chronic pain patients but could have useful applications with other populations as well (Yu et al., 2016). The SEQ contains 15 items that appear to cluster into two behavioral processes: self as distinction and self as observer. Scores on both factors have been shown to be predictive of patient functioning for those with chronic pain, suggesting that self-as-context can mediate suffering in the context of persistent painful experiences.

A closely related concept to self-as-context is self-compassion. According to Neff and colleagues (e.g., Neff & Vonk, 2009), self-compassion describes three highly interrelated behavioral repertoires including self-kindness, shared humanity, and mindfulness. Self-kindness is the opposite of self-judgement and occurs when personal struggles are met with understanding and kindness. To illustrate, imagine what you might say to a friend who is struggling. Most of us would say things that are supportive and understanding of the context within which struggle occurs. We respond in ways that are consistent with others-in-context; yet we blame ourselves when we struggle in these same ways. Self-kindness occurs when we can achieve distance and treat ourselves as we might treat a friend or loved one. Shared humanity is the understanding that we all suffer – that suffering is part of being human and can be a shared experience. This sense of shared suffering emerged as a protective factor during the coronavirus pandemic against elevated depression and anxiety during this time (Kavakli et al., 2020). Finally, mindfulness is noticing a response to events here-now. It is clear that deictic relations are at the core of both self-compassion and self-as-context.

One measure of self-compassion in the "Self Compassion Scale" (SCS) and the "Self-Compassion Scale Short Form" (SCS-SF). These scales also provide Likert-type questions that estimate performance in each of these domains of self-compassion, including self-kindness, self-judgement, common humanity, isolation, mindfulness, and overidentification. The SCS-SF shows strong internal consistency and low social desirability bias (Raes et al., 2011). Moreover, the SCS is highly correlated with measures of psychological flexibility and emotional well-being (Marshall & Brockman, 2016).

According to Moran et al. (2018), the concurrent use of the SACS, the SCS, and the Childhood and Adolescent Mindfulness Measure (CAMM) (which we reviewed in earlier chapters) can be used to model three selves: self-as-content, self-as-process, and self-as-context. Because no measure exists to directly measure self-as-content, the researchers used a composite of subscales from the SCS to estimate fusion to a conceptualized self. No measure exists to directly measure self-as-process, which is approximately synonymous with the process of mindfulness (Foody et al., 2015). Therefore, the CAMM was used to estimate self-as-process. Finally, self-as-context was estimated using the SACS. Their results showed that all three measures operated together as a strong predictor of depression in an adolescent sample, supporting this conceptualization of self within ACT-based approaches.

Although not explicitly used in the existing ACT literature, the Questionnaire on Self Transcendence (QUEST; Fishbein et al., 2022) could provide a measure that specifically targets trait experiences of transcendence within contextual cognitive behavioral therapies. The QUEST supports a three-factor structure of trait transcendence that includes intertranscendence, the observing self, and distancing. Intertranscendence is the feeling of connectedness with others and is ancoralogous to a sense of shared humanity within self-compassion. The observing self represents noticing one's own experience as if distinct from the person who is having the experience (i.e., transcendence). Finally, distancing refers to noticing and deliteralizing thoughts and feelings as they occur here and now. Early results of this assessment support the internal structure and factors, as well as correlations with outcomes such as stress, anxiety, and depression.

PROMOTING SELF-AS-CONTEXT AS AN INDEPENDENT VARIABLE

Self-as-context, like the other flexibility processes, is a means to achieve other outcomes or to change behaviors of interest. Two examples that were already given were experiences of depression by adolescents and overall quality of life in individuals experiencing chronic pain. It appears that responding contextually is associated with outcomes like these and potentially other measurable behavior, but how can we encourage self-as-context using behavior change principles?

As mentioned above, metaphors play an important role in establishing self-as-context. This is for at least two reasons. First, rigid conceptualizations of self can be highly resistant to change, where metaphors allow the behavior analyst to build competing patterns of relational responding prior to initiating a conversation about self-concepts. Second, metaphors can allow for experiencing the process of self-as-context beyond an academic understanding of this process. Admittedly, understanding the process academically or descriptively can be challenging, but experiencing self-as-context and transcendence is much less complex. It is something we all experience at some level every single day, even if we do not have a name for it.

Examples of metaphors that we have provided are the house metaphor and the chessboard metaphor. The basic assumption of both is that the content contained in the experience is dynamic and ever-changing, yet something about the context remains constant. These metaphors illustrate the push and pull of self-conceptualization and identity and hold these identifiers loosely and within the framework of chosen values. This basic metaphor can be adapted to cohere with any client's interests. For example, in video games, the levels change and new bosses emerge, yet the hero remains the same and all of these experiences exist in the service of saving the world from evil villains in the game.

Experiential exercises can also be used to bring experiencing self-as-context to life. Luoma et al. (2010) give the example of the observer exercise. Take a moment to do this exercise as you read along.

> Now, I'd like you to take a moment and think back to a memory of something you did this morning, such as eating breakfast or getting ready for work. Take a look around that memory; notice what you were doing and who was there, if anyone. See if you can remember the sights and sounds of this memory...
>
> Now, as you notice this memory, as you observe it, also notice who is noticing...
>
> Now release this memory and travel back in time to find another one – from perhaps a month or a year ago. Once you have found this memory, also take a look around this one. What were the sights and sounds of this memory?

> And again, as you notice this memory, notice who is noticing. Notice there is a "you" there who is observing that you have this memory.
>
> *(p. 175)*

Behavior analysts may be especially adept at using metaphors and experiential exercises at the correct time to influence behavior. For example, self-monitoring data could be used to identify times and contexts where clients are most likely to engage in self-statements that appear inflexible and are predictive of the onset of other challenging behaviors. Given a robust enough assessment, behavior analysts could begin to use self-as-context activities as an antecedent strategy. For example, for the student who engages in self-defeating statements around their academic performance, introducing qualifying statements such as "I am having the feeling I cannot do this" before engaging in studying could increase the amount of time that the student actually spends studying instead of procrastinating.

Deictic relational framing and defusion exercises can also influence self-as-context statements of individuals with disabilities. Garcia-Zambrano et al. (2019) evaluated a combined intervention including a deictic relational training protocol along with a defusion exercise across individuals with disabilities in a control trial evaluation. The experimental group completed the protocol and the control group discussed social skills with the experimenter. Results showed that this intervention was effective in decreasing self-as-content statements and increasing self-as-context statements for the experimental group in the study. This study shows that even brief self-as-context interventions can lead to changes in directly observable behavior.

In intervention packages that target multiple ACT processes, such as the AIM curriculum that we discussed in earlier chapters, activities can be weighted to differentially target self-as-context processes when assessments suggest highlighting this process. In this way, researchers can evaluate how the percentage of intervention allocated to self-as-context processes (e.g., 16%, 50%, or 100%) influences intervention outcomes when looking for broader patterns of behavior change.

Moreover, we can work self-as-context into the ACT matrix by being explicit about the context within which the matrix is being completed. We are used to thinking of processes like values and committed action as relatively fixed processes. However, these too can occur in a context. For example, a person's deepest-held values at home (e.g., connectedness and spending time together) might not be the same values that they hold at work (e.g., producing good work). In fact, feeling overly connected to people in the context of work may be the opposite of what someone values. Consideration of context when completing something like the ACT matrix challenges clients to see themselves through this contextual lens and can augment flexibility when determining committed actions. For example, the same person may engage in actions such as planning a family dinner while also planning the best way to set personal boundaries in their work life. In practice, comparing matrix responses with and without the inclusion of context could be an effective way to target self-as-context as part of a more comprehensive intervention package.

SELF-AS-CONTEXT WITHIN SELF-COMPASSION TRAINING

Considerable research exists in the area of self-compassion training as a theoretical extension of self-as-context processes. These outcomes suggest that self-related processes can be used to influence behavior change (although, self-compassion training necessarily involves mindfulness-based strategies as well). Self-compassion training often takes the form of one or multiple lessons that can be brief in duration (e.g., ten minutes) or extended in duration (e.g., two hours). Training often involves an educational component around the three behavioral repertoires of self-kindness, shared humanity, and mindfulness, as well as experiential exercises designed to practice these skills in session. Participants are then assigned homework to practice the skills in their own lives and to reflect on their performance between sessions.

Despite different forms of self-compassion training, results have shown a variety of positive impacts such as improvements in binge eating (Kelley & Carter, 2015), heart rate variability in perceived social threats experienced by women (Arch et al., 2014), stress and burnout among practicing psychologists (Eriksson et al., 2018), and much more.

Behavior analysts could again extend this by delineating between self-kindness, shared humanity, and mindfulness as potential separate yet interacting behavioral processes (as we have done with the six core ACT processes here). In doing so, functional analytic work applied at the level of the single subject could selectively promote these processes within the context where behavior actually occurs. In this case, self-compassion activities, much like more traditional self-as-context activities, could operate as an antecedent solution to influence target behaviors of interest.

SPIRITUALITY AND A SENSE OF TRANSCENDENCE

When we start talking about self-identity and experiences of transcendence, we inevitably enter into discussions surrounding religion and spirituality. The conventional wisdom in fields like clinical psychology and even behavior analysis is to avoid these topics because they are outside of the ambit of intervention. They are assumed to be something that is sacred to the individual. However, when implementing ACT-based interventions, spirituality and religion could play a large role in the experiences of clients, their successes, as well as their suffering. On the one hand, religion and spirituality can be a value in their own right. Spiritual transcendence has been a part of human cultures as long as there have been human cultures, and organized religion can be a major part of a person's self-conceptualization.

For many clients, religion or spirituality can operate as core beliefs or extended rules that influence a number of behaviors that we are interested in. This is not always a good thing. Many religions have historically operated under patriarchal ruling structures with conceptualized and real social negative reinforcers and punishers for defecting from the status quo. Experiential avoidance can be not only permitted but encouraged in some contexts. Noticing these sources of control may be part of the ACT journey for some clients as they navigate their deepest-held rules and convictions throughout the process.

But it does not have to be all bad. Embedded within most religions are these centralized ideas of transcendence, flexibility, and forgiveness. In Christianity, the idea of grace is similar to the ACT process of acceptance. Where these rules already exist for clients due to religious or spiritual beliefs, there may be inroads to building new behavioral repertoires that build on existing belief systems. Can we as behavior analysts be flexible enough to work with these belief structures, especially when spirituality is identified as something that is highly valued? Can we move from spirituality as a competing value to spirituality as a complementary value?

Hayes et al. (1999) advocate for using spirituality while not necessarily promoting spirituality. It is not our job to change or alter a person's spiritual or religious beliefs, but it is our job to meet our clients where they are and to help them find meaning in their own existence. Examples include the use of religious-based stories in metaphor. Noah's Ark for example provides a clear example of committed action over time to avoid catastrophic negative events later. Religious or spiritual events can also provide an opportunity for self-reflection and self-growth when such reflection occurs in the context of chosen personal values. Finally, there may be utility in deliteralizing rules that are incompatible with chosen values with an emphasis on the context within which those rules may have been developed and operated. How do clients want their spirituality to feel? And when their experiences with spirituality are negative, to rethink the function that spirituality serves in their life and to commit to altering those functions to feel more connected with this value and others.

ANTECEDENT AND CONSEQUENCE STRATEGIES TO PROMOTE SELF-AS-CONTEXT

Because self-as-context involves relational behavior that contextualizes self-statements and self-judgement, antecedents can be placed in the immediate environment to encourage this verbal behavior. For example, the classroom teacher might place a sign in the classroom that says, "Right now I feel ________________ and that is okay." As an antecedent strategy, the teacher might encourage students to openly state how they feel today in this moment and to encourage acceptance and willingness to experience that emotion. The students may also have the option of changing out "that is okay," with "I need help," which would prompt the teacher to either assist with the situation or, even better, to utilize the other ACT-based strategies that we have reviewed so far to help the student to navigate their emotions. This is just an example, but it shows how visual prompts in the environment can be modified to be made ACT consistent to prompt more workable language, in this case centered around self-as-context.

As a setting event, self-as-context exercises can be embedded within the day to help defuse unworkable self-conceptualizations. There are a number of daily lessons within the AIM curriculum that are designed to target self-as-context. For example, in a lesson called "Water Droplet," the instructor draws a droplet of water on the board and the group brainstorms the different forms the droplet can take, such as snow, or ice, or a puddle, and then imagines interacting with the water in different ways. The takeaway from this lesson is that even though the water can take different forms, it is still water. It can be good in the case of addressing thirst, and it can feel bad when it's raining. And despite these evaluations, at the end of the day, it is still just water. In later tiers, learners will relate this back to their own behavior and activities like these are designed to set the occasion for more adaptive forms of relating throughout the day.

We can reinforce more flexible ways of conceptualizing oneself and one's experience socially, and there may be important utility in doing so when self-as-content operates at strength within a behavior-behavior relation. Consider that pliance with these conceptual labels is likely socially mediated (i.e., how others define us) and may be socially convenient for others in the short term but can come at a cost for the individual and for society more broadly in the long term. Many people arrive in the moment with a history of being labeled and conceptualized by others for specific ways and have contacted social reinforcers for behaving consistently with these conceptualizations. By reinforcing the alternative, self-as-context, we are challenging this social narrative around conformity, groupthink, or more broadly nomothetic normalization that has become so commonplace. By socially reinforcing contextualization of these labels, "different" is what's normal, and we can help to create a space that feels safer for people who *are* different. The implications of this within the realm of neurodiversity are obvious and in areas like supporting groups who have been historically disadvantaged because of their identity and/or heredity. What is less obvious is that we are all *different* from one another and we are all *different* from ourselves across time and space. Along with other dimensions of experience, we are also the same as one another and there is that element of transcendence that remains the same within ourselves across time and space. These are the types of relations that we ultimately want to reinforce and build social systems around if we are being ACT-consistent.

COMBINING SELF-AS-CONTEXT WITH PRESENT-MOMENT AWARENESS, ACCEPTANCE, DEFUSION, VALUES, AND COMMITTED ACTION

Self-as-context is deeply embedded within each of the other five core ACT processes. Ultimately, ACT-based interventions are designed to promote greater contextual sensitivity, which requires seeing oneself as dynamic and flexible within an ever-changing context. Present-moment awareness is all about diminishing stimulus control of private verbal experiences about events in the past and the future to augment stimulus control of events happening here and now. "Here and now" are deictic relational frames that specify a context as well as a point in time. We cannot be constantly in the present moment. Reasoning, planning, and problem-solving all require deictic relations about events at other times and other places. Being able to ebb and flow between the self that is here-now and transcendentally experiencing to conceptualizing oneself in the past and future for the purposes of planning and committing is a necessary skill promoted within ACT. Mindfulness is also heavily involved in promoting self-compassion and in strengthening transcendental experience. If experiencing life transcendentally is a generalized operant behavioral repertoire, then mindfulness exercises provide the operant training framework to build it and to promote variability and resistance.

Reflecting on self-as-context can also be an experience that is accompanied by feelings of anxiety, self-criticism, and self-doubt. For example, the spouse who has identified with their role of a hard-working breadwinner may struggle when observing and noticing that their excessive work routine is coming at the cost of time with their family and the formation of deep personal relationships. Their rule of "I must work hard to support my family" has been built over a lifetime of relational frames of what it means to be a good family member and a good partner. Moreover, they have sacrificed opportunities to experience valued reinforcers because of this rule. To even entertain a contextual and values-centered view requires accepting the discomfort of knowing that this way of being cannot last forever. Experiential avoidance can be tempting if a sufficiently strong acceptance repertoire has not yet been developed.

When these core beliefs are likely to lead to experiential avoidance of self-as-context, defusion exercises can help to weaken those rules to prepare for a more contextualized approach to self. Ultimately, defusion is the process through which we promote self-as-context. By defusing the literalized content that we define ourselves by, we can start to notice the context of here-there and now-then where the content is most likely to occur. We can create separation from the observer and the things observed. Self-as-context is all about becoming the master of one's own thoughts and perceptions to identify more abstract and transcendental ways of thinking that are more in line with one's chosen values.

Ultimately, values are the compass with which to orient a contextualized view of self that is sufficiently persistent to allow for flexibility and adaptability in context. Values transcend experience from context to context and moment to moment. Some values are contextually bound, and others are contextually ubiquitous. Identifying those values that exist in all contexts can help clients to identify things in their life that bring about feelings of vitality and purpose.

Finally, engaging in self-as-context, or even self-reflection more broadly, is in itself a committed action. Setting aside the time and space needed to visit and revisit the content and the context of one's life can be a deeply rewarding experience. Mindfulness is also central to experiences of transcendence, where the act of dedicatedly practicing mindfulness is also a committed action. Setting these as targets throughout intervention can help build self-as-context as a generalized behavioral repertoire.

Who we are is a very important question that we all must answer in our time. We cannot ignore the importance of this experiential reflection for the clients that we serve. Even more important is the realization that we can define who we are, and we can continuously redefine who we are, as the situation affords it. Each of the six core processes that we have reviewed builds on one another to promote a way of being that can bring about vitality and situational flexibility. All in the service of living the life that we are all capable of living, and experiencing the life we are all capable of experiencing.

PART 3

Promoting Psychological Flexibility with Clients and in our Field

11

The ACT Assessment Process

The hallmark of behavioral assessment is direct observation of behavior. This characteristic is one that distinguishes the behavioral approach from most others in psychology. That is to say that behavior is not evidence of some internalized construct; rather, behavior *is* the event of interest in its own right.

Overt behavior can often be readily observed in a scientifically accountable way, and the direct observation of overt behavior complete with interobserver agreement has yielded substantial benefits for countless numbers of clients, and for the field of behavior analysis itself. It nevertheless creates a challenge when the full range of behaviors (thinking, feeling, attending, valuing, and so on) are considered.

Skinner opened the door to observing private actions in the very article that first used the term "radical behaviorism" (1945), but in that instance, direct observation begins to show its limitations since it can be limited to an audience of one. That can be true with overt actions as well, since some forms (e.g., drug use, sexual behavior) may not be readily seen or evoked during a relatively short assessment process due to privacy or other contextual factors. When behavior analysts try to deal with private behaviors such as worrying, anxiety, or loneliness, it becomes difficult to link the goal of reliable observation to all scientifically interesting forms of behavior.

One historical solution has been to look for residual observables of such covert behaviors such as the number of tranquilizers taken by a person struggling with anxiety. In theory, this sounds like a rational approach to take but just a brief search for empirical studies on such extensions will reveal that the field has next to nothing to show for the conditions that most human beings struggle with.

In many areas of psychology, most measures are self-report, but treating client self-reports as a sole determiner of overt action can easily threaten the functional utility of the assessment process from a behavior analytic point of view. The problem is not just reliability – after all, parental or caregiver observations can substitute for some aspects of direct observations by behavior analytic staff and sometimes reliability can be checked such as that between parents, but there is still a fear of these reports blending into mere interpretations rather than observations, which also can undermine the integrity of assessment. That shows that the concern is deeper than observation or reliability per se – it is about the need to link assessment, however it is done, to valid functional analyses of actions to direct intervention and support decisions.

If the valid functional analysis of verbally able persons is the target, behavior analytic assessment needs to become more multi-faceted and sophisticated. Based on what we know

DOI: 10.4324/9781003250371-14

about relational operants, the need to somehow assess the possible involvement of private events becomes central – simply because we know that relational framing alters how direct contingencies work. For example, punishers can become conditioned reinforcers due to their participation in relational frames but without any pairing with reinforcement (Whelan & Barnes-Holmes, 2004); stimuli can elicit classically conditioned responses that are greater than those established via direct pairing due to their participant in relational frames alone but controlling for any possible associative basis for that effect (Dougher et al., 2007). This presents a challenge to functional analysis.

Functional analysis was not invented by behavior analysts as we conceptualize that term today in the treatment of aberrant behaviors. The early behavior therapists devised functional analytic approaches to unpacking complex human behavior cast in terms of direct contingencies and social learning processes (e.g., Kanfer & Saslow, 1965; Kanfer & Grimm, 1977). That approach still exists today, although in a more sophisticated form, in clinical psychology (Haynes et al., 2011). In behavior analysis, however, standardized experimental examination procedures have emerged that assess the impact of different kinds of contingencies on objective metrics of behavior. Brian Iwata in particular is credited with the development of this approach, beginning with the analysis of self-injury (e.g., Iwata et al., 1982) and then extending more broadly (Hanley et al., 2003) that we discussed earlier. It has become the most common contemporary assessment approach of functional analysis or functional assessment in behavior analysis. Behavior analysts are quite proud of these methods, but their historical roots in clinical psychology are often forgotten.

Behavior analysts have enjoyed their own constricted variety of what a functional analysis is but once the focus expands to include more verbally capable clients, that history becomes more relevant. As soon as verbal abilities pass a certain point, an adequate analysis of human functioning cannot succeed without a parallel analysis of relational abilities. For example, a standard empirical functional analysis can be successfully used to categorize human behavior in most children showing problem behaviors until they can successfully derive mutually entailed relations – after that, using the standard tools deployed by board certified behavior analysts (BCBAs), the functions of problem behaviors are three-and-a-half times less likely to be successfully categorized (Belisle et al., 2017). Said in another way, relational operants have forced the field of behavior analysis to confront how it is possible to study behavior-behavior relations as a central topic, but without the emergence of mentalism or the loss of a pragmatic view of causality linked to experimental manipulation. Because of that overall purpose, the inclusion of self-reports, the reports of others, the assessment of relational skills, the assessment of implicit relational actions, and so on need to come not at the expense of direct observation of overt behavior, but rather as a parallel supplemental source of information that may enhance the overall assessment process.

If the field of behavior analysis is going to live up to the aspirational goal of a comprehensive account of human behavior, the quest for understanding all human behavior will have to be re-invigorated and the assessment approach will need to evolve. process, in which we discover the various conditions under which a specific behavior occurs, will have to expand. It is naïve to think that many of the maladaptive behaviors we struggle with, from excessive eating, drug use, and gambling, to depression, would readily be evoked in a ten-minute functional analysis based on conditions contrived by an experimenter that distill actions down to four possible reinforcers: tangible, escape, attentional, or intrinsic. Perhaps this is why such data have yet to exist – the methods do not match the behaviors of concern. This is of grave concern if we define our entire field by this singular procedure as many do – the consequence is that our range of application is restricted to only those challenges maintained by those four immediate reinforcers. That isn't a comprehensive field.

Fortunately, direct observation of most of these behaviors is clearly possible, but most if not, all may be hindered by an assessor's presence, social contingencies, or the limited time allocated for assessment, and most if not all likely involve private events. To stop the cycle of omitting the presenting challenges of so many people and move forward towards the aspiration of becoming a "science of (all) human behavior," a multi-level multi-dimension assessment process will need to replace the antiquated ideal of direct observation of overt behavior or bust.

In what follows we will give advice for how behavior analysts can practice inside the expanded set of issues human relational framing demands. Grey boxes show clinical examples of our recommendations. We will also periodically point to areas where future research will be needed but filling in those gaps will require years of hard work by the field itself. Our concerns here are more immediate and practical. Thus, all of these recommendations should be tempered by a "try it and see" attitude that is held to account by actual client progress as is revealed in overt behavior.

INITIAL ASSESSMENT OF A CLIENT

When considering if a client may benefit from acceptance and commitment therapy (ACT), the first step is to determine if the person's repertoire is sophisticated enough to reap the benefits of a talk-based intervention. A simple query to the caregiver about whether the client ever speaks about the past or the future (in any modality) or takes the perspective of another may provide insight as to the degree to which relational behavior is an existing part of the repertoire. If the answer is less than clear, say along the lines of "sometimes" or "a little bit," this alone does not mean that ACT will be too advanced or inapplicable; however, the expectations for ACT, the delivery method of ACT, and supplemental remediations to build a more complex language repertoire will need to be considered as part of the treatment package.

During the initial meeting with parents, it was concluded that the client frequently speaks about events distant in time and place or takes the perspective of others – indicating a potential match between client and the ACT treatment approach.

Although parents requested a possible treatment involving the usage of ACT, it is clear that the client's behavior remains almost exclusively under direct contingency control.

Beyond the initial subjective appraisal of language complexity, the intake process will likely need to include a series of questionnaires, semi-structured interview, and direct interaction with the client. Some of this work can be done by stakeholders prior to the initial meeting, while others benefit from completion live within the proposed treatment environment. This multi-model assessment approach allows for a more contextually centered functional assessment in which the behavior analyst can render an informed direction for treatment.

Another means to evaluate the potential for ACT to serve as an effective treatment model is to directly appraise the degree to which the client can derive relations among stimuli. This is even more precise than probing for speaking, where the ability to derive simple relations is likely the minimum requirement. That is, ACT intervenes in derived relational processes, thus if one cannot derive relations, there should be no expected benefit to this kind of interventions. This ability sits at the foundation of ACT and depending on the depth of a client's ability to actually derive, may mitigate how much understanding a talk-based treatment may have on resulting behaviors. One way this task may be accomplished is by using a direct test of relational skills. The PEAK Comprehensive Assessment (PCA; Dixon, 2019) Transformation Subtest may serve as an effective tool, as it identifies the strength of six types of relational frames and takes approximately 15 minutes to administer. If results reveal the client has little ability to derive stimulus relations, remediation of such deficits may be necessary prior to ACT-based treatments. Recent evidence suggests that a sequential approach can be useful, in which relational framing is strengthened before ACT itself is used (Gilsenan et al., 2022). Other non-standardized appraisals of relational repertoires are also possible whereby the therapist simply constructs certain relations among stimuli and then evaluates if the client has the ability to derive novel relations among those same stimuli or transform the response to solve another verbal puzzle.

Administration of the PCA (Dixon, 2019) provided supplemental insight into the relational repertoire of Candice, thus allowing for a determination as to her ability to engage in relevant relational tasks that form the basis of an ACT intervention. Her scores on the PCA's Transformation Module (expressive/receptive) were: Coordination (15/16); Opposition (12/9); Distinction (14/12); Comparison (5/4); Hierarchy (11/5); and Deictic (4/5). These scores indicate a fair degree of relational abilities with greatest strengths in coordination and distinction and relative weaknesses in comparisons and deictic framing.

A series of tasks were delivered to Jobo whereby stimuli were arranged to teach an A-B relation, a B-C relation, and evaluate the ability of the client to infer an A-C and C-A relation. Stimuli used for A were three spoken words, B were pictures of items, and C were 3-dimensional items. Jobo was unsuccessful at speaking the A response in the presence of a C stimulus item, and minimally successful selecting a C stimulus when presented with an A stimulus from the evaluator.

CAREGIVER INTERVIEW PRIOR TO CLIENT ARRIVAL

The presenting conditions of the client are typically certain types of overt behavioral excesses or deficits. If these are not articulated by the caregiver upon initial contact, it would be wise for the behavior analyst to attempt to discover the behavior of concern. If this line of questioning is met with "my son could use ACT I have been told," or "someone recommended ACT because my child is not flexible," or "I think my daughter is stressed," the behavior analyst should follow up with questioning about the actual overt behavior that results as an effect of the interpretive processes or constructs the caregiver is bringing to the situation. Interpretations are not observations, so questions about "what happens when" are key to transforming caregiver concerns into behavioral targets. If there are no overt behavioral outcomes of the supposed condition, it may be wise to decline further services or to refer to other professionals. Perhaps there are times to use ACT as a treatment for, say, obsessive thoughts alone, but it will be difficult to justify to third-party payers and appears to reside outside the scope of applied behavior analysis (ABA) at the present time. That is especially the case when concerns are being raised by caregivers and not clients themselves. Even in clinical psychology, ACT providers are reluctant to intervene with targets that never touch on habits of values-based actions.

If it is determined that behaviors indeed are manifesting in ways that might benefit from ACT interventions, the caregiver should be given a series of additional questions that continues to tap into the functional relations that surround these behaviors. A number of semi-structured interviews are readily available that are easy to administer and have caregivers complete. The Functional Assessment Interview (FAI) and the Open-Ended Functional Assessment Interview are two commonly used tools to identify the causes which may in part underly behavior challenges.

The perspective we have taken throughout this book is that once human beings begin to talk, derive stimulus relations, and referentially transcend time, place, and person in their perspective-taking skills, direct contingency control cannot be assumed to fully explain overt behavior. Additionally, the behavior analyst must take into account how language interacts with contingencies. Thus, the functional clarity of any presenting condition will necessitate unpacking the verbal contributions of the client.

In order to do this, the behavior analyst first needs to determine how complex the client's language repertoire actually is. Does the client speak in complete sentences? Do they understand metaphor? Is empathy towards others ever shown? Questions such as these help complete the picture as to the degree to which relational responding can influence the contingencies surrounding the behavior. Whether the clinician uses these types of questions directed at a parent, or crafts their own probes directly with the client, their purpose is to determine the relative fit of the client's repertoire to the ACT approach. If significant deficits in language are indicated across many of such items, it is highly probable that a more traditional ABA intervention that focuses on direct contingency manipulations may be sufficient to produce treatment gains and is the place to start.

A series of questions regarding language complexity were administered to Sasha's mother on 3/1/2022 and resulted in positive endorsements on 13 of 16, which suggests that Sasha most likely has existing language skills that are necessary for understanding the ACT treatment approach.

Upon direct observation of the client in their special education classroom it is concluded that Toyna fails to follow multi-step directions consistently. Upon my direct probing of what she had for lunch just an hour ago, Toyna could not answer and appeared to not understand the question being presented to her. I also told her a basic joke about chickens. She did not appear to understand any elements of the joke. It remains uncertain if basic precursors for understanding an ACT treatment are currently existing within her repertoire.

MEETING THE CLIENT AND RECORDING THE OBSERVATIONS

The initial client meeting provides the behavior analyst with ample opportunity to strengthen or modify the existing hypotheses regarding functional control over behavior. At the onset of this meeting, the clinician should have obtained some information about possible controlling environmental variables, language complexity, and the relative interaction between the two. These pre-meeting assumptions should be held lightly, as there is no substitute for direct interaction with the client.

Upon meeting, begin interaction at the hypothesized level of verbal complexity. That is, if the caregiver has reported the client does not understand humor or sarcasm, be careful not to lead into the meeting with such utterances. Furthermore, if it is disclosed that the client often engages in escape behavior, be careful to not introduce too many intense demands from the get-go. Such soft skills are often difficult to define and vary in each client-therapist dyad. Take note of the subtle interaction characteristics that may provide confirmation or negation to what has been previously disclosed.

This initial meeting is a prime opportunity to record your own observations about the client both formally and informally. There may be value in using frequency or interval recording of overt behaviors as well as vocal utterances that may address underlying functional relations of the behavior. Data sheets that incorporate a more direct approach to identifying function, such as ABC data sheets, may also be of utility. Do not forget the value of informal impressions and how they can play a role in understanding the presenting problem behaviors. Sometimes insight can come from the overall experience of interacting with a client, the subtle statements, mannerisms, and affect. These soft data should not be dismissed, but rather placed within the entirety of a contextual understanding of the behavior.

Psychological flexibility processes can often be functionally inferred from a variety of overt behaviors. Here are concrete examples in each of the flexibility areas. Not all of these apply to clients at a given stage of development, and thus expectations need to be adjusted by mental age and verbal capacity.

Emotional Inflexibility

The verbal community teaches people to speak in terms of "emotions" as a way of becoming more sensitive to direct contingencies that may not be easy to describe in a rule form. For example, if the goal is to tell others whether food will function as a reinforcer it is easier and more generally useful to teach a child to say "I'm hungry" when that is the case than to speak of how many minutes or hours there has been a period of food deprivation. After all, sometimes, such as when a favorite food is available, "hunger" can be present even with short periods of food deprivation. At other times, such as after a friend has just profoundly disappointed you, food will not function as a reinforcer even after a long period of food deprivation ("I'm just not hungry" is a common statement after major disappointments). Thus, being able to speak about emotions is critical to social functioning.

Overt behavioral indications of difficulties in this area include acting in avoidant ways (withdrawing socially, being totally silent, running away, fighting, and so on) when aversive events or reminders of them appear. If the client has been avoiding for a long time (or if they grew up in an environment in which social training regarding emotions was impoverished) they may be alexithymic, and thus be unable to describe motivational conditions using emotional terms. For example, the client will not be able to say when he or she is hungry, afraid, angry, disappointed, and so on. Alexithymia predicts a number of psychological difficulties because much of our cultural knowledge about what to do in a given situation is delivered using emotional terms. Another form of emotional inflexibility is being unable to differentiate emotions (e.g., the person cannot distinguish fearful responses from angry ones; or sexual arousal from disgust; and so on); yet another is not being able to use emotional information to guide action (e.g., cannot say what to do when afraid).

Cognitive Inflexibility

A similar analysis applies to self-talk. Public forms of overt reasoning and problem-solving gradually become covert. It is possible in problem-solving tasks to ask clients to say aloud what they are thinking and then to score these protocols for reasoning skills. This method was first used by John B. Watson. In extraordinary circumstances with the proper sets of controls (the so-called "silent dog" method: see Hayes, 1986; Hayes et al., 1998) it is even arguably possible to know if these self-reports are actually what the person was thinking despite the normal wall of privacy that surrounds private events. In thumbnail form, the "silent dog" logic applies when continuously talking aloud does *not* impact performance compared to baseline, even though these transcripts are talk-relevant and they *do* impact the behavior of others on the same task, and furthermore talking aloud *does* impact performance if any one of a number of disruptions of continuous talk aloud is deployed, such as telling the person not to speak and then to summarize thoughts that occurred over the last few minutes. If all controls line up in that way, the only plausible reason that continuous talk aloud did not change performance compared to doing nothing is that even when the person is doing nothing they're still privately talking to themselves in a functionally similar way (thus the name "silent dog," after the Sherlock Holmes story, in which it was the absence of a bark by the watch dog that gave the telling clue to the mystery). Implicit relational frame theory (RFT) measures of cognition, such as the Mixed Trials Implicit Relational Assessment Procedure (MT-IRAP: Levin et al., 2010) or Function Acquisition Speed Test (FAST: O'Reilly et al., 2012) can also be used to assess cognitive networks.

When clients have problems in the area of cognitive inflexibility, they will state cognitive errors without awareness, or will show repetitive forms of talk about their own private events; and they may argue easily about who is right. In conversations, new facts will disappear into frequently stated formulations. Some of these formulations can be deliberately probed verbally by the change agent. For example, if a client is obsessed with thoughts of being inadequate, any mention of the success of others might evoke tantrums.

Attentional Inflexibility

The capacity to augment or diminish stimulus control by narrowing, broadening, shifting, or maintaining an attentional focus is key to flexible behavior in a variety of contexts. This skill can be assessed by noticing where clients look, or what they focus on. A client may fail to notice obvious sounds or visual events or may perseverate on specific stimulus events. Verbal statements about the past or future may lead to a lessened capacity to notice present events. Standardized attentional tasks (e.g., computerized signal detection tasks, table-top letter detection tasks, and so on) can also be used.

Sense of Self

A failure to be able to report events from a consistent perspective or point of view can result in inconsistent verbal reports, the inability to understand social stories, and an apparent lack of empathy or compassion. The client may be unable to take your perspective or to describe their own. Conversely, entanglement with a narrative or "storied" sense of self may result in rigidity across settings, such as with a client who must always play or must always wear certain clothes.

Lack of Values-Based Motivation

When values-based motivation is weak, the client's motives may be bound up with compliance, avoidance, or rigid rule-following. Present action may seem purposeless, and the client is unable to say why in any detail they are engaging in present action. The client may not be able to describe why heroes are looked up to or why guides give good advice.

Lack of Committed Action

The client may show a relative lack of say-do correspondence. They may avoid making promises or fail to keep them. Behavior may be characterized by an action, procrastination, or impulsivity.

During the initial meeting with Pepe it was observed that he engaged in nine instances of verbal outbursts, six of which specified irrational worries about an upcoming band concert.

Utilization of ABC data sheets during initial assessment indicated a potential relationship between diverted attention to parents and emission of the problem behavior.

After one hour of direct interaction with Splike, he remained unable to emit any response related to prior events outside of the evaluation context.

CLIENT AND CAREGIVER ASSESSMENT TASKS DURING INITIAL MEETING

Both the client and their respective caregiver should remain occupied with a variety of tasks to complete during the initial meeting. The caregiver will likely need to complete agency or school paperwork, releases of information, and background information. Additionally, this time is ideal for the caregiver to also complete a wide range of surveys or questionnaires that are designed to add to the totality of information necessary to complete a comprehensive functional assessment. Some of these instruments may examine the environmental conditions that evoke behavior, and others may address the role language has in mitigating or facilitating challenging behavior. There may also be value in examining the current state of the caregiver – their stress level, anxiety, or perceived competency to handle the presenting problem. Keep in mind that the caregiver is never the client in these kinds of situations, they are a potential agent of change that can either help or hinder the behavior analyst's treatment program. The client themselves will have the opportunity to generate important data for the behavior analyst. A mix of self-report scales, observed naturalistic performance, and direct assessments are all possible domains to consider. The scope of what the client can contribute in terms of data will be somewhat dependent on their level of functioning.

ACT-RELEVANT SELF-REPORT SCALES

A wide range of possible assessments is possible during the meeting with the potential client. We overviewed several in the previous chapters. Self-report scales that attempt to evaluate psychological flexibility and mindfulness skills such as the Childhood and Adolescent Mindfulness Measure (CAMM) or the Child Psychological Flexibility Questionnaire (CPFQ) can allow for examination of the child's relative strengths and weaknesses across the Hexaflex processes. A caregiver version of the CPFQ also allows for someone other than the client to provide insight into the flexibility processes. There are a number of other tools that target a single process of the Hexaflex and may be of greater utility if a certain focused treatment approach has been requested (e.g., improve values; reduce fusion; enhance self-as-context and perspective taking).

This whole area is moving quickly – far too fast for a book to capture without becoming dated almost instantly. If you go to the measurement section of the Association for

Contextual Behavioral Science (ACBS) website (https://contextualscience.org/actspecific_measures) you will see measures in 48 different languages; a dozen or more different measures for youth and children; and scores of measures for parents, staff, and other adults.

Interpreting these self-reports through a behavior-analytic lens takes a bit of skill. First, the items listed, as well as the inferred outcome (flexibility, mindfulness, self-awareness) cannot be considered the final dependent variable of interest. The behavior of concern must continue to remain the outcome of these processes. Be careful of focusing an intervention on a self-report score – instead, as a behavior analyst, use the self-report score and items to orient you toward actions and their context. This strategy is not new. The FAI and Open-Ended FAI are both self-report instruments that are used to orient behavior analysts to functional analysis methods that are direct. That is the same thing here – with many more options and necessitating a deeper understanding of the core processes covered sequentially in the previous six chapters.

Some newer self-report instruments are deliberately worded to refer to behavior only, and some of these have been established not by classical psychometrics but rather by identifying individual items that orient practitioners towards psychological flexibility processes and how they change over time. An example is the Process-Based Assessment Tool (Ciarrochi et al., 2022). It is a kind of file drawer full of individual items that are meant to be used in daily diaries or even more frequently, primarily by teenagers or adults who are higher functioning. Examples of items are "I did things only because I was complying with what others wanted me to do" or "I struggled to keep doing something that was good for me." Items of that kind are interpreted by the complex networks they form over time with both other items and with objectively assessed behavior.

Ronald was administered the AFQ-Y (Acceptance and Fusion Questionnaire for Youth) on 1/19/22 and obtained a score of 19. This indicates a high degree of rigidity with language. In other words, Ronald responds very literality to language from others, and most likely his own self-generation of rules and instructions.

Pam received a total score of 12 on the CPFQ (Childhood Psychological Flexibility Questionnaire). This score is lower than most neurotypical children of her age, revealing less flexibility (more rigidity) with thoughts. Subtest scores on Present Moment and Defusion were the lowest at 2 and 3 respectively, thus indicating potential for frequent distractibility away from stimuli and instructions in the current environment and increased referential behavior that may serve to augment challenging behaviors.

CHALLENGING BEHAVIOR SALES

Over the past couple of decades, a number of challenging behavior scales have become available for stakeholders to report possible controlling variables. These include the Questions About Behavior Function (QABF), the Motivation and Assessment Scale (MAS), Challenging Behavior Index (CBI, Dixon, 2019), and others. Although each varies to a slight degree on the number and types of questions asked, the general theme remains constant – a series of questions are presented on a Likert scale for a caregiver to rate the degree to which the statement accurately depicts a condition in which the behavior problem is evoked.

The general expectation is that a questionnaire is inferior to direct observation. This may indeed be true in most instances, especially if high-frequency behaviors are readily observed, however that logic does not hold as firmly if behaviors are of extremely low frequency or evoked under sporadic conditions. Thus, the value of such scales remains high for the behavior analyst who is unlikely to see much direct observation of a behavior problem during a brief office visit. In contrast to the ACT-type measures noted above, the challenging behavior scales have been exclusively developed for someone other than the client to complete.

Mary's challenging behavior of extreme aggressive outbursts has been reported by caregivers to occur less than one time per week. As a result, direct observation of this behavior was unlikely to occur during an intake session and parents were provided copies of the QABF to complete.

Negative self-statements typically occur in the home when in presence of her sister. Jaki's office visit yielded no instances of behavior; thus, her mother was asked to complete a FAST).

Depending on necessity, the clinician may deem it necessary to further explore challenging behavior causes through the use of interviews and synthesized functional analyses (Jessel et al., 2019). These supplemental measures may provide confirmation of hypotheses or reveal subtle characteristics that the standard questionnaires failed to detect. Again, if a traditional antecedent-behavior-consequence analysis is sufficient in its totality to explain the behaviors of concern, there may be reasonable doubt for continuing to pursue an ACT-based treatment. Or ACT-based approach should supplement a clear contingency-management system that is based on the identified function. Regardless of form or technique used, the functional assessment scale scores can serve as a dependent variable by which to measure treatment efficacy.

Some recent work suggests that the traditional way of identifying a behavioral function becomes less clear once a client begins to demonstrate derived relations (Belisle et al., 2017). Once mutually entailed stimulus relations are shown, it appears much more likely that behavior rating scales may reveal multiple possible controlling variables. For example, the non-compliance behavior of concern may be the product of attention seeking at sometimes and escape from demands at other times. Language adds a layer of complexity here, as the contingencies are constantly interacting with a verbal repertoire that may exert varying degrees of influence over that three-termed contingency. Therefore, if scores on a measure of derived relational responding are high, caregivers report having conversations with the learner, the above-listed self-report measures highlight sources of psychological inflexibility, and more traditional measures fail to yield a singular or even a synthesized function – there's a good chance private events are involved.

In conclusion, behavior scales have value, just not exclusive value in the assessment process.

Due to Scott's language complexity as measured by the PCA (Dixon, 2019), it was concluded that there was a very likely verbal influence on the ABC contingencies that were revealed on the QABF, necessitating a careful approach towards inferring a single behavior function for his property destruction.

A synthesized functional assessment coupled with relational testing concludes that the most likely cause for problem behavior is attention, which is influenced considerably by relational responding that results in thoughts about his abusive father.

TIMELINE FOLLOWBACK BASELINE

When a client is in need of treatment, it is extremely difficult to request that stakeholders refrain from intervention solely to provide an accurate baseline of challenging behaviors. Rather than rely strictly on a narrative that states present levels of behavior, it may be wise to consider the use of a timeline followback baseline. This technique is similar to a traditional baseline, except the time intervals for recording are placed backwards in time. Caregivers then estimate the approximate challenges which occurred during that time period. For example, if the client is planned for sessions once per week, this retroactive baseline might have weekly intervals going back two to three months identified for estimation. It is assumed that such data are treated with caution, as one's memory may not be completely accurate. Nonetheless, such an analysis does provide additional insight into the severity and frequency of the problem behavior as well as a benchmark which to measure treatment effects against. Furthermore, such data may be critical when attempting to seek authorization for treatment, as they provide a metric of the severity of the presenting problems and the need for intervention.

Due to urgency for treatment, a retroactive baseline was established by caregivers for the prior two weeks before this intake meeting. The resulting data estimated 15 episodes of property destruction across this timeframe, ten of which were emitted following a demand placed on Sista. The most common consequence noted for Sista was verbal redirection and likely demand delay/removal.

A series of ABC data sheets were provided to the grandmother to generate a timeline fallback baseline from the past week. The target behavior was negative self-statements that were at least of ten seconds in duration. Estimated controlling variables included diverted attention to older brother, and when left alone in a room while other tasks were being done by the grandmother. It is inferred at this time that attention-seeking may be a probable function sustaining the behavior.

RECORDS REVIEW FOR POTENTIAL CONTROLLING VARIABLES

Another important factor to consider when conducting a comprehensive functional assessment is the client's relevant records. These documents may be quite extensive if a comprehensive physical and psychological workup was completed at an earlier stage, or they may be sparse if the client is new to services or is of a very young age. Plan on spending time actually reading them, as it is possible that a single line of text on a single page within a mirid of files could hold an important key to better understanding the reasons for the presenting challenging behaviors. Too often behavior analysts take such documents as unnecessary or of limited value when compared to direct observation, but this firmly is not the case. Other peoples' impressions, tests, and data are extremely important, if nothing else to discover which attempts have failed in the past, the average length of treatment, and the amount and variation of services – all of which may impact the resulting approach you take with intervention.

Obtaining records can be challenging and their arrival may come at a point in time during assessment in which decisions have already been made in their absence. Again, it is important that such records are incorporated into the clinical decision-making process regardless of their volume or insight. At a minimum. any treatment authorization request should contain a section of text which summarizes prior records and includes a synopsis of how such history has been integrated into the current assessment process.

From a review of the existing files on Ronald that were provided by his physician, aggressive behavior has been occurring for the past three years on a weekly basis.

Due to the lack of obtaining prior records from Sandra's school district, the totality of this assessment is based on the current evaluation procedures by the behavior analyst.

Moreover, as behavior analytic methods continue to emerge in a variety of clinical areas existing assessments and diagnostic content will be available that can provide important information. For example, when working with children with ADHD, inattentiveness and hyperactivity can occur independently or concurrently with obvious implications for ACT-based intervention. If a client is diagnosed as clinically inattentive (i.e., well outside of a normal attentiveness range), then present-moment training will likely be both difficult and highly necessary along with a more robust functional analysis of the conditions within which attention and inattention are likely to occur. For a client who is hyperactive, acceptance and a willingness to experience their urges to act even when doing so gets in the way of valued outcomes will likely be both challenging and necessary. The more domains behavior analysts step into, the more familiar we will have to become with existing tools and diagnostic strategies in those areas and understanding that these too can help orient intervention. Consider that "autism" is also a clinical diagnosis and much of our functional analysis and intervention technologies evolved to support individuals with autism through things like social skills training and communication support. Interventions will not necessarily look the same with other populations because their problems may not be the same as those with autism – nonetheless that their behavior operates as an adaptation to their environment opens the door for functional analysis as we have defined it above.

POST-MEETING ASSIGNMENTS FOR CLIENT AND CAREGIVER TO OBTAIN ACTUAL BASELINES

Following the initial meeting with the client and caregiver, it is advantageous to provide each with some follow-up data collection. Caregivers should be given a simplified A-B-C type of data sheet in which they are to record instances of challenging behaviors that occur, along with the conditions which immediately precede and follow such occurrences. It would be preferred that such a data sheet contain checkboxes rather than open-ended categories which allow for narratives to be generated. Checkboxes are less effort, and the checks can be quantified in terms of frequencies. The lack of subjective writing also improves the objectivity of the data gathered. Following a sufficient period of time, these data can be returned to the behavior analyst for contribution towards the final functional assessment. Frequency counts or interval scoring may be considered as alternatives to an ABC sheet; however, these tools only produce rates of behavior and speak little if anything to the underlying controlling variables.

Additional value can be acquired when such data include brief examples of the language that the client is emitting during the behavioral episode, and/or caregivers are emitting when the behavior is triggered or attempted to be intervened upon. Identifying the formal structures of these narratives will be difficult, thus even some antidotal examples can help provide a layer of the cooccurring verbal behavior that participates in conjunction with the environmental continencies. For example, if a work demand from the teacher is accompanied by a statement such as "make sure you do your best on this test because it is half of your grade" or "I think you have had enough iPad for today, now do your work," a dissection of content can occur. In the first statement, the teacher is stating a performance and what may be a value to the client – their course grade. In the second statement, no value is mentioned which can be obtained, rather only a low preferred task. Utterances from the client are equally important. For example, "I don't want to be alone" may indicate the reinforcing value of social attention, and "I don't care about recess, I hate you" suggests a discounting of delayed reinforcers and potential negative social attention functions. Furthermore, this latter statement may illustrate a lack of identified values which may promote remaining more flexible with thoughts such as hate.

If the client is of appropriate cognitive capacity and in compliance with a data collection task, there may be advantages for the client themselves to record some of their own behavior. In addition to the observable elements which could mirror those provided by the caregivers, it may be possible for the client to self-report their own thoughts and feelings during the emission of challenging behavior. For example, following the property destruction of a classroom, the client could be asked to recall if they lost contact with the present moment, if they couldn't get a thought out of their head, if they lost track of what really mattered to them, or if they felt upset and were trying hard to remove such feelings. These broad categories will likely need to be honed for a specific client's functioning level. Such themes of questioning can potentially reveal elements of the Hexaflex that are participating in the functional relations surrounding the maladaptive behavior, and thus should be targeted for intervention. Self-monitoring can also be considered one aspect of the intervention that begins immediately by helping to orient the client's awareness of their own behavior and to the contingencies that surround it. ACT, then, can provide the strategies to work more effectively with those contingencies once realized as part of a broader self-management and skills training intervention.

THE PRIVATE CONVERSATION WITH THE CAREGIVER

When circumstances permit, it is wise to have a separate conversation with the caregiver on ways in which more optimal reporting on their part could occur. This caregiver may have had little to no experience with ACT or how certain ways of speaking to the client could strengthen psychological inflexibility. When presented with concerns from the client on not feeling happy, it is easy enough to think the optimal way to respond would be along the lines of "you are ok, and you should be happy." This seemingly benign phrase is really working against flexibility, as it speaks to the inappropriateness of the thought and contains a directive for the client to remove it from their repertoire. Instead of weakening the dominance of such a self-rule, a statement like that from the caregiver is likely strengthening its literal meaning along with implying flaws in the client for not being able to delete it from their thinking.

Data collection should be encouraged immediately, and this may continue to take the form of ABCs, frequencies, or informal narratives. What should be paramount for the behavior analyst when choosing modality of data is the probably of both getting assessment compliance and assessment accuracy from the caregiver. There is always a more complex and refined way to improve upon data collection, but a common mistake is to let perfect become the enemy of the good. You cannot score and use an assessment you do not have. It is better to take a realistic stance on compliance and get data as compared to demanding optimal measurement that is impossible to collect. When a caregiver is given a data collection assignment, a considerable effort needs to be put in place to manage and reinforce such an activity. Most ACT-related conditions that necessitate intervention will be focused on relatively lower frequencies than behaviors typical of those who are less verbally sophisticated. That raises a serious possible reality – your client may never display the problem behavior of concern within your presence. This is especially true with outpatient care, and as such, you may need to exclusively rely on your caregiver to provide the needed data to make clinical decisions. As a result, make sure you provide ample training and emphasize the importance of such data right from the start of the relationship.

Table 11.1 shows a modified ABC narrative that we adapted to add an analysis of private events to the standard ABC narrative. It adds antecedent "Private Thoughts and Feelings" that occur prior to or during the behavior and following the consequences of the behavior. The external columns define an external contingency, which may also help explain the occurrence of private events. This is similar to the ACT Matrix but applied in real-time, which may reveal functional patterns that are not easily captured in a single moment or conversation. It is also similar to classical "thought records" in cognitive behavior therapy, but the last column is different. It asks for evidence of contextual processes that may help explain why the public and private events are related. That final contextual step is the key to avoiding mentalism. Thoughts and feelings are private behaviors – they are not causes of behavior – but they can be functionally related to behavior if social or other contextual events create a context in which that occurs. That is exactly what psychological flexibility and inflexibility are all about.

For example, results could reveal a pattern of a romantic partner in the context of an argument (external antecedent) having thoughts that their partner does not care about them, and when these are taken literally, having intense fears that their partner may soon abandon them. Statements of reassurance or expressions of caring by their partner could reduce that fear and the aversive qualities of those thoughts, and raising one's voice in the past may have led to such outcomes. The external consequence is that their partner attends to them more and they have the thought that their partner does in fact care about them and they feel relieved. As a result of this contingency, yelling has been increasing and their relationship is deteriorating. Alternative, relationship-enhancing behaviors might be available, but they are not at strength once fear is in the room (such as saying "I get afraid and feel very

TABLE 11.1

External Antecedent	*Private Thoughts and Feelings*	*External Behavior*	*External Consequences*	*Private Thoughts and Feelings*

Hypothesized External Contingency:
Hypothesis Flexibility Process:
Hypothesized Social-Verbal Contingency:

vulnerable when we argue because you are very important to me. And then I tend to yell – which creates an ugly moment. Would you just sit with me for a moment before we continue so I can find a way forward that is more like how I really want to be in our relationship?"). The final column might include such contextual features as taking thoughts of abandonment literally; avoiding feelings of vulnerability; or being unclear about relationship values. Psychological flexibility processes will often be of use and will point to these contextual features that are establishing a behavior-behavior relationship between private and public behaviors. If this is a common theme across multiple observations, then the intervention must also consider the private experiences and contextual processes that are turning normal disagreements into relationship-threatening forms of communication.

THE PRIVATE CONVERSATION WITH THE CLIENT

When you are closing the initial meeting with the client, make sure you provide an assurance you are going to try to help them. The depth of this conversation will be dictated by their general level of understanding of the meaning behind such dialogue; however, if you have concluded the person is right for an ACT intervention, it would be most appropriate to confirm to them your willingness to help. When working with children it is even more important to emphasize that the intervention will be fun and enjoyable; nothing that will produce a great degree of anxiety. Even adult clients need some assurance that treatment will be something that is pleasing, not a burden. Without such reassurance, the odds of success will likely be reduced.

Depending on the context of care, an additional dialogue can center around your level of confidentiality, duty to warn, and coordination of information with other professionals. Complex narratives on this content can be done with highly cognitively advanced clients and differentiated phrasing can be used as necessary. For example, explaining the duty to warn parameters to a young child could be modified by saying something along the lines of "we will keep all we talk about secret between us, unless I am really worried about your safety or someone else's." To make sure these matters are covered properly, comprehensive details around the scope of responsibilities can be put into a template for caregivers with content modified for certain client-types to create an assent process for delivery of care.

Developing rapport with the client is critical and must start at the first interaction. This rapport is more complex than stimulus-pairing, whereby the clinician is linked to a wide range of tangible and edible reinforcers. Client rapport involves a genuine interest from the clinician in the client. It requires listening, responding, attending, and caring. Be flexible with the amount of content to cover in any given session – including the initial intake. Instead, take time to learn about your client. Let them talk – don't fall into the error of encouraging them just to respond to your queries. Show an interest in their interests. Talk about the color of their shoes, a personal item they brought to the intake, or favorite activities they like to do. Make sure that your statements of interest are not mechanical, but honest. This investment will pay dividends in the development of a real relationship that can collaboratively address the treatment process lying ahead.

The ACT Matrix can also be used to guide these initial conversations in a way that is ACT consistent. Essentially, the ACT Matrix is a momentary functional assessment and is a tool to guide or orient the content of the conversation. What values are being disrupted by the behavior that is leading to treatment in the first place? What are the private experiences that occur along with the behavior? What can we do instead to move towards those identified values? With this information, the behavior analyst has a lot to guide initial versions of the intervention and to develop more specific measurement strategies as described above.

SYNTHESIS OF MEETING, RECORDS, AND OBTAINED DATA TO CREATE A FUNCTIONAL ANALYSIS

A real functional analysis is broad, multimodal, and comprehensive. In order to meet such expectations, the behavior analyst will need to incorporate all dimensions listed above into the final determination of the treatment approach. This will include justification that ACT is appropriate, the degree to which verbal stimuli are impacting the environmental contingencies, the maintaining variables at both a verbal and contingency level, the confidence level of such hypotheses, and the potential for treatment adherence by the client and their associated stakeholders. In Figure 11.1, we provide a flowchart that details the multi-model process of conducting a functional assessment. The first step is to determine if the presenting problem can be articulated in a directly observable and countable form. This is critical for a behavior analyst, because not having it impedes reliability between observers, puts excessive focus on private events, and begins to blur the boundaries of behavior-analytic care. When such operationalization of the presenting problem is not possible, it is generally

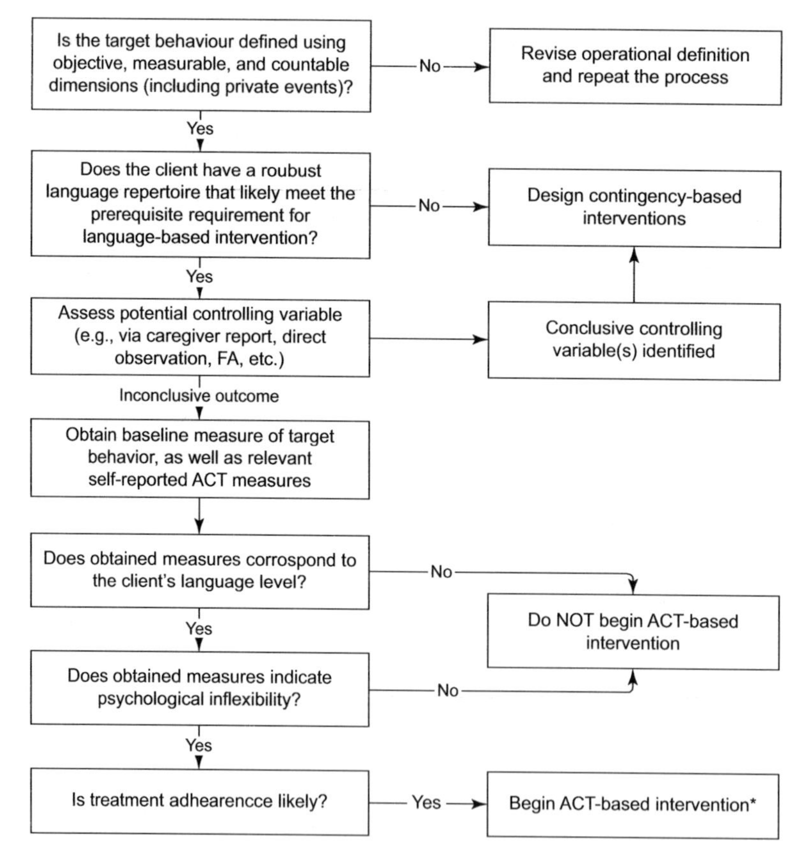

FIGURE 11.1 Multi-model process of conducting a functional assessment flowchart.

wise to terminate potential care as a BCBA or to bring in other skilled professionals and play an ancillary role in their primary treatment.

The second step of synthesis involves appraising the language level of the client. When a formal or informal assessment has been conducted, those individuals who fail to demonstrate the necessary precursors to understand a talk-based therapy that relies heavily on metaphors should be assigned a treatment approach focused on contingency manipulations. However, when language skills are robust, ACT can serve as a logical treatment of choice and a structure in which a wide variety of treatment elements (including direct contingency elements) can be included. For those clients somewhere in the middle, a combination of basic ACT treatment and strengthening of relational framing might be considered.

The third step involves determining if a conclusive function of the challenging behavior is readily available using traditional FA methods. If the answer is "yes," this suggests that a "contingency only" intervention may be sufficient to bring about behavior change. The degree to which language rests upon these contingencies and influences eventual behavior limits the need for an exclusive ACT treatment approach to behavior management.

Finally, the baseline data and metrics around psychological flexibility should be examined to determine the need for ACT care. If such information suggests that the manifesting problem is related to the inflexibility of language and behavior, ACT treatment may be warranted. Compliance with treatment is equally important, as any intervention is only as good as its ability to actually be adopted by the client. If adherence is low, ACT could still hold potential if the intervention could concurrently address compliance. In that case, it may be necessary to scale back treatment expectations initially, so that the feedback process remains relatively positive.

WRITING THE FUNCTIONAL ANALYSIS EVALUATION REPORT

In most instances of client care, it will be necessary to provide a written document that outlines the entirety of the functional analysis. This document will need to include the operational definition of the target behavior, current presenting instances of such behavior, the setting conditions that modulate probability of emission, antecedents, consequences, and any related co-occurring variables that increase or decrease probability of emission. Finally, a hypothesis will need to be made as to what is likely possible as to the cause of the behavior, and how that decision was rendered.

Operational Definition of the Target Behavior

The definition of the targeted behavior for treatment rests upon what has been described as the presenting problem. There may be some negotiation with caregivers as to what this target behavior eventually is agreed upon. For example, when a caregiver says they would like you to treat their child's anxiety, you may find it necessary to probe more directly into what the child does when they are anxious, or what limitations in functioning are occurring given this anxiety. You may have supplemental insight into the presenting problem, based on the self-reported thoughts of the client that were revealed using tools designed to evaluate psychological flexibility. Keep in mind that the goal is to ensure that a behavioral product is available – not to dismiss any possible underlying psychological condition that is more based on private events. Consider something like fear of a public performance. This is often accompanied by poor overt performance, avoidance of tasks requiring a public performance, overt emotional displays (e.g., crying, aggression), and so on. If there is no behavioral manifestation that might be labeled as "anxiety" (e.g., failure to take tests at school to avoid work demands; avoidance of speaking in class), it is time for the behavior analyst to refer elsewhere. If the target behavior can be agreed upon and within the scope of competency of the behavior analyst, it will be important to put relevant parameters within the operational definition such as rate, frequency, intensity, and/or duration.

Ronald's target behavior for intervention is defined as verbal outbursts to peers. The frequency of such behavior during the past two weeks has been 19 episodes. Duration of behavior is less than five seconds, is of a loud volume intensity, and typically consists of statements such as "I hope you die," "you are ugly," or "I hate your guts."

Pam's target behavior is work non-compliance. This behavior takes the form of throwing items, eloping from the classroom, and asking to get a drink. Frequency over the past seven days, as estimated by caregivers in a timeline followback baseline, is around five times each day. The duration of these behaviors range from one min to over one hour, and are of significant intensity – often requiring multiple staff to encourage her to return to work.

Setting Conditions

A setting condition is a momentary modulator of the three termed contingencies. These conditions come and go, they are not static traits of the client. Examples of such may include medication consumption, sleep difficulty, illness, food satiation, sleeping at a grandparent's house, a hangover, or certain times of day. These may include changes in response emission under certain sorts of language control such as the present of memories or thoughts. When providing setting condition information, it is critical to describe how such events both set the occasion for and reduce the probability of emission of the targeted behavior. Language itself may serve as a setting condition whereby a rule generated by the client, or a rule emitted by another could set the occasion for altered performance. Such rules may have been revealed during the initial interview with the client or caregiver, or on self-reported flexibility process assessments.

Frequent setting conditions reported during parent interview include staying at Father's house on alternating weekends, medication changes, and when chicken nuggets are not included on the hot lunch menu. Additionally, if a peer tells Shilo that she is ugly, that thought appears to stick with her throughout the remainder of the day.

No setting conditions have been observed which make the behavior more probable, however it was noted that there has never been an episode of concern during after-school part-time employment at a local grocery store.

Antecedents

Discrete stimuli that signal the availability of access to reinforcers are often described as antecedent or discriminative stimuli. More colloquially these "triggers" of behavior can take many forms such as unpreferred tasks, diverted attention to others, being left alone, asked to transition to another activity, or told "no." In contrast to the setting conditions, antecedents are not wrapped around the entire contingency event, but rather are part of the event itself. Most verbally sophisticated humans have a few antecedents that precede their challenging behavior, not just one. As a result, a frequency distribution of common antecedents is most practical to report, rather than attempt to determine a single trigger. Antecedents may not only trigger a response from the client but also the cooccurring language processes that may in turn cause the behavior of interest to be emitted. For example, when hearing a Backstreet Boys song on the radio, it may occasion a brief removal from the present moment as the client derives relations between that song and their long-lost love, and now when asked a question by a peer, a verbally aggressive response of "leave me alone, I hate you" is emitted. The likelihood of such a response is drastically increased by the song, as it serves as a trigger of a private event which in turn triggers an overt behavior.

Consequences

Events that reliably follow the behavior of interest are often described as consequences. When such events serve a reinforcing function, the behavior will increase in frequency. And when such events fail to strengthen behavior, they may weaken emission, or terminate such altogether. For the purposes of assessment, a behavior of concern is generally assumed to be occurring because there is some sort of consequence sustaining its emission. Given the necessity of treatment, such consequences may be increasing the likelihood of emission.

The first step towards consequence identification is to see if something reliably follows emission of a targeted behavior. Sometimes even seemingly irrelevant events can in fact be powerful consequences. Thus, any event often occurring needs to be documented. Consequences may also occur at a covert level within the client, and as such will be difficult to discover without dialogue with the client. Direct probes such as "when you were running down the hall yelling 'fuck this school,' what were you thinking about?" or "can you tell me what thoughts you had when you kicked Sally in the back?" These self-generated rules and thoughts may be initially difficult to include within a description of consequential events, however effort should be made to explore their presence.

Co-occurring Variables

Perhaps the most important section of a functional behavior assessment that seeks to eventually implore ACT intervention is that which describes co-occurring variables. Such variables really should be dedicated to the degree of presence or absence of the six psychological flexibility processes. When conceptualized as a blanket that can wrap within it the antecedents, behaviors, and consequences, these language influences ripple across the client's interaction with the environment. Here is where the behavior analyst might report flexibility assessment scores, relational framing complexity, interview outcomes, or all. When synthesized with the above elements, a case can be made for a treatment approach that includes language intervention.

Pam exhibits a variety of behaviors that may be co-occurring with the environmental contingencies that are sustaining her behavior. During her initial intake she repeatedly stated that she has problems "letting go of things that happened in the past," thus suggesting when she is experiencing attention diverted to others by caregivers (antecedent) that she may likely be thinking about private aversive events, thus increasing the aversive function of lack of social attention from adults.

Rick was administered the Acceptance and Action Questionnaire 2 (AAQ-2) and resulting scores suggest that his ability to self-manage behavior is limited. For example, he reported that "emotions cause problems in my life" at the most severe level with a score of 7. This may suggest that Rick fails to contact reinforcers in his environment because of self-generated rules that impact engaging in positive behavior by serving as verbal abolishing operations.

Hypothesis of Function

Concluding inferences regarding the function of behavior should remain within the parameters of behavior analytic science. Typical categories include attention, escape, tangible, sensory, and physical. The latter suggested the need for medical care, while the four others highlight behavior-environment relations. Where ACT and the relevant language contributions position themselves remain as modulators of these behavior-environment conditions. For example, values work may serve as a verbal motivative operation for consequences that are intrinsic to action; fusion may establish unhelpful antecedent control via a transformation of stimulus functions; and so on. There will be times in which multiple functions are possible for a presenting condition, and the probability of such complexity increases with developed language. Furthermore, there may be sequential functions, whereby a behavior may initially occur to remove demands, only to change upon demand removal to gain attention from the caregiver. The description of function should be objective, clear, and follow naturally from the prior elements of the functional assessment.

The function of Jackie's verbal aggression is to escape from work demands. Such escape is most likely when she fails to be able to describe her own values and the committed actions necessary to engage in to obtain such delayed reinforcers.

Based on the analysis reported above, negative social attention is the hypothesized function for Jace's elopement from the classroom.

INSURANCE AND MEDICAL NECESSITY FOR BEHAVIORAL TREATMENT

When the behavior analyst seeks third-party reimbursement for services, they may find themselves confronted with a reality in which that payee is unfamiliar with ACT. Worse yet, misinformation about ACT may have been provided, thus making the request for services even more difficult. In order to ensure a careful and fair appraisal of services that are being proposed, it is critical for a clear operational definition of behavior, countable and measurable goals, and clear objectives that serve as intermediate steps towards achieving more global performance improvement. When working specifically with children with autism, relating such goals to the core deficits of autism may also be necessary. Be careful to not make the mistake of proposing services that "seek to improve psychological flexibility," "decrease fusion," or "improve a value-driven life." Although there may be some truth to such language, these sorts of phrasings are meant to discern processes that lead to a behavioral end, and that is what needs to be articulated. Below we provide an example of how an authorization request might address limitations in functioning across each of the six ACT processes. From a review of this content, you will see a measurable goal, each aligned with the Hexaflex process, the environment it will occur within, and the relation of such to the core symptoms of autism. Additional information is provided related to the problem behavior areas addressed and the client's current level of performance. Such present levels can be obtained via the caregiver and/or client interview. The example below is based on a diagnosis of autism and is not to imply that behavior analysts only work with Autistic populations – rather, the report form will be familiar to many practicing behavior analysts interested in integrating ACT-based approaches.

Specific Behavior Goals and Objectives

Sample goals are shown in Table 11.2. Coordination of care with other individuals within the life of the client is often expected of the behavior analyst. As a result, many third-party payees request such details in order to approve a request for services. This task requires coaching, modeling, reinforcing, and monitoring of caregivers – all of which are a part of the repertoire of a well-skilled behavior analyst. When treatment involves ACT intervention there may be value in ensuring that the language of treatment is embedded into such care coordination.

Table 11.3 illustrates ways in which care is transferred to a parent such that they use prompting strategies when disengagement is noticed by the client for unpreferred tasks, redirection when aggression occurs, and the embedding of ACT language emitted throughout the home environment. Of course, all such metrics will require self-report of their utilization by the caregiver. Even so, such information can serve as the basis for dialogue between the caregiver and behavior analyst during coaching sessions.

It is important that third-party forms be accurate and honest. You should never be in a position of "gaming the system." Remember, psychological flexibility terms are meant to orient you towards functional analyses within a domain. Because ACT is based on behavioral principles as augmented by verbal rules and relational operants, if it is appropriate given the difficulties your client is facing, you should always be able to provide more specific functional analysis within the domain that you believe applies to your client. For example, you can speak of the degree to which stimulus control needs to be augmented or diminished in a particular problematic context without necessarily using terms such as "increasing mindfulness" or "altering flexible attention to the now."

DOCUMENTING AND REPORTING CLIENT PROGRESS

A wide range of metrics can be used to document the progress of a client during a reassessment. Done at regular intervals, the reassessment allows for a summary of change from baseline to current ability. Depending on what tools were used during the initial evaluation, it may be wise to consider using the same instruments to form a before-after picture of change. Frequencies of challenging behavior, emission of inflexible verbal utterances, and scores on behavioral and flexibility assessments all should be considered as evidence of change. When all such indices show improvements, a clear case can be made regarding treatment effects. However, when some metrics change and others do not, a more careful clinical interpretation may be warranted.

TABLE 11.2

Goal	*Domain*	*Core ASD Symptom Addressed*	*Problem Behavior Area Addressed*	*Current levels of Performance*
Sammy will identify at least three personal qualities about himself with 90% independence across two different settings, with two different people, and over three consecutive sessions. (Self-as-Context)	Adaptive, social, emotional	B.3	Inappropriate language	Sammy can label one quality independently.
Sammy will set one goal per day and identify the steps to achieve that goal. He will work towards this goal without engaging in maladaptive behaviors with 80% independence for three consecutive weeks across two or more settings. (Value)	Adaptive, social, emotional	B.3	Perseveration of topic, inappropriate language, physical aggression	Sammy can identify goals and steps but does not consistently follow steps or complete them independent of maladaptive behavior
Sammy will define and apply six methods to promote appropriate social interactions when he gets upset with 90% independence across two different settings, with two different people, and over three consecutive sessions. (Defusion)	Adaptive, social, emotional	B.3	Inappropriate language	Sammy can describe ways but is not applying them consistently.
Sammy will describe three goals and steps to take to achieve self-management goals without help from an adult with 90% independence across two different settings, with two different people over three consecutive sessions. (Committed Action)	Adaptive, social, emotional	B.3	Perseveration of topic, inappropriate language	On average Sammy can describe two goals or values without help from an adult.
With one prompt or less, Sammy will refocus his attention to the present environment by use of self-management strategies with 90% independence over three consecutive sessions. (Present Moment)	Adaptive, social, emotional	B.3	Perseveration of topic, inappropriate language	Sammy can refocus his attention with one prompt or less about 25% of the time.
Sammy will tolerate aversive stimuli or situations (i.e., unpreferred topics, loud noises) without engaging in challenging behaviors with 90% independence over three consecutive sessions. (Acceptance)	Adaptive, social, emotional	B.3	Inappropriate Language, Physical Aggression	Sammy demonstrates tolerance approximately 10% of the time.

TABLE 11.3

Goal	*Baseline*	*Present Level*	*Discharge Level*
Verbal prompting upon observed disengagement from non-preferred task	< 50% per day	+/- 50% per day	> 90% per day
Verbal redirection when verbal outbursts occur using attending to present environment	< 50% per day	80% per day	> 90% per day
Embedding of treatment language (accepting difficult situations; stepping back from emotions; moving towards values/reinforcers) into routine communication throughout the week	< 10% per day	+/- 50% per day	> 90% per day
Attending and engaging in weekly 1:1 parent meeting session with BCBA	n/a	100	100

Sammy was administered the Children's Psychological Flexibility Questionnaire (CPFQ; Dixon & Paliliunas, 2018) on 2/6/22. It was readministered on 9/12/22 (Table 11.4). The CPFQ is a 24-item questionnaire designed to provide a quantitative measurement of an individual's psychological and behavioral flexibility. Higher scores indicate greater flexibility while lower scores suggest greater inflexibility. Each section has a range of 0–16 points, for a total score of 96. The CPFQ examines six domains that aid in promoting adaptive functioning, reducing negative self-talk and its effects on behavior, and aligning goals and values with necessary self-management behavior. According to the Center for Disease Control and Prevention (CDC), one of the core deficits of autism spectrum disorder (ASD) is "restricted or repetitive patterns of behaviors." Moreover, this can be seen through insistence on sameness inflexible adherence to routines, or ritualized patterns of verbal or nonverbal behavior (e.g., extreme distress

TABLE 11.4

Flexibility Process	*Definition*	*Max Score*	SCORE *Initial DATE*	SCORE *Current DATE*	*Improvement Score*
Present Moment	An individual's ability to interact effectively in the present context; refrain from rumination on past thoughts/events or worrying about future events.	16	2	9	+7
Acceptance	An individual's ability to accept negative *and* positive events during the day, even when it feels uncomfortable.	16	5	12	+7
Defusion	An individual's ability to create distance between inflexible and negative thoughts and understand that thoughts are not the same as behaviors.	16	4	7	+3

TABLE 11.4
Continued

Flexibility Process	*Definition*	*Max Score*	SCORE *Initial DATE*	SCORE *Current DATE*	*Improvement Score*
Self-as-Context	The individual's ability to take perspectives in order to create a distinction in context to his or her past experiences without attachment to those experiences.	16	9	11	+2
Values	An individual's ability to know what is important to them; what drives the person; things the person cares about.	16	9	8	-1
Committed Action	Committed action refers to the patterns of behavior change one makes to get closer to their values.	16	4	12	+8
Total		96	34	59	+25

at small changes, difficulties with transitions, rigid thinking patterns, greeting rituals, needing to take the same route or eat the same food every day) (B.2). Helping to remediate deficits in psychological flexibility associated with ASD is imperative for an individual's long-term prognosis with ASD.

Behavior Assessment Interpretation

Sammy displays challenging behavior that can be of considerable intensity, but the frequency and intensity have reduced from pre-treatment levels. The complexity of his multiple function-controlled behaviors is not surprising given the relatively high levels of language, yet its limits in abstract thinking and reasoning. These shortcomings are improving considerably as revealed by the marked gains in flexibility revealed on the CPFQ. Furthermore, Sammy is improving in self-management, understanding that thoughts are not always descriptions of reality, and that engaging in behavior, albeit sometimes difficult, can yield important outcomes tied to things he values.

Extending Assessment Beyond Clinical Care

Although the majority of practicing behavior analysts are involved in service delivery to clients with disabilities, there remains a need to ensure the extension of ACT interventions beyond this population. Logical extensions of the ACT approach apply to the caregivers or parents of these clients, agency staff, business and industry employees, athletes, college students, and even to the behavior analyst themselves. As a result, the ACT assessment approach will vary to some degree from that listed above, but the general theme of ensuring a functional eye towards intervention needs must be retained. Certain portions of the above details will logically be minimized while others extended.

For example, when attempting to implement ACT with staff, interviewing parents of those staff will obviously not be necessary, nor in general will a medical or psychological records review. While it is important even in these areas as a behavior analyst to maintain a behavioral focus, and the bottom line is still patterns of effective action – habits of values-based behavior, this is typically not that difficult to do. For example, the section above in which we described behavioral indicators of rigidity or inflexibility and each of the various domains of the psychological flexibility model can easily be expanded with higher functioning or neurotypical clients to include a deeper exploration of emotional, cognitive, attentional, sense of self, values, and committed action domains.

In neurotypical adults, it is not hard to evoke discussions about the impact of difficult emotions or thoughts; or patterns of attentional control; or statements of values; and so on. The "mentalistic error" can be avoided if the analyst views these reports and overt behavioral observations related to them as part of a "behavior-behavior" relation in which each element is contextually bound as well as the overall relationship between the elements.

For example, suppose a neurotypical adult client reports being afraid to speak in public. She is avoiding giving talks at work and when she has to do so, the talks are disrupted by overt expressions of emotional arousal and apparent difficulty in breathing, sudden pauses in speaking, frequent sips of water, losing her place in the talk, sweating, and shaking. After such episodes, she states she was "nearly overwhelmed with anxiety," that during the talk she was verbally focused on possible humiliation and ultimately being fired. She reports being afraid she has "embarrassed herself in front of her boss who will eventually get tired of this kind of thing."

It would be mentalistic to treat anxiety, arousal, thoughts of being fired, and so on as *causes* of poor public speaking performance, not because these are private events but because they are dependent variables rather than manipulable contextual variables, so the contingencies responsible for a "behavior-behavior relation" are unstated and unexplored. Because of the multiple channels of information, however, there is nothing wrong in supposing that negative emotional arousal is part of the context for poor public speaking. If a careful examination of the client's history and actions while speaking supported it, the behavior analysts might focus especially on culturally supported patterns of emotional avoidance and negative self-judgement as being responsible for amplifying initially normal levels of arousal into levels that disrupt the ability to speak aloud.

Suppose the behavior analyst decided to do exposure work in which the client gives talks aloud while learning to notice the arousal, describe and name the private events that occur, treat oneself with self-kindness, and then reorient oneself toward the task at hand. An ACT approach like that this known to improve public speaking and to do so better than traditional cognitive behavioral methods, despite the fact that subjective reports of anxiety come down more slowly (Glassman et al., 2016). There is no reason that training in speaking skills should be viewed *a priori* as residing outside of the skill set of behavior analysts.

Interventions such as this do require compassion and perspective-taking skills, which clients of behavior analysts report are often missing (Taylor et al., 2019). Ironically behavior analysts themselves report both that they received no training in how to deliver such compassionate care, and that they need these skills on a daily basis (LeBlanc et al., 2020).

We will address this issue in more detail later but our point now in this chapter on assessment is that as verbal abilities expand, it is more important to assess a full range of psychological and social actions (e.g., emotion, thinking, sense of self, attention, motivation, relationship skills). Let's take a very common example.

Assessment of Caregivers

The psychological flexibility or inflexibility of the persons that care for clients that are served will have an impact on behavior-analytic treatment efficacy. Although these individuals are typically not actively seeking their own evaluations by a behavior analyst, they are part of the contextual system that the client is contained within. Parental assessment measures may include indirect assessments noted above such as the Parental Acceptance and Action Questionnaire (Cheron et al., 2009), along with other indices that may provide insight into their general levels of stress, depressed mood, or struggles with anxiety such as the Depression, Anxiety, and Stress Scales (Lovibond & Lovibond, 1995), and free to use and widely known instrument. If the behavior analysts tried to use ACT as a psychotherapy for depression in caregivers and parents, this would generally stretch beyond the scope of services that a behavior analyst would be prepared to deliver and as such there may need to be coordinated care with other professionals. But if the focus is on how to handle difficult emotions while delivering needed care there are many easy ways forward as we will cover in later chapters.

In anticipation of this possible need, it is good to assess how caregivers' openness to ACT ideas. Woven into the content of an initial meeting and probed during subsequent evaluations of treatment efficacy, it is helpful to ask these caregivers about what they are doing to cope with the situation and how well their various strategies are working. If a parent believes that, say, thought suppression is both necessary and helpful it's very unlikely that you will be able to implement an ACT program with that parent and perhaps not even with her or his child. The behavior analyst should avoid using technical terms when exploring these matters and also should be aware that some religious and cultural groups are opposed to things like "mindfulness" (a safer term initially might be "attentional flexibility" or "situational awareness."

Assessment of Staff

One of the most critical resources for a behavior analyst is their staff. Depending on the size and nature of their practice, staff could be a couple of behavioral technicians who carry out weekly sessions for an identified client, or hundreds of behavior analysts who span across the country implementing services to even many hundreds of clients. It may also be possible that staff means a group of warehouse employees at a trucking company that has absolutely nothing to do with client care. Regardless of how one may define their "staff," the psychological well-being of employees can be of great concern and potential benefit to an organization.

As in other areas, standardized self-report measures can be helpful, but so too can assessment of psychological flexibility processes in the organization itself. For example, using programs such as "Mentimeter" it is not difficult to collect individual Matrix for each staff member electronically but to display them only in anonymized collectivist forms during staff meetings. A group Matrix can also be collected in a similar way ("what behavioral qualities do we as a clinic value or wish move towards as a team?").

Once the staff has had ACT training they themselves can begin to assess the degree to which the work environment is emotionally open or closed, is cognitively flexible or not, is focused on values-based outcomes or not, and so on through the various flexibility processes.

Self-Assessment

Almost all tools we have referred to throughout this chapter could be administered directly to oneself. Although it is most likely best to seek help from others when under conditions of psychological distress, ACT is based on the psychology of the normal and thus one of the best ways to learn is to begin to apply these concepts to your own behavior.

There have been a wide variety of ACT exercises that strive to have the user self-appraise deviations between current and optimal living. For example, a piece of paper may be divided into four quadrants each labeled "family," "health," "education," and "career." Afterwards in the center of the paper, a small circle is drawn to intersect the quadrants to resemble a bullseye of a target, with a very large circle on the edge of the paper indicating the outer edges of the target. The task for the appraiser is then to place an "X" in each square indicating how close that aspect of their life is currently to the ideal. Ideal being right on the bullseye. During this self-discovery, it is oftentimes revealed a give and take between these life domains. Excelling at work takes a toll on the family, and personal health is often neglected while chasing after educational aspirations. The key here is to appraise, reflect, and realign. Appraise the current state of affairs as to how one is living. Reflect on the obtained data reported and determine if this distribution of efforts is yielding results that are desired. Realign priorities and associated response patterns to more effectively move towards a value-driven life. A toil of this kind helps us understand how every moment of every day has an accumulating effect on the overall scatter of Xs on this target.

SUMMARY

The assessment process of ACT remains broad, multimodal, and comprehensive. Behavior analysts will need to prepare for a significant departure from their traditional assessment methods and limited scope of functional evaluation. Expanding the assessment process to include a wide range of tools and modalities will strengthen the confidence that a client is able to understand ACT, benefit from an ACT treatment approach, and yield measurable outcomes that matter. We have provided a wide range of approaches to obtaining the necessary information to formulate treatment, but we did not generate a finite checklist of steps for the behavior analyst to complete. The complexity of presenting conditions necessitates interpretation on behalf of the behavior analyst. Much akin to the clinical psychologist or speech pathologist needing to make a series of choices as to what tests to administer to evaluate present levels of performance, the behavior analyst will need to make educated informed choices as to how to approach the ACT assessment process. Careful consideration of language complexity, dependent variable identification, Hexaflex strengths and weaknesses, and targeted goals all will need to remain at the forefront of an ACT based behavioral assessment. How one assesses their clients should never be a one-size-fits-all process. Rather the optimal evaluation is one based on clinical impressions that are rooted in a comprehensive case conceptualization, scientific discoveries, and practical utility.

12

The ACT Treatment Process

Behavioral intervention is individualized intervention taking place at the level of the single subject. When multiple clients present similar problem areas or "symptoms," there can be no assumption that a similar treatment will be delivered unlike in many other therapeutic frameworks that emphasize "symptom reduction." Instead, the treatment approach will be customized based on the empirical and conceptual linkages between the areas of difficulty, areas of strength, and those historical and situational variables that may bear on these areas (i.e., the on-going behavior environment interaction) made by the clinician. The rationale for this approach rests upon the uniqueness of the functional relationships between a presenting problem and its maintaining variables. Although two clients may engage in a targeted behavior problem of work non-compliance, it is very possible that one does so to gain attention from the teacher, and the other to escape the nonpreferred work demands. One may have alternative behaviors readily available while the other does not. A functional treatment for each client would be radically different, as one will require more appropriate ways to gain social attention, and the other teaching tolerance for work and more appropriate means of escaping under conditions of distress. As behaviors become more complex, the analysis and subsequent intervention also increase in intricacy. Derived relational responding overlays a distinguishable set of actions atop the four termed contingencies, and thus any effective intervention for a verbally sophisticated individual will necessitate concurrently treating the stream of interaction with language and environmental contingencies and setting variables or motivative operations.

That is to say, psychological flexibility *is not* "inside" the client and causing this or that behavior. Psychological flexibility *is* a broad description of how behavior interacts functionally within the environment. A strong intervention will necessitate determining under which conditions this kind of interaction is the most likely and those situations where this interaction is the least likely to occur – and in those situations where inflexibility shows up, to strengthen it using the variety of methods we have overviewed to this point.

Treatment of clients in need of acceptance and commitment therapy (ACT) interventions will by definition require extensive coordination with others. Low-frequency behaviors may be rarely captured during dedicated treatment sessions, and thus plans will need to be consistent across all aspects of the client's day, and data will need to be captured by multiple stakeholders. Furthermore, the entire makeup of a treatment session may be quite different from what a behavior analyst typically conducts, as an ACT session may involve simply talking to another person – the client. It is functional behavioral processes altered by the content of that dialogue that one hopes will transcend beyond the treatment session and

DOI: 10.4324/9781003250371-15

alter the influence of language's impact on subsequent four-termed contingencies that the client encounters. This idea that talking to someone in a session context may sound intimidating to behavior-analytic readers. Can we do that? Isn't that psychotherapy? Consider at least two other already established behavioral procedures that most of us have conducted without much concern. We know that challenging behavior maintained by tangible reinforcers can be reduced by having an extended play session prior-to introducing demands to act as an abolishing operation. This approach is less skill-based than ACT, but consider a verbal behavior training session where, in many cases, verbal stimuli are presented to the learner and, on some trials, reinforcement is provided contingent on the nature of the correct responses in order to select certain functional topographies of language. The idea is that by training this skill in one context the skill will transfer to the context where it is the most needed. In this way, ACT sessions are not different. Exercises occur in a session-based context to strengthen skills that may generalize in the contexts that really matter.

And just like with any behavioral technology, it is not enough to simply train and hope and we do not want to get in the habit of conducting ACT sessions and then waiting for the next scheduled meeting to "check in." That is when, in our opinion, the professional lines start to blur. Instead, we need to define our behaviors of interest that will include some combination of direct observation, self-monitoring, and self-report, and track the degree to which these behaviors are happening at the desired times and in the desired contexts. Did our intervention *change* behavior?

The degree to which an ACT session can have such an effect on the behavior of the client is determined by at least four factors – the client's complexity of relational framing, understanding of metaphors, level of impulsivity, and memory skills. None of these factors appear behavior analytic at first glance, however each clearly can be described with the technical precision necessary to remain within a behavioral account of human behavior.

The *complexity relational framing* will matter. If the verbal repertoire is only beginning to imply transcendence of time and place, you will need to talk differently to the client than if the repertoire is fully matured. Expectations will need to also be adjusted based on language complexity, as robust articulated referential inferencing from an ACT metaphor to the challenges of a client's life can only occur when language is at a certain depth. This does not mean ACT is not a good fit for a younger or language-early client. Rather it means that there needs to be a match of ability, precise features of the intervention method, and expectations. Often this is done concurrently with an eye toward development of the verbal skills such that greater depth of intervention using verbal methods can eventually occur. If the language repertoire is rote and is a product of pure contingency-based learning, it is very possible that no relational framing skills are present. This veneer of a true verbal repertoire is revealed all too often when such a client is exposed to a relational framing evaluation such as used in the Promoting the Emergence of Advanced Knowledge (PEAK) Comprehensive Assessment (PCA), and while obtaining correct scores on many directly reinforced test items, fails considerably on items that require relational responses derived during test administration. Even here there is no reason to dismiss ACT as an eventual viable treatment – it just means that further development of relational skills is necessary initially.

Metaphor is often an active vehicle of an ACT intervention. By using metaphors, the clinician presents a less-intrusive directive on the importance of one or more of the Hexaflex processes. It is then left to the client to make the relevant derived relational responses to their own life, in order to obtain meaning behind the metaphor. For example, say that the clinician is describing sand at the beach, and how impossible it is to avoid getting sand in your shoes, on your clothes, or in your hair when you go to the beach. No one really likes all this sand on them; however, it is tolerated because of the good times one can have playing on the beach. This narrative might be expanded with some sort of experiential sand activity, whereby the client builds a few designs with kinetic sand toys. More than likely, even during the activity, small amounts of sand will be spilled, or remain on the client's hands. Afterwards. the therapist may ask the client how the sand at the beach situation (getting sand on self) is like (relational frame of coordination) going to school (event the client wishes to avoid). With the ability to relate these concepts, the client may emit a response along the lines of "I like going to school, but there are parts that make me scared. The sand that gets stuck on me is like the scary parts, but school is like the beach." A subsequent narrative can be then had by the clinician who assures the client that tolerance of a little sand (acceptance process) might be worth the hassle if you really like the beach (value process). With sufficient relational abilities, the client may then deduce that scary parts of school are worth dealing with because the greater value of being at school is worth the hassle. When such metaphor skills are in deficit, the client may not see how sand is related to their life and fail to grasp the connection between school and the beach, or most importantly fail to grasp the impossibility of doing well at school without acceptance of some difficult thoughts and feelings. When such limitations in metaphor are detected, remediations will be necessary to ensure the client gets the most out of any ACT intervention.

Impulsivity tempts us all, every single day, multiple times per day. It is sometimes baffling that we ever opt for the more optimal and often delayed consequences of an alternative form of action. However, at times we may impress ourselves with the more rational choices we make. The degree to which someone can stand at the crossroads and effectively evaluate the various paths upon them, and make an optimal decision and stick with it, might be conceptualized as one's self-control skillset. Self-control is the inverse of impulsivity and it can be relatively lacking in children with disabilities, or persons with all sorts of mental health conditions. *Relatively lacking* is key, as even most impulsive people will occasionally choose a more ideal self-controlled option. When and under what conditions, remains the source of research for many within and outside of behavior analysis. Where impulsivity and self-control intersect within the world of ACT involves engaging in value-oriented behavior – deliberately aligning one's behavior to values choices. It is very common to know what one should do, but to engage in behavior that is counterproductive to this "should." Everyone knows diet and exercise are good to do, because most people value healthy living, however impulsive temptations reorient our good intensions to a life of junk food and sedentary existence. A key aspect of the ACT approach is to refocus choice-making to become more advantageous in the long run. The focus is on making room for the hassle of the now, in order to get to the joy of the future. When that future is down the road, and the hassle is here, avoidance often reigns supreme. There have been many techniques within behavior analysis to alter responding from impulsive to self-controlled choices (e.g., Whiting et al., 2022). Most focus around finding ways of making the delay to more optimal reinforcers appear somewhat shorter, more meaningful, and tolerable. One way this is done within ACT is to describe the future consequences (values) in the present, such that the motivative elements of these delayed events are brought into the present. That values are freely chosen is critical as tolerance without an intrinsically rewarding valued outcome is simply compliance training – and "compliance" just like pliance as a rule-following repertoire is very much the opposite of what we are trying to promote from within an ACT-based approach.

For example, upon presentation of a math worksheet, which reliably occasions avoidance and tearing up the assignment, the clinician might state to the client "tell me about the swings on the playground you like to use at recess." Here the crossroads remains the same – option A is to complete the worksheet and go outside to recess (delayed social peer value), and option B is to avoid work and destroy the worksheet (immediate demand escape). There may be a bias towards option B, as the consequence of this course of action is obtained immediately. However, upon hearing the utterance from the clinician about all the fun outside, a slight enhancement of the choice towards option A may have occurred. Again, derived relational responding is at work here, as the words "the swings" may be in a frame of coordination with the actual swing items, "recess" may be in a frame with the actual experience, and as a result there is a bit of psychological interaction with the words just as if the client was there experiencing recess at actual recess time. The thoughts, emotions, and experience of recess are discounted, or shall we say were discounted at the choice point crossroads, until the therapist rekindled a portion of it with their utterance "tell me about the swings." With this verbally established "taste" for recess now happening for the client via a transformation of stimulus functions, a nudge towards option A is more likely. When a client has the ability to make such derivations, a wide variety of value-driven ACT techniques can be used to decrease impulsive behavior. Yet when such skills are missing, remediations will be needed in order to maximize treatment outcome potential.

Memory skills are not often discussed within the behavioral vernacular, as we are often told to dismiss the idea that memory is even a real concept. The word traditionally implies some sort of internal working of a hypothetical mind, storing and retrieving information. That overall construct fails to fit within the behavioral tradition. It would be safe to assume however that every single behavior analyst uses the term memory casually in everyday discourse, even if they have banished it from technical talk. One's ability to recall events from the past is essentially memory, and more behaviorally speaking "memory" involves the persistence of "stimulus control." Treating memory as a form of stimulus control has been noted before (see Sidman, 2008 and Palmer, 1991) and is useful as the clinician conceptualizes the relative ability of their client to recall ACT concepts that were talked about during sessions and use those problem-solving strategies outside of sessions where they are needed the most. It is one thing to understand the metaphor of sand at the beach as it relates to accepting the good and bad of a school day, but it is another thing altogether to wake up on a school morning, accept the thoughts of avoidance, recall (memory) the dialogue from the prior ACT session about the sand and beach, make a choice to tolerate the hassle of school (sand), get out of bed and get ready for school (committed action), and go to school (value). In short, to take the lessons of ACT and apply them when needed requires good stimulus control over extended periods – or "memory." When the client has the ability to link their life to ACT treatment sessions, great successes may begin to occur. However, when memory skills are deficit, and treatment techniques are forgotten (poor stimulus control), the effectiveness of ACT is weakened considerably. Enhancing the memory abilities of a client is critical in order to get the most out of any ACT intervention.

LINKING ASSESSMENT RESULTS TO TREATMENT

Upon discovery of the controlling variables for challenging behavior that occurred during the functional assessment, attention should be paid to the resources at disposal that can produce treatment changes. This evaluation-to-treatment approach should be the foundation upon which all subsequent interactions with the client should rest. A comprehensive assessment provides the necessary information to construct a rationale treatment plan, and such a plan's outcomes should be routinely monitored for success, modification, or abandonment. Typical timeframes for re-evaluation range from six months to one year, but ongoing progress monitoring should occur every session at a less formal level to ensure that the treatment approach matches client need, and also that the treatment approach produces observable gains.

There will also need to be dedicated time and energy given to the development of treatment priorities. By now as you read this book, you may find that even you yourself could stand to benefit from all that ACT can improve upon. Your client too likely has a long list of matters with potential for intervention. You cannot address everything at once. A set of urgencies need prioritization that should occur with the relevant stakeholders. Once established, this list of three to five big issues can serve as the main thrust to intervention, and specific targets of measurable change can be identified. The hope is that akin to building a repertoire of generalized relational responding, with ACT we can build a skillset of generalized flexibility, such that any sort of challenge that presents itself can be encountered with a willingness to adapt because doing so serves valued ends. Consequently, making subsequent treatment goals even quicker to attain.

Functional assessment should also directly guide the intervention approach. "Experiential avoidance" and "cognitive fusion" are umbrella terms that describe a myriad of different topographies and functional interactions that can contribute to suffering and undesired behavior. It is critical that behavior analysts can describe this stream of interaction at the level of the individual client. For example, the client who is engaging in work refusal may be said to be experientially avoiding their work – and this really is no different than what we mean by "escape-maintained behavior." If we obtain more data from an assessment including tools such as present-moment awareness probes and responses recorded using the ACT Matrix, results may reveal deficits in attending to academic stimuli (i.e., academic stimuli evoke attending to events other than the academic task) and reports in the private-away quadrant of the Matrix suggesting that the client is instead attending to a stream of thoughts about their inability to succeed in math, the negative judgements of their peers, and the urge to run out of the classroom. Therefore, the intervention will likely need to train present-moment awareness and locate ACT-based exercises that work directly with unworkable rules around self-judgement, self-doubt, and how they perceive the reactions of others. Additional data may also link into this analysis. For example, the Child Psychological Flexibility Questionnaire (CPFQ) provides a skill profile across each of the core processes of the Hexaflex. For a client who shows strong defusion skills, embedding defusion activities prior-to the math class may be an effective antecedent self-management strategy. If the same client shows weak defusion skills, then additional session-based training will be required, and once the skill reaches a mastery criterion, then the skill is introduced as a self-management strategy along with monitoring the success of this intervention component. This strategy will work in every single case. In fact, this specific strategy may only work in *this* case, which highlights why analysis is so critical when implementing ACT behavior analytically.

As another example, a client is engaging in overall suppressed levels of behavior that may be labeled as "depressed." There is an elaborate history of behavior scientists exploring how depression develops, including the idea that avoidance at one point in time both diminishes the conditioned reinforcing value of life's events that have historically maintained behavior and increases the response effort to act as inaction becomes habitual (see Sturmey, 2020). Behavior analysts are not just tasked with reducing challenging behavior but with increasing desired behavior – but what is the behavior that the client desires? In this case, we cannot simply go off of a diagnostic checklist and attempt to reinforce our way through alleviating the symptoms of depression as prescribed in the *Diagnostic and Statistical Manual of Mental Disorders, Fifth Edition* (DSM-V) – we must focus on behavior. After a semi-structured interview and completion of the Valued Living Questionnaire (VLQ) and the Valuing Questionnaire (VQ), behaviors that the client is finding most disruptive are avoidance of social engagement and feelings of guilt and shame around not attending their religious services regularly. Although both of these are reported as highly valued, the client reports that they "just do not feel motivated" and rate their behavioral engagement in both as low. More than that, after having the client record their experiences for two weeks using our modified ABC log from the last chapter, the client reports that they feel guilty in the moments leading up to choosing not to go to see friends or family or attending their religious service, and that this guilt is alleviated as they construct reasons that they cannot go and they hear back from their family that everything is okay and that they should just "take it easy." They think, "I will see them next time" and next time rarely comes. Results on the CompACT also showed low levels of openness to experience that could provide important information.

We need to separate the part of wanting to see friends and family and attend spiritual events that is driven by shame and guilt (i.e., negative reinforcement) and those aspects that operate as sources of positive reinforcement as well as to augment or strengthen those conditions, so sessions might initially focus on values clarification. Beyond avoiding shame and guilt, why does doing these things matter? This is accomplished through metaphor, experiential exercises, and on-going discussion. Acceptance is another process that may be important. That is, those feelings as they exist now may override any potentially valued reinforcers. We carry the weight of our past decisions. In this case, we practice "letting go" of the past and orienting thinking to the present moment and accomplishing committed actions that involve engaging with peers and attending services. Finally, we may want to shape engagement by setting small, committed actions that can be more easily accomplished knowing the high response effort currently associated with engagement while promoting a greater willingness to "do the small things, right here right now." Shaping is a powerful strategy and can build momentum that is alignment with one's values once those values have been established. Data on engagement in these events can be easily self-monitored and different antecedent strategies can be tested along the way. Once again, this may work for this client, or it might not. If not, we will know this because data were collected, and the information obtained will allow for generating a new functional hypothesis and refining the intervention until it does work. This has always been a staple of behavior analytic intervention.

This also does not mean that every intervention component needs to be made from scratch. So many resources have been developed and are being developed to assist behavior analysts (and others) to develop this training. We have discussed the Accept. Identify. Move. (AIM) curriculum. This can be conducted as a general training strategy by moving from the start to the end of the book and embedding the lessons at the same time each day that operate as a setting event. This can also be individualized, for example by emphasizing AIM lessons that target the core processes that are most related to the individualized behavior plan and/or timing the activities strategically throughout the day based on scatterplot data. *The Big Book of ACT Metaphors* (Stoddard & Afari, 2014) also provides several programs that can be used as described or adapted to help guide training sessions and additional efforts can be used to locate metaphors that directly link to the challenges that clients are experiencing. Again, when and where these metaphors are located can be guided by additional information and when data are being collected on the efficacy of this or that program, results can further guide the effective intervention to port.

IDENTIFICATION OF TREATMENT GOALS AND OBJECTIVES

When designing an ACT intervention for a client of behavior analytic services it will remain paramount that treatment has a measurable effect on the behavioral condition which brought that person in for treatment. Treatment goals should never be to move Hexaflex processes or any sort of hypothetical constructs. Intervention needs to remain within the very domain of the service that has been sought and approved by caregivers, funders, or school personnel. As such, the only ambition of a behavior analytic treatment involving ACT is to change behavior – period. The means by which one goes about achieving this end can hopefully be augmented using language-based interventions such as ACT – not using ACT as an alternative to behavior analysis treatment.

When a Hexaflex process, or processes, have been detected to be in deficit for a client, the behavior analyst will need to operationalize each in order to develop empirical goals by which to work towards. It will be difficult to convince payees that improving a client's "committed action" is a clearly worthy endeavor if committed action remains a loosely defined buzz word that you really care about. Also, agreement between implementers and evaluators as to what exactly is "committed action behavior" will likely suffer when such terms remain at their more colloquial level of discourse. Table 12.1 provides behaviorally defined global translations for the six Hexaflex processes that can serve as the initial conceptualization for

TABLE 12.1
Broad and client specific definitions along with measurement parameters for all six ACT processes

Flexibility Process	*Global Functional Definition*	*Client and Situation Specific Definition*	*Measurement Parameters*
Present Moment	An individual's ability to interact effective in the present context; refrain from needless rumination in past thoughts/ events or worrying about future events.	Sally will sit in her seat during math class and sustain eye contact with teacher/materials throughout the entire class period.	Five math class periods per week during school semesters. Momentary time sampling of eye gaze at five min time blocks.
Acceptance	An individual's ability to accept negative *and* positive events during the day, even when it feels uncomfortable.	Sally will make a socially appropriate congratulatory statement to a peer when that peer wins (and Sally loses) at a board game.	Two board games played per week during social group. Frequency counting of positive vocalizations.
Defusion	An individual's ability to create distance between inflexible and negative thoughts and understand that thoughts are not the same as behaviors.	Sally will initiate social exchanges with previously avoided peers on the playground.	Two recess periods per school day. One social exchange within the first five min of recess. Percentage of self-initiated social exchanges per week.
Self as Context	The individual's ability to take perspectives in order to create distinction context to his or her past experiences without attachment to those experiences.	Sally will provide an empathetic statement to a peer who is struggling with an emotion.	Naturally occurring. 50% of opportunities for such an utterance. Percentage of self-initiated statements occurring per week.
Values	An individual's ability to know what is important to them; what drives the person; things the person cares about.	When provided a choice between a healthy and unhealthy snack item, Sally will make food choices that are consistent with her diet.	Three snack periods per day each containing a relatively healthy and non-healthy option. Frequency count of healthy option chosen per day.
Committed Action	Committed action refers to the patterns of behavior change one makes to get closer to their values.	Sally will participate in physical education class by completing all warm-up exercises without talking to peers.	One PE class per day, with endless opportunities to disengage from warm-ups. Partial interval recording at 15-second intervals for non-talking to peers.

goals and objectives for a client undergoing treatment. It also provides an example of how these global functional definitions can be made topographically specific for a given client and a given situational goal, along with potential measurement parameters.

An isolated review of the Client Specific Definition may trigger concerns as to the need for an ACT intervention altogether. For if the changes we wish to see from the client appear now to be nothing more than behavior changes, what added value does an ACT approach provide? Nothing could be further from the truth, as Sally's behavioral skill set is influenced by how she interacts with the Hexaflex processes. Of course, we could provide massive reinforcers to promote eye contact during math class, but by doing so we never are really treating the underlying cause of the behavior. In Sally's case, the disengagement is brought to bear by a series of private events, that serve as setting conditions, which create the ripe conditions to disengage. It is only by teaching Sally to better identify such events, and how to subsequently manage them, will long-term functional change occur and thus produce more attention in class.

One ACT process that will be critical when developing treatment goals and objectives is that of values. Person-centered planning is guided by clients' values systems and involves the active participation of the client in creating goals and objectives. In the case of ACT, we have taken the time to define what is meant by values in a deeper way than "what does this person prefer or not prefer?" to describe those larger-later abstract categories of reinforcement. For many clients, they will be able to describe these values with some prompting and education on what is meant by the term "values," and developing treatment goals and objectives can extend from personalized committed actions with sub-objectives that seek to build momentum throughout the intervention. For others, additional work may be needed based on low values clarity or early language learning. For example, a client may express that they value becoming an astronaut. Without additional values clarification, goals and objectives would include those that allow access to astronaut training programs to eventually go to space. None of this is to say that they will not become an astronaut – they very well could, but the risk is that a career pivot to any other profession would be disastrous. Or pending failed admission into the astronaut training program, all of this work serves as yet another exemplar of why putting in the work does not yield desired outcomes. Values clarification necessitates digging deeper. What about the thought of being an astronaut brings about feeling good and excited? We might find that exploration and friendship like those expressed in television programming are values and being an astronaut is one single topography of how those values are realized – among an infinite number of ways to experience those experiences. Therefore, building the skills necessary for exploration and friendship can become center stage of this planning process and will include things like building the necessary ACT core processes, social skills training, and other necessary elements in ways that are topographically broad and dynamic.

The on-going practice of values-clarification can even further ensure that planning is person-centered. The better able we are to identify not only what matters to us in this or that moment but to also identify those longer, temporally extended values, the more those values can participate in the planning process. When we define "person-centered" topographically as "the client is in the room and answers questions about their program," then this creates a false dichotomy between what is person-centered and what is not. The client who is simply repeating back the last option given is no more a part of the process than the client who was left at home. In the same way, the client who has done the work to identify core values and to advocate for them can be the most involved in this process. Therefore, behavior analysts have a responsibility to work with clients to do this work. Person-centeredness does not need to occur exclusively during the one or two hours when everyone is together in the room. Strengthening values clarity and training self-flexible advocacy skills can occur throughout the intervention process and aid in optimizing the role of the client in determining their own scope of treatment. This may be one of the greatest contributions of ACT-based programming in the interest of promoting functional self-advocacy.

Goal creation should focus on the SMART acronym we discussed earlier, thus entailing Specific, Measurable, Attainable, Relevant and Time-based. The sub-steps to achieving these goals, often termed "objectives," need to contain this SMART conceptualization. We introduced SMART in Part 2. In addition to these goals, we recommend linking each to the specific values that the goals are in service of for a comprehensive, person-centered approach to goal setting and measurement.

MEASUREMENT OF GOALS AND OBJECTIVES

Specific refers to the idea that a goal should be narrow enough to allow for effective planning. For example, if Sally needs to improve her peer interactions, there needs to be a specific instance of this behavior we need to initially target. Although the loftier outcome of "having more friends" is surely on one's mind, it cannot be forced into a goal at that level of vagueness. Rather the clinician must tolerate losing a bit of scope for the enhanced precision achieved by keeping the goal within a specific set of parameters.

Measurable in this context means seeable and countable. This can be obtained by having objective visible demonstrations of behavior that people can agree upon. In the examples above, all of Sally's identified measurement parameters specified what is to be counted with a specific type of data collection method. Keep in mind the concept of numerator and denominator as often as possible. This fraction allows you to capture percentages of optimal performance. For example, Sally's two board games played per week serve as a denominator while her socially appropriate congratulatory statements can be used as the numerator. When providing monthly summaries of her goal achievement, we take two games per week times four weeks to produce a denominator of eight, and her attained performance of four during that same time period as numerator. Thus, her monthly goal performance here would be 50% (4/8). The focus on behavior-behavior relations that occur in ACT and psychological flexibility easily lend themselves to measurable goal setting as well, especially if the functional analysis of factors that support or interfere with a targeted flexibility process contains public accompaniments. For example, suppose Sally shows overt signs of anxious arousal when she is around peers (flushed face; rapid breathing; difficulty speaking smoothly in a normal tone of voice). If the behavior analyst concludes that there may be an unhelpful behavior-behavior relation between anxious arousal and avoidance of peer interactions, part of the treatment may include the deliberate creation of measurable arousal and then creating measurable behavior change in their presence. For instance, social interactions could be practiced for a given number of minutes in role-plays after doing jumping jacks to raise one's heart rate to a given level.

Attainable goals involve the setting of targets that are sensitive to baseline measures. That is if performance during baseline revealed Sally has never made it through PE class without disengagement from activities by talking to peers, it would be logical to select a goal for this behavior that was not too drastic of a change in her behavior. For example, five days without talking to peers is much less likely to be obtained than two days. Even better, a dialed-in baseline might reveal that her chatter with peers usually happens after five minutes of PE, thus suggesting her behavior is in line with the goal during that first five minutes. Making the goal more attainable might require setting it at six minutes each day and increasing this criterion upon successive successes, rather than forcing an entire X number of days to be chatter-free.

Relevance of a goal is paramount to a good overall treatment approach, as it is only from relevant goals that relevant behavior change will occur. The scope of what is relevant will vary, and input should be sought from appropriate stakeholders. Also keep in mind that relevancy should include an eye towards generalization, adaptive functioning, and treatment maintenance. Thus, it is best to craft a goal that has embedded natural supports rather than one which requires contrived mechanisms to occasion the behavior. As you can see from Sally's goals noted above, they are all embedded within a natural environment rather than just articulations of future performances during ACT treatment sessions such as "What should you do when you lose a game (accept, congratulate)?" The appearance of relevance can be key to compliance with work on needed behavior-behavior relations. For example, suppose the behavior analyst decides to target defusion skills by together saying difficult thoughts aloud that Sally admits to, but using silly voices of her choosing (e.g., Donald Duck saying "I'm afraid they don't like me") before Sally goes out to the playground with peers. The goal may be to say at least five such thoughts for at least two minutes total. This is a procedure with known positive benefits for children with developmental disabilities (Eilers & Hayes, 2015) but clients are far more likely to comply with an exercise like this if the actual thoughts being practiced are very close to the private events experienced by the client – that overlap is what makes this exercise and this goal relevant.

Finally keep the goal *time-based*, allowing for a deadline by which to evaluate the success or failure of performance to match the goal. In regard to ACT goals, time-based matters, because if the goal is not achieved, it can be deduced that the treatment itself is not successful at changing targeted behavior. Any number of reasons might be responsible for such failures – language skills, metaphors, impulsivity, or memory. Regardless of cause, the functional outcome is not what was expected. This reality check allows the clinician the necessary information to either modify the goal, the treatment approach or both. Set times sooner rather than later, as one-year goals only evaluated at the end of the year may create voids of information that if gathered sooner, would have allowed for much quicker modifications, and a potentially better performance.

THE FIRST TREATMENT SESSION

The first treatment session should involve considerable introduction to the ACT model. The level of this introduction will logically match the abilities of the client you are treating. For example, if you are working with a young pre-school child, you might show a diagram of the Hexaflex and inform them that you are going to tell them about six different ways that can be helpful in managing their feelings. If working with a teen who has an intellectual disability, a discussion about flexibility might begin with speaking about ideas that could help them "bounce off" of problems they encounter during the course of the day. The Hexaflex can then serve as a kind of cheat sheet for tricks to "bounce" better and not get so wrapped up in drama. There is also a level of dialogue here that might be contextually related to the presenting condition the client faces. Placing the treatment introduction into the very stuff the client struggles with, can be of considerable help, as it then can reveal itself as serving as the means to a better end.

Mom says you have been having a hard time during school trying to make friends. Sometimes it is scary to talk to new people, or even people that you know. We are going to work on different ways to make more friends and all along have some fun. Ok?

During our last (assessment) meeting, you mentioned in some of things we did together (questionnaires) that you had a hard time letting go of bad thoughts. This type of stuff is hard for everyone to do. The cool thing is, I have some different ways of making letting go easier to do. During our time together, I will show you some of these ways, and hopefully they can help you focus better during the school day.

The actual introduction of the ACT model might take the form of a brief overview of all six processes, or the sequential roll-out of each individual process over a few additional sessions. A visual representation of the model is nice to refer to and can be modified for different types of clients. For example, a younger child version might include tag lines that follow each process, such as "Present Moment – Be Here" or "Acceptance – Everything Is Ok," to provide a bit of additional information to connect the process to rules the client can try and follow. More sophisticated tag lines for older clients could represent more complex rules such as "Present Moment – Right Here Right Now," or "Acceptance – Ride the Tides of both Good and Bad," or "Committed Action – Practice Makes Permanent." During this initial meeting, the clinician can walk through the Hexaflex and describe the various ways one can become more flexible, and why such flexibility is a good thing.

Acceptance is about being ok with everything that comes our way. It is not about being excited about bad stuff, but rather that bad stuff happens to everyone and it is not our fault. Or worse yet, it is not possible to try and fix things that have already happened.

Self-as-context is kind of weird. It is like understanding there are multiple types of you, and then there is this bigger single you. For example, sometimes you are a brother, a son, a school kid, a friend. Yet within those various "yous," there is a part of you that remains the same. The person who likes French fries. The person that loves kittens. The person who wants to be part of their family. This bigger you – is what we say is "self-as-context."

In addition to verbally walking around the Hexaflex during this introduction session, it may be useful to introduce more visual metaphors of the processes to clients. To aid in this task, one of this text's authors (Mark R. Dixon) has created a series of six animal characters for younger children, shown in Figures 12.1 and 12.2, and superhero-like characters for older teens to hopefully assist in linking the Hexaflex processes to things the client may already understand. The animals remain the same for both groups of clients, but their visual representation and abilities are different. Regardless of their form as a drawing or a plush toy, these animals help bring the Hexaflex to life. Describing each character and why they represent a specific process, as shown in Table 12.1, can be a great ice breaker during the initial treatment session.

It is during this first treatment session that goals should be shared and agreed upon with the client. These goals will be used to justify the "hassle" of learning about the Hexaflex, tolerating coming to sessions, and the benefits of trying one's best every time there is a meeting. Furthermore, it is up to the clinician to instill a motivation for the client to "work on these techniques" outside of sessions and report such successes or failures the next time of meeting. Getting buy-in from the client matters, and there is no clear prescription to give you on how this will be accomplished.

FIGURE 12.1 Animal characters to link with Hexaflex processes for children.

FIGURE 12.2 Animal characters to link with Hexaflex processes.

Each of the flexibility processes can include seeds of buy-in. Sometimes the buy-in involves negative reinforcement. For example, clients with a history of experiential avoidance or cognitive fusion will have often experienced failure caused by these two processes. Using language or exercises appropriate to the client's ability, it is not hard to act that failure. For example, suppose a client has been trying to "throw away" a painful memory of rejection by peers who told the client to "go away" but every time she focuses on this she gets very angry and start telling peers they stink and she hates them. To act out how this works the

TABLE 12.2
Example of anthropomorphizing the relationship between ACT process and animal

Present Moment	*Acceptance*	*Defusion*	*Values*	*Committed Action*	*Self-As-Context*
Seahorse – The seahorse must remain actively engaged in trying to stay floating upwards. Too many distractions and thinking about distant thoughts will pull its body sideways as it forgets about the present.	Penguin – One of the rare birds that cannot fly. All other birds have a wonderful ability to use their wings, and the penguin must accept that no matter what, it cannot fly.	Owl – The owl is wise. It can see things for what they really are. It is able to stand back from thoughts, notice them, and not judge or get trapped in such thoughts.	Bear – The bear has to always be looking towards the future. It has to hibernate every winter, and if it makes too many impulsive choices each day, it will not have saved up enough energy to survive the winter.	Turtle – The turtle takes a long time to get to where it is going. It must set a goal, and never give up. It might be slower than others, but with focus, the turtle gets to its goals.	Octopus – The octopus changes colors. It blends into the background of wherever it is. So what is the real color of an octopus? It's constantly changing, but the octopus itself is always the same.

client is told that a bag of high static foam packing popcorn is like that painful memory and that telling peers they stink is like reaching into that bag and trying to throw away the memory of them saying "go away." Unfortunately, the packing popcorn immediately sticks to the client and no matter how hard she tries to throw them away that only increases the static and they get all over her. After wiping the foam pellets off, the behavior analyst might note that trying to throw away the pellets means touching them – whereas the only way really to keep the pellets off her is to keep her hand out of the bag in the first place. In the same way, trying to get rid of a memory by saying bad words to friends only makes the memory more sticky. If the client related well through this exercise then working on flexibility processes might be cast as "learning to keep your hand out of the bag." Said in another way, the pain of rejection might now motivate working on ACT processes by negative reinforcement since the client may have experienced how alternative behaviors make the painful memory sticky.

Quite a number of such exercises have been used in ACT protocols. For example, fusion can be represented by putting a piece of cardboard in front of your face; the conceptualized self by wearing a mask, rumination or worry by having someone constantly saying worries or past concerns aloud, and so on. Values are not the only motivative operation in the psychological flexibility model. Virtually every one of the flexibility processes can help the client once they are made fully relevant to the client's situation.

REGULAR TREATMENT SESSION STRUCTURE

Once the general theme of treatment has been established, it is important to create a session workflow that can be used on a regular basis. We suggest the first few minutes of each session consists of any pre-session reinforcer pairing where repour is established and compliance probability is increased. Afterwards, there should be some sort of data review involving notes from home, technician data, and/or self-reports of how things have been going since the last session. Use this time not to fall back into the past, but rather to present a general interest in the life of your client outside of your treatment environment. Celebrate the successes, and grant permission to move past the messes.

A brief present-moment activity is a great way to ensure that the client can begin the session somewhat focused on the here and now, and let go of any psychological baggage brought into the environment. For younger clients this also helps orientate them to the general compliance necessities of the treatment session with low-effort tasks such as deep breathing, noticing stimuli, or expanding focus.

The majority of each ACT session involves a blend of dialogue and active participation by the client. The latter may vary based on environment, cognitive level, challenging behaviors, and therapist resources. For example, you might discuss Self-as-Context as the transcendental self, and try to bring it into an experience by creating a craft project of a tree with a variety of leaves. The tree may be the client, and the leaves their thoughts. Some leaves are pretty, and some are ugly, but the tree is different than an individual leaf. The tree and leaf project might be drawn on a whiteboard, a coloring sheet to complete, a three-dimensional paper mâché project, or a computer-drawn graphic. For more verbally advanced clients, it is possible to forgo the experience altogether and just discuss the tree and leaves with a higher-level dialogue. The topography of the experience is less important than the message it is designed to represent. Keep in mind the metaphor of the tree needs to be explained and discussed, otherwise the art and craft project of making a tree and leaves serves no substantial therapeutic function.

In addition to the surface-level narratives of understanding process and activities which represent one or more such processes, each treatment session should also address the behavioral challenges that the client has been exhibiting. A direct connection needs to be made by which the client learns to become aware of when they are stuck – rigid, not present, not accepting, making non-valued choices, and to use the Hexaflex tools to pull themselves out of such a place. For example, when the fear of completing a homework assignment creates non-compliance and its associated self-rules ("I like to play games more than doing my homework"; "I am always going to be stupid"; "I hate myself"), the first step is to realize when one is stuck in this type of predicament. Next, an attempt to use the Hexaflex should occur – whereby the client tries to reorientate more flexibly. Once such attempts are made, the client could likely benefit from opening up and expanding rather than suppressing their emotions – both the good and bad. Finally, once willingness has occurred, teach the client to pivot towards a path consistent with their values.

A variety of visuals may aide younger clients with this process. The "Steps to Flexibility" is illustrated in Figure 12.3, as well as an example of the "ACT Matrix" in Figure 12.4. The Matrix may involve interaction whereby the clinician places an image of the client anywhere on the diagram, and literally moves it towards or away from a given position based on what is being said or performed during a session. A great way to do this is by using a magnet or whiteboard.

THE USE OF METAPHOR AND CLIENT LIMITATIONS

There is a real dilemma a clinician will face if their client is not able to understand metaphor. It is not that the concepts that are inside ACT are especially complicated. Rather, the reason metaphor is so critical is that ACT concepts involve both direct contingency learning and an interaction with relational learning. Talking about that interaction using only abstract verbal terms is often inherently confusing. A good metaphor is not only apt – it also allows the client to test out the plausibility of ACT recommendations that are sometimes counterintuitive. This can increase credibility and augment the impact of the ACT method.

Given that ACT is a predominantly metaphoric-driven intervention, designed to rest upon derived relational responding, treatment will suffer when the client fails to grasp how a metaphor is related to their own life. It will require a fair amount of effort from the clinician to teach metaphors using repetition and multiple exemplars. The sorts of metaphors

FIGURE 12.3 The "Steps to Flexibility" model.

taught might need to begin even more basic than the treatment content. For example, if the client is not clear on how getting out of quicksand by not struggling is akin to getting out of scary thoughts by not trying to suppress them, the clinician may need to start with a dialogue focused on how bad thoughts are the same as bad experiences. If that does not land well, the behavior analyst may need to begin on an even more basic level, for example, asking how the hum of the air conditioner is like the hum of thoughts in your head. The moral of the story is that if you concentrate too much on the hum of the air conditioner, you will likely not notice or do anything else. After observing an understanding of these connections, the clinician might again revisit the quicksand metaphor.

Each process of the Hexaflex is best actualized by the client through metaphors and acted-out physical exercises – experiential metaphors. The latter requires additional creativity on behalf of the clinician to bring to life the lesson being taught. Take for example a session in which the overall message is that values are hard to obtain and require committed actions on a regular basis. To illustrate this idea via an experiential metaphor, the clinician may arrange a game of beanbag toss whereby the values for the client are placed at a distance, and the task is to "toss" items (beanbag, or pieces of crumbled paper) that represent committed actions towards the target (values). As the client experiences a less

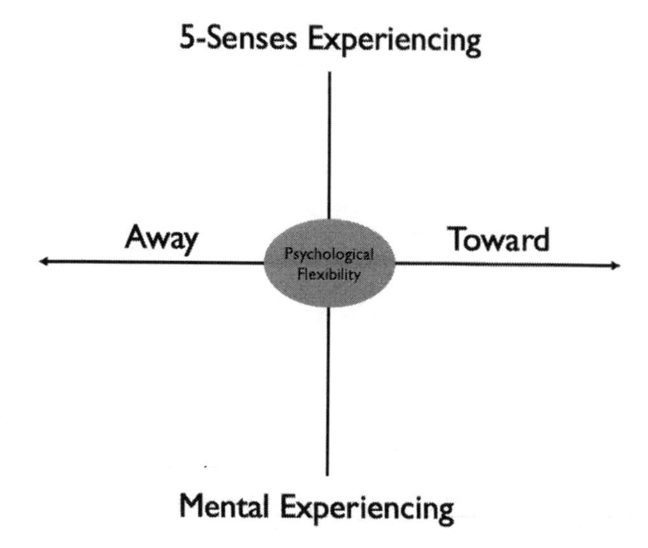

FIGURE 12.4 The ACT Matrix model.

than optimal toss of an item to the goal, the clinician can remind them of how just one toss is like one try to get to a real value. It is never enough, and with repeated attempts, more frequent and precise value attainment is possible. Afterwards, dialogue could be directed to the relationships between the experience and the real values and committed actions the client is working on.

The power of experience to teach metaphors is substantial. If the game involved crumpled paper the pieces of paper tossed might contain written text by the client of their committed actions. The target could also depict value statements, allowing the physical metaphor to establish by direct pairing the client's commitments and values.

Let us start by writing a value you have on this target. You said you valued making friends. Now I will put the target on the other side of the room. It will be hard for us to toss these crumbled papers to the target but the more we try, the better we will get. Before we crumble the paper, write a committed action, or a behavior you can do, that will help you move towards making friends. How about you write "approaching and asking questions" on this first piece of paper. And on this second piece, write "giving compliments." What do you think you could write on these last two pieces? Now, let's stand here, and toss our committed actions, towards our values. Make sure you notice, how the more we practice, or stay committed, the better we get at moving close to our value. Keep in mind, if we just give up and don't toss our paper, we will not reach our values.

It is acknowledged here that the example dialogue above takes some liberties with technical vocabulary and ACT processes. The distinction between values and goals is blurred, and frequency of commitment is not necessarily the critical element to sustain value-driven results. However, much akin to the mid-level terms of ACT used throughout and the deeper technical vocabulary, building an understanding of metaphor will require teaching loosely. This is even more crucial with young and verbally developing clients who will need a variety of ways to shape the concept of metaphors, processes, and necessary behavior change.

ACTIVITIES VERSUS TALKING

Only a small percentage of the clients seen by behavior analysts will be able to spend an hour or more simply talking. Oftentimes, the behavior analyst's clients are young, have attention difficulties, or find the subtle nuances of conversation with an adult not very interesting. It is your goal as a behavior analyst to make ACT come to life for your client. This means you will need to be creative in developing a treatment approach that fits the needs of your specific case and realize that it may involve you engaging in generative and product activities instead of a basic conversation. Young children will likely need exploratory tasks, that involve movement and creative design. Persons with disabilities too will likely need multiple experiences during an hour session to break the treatment into smaller units of demands, as well as variation needed to get the main point of a lesson across. Multiple exemplars that involve talking, experiencing, and deriving metaphors will be the best way to approach session design.

CLIENT (AND CAREGIVER) HOMEWORK BETWEEN SESSIONS

Between sessions, it is critical to ensure that the ACT language remains at the forefront of the client's life. This is best accomplished if the caregivers who surround the client are skilled on how to speak the relevant dialogue of acceptance, values, and remaining present. There is utility in spending time directing the caregiver on this line of dialogue, as well as reducing the probability of using typical phrasings that run contra-therapeutic to the ACT approach. Thought suppression, lamenting on the past, dismissing delayed values, and not articulating committed actions can all have negative effects on the robustness of treatment adherence. It may be helpful to give parents and caregivers phrases to use as a starting strategy, and over time and repeated dialogue, these initially generic phrases can be enhanced and adapted for the various changing interactions they will have with the client between sessions.

> *Instead of you saying, "Don't think about those types of things" or "Get over it," maybe you could say something like "It is ok to have those thoughts, but they are just thoughts. Everyone gets tricked into thinking that thoughts are always real." You could also try teaching more acceptance rather than suppression. For example, "Maybe you hated that experience. That sucks. Instead of putting it in front of you and blocking your path forward, you can put it to the side. I know you want it gone, but it never will be. We all have to keep moving even when our thoughts and experiences keep trying to pull us backwards."*

The client too needs a set of skills that transcend the therapy session. These skills may take the form of a cheat sheet or handout given to them for the purposes of self-monitoring. It may also be possible for the client to create a series of short-term goals that could be worked on between sessions, and progress could be reported back to the clinician at the next session. Finally, it may be helpful if brief between-session prompts/feedback occur to bridge the treatment gaps. For example, a client with a cell phone might receive a daily text message from the clinician asking for an example each day of how they put a Hexaflex process into practice that day.

I am giving you a personalized Hexaflex you can keep on your desk at school. When you find yourself drifting from the present moment, or not being committed to the things that matter, I want you to look at this thing, recall some of the stuff we have been talking about, and bring yourself towards what really matters.

When you find yourself getting upset about stuff, I want you to pull out this list of values we created and ask yourself if getting upset is moving you closer to or farther away from what really matters.

Here is a stuffed animal. She is an octopus named Ophelia. Remember that an octopus changes colors depending on her environment. You too change colors. Not real colors, but how you behave and who you are around. So, when you start to worry about not fitting in or having friends, maybe think about Ophelia. She needs to adapt, and so do you. When you are outside on the playground, be like Ophelia and change. Be more talkative, and outgoing. I know it is hard. But you value friends, so change. Then, when back inside you can change colors again – just like Ophelia – and become quiet. Which is the real you? All of them. Next week when we meet, I want you to tell me how you were like Ophelia and adapted to the stuff around you.

MANUALIZATION OR CUSTOMIZATION

As the behavior analyst embarks on the delivery of ACT services for clients, staff, or self, they will need to make a decision on whether to use existing materials or create materials themselves. There are advantages to adopting a curriculum such as *ACT for Children* (Dixon, 2014) or AIM (Dixon & Paliliunas, 2018) and its affiliated appendages, as such tools have been already vetted to some degree in the professional literature as having a degree of utility. Such easy-to-use tools save considerable time for the behavior analyst, as a lesson can be selected, read, and implemented with minimal preparation. However, a downside may also exist, as no curriculum can be a one-size-fits-all. There will be clients and situations that do not ideally fit the prepared scripts; also, even within such curricula, there is a bit of formulation for a specific age and ability level that will need to occur.

When the behavior analyst ventures beyond existing resources into the domain of building their own ACT treatment sessions, it is advised to have a primary focus on a single process and allow the discussion to naturally cascade to the relevant others. After process selection, there should be some time dedicated to the intensity of the intervention; which will be based on available time, client skill level, ability to understand metaphor, and finally modality limitations (talk; experience; materials needed). We provide a general framework for working through possible treatment options below at both a low and high-intensity level using the process of acceptance as an illustrative example.

Low-intensity interventions, for instance those shown in Table 12.3, allow for brief or quick applications of acceptance that can be useful at many times throughout the day. Such techniques can help clients complete non-preferred tasks, take feedback more effectively, and improve success in their quest for present-moment awareness. The purpose of such

TABLE 12.3

Low-Intensity Practice Interventions

Willingness to let a single unwanted thought stay front and center	**Acceptance of physical distress of specific body part or activity**	**Focusing on the interaction between one's body and the environmental space surrounding them**	**Broaden or narrow the stimulus control of local conditions of the environment**	**Noticing self-accepting**
1. Place a post-it note with your single worst thought on it on your desk all day. 2. Answering the question: "If X could never be deleted from your life, what would you do instead of trying to fix it?"	1. One bad-tasting jellybean in a handful of good-tasting jellybeans 2. Put your shoes on the opposite feet and walk across the room. Notice how while not perfect, you can let go and still walk.	1. Put on music you absolutely hate. Engage in a preferred task and notice how the music and task compete for your attention 2. Try and color an image with your non-dominant hand and try to stay within the lines. Put under time pressure to make the task even harder.	1. Write down two thoughts you try and hide and two thoughts you wish would show themselves. What is preventing the latter from happening? 2. Rewind the clock 1 hour from current time. Describe how acceptance could have impacted what you accomplished during this past hour that was potentially "wasted."	1. Pick a common situation that you usually get through by adopting a "style" that you present to the world as "you,"such as feigning competence, humor, or disinterest. This time as you adopt that "persona" deploy each element a bit more slowly and deliberately and notice its features as if you were an "internal scientist."

interventions is to embed the process of acceptance with little effort for oneself or the person being addressed with such an intervention. The intervention here is brief and can serve as the additional nudge towards a more appropriate behavior. It would be expected that such tasks could be completed in five to ten minutes.

High-intensity interventions such as those shown in Table 12.4 require much longer dedicated time and dedicated space to complete. Such techniques explore not only the actual experience of allowing acceptance but also incorporate dialogue to enhance subsequent self-initiated attempts at accepting events that are currently underway. The purpose of such interventions is to strengthen the how and the why one might wish to tolerate the less-than-optimal state of affairs and illustrate the natural variability in the topographies of achieving this degree of flexibility. The intervention here requires a committed time frame and should be a teaching experience that can hopefully be used at a later time when the contingencies arise which deem it necessary. It would be expected that such tasks could be completed in 30–60 minutes.

BUILDING CUSTOM ACT LESSONS FROM SCRATCH

The anatomy of a lesson that is conducted for a specific client will vary considerably. Factors to consider include age, disability level, experience with ACT, frequency of treatment, co-occurring challenging behaviors, work tolerance, and setting of the session. We provide you with multiple exemplars that can be used as inspiration for creating your own ACT lessons with clients. Although this takes more work than premade curricula, existing content may ultimately necessitate a degree of customization itself. The core task at hand is to deliver content that is engaging, matched appropriately to the client, and has therapeutic value. If all three of these elements exist within a lesson, it is likely that treatment success will be achieved.

TABLE 12.4

High-Intensity Practice Interventions

Willingness to let a single unwanted thought stay front and center	Acceptance of physical distress of specific body part or activity	Focusing on the interaction between one's body and the environmental space surrounding them	Broaden or narrow the stimulus control of local conditions of the environment	Noticing self-accepting
1. Use face paint to place on the outside of one's face, a thought that is being experienced on the inside. 2. Write a short story that centers around the difficult thought and how the main character never can remove the problem. Detail how that character must go on with life trapped with the problem yet still manages to live close to "happily ever after."	1. Use a rope or a string to bind an appendage of your body. For example, tie your one arm to your torso, your feet together, or your arms behind your back. Complete a few previously easy chores or tasks under these new conditions of distress. 2. Put a puzzle together with all the pieces upside down. Notice the constant temptation to turn the pieces over to make the task easier.	1. Play your absolutely worst genre of music while doing a preferred task. Notice the push and pull towards trying to turn the music off or enjoying your task. 2. Create your own new way of performing a swimming stroke, riding a bike, or doing a common routine task. Embrace the struggle of wanting to abandon this new more complicated and novel performance for the old routine.	1. Coin toss. Heads you say something nice to yourself, and tails you say something mean. Push each a bit more extreme than usual and notice how you react. 2. Write a terrible thought you have on a piece of paper. Examine the word with a magnifying glass, or microscope. Describe not only the feelings of the word but the various textures you now newly see in your writing.	1. Pick a common situation that you usually get through by adopting a "style" that you present to the world as "you" feigning such as competence, humor, or disinterest. This time as you touch on behavioral choice points deliberately adopt a very new way of behaving and deliberately notice its features as if you were an "internal scientist" filled with dispassionate curiosity about what you were observing.

Step 1: Script and Theme

The first step to building an ACT lesson involves developing a theme. Operating under the assumption that the entire world can be related together, create a theme that fits with a client's interest. Perhaps they watch a lot of superhero movies. Or maybe they like to bake cookies. Capitalize on client interests in building themes for lessons, such that there is a surface level of interest right from the start. Once a topical area has been established, there may be some advantage to crafting a bit of scripted language on how the lesson is introduced to the client. This is extremely helpful if the behavior analyst is developing the lesson, but a different implementer is delivering the content.

Superheroes are so cool. They appear to be able to do much more fun stuff than us simple humans. They are always having exciting events happen to them and helping save people who find themselves in trouble.

Making cookies is an enjoyable task. Yet every cookie comes out just a little bit different from the next. Even when you follow the exact same recipe. The same oven, the same baking sheet, the same temperature.

Step 2: Discussion

The second step to developing an engaging lesson is to craft a series of dialogue starters for the client to talk with you about their interests, and how they align with the topic of the lesson. How the questions are asked can be as important as the questions themselves. For example, it will be common for many clients to disengage from answering novel "wh" questions, as doing so may allow you as the implementer to simply provide an answer for them. This is extremely common for clients who have had experience with very basic applied behavior analysis (ABA)-types of intervention where such responses are often just memorized. When such dead ends are met, altering open-ended questions to more dichotomous choices will be advantageous. For example, instead of asking what type of superhero the client would like to be, the clinician may find themselves needing to rephrase by asking if they would rather have the ability to fly or have x-ray vision. Furthermore, the clinician themselves should participate in this discussion rather than just be the deliverer of questions. A genuine two-sided conversation should occur.

Tell me about the most awesome superpower you think there is. What type of power would you want if you could pick between flying and super strength? Personally, I would like to fly. Birds seem like they can do really cool things in the air. Imagine how fast you could travel. I also think the freedom of flight could help me just drift away from the problems that sometimes get me trapped.

If you were a cookie, what type would you want to be? For me I would want to be a chocolate chip cookie. I like that type because like me, it contains two very different parts. The cookie part and the chocolate part. Sometimes I show my more cookie part – the part of me that is sugary and it occurs more. However, sometimes I am like the chocolate chip – dark, mysterious, and a little bit bitter. What about you? Would you be more of a sugar cookie all nice and sweet or maybe a holiday cookie covered with sprinkles?

Step 3: Participation

After some time spent in meaningful discussion, there may be added value in trying to bring the message you are trying to convey to life with some sort of interactive participation with the client. This might take the form of a worksheet, writing in a journal, engaging in some sort of product generation, or gross motor movement tasks. For example, it might be possible to expand on the idea of a superhero power as akin to a process of the Hexaflex by asking the client if they would create their own ACT superhero called "Defusion Man" and list the powers he has. Making the cookie metaphor come to life could entail baking some cookies, noticing the various shapes and sizes, and how different ingredients are similar to the different parts of one's life. The key here is to begin linking the metaphors of the lesson to the activity, and then the activity to the ACT process.

I have a chunk of molding clay for each of us. Why don't we take about ten minutes and try to mold a figure that represents a superhero. I will make one on Acceptance, and you try and make one on Present Moment. When you create your hero make sure to exemplify the special power they have that is part of the Hexaflex. Me, I am going to have my hero not be able to see, but have really good hearing. Like giant ears. The special power he has comes with the need to accept he lacks other power too – in this case the power to see.

Give me a name for each of these ingredients for the cookies we are going to now bake. Instead of telling me the actual name like sugar, flour, chocolate – give me names that describe how these ingredients are like the parts of you. For me the flour I am going to call "family." It is the biggest ingredient in our recipe and the biggest part of my life. The sugar, I am going to call "my son." He is the sweetening part of my existence. The oil is my back pain. I don't really like it, but it is part of who I am and part of what it takes to make a cookie. Now you try, tell me what is the flour for you and why?

Step 4: Process Connection

The final step when delivering an ACT lesson to your client is to ensure there is a link between the theme, dialogue, and activity to the actual behavior change you are hoping to accomplish. This task will involve more explicit directives for some clients over others. What is preferred, at least in the long term, will be the development within the client of an ability to make such derived responding on their own, so that you might be able to say to the client "how are the cookies like your life?" or "tell me about your own current superpowers." Here the client should be able to reflect back on the lesson and discuss the application to their life, and how such knowledge and skills could be used for better self-management. For instance, in the case of the superhero being able to deduce that they have their own strengths and weaknesses and utilizing their strengths to move closer to values would be an advantageous repertoire to develop.

It sure was fun to make these superheroes out of clay. Even me and you, just as we are, have a variety of superpowers. I am really good at remembering directions, and you are awesome at basketball. All of our strengths can help us get through things that are tough. You are good at basketball because you share, work as a team member, and can listen well to the coach. Keep that in mind when it is time for schoolwork that you hate. The coach is like your teacher. She gives you directions. Making baskets is like getting assignments done. Some are hard and some are easy. And the points on the scoreboard are like your grades. The more work you do, the better grades you get. And when you tell me you value graduating, well that means we know what we have to do, right? We can use our superpower to accept that things can be tough, like a tough opponent on the court, and work hard to get to the basket – or our grades.

These cookies are going to taste great. However, before we eat them, let's take a moment to notice how they are all different sizes and shapes – maybe just a tiny bit different. The cookies are just like us, as we are all different. However even with the same stuff that makes all these cookies, that stuff is not really the cookie. We don't see the oil, or the flour anymore. We see the entire thing. The entire cookie. Perhaps we are just like the cookie, and our thoughts and experiences are the ingredients. Some are good on their own, like the chocolate, and some are not so tasty like the flour. Remember the flour was my back pain. I sure don't want that to be my whole life. It is just a part of a bigger me. A me that is whole cookie – not just a collection of ingredients. When you go to work tomorrow, don't think of yourself as just one ingredient, but a much bigger whole. And when you start focusing on just one thing, like how you worry you will bag groceries incorrectly and be yelled at by the customer, step back from that thought and notice the bigger you that is at work. You are the cookie, made up of a lot of thoughts and experiences, and they blend together to make you. And accepting we all have some flour in our lives, can make even the bad stuff feel just a little better and get us through that work shift.

TELEHEALTH AND TECHNOLOGY ENHANCEMENTS

Advances in technology have resulted in many ways to expand the creative nature of the therapeutic relationship. Geographical distances no longer serve as a rigid boundary for access to good ACT services. Telehealth or remote treatments have become more common during the past few years and are a prime environment for the delivery of innovative ACT lessons to clients. Each therapist and client location will need to be examined for the feasibility and legality of such a relationship, but when no limitations are serving as barriers, an outstanding treatment approach remains possible. The general approach to telehealth ACT treatment remains the same as described above yet poses some additional considerations that may warrant attention from the clinician. First, the level of engagement is often difficult to detect remotely. Are there distractions in the client's environment diverting attention away from the session? Is the client an appropriate match for the technology that is needed for a remote session? Can effective behavior management occur via local resources, while the ACT sessions are done remotely? If appropriate checks and balances are in place, treatment may be useful. This may be especially the case when local resources are unskilled or unfamiliar with the ACT approach to behavioral care.

The flow of a telehealth session will closely resemble a live session; however, the utilization of technology could allow for computer screen sharing, video presentations, camera usage, and project completions with whiteboards. The following example of an entire session uses computer slides, videos, dialogue, and client participation below.

Lesson: Fish View

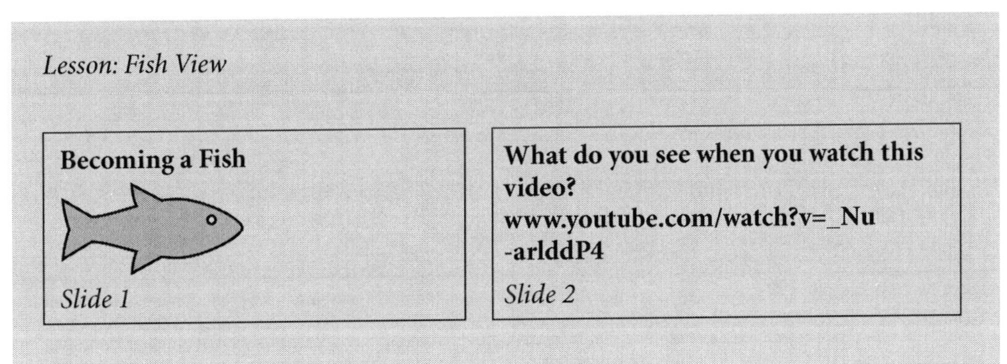

Start with a theme, and some sort of experience that is low demand. In this case, watch a video of fish swimming in the ocean.

What does the fish see?
www.youtube.com/watch?v=KSh55cVEGto

Slide 3

How does the perspective of your viewing change?

- What did you notice more as a fish?
- What did you notice more as an observer of the fish?

Slide 4

Discussion of the video and how each person/fish sees things differently. Introduce the idea of multiple views, and positions in reality.

What about yourself?

- What do people notice most about you?
- What do you notice about yourself as other people are noticing you?

Slide 5

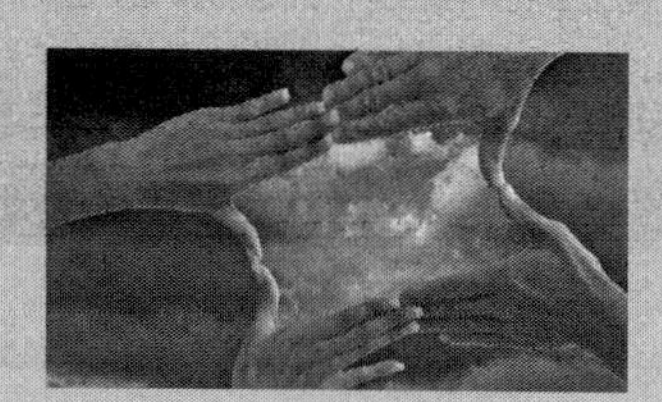

FIGURE 12.5

FIGURE 12.6

Think about a bad experience

- Something that happened during the past month
- What about it was bad from how you looked at it?
- What was something good, from how SOMEONE ELSE looked at it?
- Can you find anything good in it now?

Slide 6

Linkage to the client's world and how that experience of seeing an event can be looked at through different perspectives. Relate to a behavior episode they have recently had.

FIGURE 12.7

Slide 7

Expand the metaphor to other people and how client is looked at by these others. Reflect on the relevant Hexaflex process(es).

GROUP SESSIONS AND COLLECTIVE GOALS

When treatment content is designed for delivery to multiple clients at the same time, the general approach can be retained but clinical expectations should be adjusted. The dynamics of any group of clients will likely alter the sorts of participation and responses that are emitted by any individual group member. There are certain types of groups that are commonly configured, and each necessitates its own unique therapeutic style to promote more optimal treatment effects. The silent group is most common, whereby the presence of others simply reduces the demands for a single member to speak. Here the therapist will likely need to provide additional exemplars to stimulate discussion and may also need to call on individuals to provide a response rather than hope for a volunteer. When this is done, be careful not to push too hard on too sensitive of a topic, as the potential social punishers for sharing too much may be at work. Another type of group is the grandstander. Here a single or few members try and dominate the totality of the conversation with remaining members remaining silent. The fact that someone is talking often allows for other nonsocial members to step back and rely on the clinician's attention to the talkers. Similar to the grandstander is the anti-ACT group. This group often contains a single member who is just not going to do anything, no matter what. Here the message is that they are just too cool for ACT and will try and sabotage anything that is being attempted by the clinician. Such problems are often attention-seeking in function, and depending on extremes may unfortunately require attention from the clinician in attempts to hold the group together. Oftentimes, differentially reinforcing other group members for appropriate answers and engagement can likely improve the attention-seeking behavior of the single deficit member. Depending on scheduling logistics, removal of this person from the group can also positively alter the dynamics of the remaining members. However, that removal needs to be met with some sort of intervention for reintroducing, individualized session time, or increased session time in other contexts to incentives reintroduction into the original group and displaying of a more appropriate behavioral repertoire. Finally, there is the chatty group who shares too much on tangentially related topics. This may be done to postpone post-ACT session activities like getting back to schoolwork, to acquire additional social reinforcement from peers for storytelling, or to demonstrate how much they think they know about the topic of the session. This type of group will require the clinician to time manage effectively such that the eventual message and teaching elements of the lesson are not omitted due to running out of session time.

POPULATION SPECIFIC SPECIFICS

When the behavior analyst embarks on delivery of ACT services, attention will need to be paid to the type of population involved. Age, disability, cognitive skills, mental health, and compliance likelihood all factor into the general approach that needs to be taken to optimize intervention effectiveness. Although the ACT model conceptually does not need to be altered from a contextual integrated system, the methods of introduction and regular treatment may be in need of modification. Many of these guidelines are general, as there is a range of abilities within any specific population subgroup. However, the best way to gauge the need to adapt or sustain any approach to treatment with an individual client should be based on how that client is responding or failing to respond to the existing configuration of services.

The age of a client is a major variable to consider when delivering ACT. A quick review of the ACT peer-reviewed literature will reveal only a small fraction of studies conducted with children (see Fang & Ding, 2020 for some exceptions). This is not to say no work with children has been conducted, but rather the documented research is not as robust as it is for adults. Perhaps one of the reasons why this discrepancy exists is because children are more prone to delay mental health care than adults (Whitney & Peterson, 2019), obtain services within the existing school support system (Sanchez et al., 2018), or simply more ACT researchers have been involved with adult populations. Given the nature and complexity of ACT as a talk-based intervention, children may take longer to develop a relation with, show more defenses, and be placed into treatment by a guardian rather than seek it themselves, although barriers may be highly variable for children and their families (Kazdin, 2000). As a result, the behavior analyst will need to spend additional time dedicated to meeting the child at their age level, show interest in what the child is interested in, speak in a way that the child can relate to, and keep metaphors and the ACT agenda engaging to the child – not the therapist. There is a real additional level of effort needed to reconfigure the ACT active treatment processes into concepts that can be understood and engaging to children of any age.

The level of disability, or ability, a client possesses will impact how the ACT message delivered becomes the ACT message received. When a person of a certain ability level has difficulty understanding the consequences of future behavior, more responses may be allocated to sooner smaller reinforcers and their less adaptive behaviors emitted. If the client has a fair amount of distractibility, there may be challenges with attempting to deliver a long discussion-based treatment session. In this case, it may be best to have a variety of experiential and vocal dialogue, to ensure that a clearer relating to the client's life can occur.

There may be an increased need to repeat messages within a single treatment session, as well as revisit such messages at follow-up sessions. It is not uncommon for persons possessing a range of disabilities from autism to social-emotional challenges, and histories of trauma and abuse, to require regular checks on what the Hexaflex processes represent, and how to apply them in their life – more than what would be expected from a neurotypical client. Ability limitations, when combined with a younger age, may compound the challenges to effective treatment delivery. Again, it will be necessary for the behavior analyst to now not only use ability-related modifications to a standard treatment approach, but now they must also consider age challenges to ACT delivery as well.

Cognitive skills clearly vary with age and ability levels. The parameters of cognition that one must be most concerned with regarding treatment with ACT involve the capacity to perspective take, demonstrate theory of mind, logically deduce and induce, and engage in derived relational responding. Such capacities are assumed to be intact when speaking with neurotypical adults yet should be evaluated in clients where there are suspected limitations in cognition. These evaluations may include intelligence tests, adaptive behavior scales, executive functioning inventories, and tests of relational abilities. Some of these tools may require involving additional professionals skilled in a certain cognitive area, while others can be easily administered by the behavior analyst. Once such parameters have been obtained, the behavior analyst may need to make modifications in terms of delivery method as well as expectations for understanding. Keep in mind that someone's current state of cognitive ability is not a fixed permanent condition. Rather such skills can be taught, oftentimes using relational training procedures (Colbert et al., 2018; Dixon et al., 2021), and thus improvements in cognition can allow for a more substantive ACT agenda over time.

The mental health status of the client targeted for intervention is critical to consider. Persons struggling with co-occurring mental disorders will need supplemental supports beyond that typically provided by the behavior analyst. Perhaps the decision as to what direction treatment should take should be based on the degree the mental health condition is impacting the presenting conditions the client is seeking services for. If it is concluded that the mental health disorder is heavily impacting behavior, a logical step would be to consult and co-treat with another more specialized mental health therapist. However, if the mental disorder has little to nothing to do with the presenting problems the behavior analyst is concerned with, then it may be unnecessary to coordinate care. The evaluation to determine the necessity of collaborative care should be approached cautiously – with the primary objective of doing no harm. For example, if a child with an anxiety disorder engages in problem behaviors in typically anxious environments (public speaking, competitions, testing in school) it is more likely that the anxiety plays a relevant role in potential treatment. Yet if that same child has no signs of anxiety, has an obsession with tornados, and engages in the same challenging behaviors in the same situations noted above, it is less likely that the mental health condition is impacting the scope of variables that could be impacting treatment outcomes. Even here however there may be a future obscured link between tornados and behavior that is eventually revealed. In short, it is wise for the behavior analyst to be respectful, attentive, and willing to collaborate when necessary with other skilled professionals.

Given that T-Bone has a history with selective mutism, and is not making friends at school, I am going to not only put together a contingency plan for increasing the probability of him socializing with others, I am also going to discuss how some of the things he values – like playing with others at recess – might be able to happen if he tries harder to talk to people. Yet, I want to also make sure that any underlying social anxiety is being addressed so I have asked my friend Gretta who is a social worker to collaborate with me on overall approach.

After working with Jamba for the past two weeks it appears to me that although you say she only eats chicken nuggets and you believe this is causing her to have behavior problems in class, I do not believe her food selectivity is a major contributing factor that could limit my ability to treat her non-compliance with classwork.

The probability of compliance with services should dictate the path taken towards ACT treatment by the behavior analyst. When the client has a history of poor adherence with tasks such as self-monitoring, goal setting, or even participating during treatment, there is likely a reason to slow treatment demands to a level that can increase compliance. Additionally, there may be a need to introduce extrinsic reinforcers to the client to improve motivation conditions that could spark treatment adherence. It is hoped that over time and successful contacting of the consequences of ACT on presenting conditions that the client will begin to see the utility of adhering more carefully to treatment. In other words, the positive outcomes of treatment will reinforce treatment compliance in such a way that "compliance" is no longer a necessary goal as the client comes to enjoy and see intrinsic value in participating in ACT.

I know these sessions are a lot of work for you. And you hate the homework I give you to track how you are doing with the Hexaflex each day when I send you that text. So how about this, if we can get everything accomplished in session today, I will let you out ten minutes early so you can get back to your video games.

When you notice yourself not being so entangled in your thoughts, that is proof our time together, even though it is a hassle, might just be working. I want you to reflect on those times from the past week. Also, when you find yourself at the crossroads of value-added and value-subtracted choices this coming week, remember how good it feels to step back from those thoughts. Doing so will help nudge you towards making a choice that yields outcomes consistent with your values.

LOCATION-SPECIFIC SPECIFICS

There are a variety of factors to consider when the behavior analyst delivers ACT in a specific setting. Adjustments to the care model may need to occur when treatment is delivered in a school, clinic, home, or workplace. Certain environments may wish for treatment to be isolated to medical necessity, educational goals, parental concerns, or cultural change. As a result, the behavior analyst will need to carefully determine how the location they are providing services defines and limits what exactly the ACT intervention should contain.

ACT treatments within the educational system may take a variety of forms. A schoolwide intervention could be designed as a preventative means for social and emotional well-being. Here the purpose of ACT is to teach all students valuable life skills such that they are better able to encounter and respond to the various challenges and choices occurring each day.

Nothing is wrong per se, but rather ACT treatment is designed as the prevention not the solution to a presenting problem. Other levels of intervention within a school might target students with social and emotional disorders in restrictive classrooms or alternative placements. In these situations, ACT moves from a preventative life skill set to a more focused intervention designed to address specific social challenges exhibited by this population. A need may be present for both group and individualized sessions, as each can capitalize on the limitations of the other modality. Individual sessions strengthen the trust with the behavior analyst as well as provide a student-specific intervention agenda. Yet the group sessions with peers also serve as great opportunities for multiple exemplars of struggles and successes. Another treatment alternative involves students who are simply at risk for various larger behavioral infractions or emotional setbacks due to histories of trauma and abuse. These students may benefit from services at higher intensities than general education prevention methods, yet not need the intensity of care that is required for students in full-time alternative placements. The behavior analyst should remember that other skilled professionals exist within the school system – ranging from social workers to psychologists. Therefore, it would be wise to collaborate with these other care providers to wrap around their efforts as well in a systemic fashion.

Clinical settings commonly offer individualized care for clients who may stand to benefit from an ACT approach. Such an environment is common within behavior analysis whereby certain amounts of weekly hours are allocated for treatment in outpatient services. Less common is inpatient treatment where the client lives at the service facility. Regardless of intensity of care, a clinical setting is an effective location to deliver services because many elements of the environment can be controlled. In such environments, the behavior analyst can carefully install stimulus elements that might encourage greater present-moment awareness (soft lighting, comfortable seating, reduce distractors), or values identification (goal-setting charts, reinforcer economies). Although similar enhancements are possible in other settings, when a clinic is exclusively operated by a behavior analyst, limited concessions regarding space and budget need to occur. In the treatment room itself it may be advantageous to display a Hexaflex on the wall, posters with ACT phrasing (e.g., "Everyone feels everything"; "Nowhere is more important than here"; "Are you moving towards what matters?"), or even completed ACT worksheets and lessons by other clients to increase the believability that everyone struggles with flexibility.

Home care services create unique benefits and challenges for the behavior analyst. The home is the natural environment where the client very likely exhibits a portion of the behaviors that have brought them into treatment. As a result, it may be possible that emersion into that environment may reveal critical yet subtle variables that may have been omitted during the functional assessment process. The home also contains a variety of more naturalistic reinforcers than any other location, and thus capitalizing on the building interventions which incorporate such consequences can be quite beneficial. The home also contains a set of challenges to delivering effective treatment. In contrast to the clinic where every element of the physical space can be controlled, the home space varies freely. Other people, pets, and competing sources of reinforcement can all draw the client into a level of unpreferred disengagement in the therapeutic process. When working in the home a behavior analyst will likely need to ensure a controlled space, minimize distractions, and incorporate additional novel reinforcers not typically found in the house. Caution should be taken to ensure that the professional relationship remains professional and that the behavior analyst refrains from developing connections with family members or engaging in blurred conversations that are beyond the boundaries of the treatment. It is recommended that the home environment only be sought as treatment space if other options have been deemed unavailable or clinically necessary, as most health care services are done at dedicated usage centers rather than within patient homes.

Thank you for introducing me to Ronald's sister and showing me the tricks the family pig can do. I honestly have to really concentrate on my time with Ronald when I am here so we can make sure everything gets completed in time. Don't get me wrong, that pig is totally cool, but I just have to focus on Ronald during our hour together.

If you don't mind, I would like to bring in my own iPad when I come next time and have Sierra play some games she doesn't have at home. I think these games might motivate her more to participate when we run ACT sessions because they are not played on a regular basis.

The workplace may seem like an afterthought for implementing an ACT session, but when the client demonstrates the presenting behavioral issues on the job – treatment may be warranted directly within that environment. When working within another party's establishment, a variety of clearances may need to occur prior to beginning. These may include background checks, confidentiality releases, and a defined set of parameters under which treatment can be delivered. Given that many workplaces contain additional workers beyond the targeted client, some discussion will likely also need to occur with those employees by management prior to the behavior analyst's arrival. Even afterwards, the behavior analyst may need to field questions from co-workers and need to deflect certain answers to sustain the confidential relationship with the client. All these issues aside, the workplace can be a great spot to promote more adaptive behavior under constantly varying conditions directly in the real world. Delivering treatment at work might be a move towards naturalistic generalization beyond sessions that are conducted at school or clinic, and thus content may differ to a certain degree. A common distinction is that discussion of Hexaflex processes and problem-solving within the workplace are discussed in center treatment, and the actual engaging of behavior that mirrors such discussion is now implemented at work under the coaching of the behavior analyst.

Hey Frankie, it looks like it is getting pretty busy and you are going to be bagging a lot of groceries today. Let's use the time as we walk to the checkout line to just notice the sounds of the store, the floor as you walk across it and how it feels on your feet. Notice the thoughts you have about feeling like you cannot work fast enough. Just notice those thoughts as nothing more than just another sound in the store. You have worked hard before, and it feels sometimes like you cannot do it. But you can, and you have. As we walk let's breathe deep and feel everything. After work, you are going to the movies, so let's keep moving towards the movies shall we.

Thanks for asking me why I am here at work with Barb. She is really cool, and I am just hanging out with her today because I think her job here at the zoo is fun. You can talk to your manager a bit more about me if you like, but now I have to get ready for Barb.

It really is appreciated that you are letting me help Heather on her job. I am her therapist outside of work and getting some additional time with her at work may allow her to use the skills we have been using in therapy right in the place where sometimes she has problems. I will keep to myself and just interact with Heather when necessary. If you don't mind, my relationship with her is confidential, so if your other employees ask questions about me, just tell them I am her friend who wants to learn more about her job or something like that.

RELATIONAL FRAMES IN TREATMENT

The degree to which a client can engage in relational responding is critical for effective understanding of what ACT is all about. Depending on the complexity a client can derive the ACT treatment may not be as effective as expected. The first step is to determine the depth of the relational repertoire and subsequently to build upon deficit relational processes concurrently along with the delivery of ACT treatment. It may be thought that ACT treatment should be placed on hold until deficits in relational framing can be brought to sufficient levels of proficiency. However, if the client has already met thresholds for potential ACT treatment noted in the preceding chapter of this text, the agenda for improving framing should remain concurrent. In such a design the first portion of a treatment session may be dedicated to building the relational repertoire, while the latter portion remains concentrated on using those framing skills to comprehend the ACT treatment. Prior work has shown such a configuration is both possible and successful at improving ACT participation along with a suppression of challenging behaviors (Gilsenan et al., 2021). Other configurations may mix framing tasks with ACT treatment tasks within a single session to enhance engagement via session variability. A wealth of research into this area remains to be done, however the underlying implications are clear. Build framing and obtain more impact from the ACT intervention. It may be useful to categorize a client into one of four increasingly complex levels of relational framing abilities and strive for development of skills across higher levels and a range of the relational frame families (coordination, opposition, comparison, distinction, hierarchy, and diectic) to improve ACT performance and comprehension. The examples shown in Table 12.5 are only a tiny fraction of the possibilities that exist for building relational abilities in the clients served by behavior analysts.

KEEPING DATA AND TRACKING PROGRESS

The need to keep data and summarize the progress of your client is a defining characteristic of the job of a behavior analyst. How one collects ACT data is much less defined or well understood yet needs to be crafted in extensive detail to ensure that persons unfamiliar with the treatment model can be assured that is clearly linked to the presenting behavioral concerns that brought the client into treatment. The obtained ACT data can be broadly categorized into two areas – indirect and direct measures of behavior change. These sorts of data were discussed under the assessment process, and thus we return to the topic here strictly in regard to evaluating progress. Below we organize the entirety of data collection into an overall summary and then unpack the main features of the document. The first section of Table 12.5 depicts indirect assessments that were chosen for this hypothetical client that were completed at set intervals. These tools include a variety of mindfulness, flexibility, and behavior scales. Some of this information may have been captured by the client themselves, and others from relevant stakeholders. Typically the Avoidance and Fusion Questionnaire – Youth (AFQ-Y) and Childhood and Adolescent Mindfulness Measure (CAMM) are done as self-reports by the client, the CPFQ is done by either the client themselves or a caregiver, and the Questions About Behavior Function (QABF) is completed by those caregivers who see exhibition of the challenging behaviors. The progress direction is also described here because it is not intuitive as to if scores moving up are better or worse. Thus ideal performance changes are indicated as progress up or down.

The Observational Processes consist of both the basic performance of the client in terms of attendance and participation in ACT sessions, but also their utilization of engagement with the active treatment elements of the ACT model. As a result, data are gathered on their

TABLE 12.5

Framing Ability	*Definition*	*Example*
Level 1: Non-arbitrary skills	Ability to be trained and transfer relationships among stimuli based on physical features of the stimuli.	**Training conditions:** when provided with a small and medium block as options, the client can select the small block when given the directive "Show me smaller" and select the medium block when asked "Show me bigger." When provided with a medium and large block as options, the client can select the medium block when asked "Show me smaller," and the larger block when asked "Show me bigger." **Testing conditions:** without any prior training or reinforcement, the client will transfer the concept of smaller and bigger to glasses of water, marker lines, or any other stimuli varying in size.
Level 2: Cultural skills	Ability to be trained and transfer relationships among stimuli that are typically established with the verbal community as conventions of language.	**Training conditions:** when provided with pictures of a cat, dog, and a stapler, the client will identify the one item without shared features. **Testing conditions:** when presented with two yellow cups and a red cup and asked to match with the array of cat, dog, and stapler that the client will sort based on the distinct feature.
Level 3: Arbitrary skills	Ability to form abstract relationships and transfer such relations between stimuli that are established exclusively within the therapeutic environment for the purposes of promoting derived relating as a generalized operant.	**Training conditions:** when presented with a sample textual actual word, the client will be taught to select a designated textual nonsense word when provided with an array of such nonsense words. (ex. baseball = VAX; football = SAN) **Testing conditions:** when presented with a word problem in the form of a spoken sentence, the client will be requested to repeat the vocalization using a different (nonsense) word and an identical (nonsense) word than what was emitted in that sentence. (ex. "I like to play baseball. Replace baseball with a different word and an identical word").
Level 4: Complex Transformations	Ability to form abstract relationships between stimuli that are established exclusively within the therapeutic environment for the purposes of promoting derived relating as a generalized operant, and then transfer the newly acquired abstract derived relation to solve a novel verbal problem or puzzle.	**Training conditions:** when provided a sample object and an array of nonsense words, the client will be taught to select the "louder" and "softer" nonsense words (ex. red block = louder; blue block = softer). When presented with a nonsense word and an array of 3D objects, client will be able to select louder/softer (ex. VUG = cup; ZOP = glass). **Testing conditions:** when presented with a sequence of sounds from a piano keyboard that create a pattern of loud/soft, the client will be able to select either the object derived as louder or softer (ex. cup or glass) when asked "what type of sound comes next" to complete the pattern.

* Table adapted from programs contained within the PEAK Transformation Module (Dixon, 2016).

ability to independently articulate how they can relate the various flexibility processes to areas of their own life, the derived relating of the session metaphors to their presenting behavioral conditions of concern, and homework completion of self-monitoring connections between their behavior and flexibility. The supports section provides information as to the degree to which the relevant stakeholders for the client are engaging in the intervention process as agreed upon at intake. Here both the actual attendance is taken on the proportion of scheduled meetings or coaching sessions the behavior analyst has with these individuals, as well as a tracking of the number of recommendations made during these meetings compared to the number of actual follow-throughs on such recommendations. The section on relational framing skills may be added when it has been determined that the client is performing relational tasks at levels lower than ideal. This evaluation metric might be added only after insufficient treatment progress has been documented, or it might have been established as necessary from initial intake. More detail might be included here depending on client abilities, as the PCA score could be broken down into specific relational frame families and/or reported age norms.

The final section regarding observed behaviors is probably the most important. Here we see an objective appraisal of the actual behaviors that the client was seeking reduction of when entering treatment. These data often require others to collect (including self-monitoring), as it is quite possible the concerns are taking place beyond the walls of the treatment session. Remember to keep data collection at equal windows across evaluation periods when computing averages, as the overall numbers could vary in unpredictable ways if the observations are of different intensities or durations and means are being calculated and subsequently compared to each other. When overall frequencies are used, this risk is somewhat reduced only if the total opportunities to engage in such behavior are relatively constant. Percentages and ratios can assist in clarifying any confusion in the raw numbers when such variations in collection are present.

In the example of a completed form shown in Table 12.6, it can be concluded that this client is making progress with the ACT intervention. We see behavior reductions occurring, participation in sessions improving, caregiver adherence slowly gaining, self-reports moving in the ideal directions, and relational framing skills strengthened. In short, progress is great, and the treatment approach appears to match the needs of the client. Of course, this example is ideal, and no real case will necessarily mirror these types of numbers exactly, however the content described herein provide an illustration of how progress can be reported and hints at the sorts of data collection which was necessary to eventually arrive at this summary. A lengthy narrative report could supplement these summary data whereby the nuances of the individual case can be presented in sufficient detail to more clearly describe the various elements of treatment, the types of gains recorded, and elements of intervention that still need to be targeted for more optimal eventual behaviors.

Client Treatment Data and Progress Report Summary

Keep in mind that at the end of the day, it is going to be the clear objectively measurable decrease in problematic behaviors and improvements in adaptive behaviors that define treatment success or failure. All the self-reports in the world or all the conceptualizations of verbal dialogue emitted will mean nothing if the client's behavior fails to move in the targeted direction. The behavior analyst must see ACT and the flexibility processes as the means toward a behavioral end not the end in itself. As a result, the bulk of treatment progress rests on the dependent variable of changed behavior. ACT treatment remains the independent variable which plays a critical role in altering levels of the dependent variable.

TABLE 12.6

Measure	*Initial Level Date*	*Follow Up 1 Date*	*Follow Up 2 Date*
Indirect			
AFQ-Y (progress down)	18	22	14
CAMM (progress up)	23	27	27
CPFQ (progress up)	22	33	39
QABF Total (progress down)	34	22	18
Observational processes			
Participation in session (attendance/scheduled)	22/27	18/24	24/24
Completion of session lesson (completion/assigned)	18/27	18/24	21/24
Independent vocalization of process in own life (during session)	29	49	55
Relating session metaphors to challenging behaviors	0	3	17
Self-monitoring flexibility processes between sessions	10/23	10/24	15/24
Supports			
Caregiver session attendance	10/18	13/16	19/19
Caregiver follow through with recommendations	0/110	40/132	60/115
Relational framing			
PEAK PCA total score (progress up)	232	267	304
PEAK programs mastered	--	23	19
Behavioral outcomes			
Target behavior 1: *Negative statements to others* (frequency per day averaged)	22	30	11
Target behavior 2: *Physical aggression* (frequency total during reporting period)	19	24	4

Extending Treatment Beyond Clinical Care

The methods and processes described in this chapter extend far beyond typical clinical care delivered by behavior analysts. The ACT model has advantages for utilization with caregivers, staff, cultural systems, and even the behavior analyst themselves.

The literature on ACT methods in these areas is voluminous. In the area of self-care for behavior analysts themselves, ACT self-help has been applied to a wide variety of professionals – physicians, social workers, nurses, clinical psychology trainees, and so on. Many of these programs are "turn key" – using books, tapes, websites, apps, videos, and so on. As these programs have expanded, they have begun to offer validated intervention methods that do not require extensive training to be deployed and can be used in a wide variety of situations.

Using "off the shelf" materials of this kind is an easy first step for behavior analysts exploring ACT for interventions beyond clinical care that does not immediately lead to a high scope of practice barriers. Consider, for example, "self-help plus" – a program of supported self-help that was originally developed by the World Health Organization (WHO) to help address the needs of refugees. The initial target was South Sudanese refugees in Uganda.

In 2013, a civil war began in the new nation of South Sudan and raged for several years. Famine and disease cruelly added to the misery. Refugees poured out of the country, mostly women and children, escaping horrific violence, sexual attacks, and starvation. One million people arrived in Uganda, usually with nothing but the clothing on their backs. WHO went looking for an intervention that could be of help.

They made the decision not to focus on the usual psychotherapy methods that target psychiatric syndromes since war can produce almost every kind of psychological problem you can name. Instead, they looked for methods that fostered personal and social resilience and they settled on ACT.

In Uganda, WHO delivered ACT in a group format using an audio tape and a graphic novel (necessary because the rate of illiteracy in South Sudan is the highest in the world – only about one-quarter of the population can read). No single problem was targeted – these survivors struggled with every kind of psychological problem from post-traumatic stress disorder (PTSD) to depression, from explosive anger to an inability to sleep. Instead, what was targeted was psychological flexibility itself.

This program significantly reduced psychological distress across the board, leading to improvements in almost all monitored areas (e.g., depression, explosive anger, well-being, disability) with an effect size as large or larger than that found for self-help in the developed world (Tol et al., 2020). Importantly, these effects occurred regardless of the degree of initial distress or the extent of the exposure to violence. No adverse events were found to be linked to the program – a major factor given the painful history of other well-meaning crisis intervention programs that have inadvertently made the problems worse when they were closely examined in controlled research.

Encouraged, WHO then turned its eye to the *prevention* of mental disorders. They used this same program with nearly 650 war-torn Syrian refugees in Turkey who were distressed but had not yet developed a mental health disorder. In the first randomized prevention trial ever conducted among war refugees who did not yet have a diagnosable disorder, the ACT self-help program was found to cut a later emergence of mental disorders by nearly half (Acarturk et al., 2022).

As a result of these successes, WHO now distributes ACT self-help free worldwide in 21 different languages, recommending this approach for "anyone who experiences stress, wherever they live, and whatever their circumstances" (bit.ly/WHO_ACT). "Self-help plus" is designated by WHO as a "fully scalable psychological intervention," meaning that it can be delivered by non-specialists.

Any behavior analyst skilled in ACT would know how to use this program with minimal additional training as a supplement for parent training, as a staff-based stress program, or for caregivers.

Behavior analysts have developed similar methods for special applications. An example is the stress and burnout management program for medical students developed in Ramona Houmanfar's lab at the University of Nevada. Dr. Houmanfar, a well-known behavior analyst, developed a series of ACT-based videos that are shown to medical students in a required online class as part of their medical training (Szarko et al., 2022)

As applied behavior analysts venture out into other forms of clinical care, it seems likely that additional models will emerge. These will need to be done in a step-by-step fashion as the scope of practice gradually expands.

SUMMARY

The treatment process of ACT remains broad, multimodal, and comprehensive. Behavior analysts will need to prepare for a significant departure from their traditional intervention methods and progress monitoring. Expanding the treatment process to include a wide range of tools and modalities will strengthen the confidence that a client is able to understand ACT, benefit from an ACT treatment approach, and yield measurable outcomes that matter. We have provided a wide range of approaches to obtaining the necessary information to deliver treatment, but we did not generate a finite checklist of steps for the behavior analyst to complete. The complexity of presenting conditions necessitates interpretation on behalf of the behavior analyst. Much akin to the clinical psychologist or speech pathologist needing to make a series of choices as to what treatment to administer to promote improved levels of performance, the behavior analyst will need to make educated informed choices of how to approach the ACT intervention process. How one treats their clients should never be a one-size-fits-all process and should be client led with on-going respect for assent throughout the treatment process. Rather the optimal intervention is one based on clinical impressions that are rooted in an effective understanding of human language and cognition, scientific discoveries in this area, and practical utility.

13

Research

THE RESEARCH AGENDA FOR BEHAVIOR ANALYSTS

Behavior analysts pride themselves on being data-driven decision makers. Our research literature is unique when compared to many other areas of psychology and human services. A notable difference is the inclusion of "intensive times series" or "single-case experimental designs" (SCED). This allows for an evaluative analytic strategy that is scientific at the level of the individual – does *this* intervention work for *this* client?

There are strengths and weaknesses to SCED research approach. Without a careful strategy for scaling idiographic data to nomothetic generalizations, the research literature often does not support sweeping generalizable claims that can have clear policy implications, such as "Treatment X is more effective in treating problem Y than is Treatment Z." Repeated demonstrations alone can point the behavior analyst in a general direction, but it is often missed that SCED is really meant to focus on an idiographic process-to-outcome interface. Our literature supports methods for analyzing the function of challenging behavior (a process issue), generating a solution from the analysis (an issue of the practical extension of process information), and evaluating if that solution was efficacious in changing behavior (a treatment outcome issue). That focus on a person-specific level is highly unusual as compared to mainstream psychology or behavioral science. Even more unusual, practicing behavior analysts are not then encouraged simply to replicate the intervention verbatim. What behavior analysts replicate is instead the analytic strategy. It is understood that the particulars of the intervention may look nothing like the original study – but the creation of that intervention will be grounded in the same basic behavior change principles from which the study emerged.

It's an amazingly powerful approach, but only if the process information is relatively adequate. This strategy was highly effective in building individualized interventions for disabled persons but only when verbal processes were not too dominant. Direct-acting contingencies alone can only go so far. As a result, our literature was dominated by strategies that largely omitted private events from the analysis, focusing almost exclusively on directly observable behavior and immediate stimulus-response (S-R) contextual variables to inform intervention that was at times more in line with methodological behaviorism than it was Skinner's view of radical behaviorism. The development of our analytic strategies occurred heavily within a population that had notable language and communication limitations. Severe questioning about the validity or reliability of self-report of private events sometimes substituted for the needed development of more thoughtful ways to assess the nature and

DOI: 10.4324/9781003250371-16

role of private events. Without those developments the needed tools to analyze processes of change were unavailable.

A certain methodological rigidity also settled in, not recognizing that some questions (especially certain population-level policy-relevant questions) are actually best answered at a group comparison level. It was not widely appreciated that it is possible to combine intensive idiographic into group comparison designs, nor that proper use of group comparison strategies is actually a lot easier for researchers once a strong program of SCED is in place. Instead of using and building upon the powerful knowledge base process-focus SCEDs can give, a barrier grew up between these analytic strategies that became impossible to cross. The methodological skills of behavior analysts were left unappreciated by behavioral science more generally and the impact of the behavior analysis of mainstream issues was diminished.

Taking things one client at a time without finalizing population-based policy issues with properly done group studies also reduced the public's appetite to invest in behavior-analytic interventions. Funders and policy makers preferring large-scale randomized control trial research that would show that a specific intervention *approach* could successfully lead to behavior change in *most cases* of a given type compared to treatment as usual or no treatment control conditions.

The unique adaptations that disabilities bring make personalization of intervention strategies critically important – but that personalization increases exponentially once relational operants are at issue because the number and impact of possibly relevant processes and their combinations also increase. Thus, if the link between functional analysis and intervention becomes over-simplified the barriers to working with neurotypical populations became higher. Overcoming those barriers is why many behavior analysts are excited about the implications of acceptance and commitment treatment (ACT) and relational frame theory (RFT), but an expanded research agenda needs to be implemented to take advantage of that opportunity.

In a data-driven science, decisions made in the clinic need to extend from the published literature – setting the framework for what are considered evidence-based practices. This research defines the field of the science, and it is expected that analysts follow these established processes. A disconnect occurs when the presenting problem a behavior analyst encounters does not have a readily available empirical resource to guide the next step – and such is the case in our literature once complex language emerges. Without a clear way to analyze it and a framework from which to develop an intervention, the only solution is to refer to other professionals who have established this literature base.

It is for this very reason that we need to begin with the fact that the body of research within behavior analysis is far from complete and the field itself has to develop a strategy to change that situation. A progressive science by its very definition is constantly changing. Thus, there is an obligation on its members to continue producing new discoveries, testing the boundaries of phenomena, refining established practices, and publishing the outcomes of such endeavors. Doing so may seem like a burden on the community's members, as it is often deemed the role of the clinician to be a clinician and the scientist to be a scientist. However, when each of these siloed groups leans a little towards each other, greater gains can be made bridging the gaps of research and practice, and informing one another as to the needs of the field. One step needed step forward is to recognize that SCEDs are not everything.

A second step forward is to recognize that verbal/cognitive processes of change may need to be modeled using new data analytic tools that take the best of an idiographic approach without oversimplification. The ACT community is actively exploring complex network analyses, using a so-called "idionomic" approach. This analytic method initially assesses the impact of processes of change against within-person variability only, but then extends these relationships to the nomothetic level if and only if doing so typically improves idiographic fit. In effect, the individual becomes the certain finding and the group becomes the error term instead of the other way around. The word idionomic is new but that has always been part of behavior analysis in concepts like "reinforcement." What is new is that the combinatorial implications of relational learning need to be modeled using innovative research strategies such as idiographic dynamical systems and complex networks. We will explain these innovative but behavior-analytically sensible approaches later on in the chapter.

A third step is that behavior analysts need to become more comfortable with the broader scientific literature. That is obvious from the first two steps we have listed since few of these studies exist in narrow-focus behavior analytic journals – but literally thousands of such studies exist elsewhere. That is why ACT is currently well established.

Historically speaking ACT research began in journals where behavior analysts are used to finding research literature but it did not stay there long. The early ACT studies appeared in outlets such as the *Analysis of Verbal Behavior* (e.g., Zettle & Hayes, 1986) or the *Psychological Record* (Hayes et al., 1999) and occasionally continued to occur in *JABA* (Twohig et al., 2007) or elsewhere when SCEDs were used in the research, but it soon focused on more mainstream psychology journals. By the turn of the century applied behavior analysis (ABA) was beginning to professionalize, and clinical behavior analysis began to drift away from applied behavior analysis. ACT studies could reach a larger audience in more mainstream journals, and large federal grants began funding ACT research. That gradually has led to an explosion of ACT research data.

As this chapter is being written in June 2022 there are over 900 randomized controlled trials (RCTs) on ACT (bit.ly/ACTRCTs), an amount expected to exceed 1,000 within a year. Over the last few years, a new ACT RCT appears every three to four days. There are thousands of other studies on assessment, the psychological flexibility model, SCEDs, open-trials, longitudinal analysis, and so on. This includes over 300 meta-analytic summaries, or systematic, scoping, and narrative reviews (bit.ly/ACTmetas), and several dozen SCEDs (https://contextualscience.org/act_and_controlled_time_series_and_singlecase_designs). When the entire literature is considered, there may well be more empirical investigations conducted on ACT-based interventions than the collective entirety of other applied behavior analytic interventions.

There are legitimate criticisms to be lodged against this body of work. As with all evidence-based methods ACT "requires more investigation" and it is true that many ACT studies fail to include high-quality behavioral measures. There has historically been an over-emphasis on RCTs. But addressing such issues are the very things that applied behavior analysts are well positioned to address so it would be truly ironic to see the need for behavior analysts to be part of the overall ACT research program used as a kind of barrier to the participation in ACT research and implementation by the behavior analytic community. Behavior analysis has so much to offer, and so much to gain in this area of research.

We have written this book with the certainty that the landscape for the use of ACT by behavior analysts is rapidly changing, but it would be a mistake for applied behavior analysis simply to use ACT methods without also taking advantage of the opportunities that abound to publish in high impact journals in the ACT/RFT area. Said in another way, ACT/RFT research can be designed not only to help refine ACT and RFT but also to help increase the reach and impact of behavior analytic research itself. As this book is being written, only one journal associated with behavior analysis has an impact factor of three or more. ACT articles can and do appear in journals with impact factors of 40 or more.

Within the context of ACT, a fair amount of research is needed to help the behavior analyst approach the presenting conditions of a client with confidence. ACT- and RFT-based functional analysis is still in its childhood. Additionally, there is needed research on the parameters of treatment delivery, dosage, frequency, content, method, and unit of analysis. The current holes in ACT research as viewed by behavior analysts are in part due to the relatively small number of behavior analysts currently doing ACT research, but it is also because behavior analytic research methods need to evolve to address this novel subject area more completely. ACT and RFT research force the field to consider that the analytic method of the basic behavior analyst working with non-human animals can only take the field so far.

Throughout this text, we have tried to demystify ACT and position it clearly within the behavior analyst's operating framework. Having done so, it is expected that a cascading of research innovations will be produced. In this chapter we provide the information needed to get started on the research agenda that lies ahead for behavior analysts. We will begin with research applications based on existing methods and then extend to group design, and finally to complex network analysis done as part of an idionomic research strategy. A range of examples are described throughout, which should make the tasks of formulating an idea and getting started just a little less effortful.

ORGANIZING A STUDY

Historically our field has embraced an inductive approach to science – we seek to discover order from data and build upward to principles and eventual to analytic-abstractive theory. Risky tests are composed of the extension and systematic replication of idiographically examined process-to-outcome results. This method has worked well for members of the behavior analytic community and can continue to do so once the barrier of fitting our methods to language-able participants is overcome.

We do need to recognize at the outset, however, that the large majority of researchers continue to follow a deductive strategy to scientific discovery. In the hypo-deductive approach, a theory is first constructed, then hypotheses are constructed and tested, and based on the data, subsequently refined. In that approach, stated hypotheses come first and falsification is emphasized, at least nominally.

There remains debate as to which approach to scientific discovery is best, and it could be that the answer is contextually bound by the field, the question at hand, and the state of the existing knowledge base. For that reason, while we remain inductive researchers, we take a rather neutral position on which path any one particular researcher or research study travels. Both methods had led to scientific gains and thus neither one should not be dismissed at the expense of the other. It is better to build the strength, flexibility, and applicability of our own inductive research program than to try to tear down the research of others.

One reason we encourage this open posture is that behavior analysts need to learn how to make friends, forge alliances, and build bridges. When behavior analysts attempt to speak outside of their own ingroup, a more inclusive approach to research design, analysis, and interpretation is helpful to reduce needless conflict. When behavior analysts see that there are times to use a broader set of methodologies, it is much easier to be inclusive. Therefore, we encourage behavior analysts to be flexible in their own use of SCEDs and population-level (i.e., group-based) designs, and their combination, focusing more closely on the *function* of the study or study element and its fit to the question at hand and less on its topography.

All research begins with curiosity about nature such as how X may be impacting Y. The first formal step to organizing a hypothetic-deductive study is to formulate a hypothesis; the first step for an inductive research study is to create a research question. The difference between the two is that hypotheses include a pre-analytic answer, not just a well-formulated question.

Refining curiosity and speculation into an actual research question requires a bit of focus. Good research questions include a careful review of where and how possible answers will be derived from the data and what they will mean. Perhaps the question hones in on the magnitude of X, the parameters of Y, X compared to A's effects on Y, or any other myriad of configurations. Issues of design should be made within the context of how best to craft the question so that an answer will be meaningful.

The research question is often related to the experiences of the researcher and in applied areas especially it is often related to their values about what is important. It is wise not to skip this step because what will keep a person persisting for months and years as a researcher is passion for the area and for a more fully adequate answer to an important question.

At times the question comes as a result of seeing a missing area within the existing literature, but this is often over-done by beginning researchers who are fearful that questions that feel important to them will be uninteresting to others. A common but often unhelpful starting point is with a research question that comes right out of the discussion section of someone else's article, or out of noting a methodological flaw in a published study. The beginning researcher needs to pause before over-replying on such strategies if the goal is to do research that makes a difference. First, no one really wants to spend their life cleaning up someone else's messes, so motivation to follow through may lag when that is the method of generating research questions, Second, often what is in the discussion sections of published studies is already guiding the original author's research – even before the research article appears. Those who "take the bait" may soon find they are scooped before a project is even done.

It is better to read widely and to understand existing research and then to hone in on ideas that are closer to your passion for the work you do, or that address the needs you see that are unmet, using that broad scientific knowledge to filter out bad ideas and to elaborate good ones. Useful research questions may be the product of experiences with clients, and hunches about what might improve their lives. It may emerge from noting theoretical contradictions or by exploring the implications of more basic findings. At other times good research questions may rise out of curiosity about parameters that enhance or weaken the effectiveness of an already known influencer of behavior. There will be many more research questions that cannot be immediately answered than can be.

One of the most common beginning researcher errors is to confuse the importance of an area and the need for a clear answer, with the quality or strategic importance of a research question itself. It is counterintuitive at first but it is almost *always* best to craft questions of nature that provide meaningful and important answers regardless of outcome. Let us explain.

Suppose there is a desperately important social problem, X, and the beginning researcher has an idea of how to help fix it (call it method Y). "Will method Y help reduce problem X?" feels like an important question because problem X is important, and it is true that if method Y has a huge impact on problem X it *will be* important. That can be a very low-probability event, however. What if method Y has no impact? A minimal impact? A good impact that quickly dissipates? Very often these outcomes would be of minimal or no importance. If so, very likely the beginning researcher has asked a bad question!

Science is like a game of 20 questions. The game is ongoing and in your life you only get to ask a limited number of questions. You do not know how many you get to ask (a truck could hit you tomorrow, no?) so you need to craft your questions well. Let's start with that metaphor of the game of 20 questions and you will realize you already know some of how to do this.

Suppose someone says "I am thinking of a living creature! Can you get it in 20 yes or no questions?" Great! Game on! You already know that it would be a really, really bad idea for your first question to be "Is it a rabbit?!"

That question is a Homer Simpson-level head slapper. Doh! It's just a terrible question. Young children will sometime actually ask questions like that, but you already know not to do it, so take a moment to think about why.

You'd win if the person is thinking of a rabbit. And they could be. But it's a terrible question because you learn next to nothing if the answer is "I'm sorry, no." A better question might be "is it an object" or (somewhat riskier) "is it an animal?" Why? It is because either "yes" or "no" is important. Many thousands of answers are instantly eliminated regardless of the specific answer.

Good science questions tend to be like that. It's fine to go for the "win" ("Is it a rabbit?") but only later on in a research program.

Now combine this game of 20 questions with the fact that processes, principles, and theory enormously simplify the world. Behavior analysts play the principles and process game very well. It is easy to find books and courses on "behavioral principles" but some other areas of psychology and behavioral science barely get around to principles. Have you seen as many books and courses on "emotional principles"? "Attentional principles"? "Cognitive principles"?

The fastest and one of the best ways to begin to narrow behavioral questions is to look at processes of change because there is only a limited set of possible answers. Is this effect motivational or discriminative? Is it under consequential or antecedent control? It is based on direct contingencies alone or does it involve relational operants? Questions like that are closer to the narrowing down strategies that good 20 questions players play when they learn that the item is an object and they try to determine "animal, plant, or mineral?"

Another filter is simple practicality. For example, it would be wonderful to know if ACT-influenced processes (e.g., perspective taking; defusion; reduced avoidance) could reduce teenagers' biases and preferences towards other cultures, and if implemented at a population level to every child in a country, whether such processes would reduce violence and enacted stigma and prejudice. This could be a great question, but not if the researcher can't put such a study into practice. Getting whole governments involved is rare. Scaling down this grand idea to fit within that researcher's world of influence might result in running a similar study within a single fifth-grade classroom to evaluate whether an ACT-based intervention that has been fit to meet the needs of this particular challenge (bias and prejudice) alters processes that impact that outcome. Perhaps another classroom experiencing the same challenge is kept in a baseline or control phase, or the intervention is introduced at a later time as in a multiple-baseline design.

The worldwide grandiosity of the former question underlines how important the problem is, but a good question is a lousy question if it cannot be answered. The humbler one-classroom comparison question can actually occur (and probably should occur, for any student readers looking for an applied thesis!). External validity of the humbler study is clearly weaker, but low external validity is preferable to the no external validity that comes from a study that was never completed. Moreover, greater internal validity can occur when the experimenter has more control over details such as needed process measures or refinement of the intervention. We may be relatively certain of ACT's impact on process and outcome in the smaller study if we arrange the conditions appropriately.

When mixed methods are used with a process-to-outcome focus, the results can begin to be good enough that they lead to funding and resources to run bigger and better studies over time, eventually grabbing the attention of the broader scientific community. That is what happened with ACT and it is the reason it is now recognized as evidence-based by the World Health Organization (WHO), the Center for Disease Control (CDC), the United States Department of Defense, the American Psychological Association, the United Kingdom's National Institute for Health and Care Excellence, and many other such bodies around the world (see https://contextualscience.org/state_of_the_act_evidence).

Science is an accumulating enterprise, not a one-shot-takes-it-all enterprise. This means research even on ACT within behavior analysis will take years and hundreds of studies to mature. Therefore, do not let the ideal be the enemy of the good. Go forward within the parameters you have available and conduct the studies you can and add to the collective body of literature.

Within the Association for Behavior Analysis International (ABAI), journals such as *Behavior Analysis in Practice* are specifically designed to review research by practicing behavior analysts that will be more tolerant of differences in one's experimental design if it means answering important questions to practitioners. Evidenced by you reading this book right now, clearly ACT intervention is such a topic.

Below are two more examples. Consider the strengths and weaknesses of each. What could be done to strengthen either?

The present study examined the impact of an eight-week ACT protocol designed to improve adherence to job duties by altering behavioral commitments to values. This intervention was comparted to a more traditional behavior skills training (BST) approach across two sets of group home staff. Measures were taken at pre, mid, post, and follow-up. Due to practical limitations, the staff were not randomly assigned to conditions, but it was randomly determined which of the two group homes would be exposed to each condition. To further ensure equality across groups, no significant differences were found when comparing the different house staff in terms of length of employment, ages of staff, or prior disciplinary reports.

We explored the effects of an ACT package composed of six modules on problem behavior frequency emitted by two individuals with autism. Using a multiple baseline across the two children we measured problem behavior frequency at one-hour intervals. The introduction of the ACT package appears to have reduced challenging behavior in both participants. No process measures were taken. The degree to which causal inferences to other children can be made is limited by research design selection and the heterogeneity of the autism disorder.

SUBJECTS

To embark upon behavioral research, one must involve participants who engage in the behaviors under investigation. The terms "research subject," "research participant," "research clients," and "experimentee" are often used interchangeably depending on culture and environment. It is possible that non-humans may be involved as subjects in research studies, but most of the processes targeted by ACT have failed to be established in non-human animals.

It is often important to try to get outside of the ivory towers inhabited by university professors and their students, but at the same time, a research study that gets done is always better than one that is only imagined. The behavior analyst interested in contributing to research should emphasize the participants that they access. For some questions that could include, say, a University subject pool, but for many questions that will be inadequate.

A choice needs to be taken at this early step of selecting subjects as to if the research question being explored is population specific (i.e., broad research question) or phenomena-specific (i.e., localized challenge; Belisle et al., 2021). Take for example a researcher interested in determining if incorporating ACT knowledge into a staff training program could benefit staff retention. Recruiting from an undergraduate introduction to psychology course would not be appropriate to answer this type of research question directly. It is possible that the incorporation of undergraduates on a mock work task could be used, however, to study persistence or work group cooperation, and using ACT as an analog to staff training in such a study could inform more applied questions that could be applied to actual staff training. In the applied environment issues may emerge that were unknown to the researcher so the arc of work on an issue in staff training will simply not be complete until that population is recruited. Researchers will need to weigh the tradeoffs of participant accessibility and sensitivity to the issues that will emerge inside actual application.

Below are two more examples. Consider the strengths and weaknesses of each. What could be done to strengthen either?

The ACT process of defusion was compared to deliberate thought suppression in their impact on cold water tolerance by college undergraduates. The findings served as a basic experimental proxy of potential therapeutic techniques for diminishing the behavioral impact of private verbal judgments of unwanted sensations such as physical pain in chronic pain patients or anxious physiological arousal among those with "anxiety disorders."

A convenience sample of participants at an all-day ACT workshop is asked to complete a self-assessment of their psychological flexibility levels before and after exposure to the workshop content. Scores on participant self-reports of stress are compared within subjects, as well as being compared to a control group who received a workshop on pig roasting.

Recruitment of subjects will necessitate a clear description of the time commitment, risks, and benefits. Most often evaluated by a third-party to ensure that ethical guidelines area being upheld, the utilization of other people for the purpose of one's research gain needs to be fair, justified, and cause no undo harm. Approval of these methods must occur from a research ethics board, either through work with a university or the development of an internal review board for larger organizations. No one can be forced into a research study and no implied coercion should ever occur.

If the researcher is finding it difficult to recruit subjects, perhaps it is the study itself and not the possible subject pool that is at fault. If an ACT laboratory study on experiential avoidance is being offered for one extra credit point in a course and takes six hours to complete, it may be better for those possible subjects to find an easier way to earn that one credit. Furthermore, consider what types of students would spend six hours in front of a computer screen for one extra point. Likely it will be those extremely desperate to pass a class or those who have implied social contingencies operating on them to complete the experiment. Similar complications occur when attempting systems-level research where one might be attempting to explore how daily ACT sessions could influence teacher-child interactions. Attempting to impose a time-intensive ACT session on each teacher daily may be met with opposition due to the existing demands on content delivery in the classroom. As a result, far few teachers will opt into a research study such as this, even though the prospects of treatment success are likely.

Further ethical challenges occur when a recruitment effort includes a control non-treatment group, or sub-standard treatment group. When recruitment of subjects notes these potentials for subjects, it is often the case that potential enrollees will be dissuaded due to the likelihood of not actually getting placed into the experimental group that might improve their current state of affairs. Incentives such as money, work breaks, course credit, gift cards, or other forms of compensation can sway a certain number of potential subjects to enroll in a less favorable research study, but they can also significantly change the participant pool in ways that can alter the science. For example, ACT self-help reliably helps people who are distressed. The World Health Organization even distributes ACT self-help (bit.ly/WHO_ACT) "for anyone who experiences stress, wherever they live and whatever their circumstances." But what about people who are not stressed? What if you, say, pay people to read ACT self-help materials even if they are not presently in need – perhaps hoping that what is learned will be there for times in the future when unforeseen challenges arise? This is called "universal prevention," and a recent meta-analysis found that the data on all forms of interventions – even very elaborate ones "tended to fall within the range of 0.07–0.16 standard deviations" (Tanner-Smith et al., 2018). Thus, solving the problem of participant interest by heavy incentives to the participant could inadvertently change your science question and ironically set you up for failure. It may be better to consider design modifications to increase the potential for obtaining the participants you are really interested in, rather than obtaining participants without considering who they really are and what they really need.

Using existing clients as research participants creates an additional challenge for researchers, because by the very nature of the existing relationship, potential conflicts of interest are likely to exist. The depth of these conflicts is often related to the type of research that is being conducted. When treatment evaluations are aggregated, summarized, and depicted in contrast to persons on genuine waitlists, minimal conflicts of potential care are likely. However, when that same control group on a waitlist is delayed treatment for the sole purpose of a research project, the potential conflict of interest increases dramatically. Furthermore, when clients are comprised of persons with limited language and cognitive abilities, their potential for genuine informed voluntary consent is reduced.

A number of checks and balances need to exist to ensure the ethical care of clients as subjects. Potential subjects need to know that their existing clinical care will not be compromised regardless of their decision to be included in a study. A legal guardian or parent may be required to provide formal consent if such an individual oversees the general care of the possible subject. When this third-party makes such a decision, the client also provides a version of their own consent termed assent in which a more content-ability match of asking the person themselves occurs, often each and every session of the experiment. Opting out of this request functionally serves as that person's voice in wanting to stop the experiment and should be granted by the researcher.

Depending on the type of research being conducted, the behavior analyst may find it useful to have a general consent process for all clients presented at initial intake. When such work is designed to examine generally natural phenomena that occur during the treatment process, such programmatic reviews of data may not necessitate a study-specific individual recruitment document. For example, if you are comparing the AAQ-2 scores of clients you see individually once a week to those clients who are seen in a group session two times per week, your analysis of such data, and subsequent reporting of these data may not require more than a general consent to the utilization of deidentified client data to compare differences in treatment delivery methods. The lines are crossed once clients are being assigned to certain types of care (group or individual) for the purpose of research and not because of clinical need, or the retaining of clients in a type of care that is not helpful to them to ensure enough subjects in the experimental group. Such arrangements will necessitate a much more extensive review process regarding the ethical parameters of participant recruitment, inclusion, and retention. The most important question to ask when considering involving clients in research is: "Is anything I do for this research altering existing client care or my decisions on future possible care?" If the answer is anything other than "absolutely no," a variety of procedures, consents, and external reviews of the project will be necessary to ensure no harm to those persons who are receiving services explicitly to improve their current conditions.

We are not saying "do not do this work." Clinical research is important. Just be aware of the issues and put into action the necessary oversight and reviews to ensure that what you are doing is both ethical and within the scope of the contracted services that the client is receiving.

Below are two more examples. Based only on what is stated what other ethical and participant selection issues might they raise?

This study incorporated the use of adolescent research subjects who were diagnosed with autism, were relatively sophisticated verbally, and were receiving ACT treatment for motivational issues by a care facility that was providing educational programming linked to the diagnosis. In order to ensure there was no coercion for participating in an evaluation of the ACT intervention, a detailed letter describing the study, its risks and benefits, was sent home to parents. In this letter it was explained that participation was in no way tied to services, and that the decision to opt out of the project would have no bearing on care provided. The potential for conflict of interest was evaluated by an institutional review board in which the researchers of this study were not members.

The current investigation utilized file data which was previously gathered by the clinic to track client progress during ACT interventions designed to reduce problem behavior. The data were provided to the researchers for inclusion in this study, but the researchers were not involved with the generation of such data, nor did they have any influence on future client care.

SETTING AND MATERIALS

A wide range of options exists for the behavior analyst when choosing the type of setting to conduct ACT research. Most often research begins based on opportunities within the behavior analyst's current primary setting. If employed at a university, a faculty laboratory or office space may serve as a functionally relevant location to deliver ACT services. Some universities may also contain health service centers, and it is possible that discussions with those persons could allow for utilization of space after hours or during low-traffic time periods. All three authors of this text have worked at multiple universities and have negotiated space for supplemental ACT research by discussing the possibilities with others within their university. If employed at a clinical treatment facility, hospital, or school, many possible settings in which to conduct research likely already exist. All that is needed is to work out the possible scheduling conflicts in existing spaces or programs. One can often even deliver services in your own office. In short, be creative. Perceived space limitations are often overcome with experience and effort.

When the research program becomes larger than a single location, complications may arise, but are not insurmountable. Care should be taken to ensure some degree of consistency across multiple sites to reduce the probability of setting variance resulting in a biasing of overall treatment effects. For example, when employing a multi-site project to evaluate how ACT impacts attention during math class, the researcher will need to ensure that classroom size and students are similar across sites, and that math content and delivery methods are also similar.

Real-world experiments can be done anywhere. Perhaps there is a desire to examine how value-based phrases placed on billboards impact recycling within a community. Here the comparison might number of recyclables collected before, after, and return to baseline conditions of the entire town.

Ideas for choosing a setting should not be constricted to whatever is the easiest to access, or the areas in which approval is most likely to be obtained quickly. It is better to let the research question drive the selection of setting. If one wishes to explore a phenomenon outside of their immediate locale, by all means do so. Pragmatics come into play of course and the logistics of accessing dispersed settings may tax the abilities of the researcher, but the most important step is to begin. Give and take will naturally occur between the ideal and realistic setting, and the gap between the two will likely shrink with successive experiments, increased collaboration, external funding, and sheer experience of putting together research projects of scale.

The materials for designing an ACT study will also vary based on the research question that is being asked. At first, it may appear that a talk-based treatment like ACT really will only require the experimenter to talk to people, and for them to talk back. Maybe a voice recorder could be used to capture such dialogue and later scored for certain types of flexible and inflexible phrases emitted by each party. At the other extreme may be a study that examines the influence of ACT on dopamine production by pathological gamblers (e.g., Habib & Dixon, 2010) whereby slot machine simulations are played within an fMRI imager at a local hospital and subjects are delivered money for every jackpot obtained. This sort of configuration will require a substantial budget, sophisticated technology, highly trained technical staff, and data analysis equipment. Neither study is necessarily better than the other in terms of advancing the field's knowledge of how ACT exposure impacts the human condition. Rather each project requires a different setting and set of materials. If one's aspirational research question falls outside of the practical acquisition of materials, it might be possible to simply rethink the project within material constraints yet still address the general theme. For example, the extremely expensive fMRI scanning project could be redesigned to involve ACT exposure to recreational gamblers in college courses, who indicate on paper Likert scales ranking how excited they feel after certain slot machine outcomes while playing a slot game on their cellphone. Although the appeal of a direct measure of neurobiological activation is eliminated, the general theme of ACT influences on excitement would be retained.

SELECTING A DEPENDENT VARIABLE

The simplest dependent variables one might wish to consider are the behavioral indices of change that are measurable and observable to the behavior analyst. These types of metrics may include rate, frequency, duration, intensity, and latency of a targeted challenging behavior or an aspirational behavior. Treatment effectiveness might be measured by decreases in the challenging behavior, or increases in positive behaviors, or sometimes both concurrently. For example, a study might attempt to increase the frequency of engagement with peers and to reduce the frequency of negative self-critical statements.

There is no reason to stop with simple countable behavioral metrics, however. Multiple dependent variables spanning multiple levels of analyses are often helpful in ACT research.

The contextual nature of the ACT-subject interaction allows for vigorous examination of behavior-behavior relations, language-overt behavior relations, and language-neurobiological relations. Remember that the strength of behavior analysis is the focus on idiographic processes of change and their relation to outcomes. The processes can include behavior-behavior relations – where the word "behavior" covers *all* activities from brain activity assessed by EEG, fMRI, or other means; to biophysiological changes such as blood pressure change, heart rate variability, or immune response; to social behavior such as cooperation or empathy; to verbal and relational framing changes such as self-statements or implicit verbal reactions.

When the researcher has the tools necessary to expand outward and address these contextual multilevel interactions, the potential for impact of one's research often can grow. Behavior analysts have an opportunity with ACT to speak to a much larger audience than behavior analysts, and that opportunity should not be squandered by adhering to historical parameters of what constitutes behavior analytic research.

Consider the new self-report instrument shown in Table 13.1. This is the "Process-Based Assessment Tool" (PBAT; Ciarrochi et al., 2022) which was set up to ask about variation, selection, and retention-based actions over the last several hours in high temporal density longitudinal assessment. It is an item pool of what are in effect behavioral reports. Items were individually vetted by a machine learning algorithm – it is not a psychometrically guided instrument seeking out a latent construct.

Table 13.1
Process targets, negative behavior and positive behavior examples

Process Target	*Negative Behavior*	*Positive behavior*
Variation	I felt stuck and unable to change my ineffective behavior.	I was able to change my behavior, when changing helped my life.
Selection		
Affect/Yearning to feel	I did not find an appropriate outlet for my emotions.	I was able to experience a range of emotions appropriate to the moment.
Cognition/Yearning for coherence	My thinking got in the way of things that were important to me.	I used my thinking in ways that helped me live better.
Attention/Yearning to be oriented	I struggled to connect with the moments in my day-to-day life.	I paid attention to important things in my daily life.
Social connection/Need for connection	I did things that hurt my connection with people who are important to me.	I did things to connect with people who are important to me.
Motivation/Need for autonomy	I did things only because I was complying with what others wanted me to do.	I chose to do things that were personally important to me.
Overt behavior/Need for competence	I did not find a meaningful way to challenge myself.	I found personally important ways to challenge myself.
Physical health behaviors	I acted in ways that hurt my physical health.	I acted in ways that helped my physical health.
Retention	I struggled to keep doing something that was good for me.	I stuck to strategies that seemed to have worked.

Items in the PBAT

If you think of ACT processes as types of behavior-behavior relations you can see that these items try to cast ACT processes as functional actions, worded both positively and negatively. Consider the area of values. The PBAT asks the person to assess whether in the last few hours she or he did things "only because I was complying with what others wanted" or the degree to which in that time frame "I chose to do things that were personally important to me."

While these items are self-report, they have a behavioral observation quality to them. If enough was known about a person it might be possible if the person was being observed externally to link a statement such as "I did things that hurt my connection with people who are important to me" to actual externally observable actions that might hurt the person's connection with people who are important to them.

We will report on how the PBAT is being used and validated below, but our point is that once processes of change are on the table, and they are understanding a behavior-behavior relation broadly speaking, a wide variety of new assessment and analytic methods open up.

Thought of that way, ACT processes can at times operate as either a dependent variable (in effect becoming the target outcome) or as a process variable (i.e., evaluated as an action that is functionally linked to other actions). Ultimately the goal of ACT is to effectuate overt behavior change; however, if the link between the six core processes and topographically broad behavior has been established, then homing in on evaluating best strategies to move these processes in their own right may be a reasonable research question. Actual verbal utterances emitted by a client can be judged in terms of their psychological flexibility or inflexibility. Self-report scales that measure mindfulness, acceptance, or rigidity (and so that) can be examined for their link to ACT interventions and to subsequent meaningful behavior change. It is important, however, to remember that no behavior should be thought of as impacting another behavior within the same person without considering the context in which that relation occurs. Devoid of context, such relations risk the error of mentalism and non-manipulable "causes" as we have discussed extensively earlier in this volume.

When the investigation involves examining the ability of others to correctly deliver ACT, a series of performance measures may be used to judge treatment effects. For example, if staff or caregivers are being observed to determine their ACT-appropriate interactions with clients, it might make sense to score their behaviors such as verbal utterance content, proactive versus reactive statements, and covering each process of the Hexaflex within a certain length of time. In summary, ACT as a unit, or ACT as a collection of specific processes, may be of value to the researcher as an isolated dependent variable or part of a multi-dependent variable analysis of treatment effects.

Below are two more examples. Based only on what is stated what issues do they raise?

A researcher is interested in why painful reminders of past traumatic incidents lead a teenager to engage in deliberate self-harm. Because this person is high in measures of experiential avoidance, the researcher says the self-injury is caused by avoidance of emotions.

A researcher wants to study ACT processes in a client with repetitive behaviors but does not want to ask the client about them because verbal reports are unreliable and mentalistic. Instead, the claim is made that repeating behaviors alone is evidence of "fusion" and thus that ACT is ideal for this client.

ACT AS THE INDEPENDENT VARIABLE

Even though the logical independent variable in ACT research is to apply ACT and measure change, many variations of this general theme are available to the behavior analytic researcher. The entire ACT model may be introduced to a single small group of subjects over time, or compared across large groups of subjects, some of whom receive a different sort of treatment. The ACT processes themselves might be examined in relative isolation, to determine if something like Defusion can be helpful to change the state of affairs for some clients following instruction. ACT methods of delivery could also be compared to determine if computerized content delivery is equal or inferior to human delivery. ACT might also be examined in conjunction with a larger treatment package, conceivably containing RFT training, medication, or neurological conditioning. Finally, ACT might be examined as to its model dependency – as changing, modifying, or deleting certain processes from the existing model may or may not yield greater treatment effects for certain populations.

The total ACT model as an independent variable is a packaged intervention which will likely vary in terms of implementation by different providers. Much akin to behavioral skills training, ACT contains a range of moving pieces that are applied in a less uniform fashion somewhat dependent on the needs of the client. Thus, it remains of great interest what exactly must be part of an ACT intervention, the duration and frequency of sessions, and the sequencing of Hexaflex processes. It is clear that ACT can be helpful in some circumstances for some people, but the microlevel variables (the treatment kernels) contained within an overall ACT approach need considerable exploration and comparison empirically, and much more idiographic linkage to client functioning and processes of change.

The same is true with the single processes in a psychological flexibility model. Variations are many in how a practitioner thinks of something as complex as Self-as-Context. One clinician may introduce this via an experiential metaphor, or contemplative practice, while another may seek to simply describe the nature of seeing oneself from afar. It is unknown as to which approach has a greater effect on uptake from a client, and how different clients may necessitate different process descriptions.

A wide range of ACT treatment delivery methods have been documented in the published literature, ranging from individual to group sessions; from telehealth to live lecture-based interventions; from self-guided slideshows and textbooks or brochures to arts and crafts projects, and even client journal entries. On one hand, this diversity speaks to the potential potency of process-based treatment as a mechanism of change. Yet on the other hand it raises questions as to which approach may be more beneficial than others. It is naïve to think that any type of ACT, delivered in any sort of format will produce equally wonderful results. The researcher of the future has a wealth of opportunities to explore the ways in which methods of care interact with client outcomes, and even coupling ACT with other more traditional behavior analytic independent variables such as behavior skills training, verbal rehearsal, goal setting, or self-management.

A final research consideration involves the interaction of RFT and ACT. Throughout this text, it has been emphasized that the underlying behavioral processes at work within ACT involve language, as explained via RFT. Although the conceptual links are well established, the empirical connections are in the early stages. We have alluded in earlier chapters to a certain level of language repertoire that is necessary for a client to benefit from ACT, but it remains unclear if such recommendations are definite with respect to a bare minimum relational threshold. Furthermore, it is unknown how best to grow the client's repertoire efficiently in order to take the greatest advantage of ACT treatments, and if such work should be done concurrently or prior to the introduction of ACT interventions. It is also possible that poor client outcomes in ACT may be the product of underdeveloped relational repertoires and improving such could aid in treatment efficacy.

RESEARCH DESIGN

ACT experiments should include SCED between group and mixed designs. The adherence to strictly single-subject explorations by many behavior analysts has marginalized the overall impact the field has had on science at large, but at the same time, many key scientific questions regarding ACT and processes of change need to be linked to new forms of idiographic research. The core behavior analytic methodological commitments are more important now than ever, but how these commitments have played out needs modification.

Take statistical inference. Behavior analysts have often resisted classical statistical methods on such grounds as statistical significance does not mean clinical significance; averages do not represent the individual; between-person variability is not the same as within-person variability; the null hypothesis as tested against a between-person distribution directs attention away from experimental control; and so on. All of these criticisms are valid, but the average behavior analytic student eventually simplifies these many messages into an overall idea that statistics are not helpful to behavior analysis. What then follows is statistical methods are barely taught in many programs, people with poor mathematical training are counseled to become behavior analysts, behavior analytic research avoids any use of statistics regardless of whether or not the analytic methods are apt, and a self-amplifying process sets in that reduces the ability of behavior analytic research to ask sophisticated research questions.

That is especially unfortunate now, precisely when new forms of statistical analysis have evolved that fit hand in glove with behavior-analytic sensibilities. With enough longitudinal data, we can now model individual development over time as a complex network based entirely on variability within an individual person (e.g., Gates et al., 2014). These methods are very well developed but they are also cutting edge, and require *more* statistical sophistication to be understood and used, not *less*. We will have more to say about these methods below, but our point here is that behavior analysis needs to keep moving forward within its core assumptions and not rest on its laurels.

In order to move beyond the constraints of the history which has led to so many people needing to read a book such as this, we will need to do better in the decades ahead to ensure that the parameters which we defined as behavioral research are extended considerably outward. This does not mean we need to abandon our history, but rather we should allow that history to factor into forward-looking decision-making when crafting a new research program, such as rising to the challenge of ACT and RFT.

We are fully aware that many behavior analysts may not have extensive knowledge or understanding of statistical analysis or group designs. There are details too extensive for a book such as this and may require additional reading. However, we provide enough material here to get researchers started thinking within and beyond the single-subject box. In the sections below we detail a wide range of examples of potential research on ACT across populations, settings, and research designs.

We do so using a Theory-to-Impact model. Introduced in a response to why behavior analysts have failed to save the world (Dixon et al., 2018), this model speaks to the necessity of our field to pursue progress concurrently across multiple levels of scientific inquiry. Instead of using a top-down approach to science whereby theory guides basic research, and then basic research guides practice, a dynamic system is encouraged in which the various levels of science are at interplay with each other – each nudging the others to drive the system forward. At the core of the model is the behaviorism theory world view. Branching out in concentric circles are basic science, translational research, applied research, and finally – impact. The optimal state of affairs for our field is when progress is made within each of these areas at the same time, rather than a gradual cascading from theory outward.

An unfortunate error our field has made, and likely the reason we have yet to save the world, is that we have been conservative in our impact. We have too slowly moved in linear rather than dynamic progress – all the while holding tightly to SCEDs as the solution to any research question. This conservative nature of our methods, analyses, and applications does protect the integrity of the field, yet it also comes at a cost. To truly save the world our field needs to challenge itself to become urgent in designing large-scale impact interventions, oftentimes necessitating the use of research design methods that are beyond SCEDs.

Correlations

When two variables are examined in regard to their relationship to each other, a correlation coefficient can be calculated. This metric describes the degree of relationship between the two, not a casual impact of one on the other. The two variables of interest might be the degree of psychological flexibility self-reported and the degree of delay discounting, or complexity of relational framing skills and weekly challenging behavior average.

Correlations typically involve gathering two scores for a single subject, and then the total group of subjects is analyzed as to the degree by which each score of one variable is related to the score on the other variable. Correlations assume independence of subjects, and also a linear relationship. A positive correlation may be said to occur between two variables when an increase in one score also reveals an increase in the other score. A negative correlation may result when the changes in the level of one variable increase when the level of the second variable decrease.

Importantly, with high temporal density data on two or more variables correlations can also be calculated within-person. If several people have such data you can then combine a series of within-person correlations (e.g., they can be averaged).

You might suppose that these two kinds of correlations would be the same, but you would be incorrect. Consider the relation between typing speed and typing errors. In any large group these two variables will be negatively correlated because experts will type faster with fewer errors. For every individual, however, efforts to type faster over man trials will produce more errors and the two will be positively correlated.

Both relations are valid but the level of analysis differs. If the goal is to model individuals over time, correlating variables within individuals over time is usually best. If the goal is to make a population-based statement that applies only at that level, group-based correlations may be best.

Examples of correlational studies include:

Basic: evaluating performance on an attentional task under a stressful condition, such as the presence of an aversive noise, and correlating the number of errors with scores on various mindfulness measures.

Translational: providing ABA service providers with the opportunity to perform a discrete trial training session and introducing rule statements about their inability to succeed and correlate their willingness to continue with the session with indices of experiential avoidance.

Applied: repeatedly measure burn-out symptoms of agency therapists and the PBAT items twice a day over a month. Examine person by person how psychological flexibility and experiential avoidance items predict burnout within the month.

Impact: comparing retention rates of staff at hundreds of agencies, where some agencies are already implementing ACT-based services with their clients and other agencies are exclusively implementing more traditional ABA-based interventions. Correlate these organizational measures of ACT involvement with staff retention data.

AB Designs

The AB design is when a baseline period elapses and is followed by a single treatment. This rather basic research design allows for a direct comparison of two conditions. No causal proof can be revealed from AB designs, as there are many threats to internal validity, however the AB design may be sufficient to provide information about the possible impact of a treatment. The baseline-treatment-only nature of this configuration may be difficult to publish but could have clinical value beyond a "B" only design whereby treatment just starts for someone on day one of services. Strengthening internal validity can be accomplished by varying the length of baseline across different subjects, replicating the effects across multiple subjects, and keeping other subjects in a baseline-only condition. Even the AB may be beneficial to an ACT researcher who wishes to examine how adding ACT to a school social-emotional curriculum could benefit students. Instead of jumping into the ACT approach, the researcher could gather dependent variable information from the prior school year such as bullying reports, attendance, and out-of-school suspensions, and compare them to the current year once ACT is introduced. This is exactly what Dixon and colleagues (2022) did in their study using the AIM Curriculum in a public middle school of over 200 students using two years before and one year during standardized testing scores as the primary dependent variable.

Basic: an unfamiliar image is paired with aversive stimuli and the participant can make the image disappear by clicking a button. A defusion exercise is then performed to weaken this relation to determine if clicking rate reduces in the intervention condition.

Translational: a procedure is developed to measure present-moment attending, such as by presenting a video where events are occurring within the video that require active attending to notice. In the baseline condition the participants are asked to attend to the video and the video is periodically disrupted to ask questions about events happening within the scene. The participants then engage in environmental scanning for ten minutes and are representing with the video. Participants are able to more accurately report back events as they are occurring within the scene.

Applied: employees are evaluated during baseline on the frequency of positive interactions with clients during a work shift. Treatment involves a weekly reflection back and projection forward of times needed to accept difficult challenges on the job. Focus groups of employees also implemented to strengthen adherence to intervention. Post-treatment measures of positive interactions with clients are compared to pre-treatment levels.

Impact: a disrupted regression design is used within a school distract evaluating the occurrence of discipline referrals and suspensions. Tier 1 and tier 2 ACT-based programming guided by the AIM curriculum is embedded in the school midway through the first semester. On-going data collection shows a reduction in disciplinary referrals compared to the regression developed from the baseline data.

Reversal Designs

A reversal design expands upon the AB conceptualization by simply replicating the A and B conditions a second time. With the subsequent return to baseline following the first treatment phase, researchers can evaluate if the dependent variable level returns to pre-treatment or baseline levels, or at least stops improving. In other words, once the independent variable is removed, does the treatment effect disappear or at least slow down as well. The eventual reinstatement of the treatment a second time ensures that if treatment is suspected to have an effect on the dependent variable, then that variable would rise again to levels or to rates of improvement displayed during the first treatment condition. There are many slight variations of the reversal, whereby an additional treatment or C condition may be introduced and compared to the B treatment, or where reversals of the AB reoccur more than once to produce an ABABAB design. The design logic remains the same across these variations – does a treatment effect wax and wane with introduction and removal of the independent variable.

A complex clinical example was provided by Harmon et al. (1980) who tried to address the age-old question of whether people who were struggling with depressed mood should get more active to help their mood or focus on improving their mood to help increase their activity. Taking advantage of the fact that self-monitoring tends to be reactive, they found in an ABACA design (where B was frequently monitoring mood and C was frequently monitoring activity), that changes in activity improved mood much more than the reverse. To control for order effects the same question was asked with others in an ACABA design and the same behaviorally sensible results were obtained.

Basic: a delay discounting task is developed where participants can choose between a smaller sum of money immediately or a larger sum of money available later. Individualized values-based stimuli are framed in a hierarchical class with an unfamiliar symbol. The symbol is then randomly placed on either the smaller-sooner or the larger-later option to determine the influence of the symbol as a motivative augmental for either choice pattern.

Translational: rock climbers attempt a relatively difficult climb with conditions of baseline and an acceptance treatment. During treatment, subjects vocalize strain on physical body and concerns about the climb path and its difficulty. During baseline, performance as usual.

Applied: a 20-minute morning meditation routine is implemented for a client with ADHD to evaluate changes in on-task behavior and reduction in disruptive social behaviors with others. Baseline establishes high rates of off-task behavior and social disruption. After establishing stability, the meditative routine is embedded until stable increases in on-task behavior and reductions in disruption to appropriate levels are observed. The meditation routine is withdrawn, and behavior returns to near baseline rates, followed by a successful replication of the intervention.

Impact: two behavior analysts are hired who specialize in ACT-based interventions in a school. The case load is too large so only a subset of the children are working with these two behavior analysts while others are receiving more traditional programming. To ensure equal access the school rotates classrooms that the new behavior analysts serve and evaluation of the data after the fact show reversals of challenging behavior rates as a function of the behavior analyst referred to the case.

Multiple Baselines

A very popular behavior analytic research design is the multiple baseline. One reason for the frequent use of this design is because it concurrently controls for greater internal validity than an AB design through the replication across multiple subjects, settings, or behaviors and at the same time providing a way to embrace interventions which may not be prone to reversals as described above. For example, if attempting to examine the effects of ACT sessions on anxiety during spelling test performances, it may be difficult to remove the added value of psychological flexibility for a subject by simply eliminating ACT sessions prior to the spelling tests. Skills taught are often difficult to unlearn, and changes in verbal relation are often persistent since they are maintained by natural consequences out of the control of the therapist such as coherence and problem-solving impact. Such persistence is not a bad thing, but research designs need to be used that eliminate the need to return to baseline conditions.

Multiple baselines do not allow for the same level of casual inference about the impact of the independent variable on the dependent variable as reversal designs, but they do provide a fair amount of control to internal validity threats such as sequence, time, maturation, and history. A recent example using the multiple baseline design examined the role that additional relational training could have on the quality of ACT session performance and subsequent behavior problems in three clients with autism (Gilsenan et al., 2022). Following poor measures on both dependent variables, researchers introduced remedial relational frame training using PEAK (Dixon, 2016) curriculum programs to boost client performance successfully.

Basic: a series of three elaborate relational networks are constructed over the course of two-weeks using unfamiliar symbols. To test the effectiveness of increasing nodal distance as a model for defusion, additional members are added to the first network initially along with tests of the strength (density) of network relations. The addition of new class members is then introduced to the second network, followed by the third network, to replicate the defusion effect.

Translational: basketball free throw shooters who are subsequently asked to ignore an onlooker yelling "you will miss it," "you are no good," "you are a loser." Subsequent condition whereby the same shooter is now instructed to accept, notice and embrace the onlooker's comments. Measure percentage of shots made.

Applied: children with autism review video of their own behavior during prior X hours of time in school or clinic. Subjects are asked to state aloud when they see themselves "accepting" in the video. Treatment condition teaches what the acceptance process is, associated feelings, and positive outcomes that may be obtained.

Impact: ten elementary schools within a district are recruited to try a new ACT-based school-wide program. Rather than introducing the program district-wide, the program is introduced to each school in a stepwise fashion over the course of two years, where implementing the program in a new school occurs immediately following initial signs of success at the previous school that operates as the preceding tier in the multiple baseline.

Alternating Treatments or Multielement Designs

The repeated alternation of experimental conditions creates a unique opportunity to evaluate relative effects of a certain independent variable, or level of such variable, on resulting behavior. A very common type of multielement design application is found within the functional analysis literature, whereby attention, demand, tangible, and sensory conditions are introduced one at a time with the hopes that over repeated sessions, a pattern of dominance will emerge indicating which condition yields the highest or lowest rates of problem behavior. The multielement design does not need to be typecast in just this application, as the design is equally useful to explore the relative influence of ACT processes on any given behavior. Here a client might be exposed to sessions of therapy that differ on which Hexaflex process is discussed, and frequency of independently emitted vocal utterances that were defined as "psychologically flexible" could be recorded. Over successive representations of these conditions, the level and trend of the obtained data could be compared by the Hexaflex process.

A similar design logic can be found in the alternating treatments design (ATD; Barlow & Hayes, 1979). Typically, two or more conditions are alternated in a random fashion to explore the relative effects of each in comparison to the other. A very practical comparison could be made between in-person and telehealth delivery of ACT for a given client, and frequency of challenging behavior could be tracked for the next 24-hour period of time post-session by parents to examine if one modality of treatment is better than the other. Keep in mind both of these design types create challenges for independent variables that may have carryover or contrast effects, as the rapid alternation of conditions is not assured to be free of residuals. For example, there may be treatment gains during a telehealth session that are not eliminated when presented with the next in-person session for a client, thus making the subsequent in-person post-session data recording contaminated by treatment gains from the prior session on telehealth.

Eilers and Hayes (2015) used an ATD to compare an ACT defusion exercise to a matched placebo exercise in the reduction of repetitive and restrictive behaviors displayed by children with autism spectrum disorder. For example, a boy cried and ran away whenever a statue was brought into a play session, repeated the words "I don't like the statue" in a silly voice, as compared to saying "the cow says moo" before play sessions. Problem behaviors were clearly lower following defusion sessions when a statue was brought into the room. This effect was replicated across three cases.

Basic: an application is developed to capture momentary attending to a computerized task. College students are recruited and asked to either attend closely to the computerized task or to attend to other stimuli in the room, such as a television, instead of the computerized task. Results support the potential use of the application to measure attending.

Translational: students are exposed or not exposed to a textual stimulus on their desk that states the biggest fear about school or taking exams. Evaluate test performance in each condition, and replicate across a few additional classrooms.

Applied: clients are presented with a decision matrix about the various courses of action that will occur following acceptance or non-acceptance of a low preferred outcome. Types of outcomes across elements include sooner/smaller and larger later; high probability/low probability; sooner less aversive and later larger aversive.

Impact: each day employees at a fast-food restaurant are given a motivational message to start the day. Using a random-number generator, the motivational phrases each day alternate between ACT-consistent metaphors and general phrases that are likely to be conveyed in a workplace setting. Data on employee motivation that day is collected and the average is compared company-wide.

Changing Criterion Designs

The eventual performance targeted as a metric of success may be far from the client's current level of performance. Such long shots at treatment success are difficult to obtain. Anyone who has struggled with dieting, exercise, quitting smoking or drinking, or even online shopping, can attest to the idea that going from "excessive" to "nothing" is often an aspirational illusion. Taking smaller steps towards harm reduction instead of complete elimination can provide opportunities to celebrate sub-goals accomplished along the path towards optimal change. The changing criterion design is thus well positioned for utilization in ACT research whereby the clinician may identify certain intermediate targets of change for the dependent variable that the client can attempt to meet and change those criteria a bit more stringently as success has been accomplished. For example, a smoker who wishes to eventually become smoke-free may be tasked with reducing the 20 cigarettes per day consumed to just 15. Surely the long-term goal remains of complete termination of the habit, however from 20 to 0 is oftentimes too big of a leap for anyone to believe is possible of making. Gradual reductions of maladaptive behaviors, or conversely the slight increasing of positive behaviors, can often times yield successes where an all-or-nothing approach is bound to fail. Here the researcher sets attainable small sub-goals, often times at or even below baseline levels of performance, and gradually alters such goals to drive towards the terminal desired behavior. The changing criterion design can be embarked upon in isolation or in combination with other designs such as the multiple baseline, or even the AB design, whereby the B condition is the changing criterion. Furthermore, any of the aforementioned designs can be entangled within each other to create custom solutions to the research question at hand. For example, the multi-element may be instated following a multiple baseline or the alternating treatment design could be used to examine the relative differences between a changing criterion for one behavior of interest and a fixed terminal criterion for a second behavior. An example of a changing criterion design is provided by Singh et al. (2011) who helped a man with developmental disabilities quit smoking using the "soles of the feet" mindfulness exercise.

Basic: a rule-statement is provided to participants describing a pattern of behavior (pressing button A) that will produce maximum reinforcement compared to the alternative behavior (pressing button B). The response requirement is gradually increased for pressing button A above the requirement for pressing button B (i.e., the rule becomes increasingly inaccurate). Some participants practice defusion of this rule before each session. Results are compared between the two groups within the changing criterion design.

Translational: high school gymnasts are provided acceptance training in minutes prior to performance. Measurement of falls and lost point performance with changing criterion thresholds.

Applied: an autistic adolescent wants to increase their social engagement throughout the day. An acceptance and willingness program is developed with sequentially increasing targets of engagement, starting at near baseline levels. As they increase their engagement to meet the criterion, the criterion is increased by ten minutes until they reach a threshold that they feel is acceptable (i.e., their social behavior is aligned with their social values).

Impact: a large ABA service provider wants to increase the amount of time staff are engaging in mindfulness activities with their clients that often gets missed due to other demands. An incentive program is put in place where staff must engage in a single mindfulness activity each week to contact the incentive. The threshold is then increased regularly as staff engagement increases.

Between Subject Studies and Randomized Controlled Trials

The very foundation of behavior analysis rests on the belief that behavior of a single subject studied for extended periods of time can yield more insight into the interrelationship of the independent and dependent variables than aggerated conclusions made from examinations of large groups of subjects. Between subjects, designs do not necessarily explain the behavior of individual participants, as the averages used to compute differences between groups dilute the contribution of any one subject, and between-person variability is needed to assess differences between groups, which does not necessarily predict the within-person variability needed to determine individual developmental trajectories. Taken on their own terms, these criticisms are fair, but they miss the point that certain kinds of "population"-based questions are best answered using group comparisons, and group studies are the most widely accepted methods in behavioral science. Group studies are the most common research approach within life science broadly and psychology specifically and rigidity on this point marginalizes the impact of behavior analysis outside of the field. However, as our field attempts to gain mainstream relevance, it will be crucial to have a few examples of our relevance within a framework that the rest of psychology and science can understand.

A group design that explicitly compares a treatment of interest as compared to a control group receiving no treatment, a placebo treatment, or treatment as usual (or sometimes a benchmark active treatment) is called a randomized controlled trial (RCT). Highly quality RCTs meet certain levels of integrity of factors such as proper methods of randomization, careful use of inclusion and exclusion criteria, and blinding of participants, assessors, and researchers to group assignment. There are over 900 RCTs that have been conducted on ACT to date, and a new one appears around every three days.

The popularity of the RCT is due to the strength of casual inference that can be made. The randomization of subject variables that might influence treatment outcomes are controlled for across groups, leaving nothing but the administration or non-administration of treatment as the sole determiner of changes across groups on the dependent variable(s). A range of demonstrations as the utility of ACT could be embarked upon within an RCT framework, including comparing ACT to behavioral skills training, a waitlist for ABA therapy, traditional staff training methods, medication, cognitive behavior therapy, or spiritual guidance. Furthermore, ACT could be compared to itself in terms of method of delivery, dosage, or full model versus constricted model elements. Yi and Dixon (2021) compared the effects of ACT on parent adherence to a telehealth treatment program which sought to teach them behavioral skills to better interact with their child with autism. When parents who had the added element of ACT instated on top of the standard parent training, those parents completed all sessions much more frequently than parents who did not receive ACT.

Basic: three groups of individuals are presented with a pairing of WDF with blasts of aversive noise. One group reads a magazine; two groups learn an equivalence class containing WDF, but also YGP and ZQM. In one of those equivalence groups, YGP is given five new functions such as meaning "Yes, Grand Poohbah." The ability of ZQM to produce skin conductance is assessed in all three groups.

Translational: subjects place their hand into a bucket of ice water and are instructed to keep it in as long as they can. One group is told to accept the cold, imagine how cold it will be, and how the pain will feel prior to hand insertion. Measure relative differences between group duration of hand insertions.

Applied: different shift staff delivered varying types of ACT training designed to improve customer relations across classroom instruction, 1:1 self-paced manual, and 1:1 direct interaction with "acceptance coach." Measure the frequency of positive comments made by customers to staff under each training exposure condition.

Impact: an entire district's high school student body is divided into two random groups. One group receives an app on their cell phone that prompts them to record one psychologically flexible thing they did daily, and the other group receives a control app that asks about how the weather was outside that day. A variety of measures are taken on each group of students including attendance, office referrals, bullying incidents, and college readiness exams.

Factorial Designs

When the basic between-group design takes on an added degree of complexity, it is often called a factorial. Here the independent variable increases in levels or in types, such that even more complex research questions can be answered. For example, if a clinician wanted to compare the number of hours of ACT treatment, say three hours or five hours per week, and also the type of treatment delivered, say manualized versus therapist-led, a group can be created based on this combination of elements. This allows a number of comparisons to be made: is there any difference in the behavioral outcomes observed when clients get three or five hours of care, regardless of type of treatment? Does the type of treatment delivered to clients matter regardless of the hours of treatment? Is there a combined or interactive effect in which, say, type of treatment matters but only if there are enough hours devoted to it?

Basic: persons high and low in psychological flexibility are assessed using an Implicit Relational Assessment Procedure (IRAP) and are also given a cognitively challenging task with and without high time demands.

Translational: adults with or without attention deficit hyperactivity disorder (ADHD) are provided present-moment, values, or full ACT model overview for ten minutes prior to engaging in a short-term memory task. Recall accuracy evaluated for all subjects and an examination is undertaken about which type of treatment works best and whether the effects are equal across adult ADHD/non-ADHD types.

Applied: gym patrons are evaluated for length of workout, or number of reps/pounds lifted. One group exposed to control conditions, while the other group engages in five minutes of interacting with negative thoughts about strength, beauty, fitness prior to working out. Measure duration or intensity of workouts before and after intervention, and across groups.

Impact: multi-state/center ABA treatment company provides various levels of ACT training to their employees. Some employees receive an ACT infographic, another receive a one-hour ACT overview video, and the third group receives a three-hour live interactive training. Measures are taken on staff turnover and burnout and examined across groups as well as by geographic region.

The weakness of all group comparison designs is the between-person variability cannot be used to model within-person variability. Said in another way, it is mathematically impossible to go from a group comparison result to even probabilistic statements about whether the differences between groups will apply to a particular person over time. The full extent of this statistical problem is only now being fully appreciated (see Molenaar, 2013, for an explanation why). If you want to know what a particular client needs, unless there are properly analyzed high temporal density idiographic longitudinal data in the RCT, the results of an RCT cannot tell you. But if you want to ask overall whether policymakers should invest in treatment X or treatment Y for a class of people with problem Z, the RCT is needed.

Idionomic Complex Network Analysis

When high temporal density idiographic longitudinal data are available an important new kind of statistical analysis is available that fits behavior analytic assumptions. We will use the example of Group Iterative Multiple Model Estimation or "GIMME" (Gates et al., 2012) as applied to the PBAT described earlier. GIMME identifies relationships present in individual longitudinal networks in the context of within-person variability assessed person by person. In an iterative fashion, it then seeks out pathways applicable at the sub-group and group level, only retaining them if they improve fit at the individual level. GIMME analyzes each person separately and only then takes a peek at additional relationships between events over time when similarities between an individual and other individuals are considered. These additional nomothetic findings are allowed in, only if most idiographic models are strengthened. In a sense, this turns classical statistics on its head. In this "idionomic" approach (a neologism that combines idiographic and nomothetic analysis) the individual analysis if considered sacrosanct and considerations of subgroup and group finding are treated as possible sources of error.

An example of this approach is a study by Sanford et al. (2022). The PBAT and items assessing common clinical outcomes were assessed twice a day for more than a month with 50 individuals in an experience sampling format, over a month, yielding at least 60 measurement occasions per person. These data were then analyzed using GIMME. Most people showed interpretable networks of processes leading to common clinical outcomes. Consider the idionomic network of a single person shown in Figure 13.1. Solid-headed arrows show positive relationships within the person over time; empty-headed arrows show negative relationships. This person gets distressed by anxiety. This person gets more anxious when they lose contact with the present environment, but that happens when they're not in a situation that allows for expression of emotion, and that tends to happen when they are not feeling meaningfully challenged, which in turn tends to happen when they lose contact with their present environment. It's a self-amplifying loop, which is likely why this person is in the upper quartile of anxiety struggles. Being more emotionally open and able to experience a range of emotions could help because it has an inhibitory relationship on distress over anxiety but unfortunately the only process that's encouraging that behavior is finding personally important challenges which is itself not currently being fostered by this person's other actions.

An empirical idionomic network for a person high in distress over anxiety is shown below.

In essence, this is a kind of empirical functional analysis. A number of possible targets could be used in an intervention program with this person. Mindfulness training might help the person connect with their present environment. Perhaps they could be given the relationship and social skills training needed to seek out social contexts to express emotion in a meaningful way. It might also be important to connect values choices (i.e., personally important challenges) to what is considered to be a "meaning challenge."

This network is based on the PBAT which is essentially a self-monitoring tool, but there is no reason that analyses of this kind could not be done with all objective, behavioral

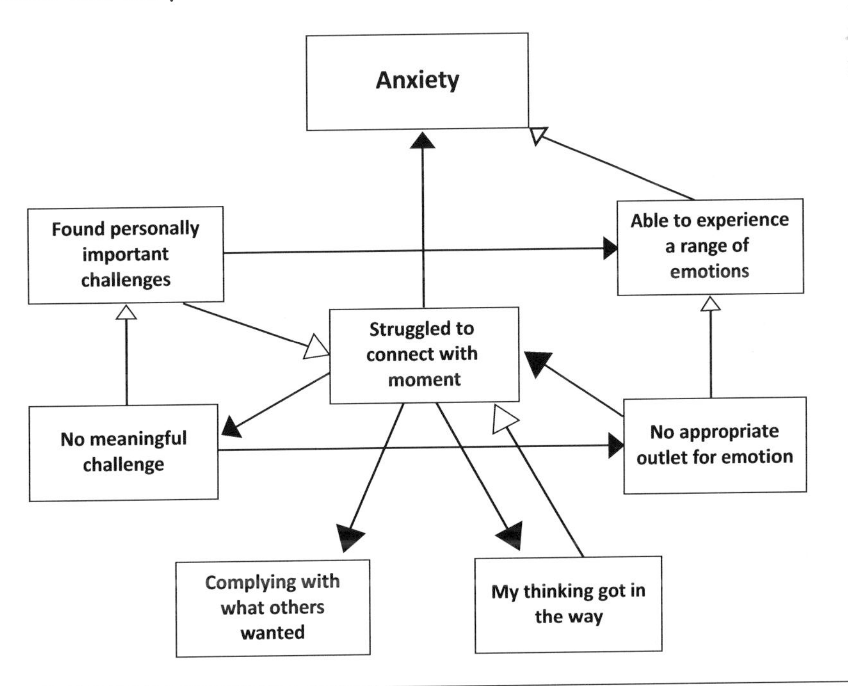

Figure 13.1 An empirical idionomic network for a person high in distress.

measures. Our point here is methodological. Very appropriate statistical tools now exist to do empirical forms of functional analysis suited to persons with high-level verbal abilities.

Person-specific idiographic data of this kind can be generalized to other individuals, just as has always been believed within behavior analysis. The trick going forward will be to combine intensive idiographic analysis on processes of change with randomized controlled trials that allow policymakers and funders to consider the overall deployment of resources in an evidence-based way while giving behavior analysts and other practitioners the knowledge they need to serve the individuals they are treating.

BI-DIRECTIONAL RETICULATED MODEL OF RESEARCH

The movement from our current state of knowledge of what ACT is and the power for it to produce change will hinge upon our field's ability to scale up and down the research agenda using the bi-directional reticulated model of theory-to-impact. Historically we moved from the basic animal laboratory to extensions of human behavior. That worked but it could only take us so far because relational learning alters the impact of direct contingency learning.

Sticking with the populations and settings in which direct contingency learning alone provided guidance makes up the majority of what is called "applied behavior analysis," but it has excessively narrowed our field.

At the same time, we cannot be content with surface-level applied demonstrations that ACT works. More proof-of-concept studies will not produce a greater understanding of the processes involved nor is it likely to increase the overall impact of ACT or RFT.

The path forward is bidirectional. It requires dancing back and forth between basic work and impact work, where each informs the other. It requires intensive idiographic work focused on processes of change and linked to increasingly sophisticated basic relational learning research. It requires idionomic research nested within group comparison studies that are the coin of the realm. The aspirational behavior analytic ACT researcher will need to wear all these hats, a kind of professional shapeshifter who one day is a basic scientist and the next a policy-changing impact-driven advocate. The ideal ACT researcher will need to practice what they preach, showing an extraordinary degree of psychological flexibility. We challenge the individual researcher and the field at large to step outside the local contingencies sustaining traditional behavioral research projects and see how they can fit their research into this larger and more impactful agenda that is designed to place behavior analysis back at the center of the cultural conversation about the role of behavioral science in human life.

14

Ethical Decision-Making

From the very beginning, acceptance and commitment therapy (ACT) has sparked controversy within the behavior analytic community. In the interests of broader understanding and use by non-behaviorally trained practitioners' promulgation, technical vocabulary was deemphasized, and the detailed connections with basic behavioral terminology were allowed to evolve slowly or in the background, while implementation by others outside of behavior analysis was emphasized. The concept of a "middle-level term" (itself a middle-level term) was introduced that could orient listeners towards the centralized themes of the approach in a way that was accurate but would require greater technical precision on the part of the applied scientist to translate into effective technologies. Those scientists, trained behaviorally and within other orientations as well, were given the skills to switch between the highly technical and the middle-level descriptors that actually mean something to the rest of society.

It was a usual developmental strategy for a behavioral method, and it fueled pushback from many within behavior analysis as a field. This has happened before, for example with the positive behavior intervention and support (PBIS) movement in schools. When the vocabulary shifted to something that the rest of the world understand, behavior analysts shied away. That is to say that what defined "behavior analysis" to many was not the effective working of a behavioral technology – both PBIS and ACT achieved that – rather the inclusion of this technical language, whether or not this language actually produced the desired outcomes and at the scale at one time envisioned by Skinner and contemporaries. It might have ended there as a simple historical disconnection – an odd anomaly of a behavioral method rarely used by behavior analysis – were it not for a gnawing unmet need.

A growing number of primarily front-line behavior analytic clinicians delivering direct services to persons with disabilities continued to notice that traditional behavioral interventions were falling short of efficacy for the presenting problems that faced their clients. Conventionally suggested tools such as self-monitoring, goal setting, and self-reinforcement missed the mark as effective interventions. When a parent began to cry, an awkward silence followed or attempts were made to redirect to the behavioral program, or perhaps worst, mentalistic platitudes began to flow from the mouths of behavior analysts. When the challenges of clients became increasingly verbal, behavior analysts were left with no other option but to refer out. We became the science of simple (at least as far as verbal behavior goes) with no room to entertain that which became complex.

As the years have passed it has been increasingly hard to deny that many behavioral challenges that face human society have yet to be alleviated by behavior analysis, and there is no

DOI: 10.4324/9781003250371-17

clear strategy to change that sad state of affairs. It is almost humorous to think of a solution to climate change in which each society member would goal set and maybe self-reinforce conservation behavior. The obesity crisis that many cultures struggle with is unlikely to end through a program of giving tickets and vouchers for healthy lifestyle behaviors. Curing the social and emotional distress of a child with autism through feedback for social appropriateness is prospectively implausible. Conducting a traditional four-factor functional analysis seems almost irrelevant to such issues as racism, the immigration crisis, or the trauma of violence and war. There is a painful and old joke that applies here. Question: how do you turn a behavior analyst into a mentalist? Answers: ask them to explain why behavior analysis is not disseminated and used. Suddenly instead of the responsible spirit of "the subject is always right," behavior analysts explain away their failures by blaming others who fail to understand or to appreciate them for what they can do.

In area after area, the behavior analyst has been left with a choice – proceed with weak tools or refer elsewhere. Both of these alternatives abandon Skinner's promise of a science of human behavior, all human behavior. And those to whom we would refer have far from succeeded at solving these most challenging and most common issues that we all face. When things get verbally complicated, science begins to take a back seat, and solutions to these problems are still needed.

A third alternative for the behavior analyst has appeared with the development of relational frame theory (RFT) and ACT, yet it carries with it a series of ethical challenges about how to proceed. The deep message of RFT is that we as a field have a lot of work to do to understand how human relational learning interacts with direct-acting contingencies. ACT is an attempt to step up to that challenge. If RFT is broadly correct and there was no "ACT" in existence, something very much like ACT would have to be invented from scratch once RFT began to take shape. Indeed, that very situation is how ACT began to be molded into an intervention model in the first place, several decades ago. Most likely, something under a different name and with alternative assumptions that extend from the basic work in RFT will take its place – but the name is inconsequential – that we need something that works (i.e., works better than other options) remains true at this moment in our shared history.

But now, with relatively few behavior analysts formally trained in ACT, and many service-regulating bodies not incorporating ACT into standards of typical care, it has remained an issue as to whether and how ACT should be used by behavior analysts. This issue contains multiple specific questions. The first set of questions is about the tickets of entry for behavioral methods. Is ACT actually behavior analytic enough to be considered a valid intervention tool? Can it be fully understood in naturalistic, monistic, behavior-analytic terms? Does it make sense given only behavioral principles as extended by relational operants and evolutionary science? Does it have an adequate evidential base?

We have spent a great deal of space on those questions in this volume because they are at the core of behavior analysis as a field. We believe this book has clarified beyond a reasonable doubt that yes, ACT is behavior analytic; understandable in natural science terms; and based on a strong empirical foundation. Where appropriate for use is time for it to be fully embraced by applied behavior analysts. ACT can help improve problem area after problem area in applied behavior analysis (ABA). The field itself appears now to have made that decision. Desperate for solutions to the problems facing the clients they serve, many behavior analysts are seeking out the education and training needed to use ACT. If you are a behavior analyst reading this book you are likely in that very group – you are arriving at the last chapter of a volume you hope will fulfill a practical need.

But we then come to the second set of questions. Even with effective self-improvement how can ACT-based treatments fall in line with the role the behavior analyst generally now has within the education, health, or mental health system? How can it fit within your scope of practice, and how can you become fully competent in its delivery? Is it ethical to use ACT in your practice? One reason these questions have a sense of urgency is that once you embrace the clinical utility of ACT for behavior analysts, a number of natural extensions begin to emerge. Said in another way, once you learn ACT, many doors open. Should you walk through them? If the answer is "perhaps in the future," what should happen before that future appears?

For example, as you add ACT to parent training, should you work with couples and families on their relationships? As you add ACT to organization consulting, should you work with executives on their sense of burnout?

Ironically, the reason these questions have not been asked with the same intensity in the past is that the technology available to behavior analysts had such obvious limitations. No one was asking these "scope of practice" questions because practice was limited by technological constraints. When behavior analysts attempted to bring their existing technologies into those spaces, usually through incentive or nonfunctional reward systems, few wanted this technology because it did not add much beyond philosophical adherence to what we believed was the scientific high ground. That is changing with ACT-based approaches because it adds to what is already in place and it is described in ways that are understandable in those spaces. We do not need to teach a new language for people to work with us, we can work with the language that has already been established within the various verbal communities where effective working can proceed.

Take the example of behavioral skills training (BST). BST is good for many things but it largely left the role of language out of intervention (i.e., language beyond simple instruction). This may be part of why variable results have always plagued behavior analytic interventions for verbal humans in areas such as staff burnout, employee performance, self-care, or social skills training. True, sometimes such interventions were powerful enough to override programmed contingencies, but at other times they were not. Couples and families with relationship issues or executives burning out due to constant stress were not lining up for BST programs. Behavior analysts did not have a technology that fit very well, so consumer demand did not cause a stretch.

When examining the published successes of behavior analytic research, there is an extreme imbalance – the vast majority of documented accomplishments have been shown with low to non speaking participants. Traditional behavior analytic interventions are simply not sophisticated enough. Performance feedback, skills training, verbal praise, and so on – all fine so far as they go – but they do not go that far. At times when they do work, the underlying behavioral processes often remain uncertain. In order to have a science that addresses the complicated nature of human beings, it will require the behavior analyst to continue to search for prediction and control at much higher levels of complexity. Science is a constantly evolving discipline, and so is behavior analysis. The inclusion of RFT and ACT into applied behavior analytic interventions is nothing more than the next chapter in our own discipline's evolution.

The world is verbally complex for the majority of humans, and human societal challenges are entangled with verbal events. It appears time that our intervention complexity matches our problem complexity. Before such a change occurs within the field of behavior analysis a number of cautionary issues must be addressed. To open the ACT toolset and apply it on another human being, ethical challenges will arise. Additionally, the behavior analyst will likely find themselves having a political challenge as well. Because if ACT really is necessary, effective, and within the repertoire of a behavior analyst, then how the field defines itself, trains its dependents, and treats its clients will all need to evolve. This will also bring us into contact with professionals who may not have even known of our existence and how they respond will be unpredictable and variable, and ensuring that this evolution occurs ethically and in the best interest of those served will be critical to ensuring this outcome is positive.

ETHICAL DILEMMAS AND ACT

The behavior analyst will undoubtedly find themselves facing a variety of ethical issues and dilemmas in regard to treating a client using ACT. Ethical dilemmas are not avoidable or optional. You will have them. The range of such issues is large – from acceptability of intervention to competency of delivering that intervention. At times issues will appear of verbal nature linked to ACT itself (are these my values or my clients' values?; am I open to my own private events in working with this particular set of client problems?). At times they will have to do with how you handle the professional issues that may arise such as confronting another behavior analyst on interventions that are less well supported than ACT, or helping a parent to abandon a non-effective treatment that conflicts with what we know about psychological flexibility. Such uncomfortable situations need to be embraced, not avoided. The key will be how to move forward when facing such challenges, not to ignore them or mindlessly paper them over. Your task is to make a choice on a course of action that serves the client and keeps yourself within the appropriate legal and professional parameters.

Ethics are typically not black and white, but rather shades of gray. Behavior analysts need to adopt an underlying set of philosophical principles or assumptions to help guide them through these murky waters. These principles are at a deeper level than the typical dos and don'ts of an external regulation body, because they serve as the very framework of your own choices. When the behavior analyst becomes clearer on what the underlying principles or assumptions are, ethical dilemmas become easier to detect and navigate.

Ethical or Not Ethical?

Donna just encountered another behavior analyst at her company attempting to treat a client that has no language abilities using the Hexaflex because she heard that ACT is an up-and-coming intervention approach that a lot of people are beginning to use. Donna is going to speak up and challenge this other professional. She was told in graduate school that no one should ever use ACT unless they are a clinical psychologist.

Ethical – Donna's challenge to the other professional is due to a mismatch of client ability and treatment approach. When there are no derived relational skills present, the conditions needed to obtain gains from an ACT intervention are absent.

Not ethical – Donna's challenge to her coworker is due to being told by her advisor that ACT was not real behavior analysis. Donna has never actually read any literature on ACT but based her opinion on the supposed skills of her former professor rather than embracing her own professional responsibility.

FUNCTIONAL CONTEXTUALISM AS A BASIS FOR ETHICAL DECISION-MAKING

Early in this text we described the scientific worldview of functional contextualism. The truth criterion (or in other words, the primary goal) is successful working toward a publicly stated purpose. Summarizing the history of our field into a sentence that reflects its origins in Bear, Wolf, and Risley's vision, applied behavior analysts seek to predict and influence socially meaningful behavior in replicable, effective, generalizable ways that are based on high precision/high scope principles of behavior change. If we link this functional view of behavior analysis to its philosophical roots in pragmatism, you can see that the very definition of our field includes treatments that work for the people that we treat. It is true that the entire field of behavior analysis is not restricted to helping others, and thus superficially speaking an applied or technological outcome is not equivalent to the broad science of human behavior. Note, however, that this single-sentence summary of our field includes the basic psychological processes that bring about behavior change, or the application of independent variables to affect a dependent variable which in turn could be used by others at some point to bring about behavior change. No basic science, and surely not that of behavior analysis, was embarked upon for tinkering purposes only. Rather it was always envisioned as the means to an end. And that end within a functional contextual worldview remains successful working toward our publicly stated purposes, which in our case among other purposes is helping others obtain meaningful gains via behavioral science.

We reviewed this philosophical foundation because it means we are ethically bound to do a better and better job of helping others in meaningful ways. That is at the core of ethical care from our pragmatic worldview of ethical care. If ACT can serve as a behaviorally sensible vehicle to produce such outcomes – we are ethically responsible to see it used and used well. When competencies are not up to a level in which this type of care can be administered correctly, then it is the ethical responsibility of the behavior analyst to obtain such skills. When the impact of ACT or any other behavioral method is not meeting the full needs of the client(s) served, there is an ethical responsibility to facilitate the necessary supplemental services to capture the care needed. In summary, the behavior analyst should keep the core belief of "successful working" near to them and allow it to influence ethical choice-making.

Ethical or Not Ethical?

Santi has a fair amount of graduate school debt and realizes that in order to make ends meet they need to put their wants and needs ahead of everyone else. They have to travel a long distance to physically see a client, and as a result will often opt to remote meet via telehealth instead. It is uncertain if the quality of care is similar, but Santi is really protective of their own self-care.

Ethical – Santi may be the only clinician that can effectively deliver an ACT intervention to their client. If they become overworked and overstressed from too much driving, another leave of absence may result. Therefore, remote care is a way to protect not only Santi's interests, but also to ensure successful working of the client-behavior analyst relationship. Santi and their team are also collecting on-going behavior change data to ensure the intervention is producing effective changes.

Not ethical –Santi enjoys sleeping in late and not putting miles in their new car. Even though it is an electric model that requires no gas, they do not want to reduce its trade-in value. Although the client has complained about remote meetings and understanding the ACT processes without experiential activities, Santi continues to use the excuse of personal stress to reduce the number of face-to-face meetings and content development that would match the needs of the client. Moreover, the data suggest that the challenging behavior that was the reason for the referral is continuing to worsen.

Perhaps the trickiest difference between previous forms of pragmatism and functional contextualism is the realization that successful working as a scientific guide requires the public statement of a purpose, goal, or value. Without that addition, any reinforced behavior is "true" and any means to obtain reinforcement is therefore "ethical."

All pragmatic philosophies have faced this dilemma. The classic questions in Philosophy 101 classes on this point include such examples as "what if Hitler had won the war?" or "is it really true that what's good for GM is good for the country?" Progressive science is not "the ends justify the means" psychopathy, and not every reinforced behavior is "good." Very early on in the ACT journey a way out of this conundrum was specified (Hayes, 1993). Pragmatism can work as a scientific guide if and only if a priori purposes are stated. Skinner did exactly that by stating that the goal of his science was the development of principles that enabled the prediction and control of behavior. Baer, Wolf, and Risleydid exactly that by adding that in the domain of applied work the changes needed to be socially meaningful, replicable, effective, and generalizable. Functional contextualism added that the principles need to have precision, scope, and depth.

The analytic and practical purposes of our science have to be publicly stated like this because science is a social enterprise and scientists need to have the freedom to choose their own paths. Skinner created needless push-back by declaring that the purpose of science itself was prediction and control (to which some other scientists said, "that's not my purpose – I just want to understand" and there we were in a needless argument about whether that's the same thing). A better way to handle this issue would have been to say that the purpose of his science was prediction and control and then to allow others to "vote with their feet."

ACT reflects this same issue when it links all therapeutic steps to chosen values, and links concrete goals to values. Values are an action – valuing. We've spent entire chapters in this book delineating the features of that action. The ACT provider needs to know what their client's values are because that is what enables them to evaluate the success of what is done. When using defusion or acceptance skills, for instance, the bottom-line issue will be "did this help increase the probability of values-based behavior?" In microcosm that shows how successful working can work, once it is linked to publicly stated purposes or goals. The ACT provider must know the client's values or they cannot be a pragmatic guide. The same is true of the provider and the same is true of the science. Reinforcement is always the issue, but not just any reinforcer. Thus, the limitation that functional contextualism places on behavior science is necessary for pragmatism to work as an ethical set of scientific assumptions.

THE SCOPE OF THE FIELD OF BEHAVIOR ANALYSIS

At its inception, the field of applied behavior analysis was defined within parameters established by the first article in the first issue of the first applied behavior analysis journal. The authors of this paper outlined seven dimensions of what they believed the field was to contain, which was designed to define the boundaries of what could and should be considered behavioral content and what should not (Baer et al., 1968). While the authors cast it as only being about "some current dimensions" as the decades passed it became one of the most cited articles in applied behavior analysis and was held in such reverence that even the authors' attempt to update it 20 years later (Bear et al., 1987) is cited less than 1/6th as often. It seems to be the case that if a treatment, theory, intervention, research study, or research program can meet the narrative thresholds outlined in BWR, 1968 then that work can be considered behavior analytic.

It is interesting – even stunning – to read their update in the context of the present volume. Most of the moves that have been made by the contextual behavior science wing of behavior analysis (i.e., the FC/RFT/ACT wing) are explicitly or implicitly anticipated or endorsed by the founders of our discipline.

In the area of "applied" work, they note that "social problems are essentially the behaviors of displaying or explaining problems" (Bear et al., 1968, p. 314) and point out that the decision to treat is a personal or societal playing out of a dialectic between "the client's problem display and willingness to pay versus the therapist's values" (p. 314). They call on behavior analysts to learn more about the stimulus control that regulates both sides of this equation – very much in line with the subtext of the present volume.

In the area of being "behavioral" they point out that when addressing "constructs of anxiety, attention, intelligence, disabilities, spontaneity, readiness, critical periods, innate releasers, storage and retrieval mechanisms, schemata, and the like," behavior analysts should "recognize that each of those labels (and many others like them) often represents some behavioral reality not yet analyzed as such" (p. 315). Doing so raises the possibility that such phenomena "might well be analyzed behavior-analytically, perhaps with great profit to us and those disciplines, and thus to our roles within those disciplines" (p. 315). The story of ACT and RFT, we believe, proves their point in this area.

They even go on to point out, however, that tightly cast behavioral accounts may need to be tempered in order for the impact of behavior analyses of issues of this kind to be obtained. They point out ruefully that

> The past 20 years have shown us again and again that our audiences respond very negatively to our systematic explanations of our programs and their underlying assumptions, yet very positively to the total spectacle of our programs… as long as they are left "unexplained" by us.
>
> *(p. 315–316)*

They saw three alternatives to solving that problem:

a) find ways to teach its culture to talk behavior-analytically (or at least to value behavior-analytic talk);
b) develop non-behavior-analytic talk for public display, and see if that talk will prove as useful for research and analysis as present behavior-analytic talk, or whether two languages must be maintained; or
c) let it be (we represent approximately 2% of American psychology, and we are currently stable at that level).

(p. 316)

Mainstream behavior analysis chose route (a) and suffered the consequences of route (c). The RFT/ACT wing chose route (b) but indeed committed itself to maintaining two languages. As a result, it has made some progress on route (a) – arguably no wing of behavior analysis has done more to maintain the visibility of behavioral thinking – and was hugely successful in avoiding the consequences of route (c). That experiment has now been fully played out over the 35 years since Bear, Wolf, and Risley's update of their now 55-year-old statement. The data are in. The very fact that the Association for Behavior Analysis International (ABAI) is publishing this volume shows that mainstream behavior analysis is ready to agree on that point.

In this area, however, they did make one mistake. They thought that carefully studying superficially mentalistic phenomena in a behavioral way might – as with the Premack principle – be quite reinforcing and popular since it would allow us some "use and consumption of inner, mentalistic explanations for behavior" (p. 316) without its cost. They were not worried that this move would "jeopardize our ability to discriminate a behavioral discipline from a nonbehavioral discipline. The various professional behavior patterns that constitute a behavioral discipline… can always be discriminated from the considerably more various patterns that constitute nonbehavioral disciplines, even if no one were any longer to display those behavior patterns" because the difference "is essentially philosophical rather than anthropological" (p. 315).

That turned out to be incorrect. What they did not fully consider is the internal struggles within behavior analysis itself. Yes, anyone with eyes to see can see that ACT and RFT is a philosophically and theoretically behavioral approach once the record is examined. And it is worth noting that by maintaining a "two language" commitment the ACT and RFT wing never abandoned the "display of those behavior patterns" despite the fact that since Bear, Wolf, and Risley could imagine even that radial step could be OK in the interests of the clients we serve – ACT/RFT developers simply added more accessible terms. That small step did indeed "jeopardize our ability to discriminate a behavioral discipline from a non-behavioral discipline" but that era is thankfully passing away. This book published under the auspices of ABAI is itself proof of that.

We (ACT and ABA) are now evolving together.

Ethical or Not Ethical?

Frank Soulmer was just featured on a podcast where he spoke about the problems of ACT being seen as a behavior analysis intervention. He references the Baar et al. (1968) article and claims that ACT does not meet the threshold of behavioral because ACT seeks to change hypothetical constructs such as flexibility, acceptance, and fusion. These are not measurable or meaningful behaviors in his opinion.

Ethical – Dr. Soulmer may have a point that if ACT attempted to obtain treatment outcomes nothing more than self-reports or clinician impressions of such midlevel terms that are not operationally defined, that indeed it would not meet the BWR (1968) criteria, and also not likely be viewed as an acceptable behavior analytic intervention. His message to the professional community would be a helpful directive.

Not ethical – Frank has failed to read this book. Frank has not become aware of decades worth of behavior-analytic ACT interventions. Most importantly Frank has spread inaccuracies about his own field, and has potentially cost clients a right to an effective treatment by their providing behavior analyst. It would be wise for a listener of the podcast to approach Frank and discuss his misuse of information and the negative effects upon clientele across the professional community.

Of course, non-behavior analysts implemented ACT-consistent procedures (clinical psychologists, psychiatrists, social workers, family counselors, and so on), and those persons do not become applied behavior analysts by doing so. No more than we become them by implementing ACT consistent procedures. But they do become friends and allies and we learn to speak the same language. That has already happened. Go to a site like Amazon and you will see that people who buy ACT books also buy books on behavioral principles. That is exactly what Baer et al. (1987) imagined when they supposed that learning how to analyze emotion, cognition, and so on might bring "great profit to us and those disciplines, and thus to our roles within those disciplines" (p. 315). Anyone looking at, say, modern-day clinical psychology can see that they were right.

What lies at the root of most resistance from within the field is that ACT is not behavioral enough. That kind of criticism is understandable and can even be helpful if delivered with the understanding that science is progressive and we should never be self-satisfied. We never have enough knowledge. We do not know enough about extinction, negative reinforcement, schedule effects, behavioral skills training, or any other countless behavior analytic principles, procedures, and interventions. We wholeheartedly agree with all of that. But "enough to be legitimately used within our field" is another matter entirely given the vast body of behaviorally sensible work done in ACT and RFT. That, we think, reveals an unwelcome and unfair double standard that has to be confronted because it harms the clients that we serve.

Is it ethical to not use an intervention that can work in favor of one that will not work because of this arbitrary, subjective, and potentially mentalistic threshold of what "is" or "is not" behavior analysis?

We believe what sits at the real forefront of opposition to ACT as a part of applied behavior analysis, is that you cannot adopt ACT without embracing Relational Frame Theory. And to do this, most everything we take for granted within the field of behavior analysis will need to change.

Relational operants operate on other behavioral principles.

That inconvenient truth is an empirical fact. For instance, punishers can become conditioned reinforcers due to their participation in relational frames but without any pairing with reinforcement (Whelan & Barnes-Holmes, 2004) which means that this effect does not fit the known parameters of conditioned reinforcement as traditionally understood. Stimuli can elicit classically conditioned responses that are greater than those established via direct pairing not only due to their participation in relational frames alone but also controlling for any possible associative basis for that effect (Dougher et al., 2007), which means that this effect does not fit the known parameters of conditioned eliciting stimuli as traditionally understood. Evocative stimuli can acquire their functions via the transformation of stimulus functions through a variety of relational frame families rather than by a history of greater reinforcement for behavior in their presence than in their absence (e.g., Hayes et al., 1987), which means that this antecedent effect does not fit the known parameters of discriminative stimuli as traditionally understood. Motivative stimuli can likewise acquire their functions via the transformation of stimulus functions (Ju & Hayes, 2008) which means that this antecedent effect does not fit the known parameters of motivative stimuli as traditionally understood.

This exciting but disruptive fact means that once verbal abilities pass a certain point, an adequate analysis of human functioning cannot succeed without a parallel analysis of relational learning abilities. We have already noted that the functions of problem behaviors are three and one-half times less likely to be successfully categorized using standard FA procedures, for example (Belisle et al., 2017) once even rudimentary relational operants are established. That means that we now have to study behavior-behavior relations as a central topic in our field and learn how to do so without mentalism or the loss of a pragmatic view of causality linked to experimental manipulation. That's not easy. This book showed you how to do it, but it took many pages and many examples to do so.

Saying "no, no, no" will not take that challenge away. If the data on ACT and RFT are to be believed (i.e., the hundreds of scientists and their entire research labs did not just agree to cook up all of these data with a coherent set of findings) the entire field of behavior analysis now faces a new ethical duty: the ethical duty to learn how relational operants impact other behavioral phenomena; the ethical duty to produce that impact on purpose by fostering relational learning abilities; and then learning how to enhance the desirable aspects of that impact and reduce their undesirable aspects. Said more simply, learning RFT and ACT when they are critical to client advancement will soon be an ethical obligation of applied behavior analysts. We are arguably already there now that equivalence-based instruction is on the task list, since there are no known methods better able to establish equivalence when it does not exist than RFT methods (Dixon et al., 2021).

Ethical or Not Ethical?

Arlo has been teaching Skinner's analysis of language for almost two decades to graduate students in behavior analysis. One of his students asked him what he thought of relational frame theory, and his response was that he refuses to read RFT work since it is nothing more than a bloated way to describe the same concepts that Skinner provided over 50 years ago, plus maybe equivalence. When a follow-up question arose as to why then Skinner's work has not produced the same kind of robust program of research that RFT has, Arlo's response was that the RFT extent of the research work is irrelevant because it's not behavioral and is nothing more than cognitive psychology pretending to be behavior analysis. He argued Skinner provided everything we needed to know about behavior analysis as a field and any student who claimed otherwise would not pass his course if he knew about it.

Ethical – Arlo has the right to make any intellectual claims that he feels are grounded in his set of pre-analytic assumptions. If behavior analysis is synonymous with Skinner's writings, then it is true that an analysis of how relational operants impact programmed contingencies has to be outside of the field because no such analysis was ever made by Skinner himself.

Not ethical – The refusal to examine a body of empirical work highly relevant to your teaching in behavior analysis is scientifically unethical once that body of work becomes sufficiently large and central. RFT and ACT have passed that threshold in the eyes of ABAI and behavior journals. As a behavior analyst informing his students that the work is just another way of speaking about Skinner cannot be ethically based on open statements of ignorance and refusals to read. Pressuring students to suppress their interest in RFT in order to pass Arlo's course or obtain a letter of recommendation from him at graduation is clearly unethical.

THE SCOPE OF EXTERNAL FORCES ON A BEHAVIOR ANALYST'S USE OF ACT

A wide range of external forces will put pressure upon the behavior analyst to use or refrain from using ACT. These entities will play a crucial role in ensuring ethical practice within the definition parameters of your credentials, the types of services you render under that credential, and how overlap with other credentials should be navigated. The practices wing of the field may have limits placed on both populations and techniques, and certain funding sources may even further define the who and what can be constituted as appropriate service delivery. These can evolve and change, but they cannot be ignored. It remains the behavior analyst's ethical, and sometimes legal, responsibility to know what external forces regulate the implementation of applied behavior analysis in their area of employment. Much akin to a surgeon who may have the education and ability to perform a certain procedure, certain licenses and permissions are required in order to actually perform the work legally. Where behavior analysts can stumble in the practice of ACT is to disconnect ACT processes from their established scope of practice as constructed by an entity that is not familiar with the unique ACT terminology, vocabulary, and outcomes.

The Behavior Analysis Certification Board (BACB) is a United States-based entity that provides a considerable amount of regulation on the practice of behavior analysis within the US. Other similar groups exist in the US, but the BACB tends to be the most commonly used mechanism for those behavior analysts wishing to obtain licensure within a given locale, or to hold a credential of being "Board Certified." At a global level, the BACB continues to provide influence on what defines the practice of behavior analysis even though in most locations they do not directly credential practitioners. The BACB also provides an ethical code of conduct that its credentialed individuals are to abide by, and not doing so may create professional and legal challenges for the behavior analyst. The latter occurs more out of a response to law violations within the local area of practice.

In regard to ACT, the BACB provides extremely limited direction as to what elements of ACT are indeed within the typical content area in which a behavior analyst is supposed to be operating within. Rather this task list of skills that the behavior analyst should be fluent in includes statements like "use instructions and rules" or "use contingency contracting." There remains a wide variety of techniques that could accomplish such objectives for a client including those within an ACT framework. What does it mean to "use" instruction or rules? ACT instead challenges the practitioner to teach clients to use rules in a psychologically flexible way. For example, "use instructions and rules" could be implemented with an intervention that attempts to alter the inaccurate inflexible rules of a client, and how teaching more adaptive rules that rest upon flexibility and adaption (ex. "When I start to get upset, I will remember what my values and engage in the relevant behavior to obtain them"). Also, the task of "use contingency contracting" could be accomplished using ACT techniques where the clinician and the client work together identifying values and the necessary committed actions by which those values can be more likely obtained ("Every day you want to go outside for extra recess, make sure that you are being flexible with your dislike for math class. Because if you can stay committed to your work, you will move closer to your values."). In order for the behavior analyst to stay within the defined parameters of the BACB's practice guidelines there will need to careful interpretation of how the various elements of ACT can serve as intervention mechanisms that directly link to specific content areas.

Ethical or Not Ethical?

Pico Dingo has been trained as a behavior analyst by a very old and strict mentor who believes that no new discoveries in the field will ever occur and has neglected to learn anything new since they graduated from graduating from their program many years ago. following the masterpiece writings of Skinner. When she (Pico) discussed using ACT with one of her clients, the mentor informed her that he would never even consider doing so. His rationale is that ACT was invented and is still a "new therapy following the death of Skinner," and therefore has no value to add to a behavioral account that has had all of the answers for many years. Furthermore, he points out that the BACB does not specifically endorse ACT as a type of treatment to use citing the BACB Task List.

Ethical – Pico Dingo's professor is correct that she might need to delay her use of ACT because she was never trained by the mentor to do so. With that professor having no idea of the work that has been done in the past 40 years on ACT, it is clear that she would never have been taught how it fits within the parameters of behavior analysis.

Not ethical – Pico Dingo's professor has failed to keep up with the relevant literature in his own field. He has become more of a historian than a clinician and thus has not prepared her for integrating empirically well-established ACT methods within the parameters of the BACB task list.

Many practitioners of applied behavior analysis operate within a medical-care model in which third-party payors place regulations on what services can be reimbursable under the umbrella of "applied behavior analysis services". As a result, many behavior analysts may find it difficult to initially obtain authorization for assessment and treatment involving ACT. There are a number of variables that come into play with successful approval for payment for ACT services. First, the behavior analyst must always keep in mind that no client is likely ever to be referred because of "inflexibility", "fusion" or any other mid-level ACT term. They have been deemed in need of care by a behavior analyst due to behavioral issues or referred to behavioral services based on a diagnosis, either by a pediatrician, clinical psychologist, or psychiatrist. As such, as a behavior analyst you will need to keep the behavioral issue as your metric of success within your intervention. It is unwise to attempt to seek services for "improving flexibility" or "teaching acceptance". These skills are themselves means to an end – to influence socially meaningful behavior change. It is far better to use ACT as the method to improve upon the behavioral manifestations that are currently being exhibited. We have attempted to clarify how these processes operate *around* behavior of interest as the independent variable within a comprehensive intervention plan, rather than as the dependent variable that we are attempting to influence.

Second, it is quite likely that third-party payors are not going to be familiar with ACT language or even its relevance within typical behavior analytic care. Therefore, it will be necessary from time to time to have discussions with insurance companies about ACT, and the parameters under which you plan to use it. Again, keeping the procedures as the means to the behavior change end is always a good idea. These entities do not typically micromanage your "use of instructions and rules", so it is a logical overstep for them to do so now using ACT techniques, methods, or kernels of intervention to produce those same change objectives. However, if ACT is being used as a packaged treatment without linkage to such measurable behaviors, of course an insurance company might second guess the value of ACT (and they should). Finally, insurance companies want to see positive changes in the client's behavior, and therefore the exclusive use of indirect measures of success such as questionnaires will not and should not suffice. Ethically, the behavior analyst's goal is to produce meaningful measurable behavior change and these targets need to be defined before the fact. To reduce pushback from goals rooted in ACT, the behavior analyst must link ACT as a treatment to measurable changes in overt behavior with clear links made to the functional assessments as we have described functional assessment here (as in a functional analytic account, not as in "the four functions" of behavior).

Ethical or Not Ethical?

A recent case has been referred to Pappy Vonshnozer for ACT implementation. Pappy has been delivering ACT for multiple years in a private school and is excited about utilizing it with her new insurance-based client. However, before she starts services, she needs to request an authorization for treatment from the care provider. She believes that challenging behavior can be reduced using ACT and is requesting 20 hours a week to improve her client's flexibility and problem-solving skills. Her initial evaluation is based on parent reports, as well as student incident reports. The school staff have also collected some ABC data suggesting that the behavior is triggered by non-preferred demands being placed on the client.

Ethical – Pappy may be correct in her attempts to incorporate ACT into her methods of treatment. The requesting of services by the treatment provider may be warranted, as the client appears inflexible with adapting to newly introduced demands by school personnel.

Not ethical – Pappy has potentially not ruled out more basic contingency-driven interventions – and such data may be important when requesting services from a third-party payer. Also, Pappy has failed to operationalize the actual behavior changes she wishes to see in her client and has focused only on the processes of ACT themselves. As such, the insurance service request will likely be denied or at least necessitate increased explanation for her approach to treatment. This may actually delay the start of treatment because Pappy has not adequately created a person and problem-specific rationale for ACT, concentrated on behavioral change measures. Such an unneeded delay can have negative consequences for the client and is unethical.

An ethical challenge may also present itself when slightly overlapping professions come together on a client case, and result in confusion as to whose role it is to deliver a talk-based intervention. Take for example a teenager with autism and depressed mood who emits negative self-statements throughout the school day. Parents are concerned he is not making friends, and grades are suffering compared to a year ago. Services include social work at school, an outside psychotherapist, and the behavior analyst. In the ideal world perhaps all three professionals would coordinate care. In principle, ACT could be highly relevant to each of these intervention areas and if so, change could occur more quickly for this student. However, things are not always ideal, and the behavior analyst may find themselves attempting to deliver ACT methods to improve academic behavior that may lead to improved change grades (improving the grades directly is the role of the educator), and decreasing the domination of negative self-statements over other sources of behavioral regulation as a direct behavior change target, while the other professionals are using a non-ACT approach for altering psychological states of "major depression". Ethically, the behavior analyst should attempt to bring all providers together to deliver comprehensive coordinated care. And if those efforts fail, the behavior analyst should very diligently address only the presenting conditions that fall within the scope of being a behavior analyst.

Ethical or Not Ethical?

Bessie Bluebottom is an experienced behavior analyst who works in areas of school refusal. In addition to direct contingency methods, she commonly adds ACT defusion skills to help deal with verbal constructions of possible aversive events that might occur at school. A recent referral was attacked by bullies at school and has begun having panic attacks and traumatic flashbacks to the incident in addition to the school refusal. The school has asked Bessie for help with school refusal but is having a hard time finding a cognitive behavior therapist to help with that – they are calling it a panic disorder and post-traumatic stress disorder (PTSD). Bessie says that is not necessary anyway since after her initial sessions with the client she knows she will be using ACT and ACT is good for panic and trauma.

Ethical – It is good to consider ACT methods for a problem like school refusal if the functional analysis includes indications of experiential avoidance and cognitive fusion or other inflexibility processes as possible sources of the behavioral problem.

Not ethical – Treating panic and PTSD is outside Bessie's scope of practice. It is possible that using ACT methods focused on school refusal will show beneficial generalization, but this should not be assumed. She should encourage the school to find a good psychotherapist as well. Since she is an ACT provider she might use her contacts there to help the school find a good resource but she should not take over features of the case that are outside her competencies and professional role.

Delivering ACT within an educational environment may produce a range of ethical difficulties whereby students who are not essentially signing up for psychotherapy, are being delivered methods that blend into other therapy areas. This is most clearly the case with ACT as a schoolwide system of preventive supports for social and emotional well-being. For example, an entire school may design a social skills program using ACT language that teaches students to "accept" their feelings, and to "defuse" from struggles within their mind. Programs such as this can be helpful but unexpected effects can confront behavior analysts with unusual requests. For example, students may begin disclosing personal information, memories, and feelings to school personnel who are not trained in effectively managing such matters. Parents may hear that their children or others are discussing previously unstated frightening thoughts and may push back against "doing therapy on my kids" as a preventative measure during a school day.

If the ACT-trained behavior analyst was part of the team that developed the program these kinds of effects could have been anticipated and avoided. For example, the program could be designed to evoke a focus on commonly experienced private events that are obviously relevant to the purposes of the group and help students themselves understand when additional therapeutic steps might be appropriate. If the ACT-trained behavior analyst was not involved in the program design, she or he should understand the issues deeply enough to expect what may be coming and to be prepared with a plan to address these types of suddenly emerging "crisis" events. Otherwise, turning to the behavior analysts for direction may lead nowhere and the social credibility of the behavior analyst may be needlessly undermined.

In pre-planning and ad hoc planning with programs of this kind the best approach is collaborative. It is unwise to step into the professional spaces of the school psychologist, or counselor, or the educators. Each is tasked with something fundamentally different even though each element is interlocking. Try to work collaboratively with these professional peers, rather than omit them from the intervention approach to decision-making. Talk about possible problems and how they will be handled if they arise. Often peer professionals are trained in non-behavior analytic methods, and the behavior analyst may need to be an information resource on ACT while concurrently respecting these professionals' own therapeutic orientations. ACT can easily be used to create bridges, which will be useful in many ways going forward.

In the era of COVID-19, telehealth behavior analytic treatments have become commonplace. This geographically boundless potential does bring with it a variety of uncertainties as to the logistics of delivering services across distant places. In addition to the legal nuances that will arise, new ethical challenges may arise as well.

A behavior analyst who is well versed in ACT may be in high demand – even for telehealth services when no local skilled options are available. The potential client may need to have local supports but also benefit from a skilled ACT intervention. The predicament that arises may involve which option is best for the client. This calls for keeping what is best for the client at the forefront and respecting professional boundaries. For example, sometimes it may be better to support local professionals and to help get them the needed additional training rather than to grab at more intervention hours regardless of the impact on professional relations.

Another ethical issue arises when the usage of telehealth may be more convenient for the behavior analyst. Because telehealth allows less travel time between clients, billable hours can sometimes be maximized across sessions within a shorter period of a day. This is not harmful unless it compromises effectiveness. For example, if the impact of ACT is likely to be stronger in a given instance via live experiential activities, deliver ACT via telehealth session might comprise treatment efficacy. The behavior analyst will need to weigh these new distant treatment challenges with each client's potential impact on therapeutic progress.

Ethical or Not Ethical?

Sam Donox is well known applied behavior analyst who is widely sought out for his skills and delivering ACT methods appropriate to his practice. He does a consistently excellent job, which is increasing his referrals exponentially. He is able to charge high fees for his skills and has recently decided he will curtail the number of hours he is "on the road" so that he can do more telehealth "whether they like it or not." He has considered training additional staff to do some of the work that requires travel but hasn't done so yet because they will "only reduce my cut". He knows good behavior analysts who can do what he does in person but he refuses to refer on the grounds that this is "money out the door."

Ethical – Delivering high-quality services and gaining a reputation for doing so is enabling him to experience financial success. There is nothing unethical about that per se. Nor is levering one's time to be efficient.

Not ethical – Failing to provide needed services in a form that is most likely to be successful cannot be viewed as a mere matter of convenience. Referral or creating staff positions to do the needed work would both be fine, but allowing money matters to overwhelm the provision of effective services is unethical.

An ACT-uneducated environment that could stand to benefit from the implementation of ACT creates an uphill battle for adoption that must be addressed skillfully by the behavior analyst. We caution against an "I'm the expert" approach whereby the behavior analyst simply tells everyone else that they are wrong, or that ACT is the newest greatest thing ever. Rather we propose a more collaborative model whereby the behavior analyst listens, respects, and contributes to the approaches used by others that are participating in the same single case, the entire school building, the insurance review board, or human resource training program. There is an ethical responsibility for the behavior analyst to nudge others to consider ACT when they believe the data and individual functional analyst's suggestions that ACT approach is beneficial. This conversation is best supported, however, with patience, data, and a direct linkage between ACT and the presenting problems that are present within the current issue of concern.

THE SCOPE OF INTERNAL FORCES ON A BEHAVIOR ANALYST'S USE OF ACT

A wide range of internal forces is at work, pressuring the behavior analyst to both use and avoid the use of ACT. These forces range from one's own ability, and history to the population targeted and related supports, to self-doubt, fears of failure, or avoidance of conflict. An ethical stance needs to be taken whenever these forces arise, with the overarching guidepost of doing no harm and promoting optimal well-being of the clients who are served.

Ironically ACT itself will help provide the behavior analyst with the tools that are needed to make some of these discriminations. It is helpful for the behavior analyst to work on emotional and cognitive openness, greater contact with the external and internal environment, and stronger values-based habits – in other words to work on her or his own psychological flexibility – so that needless barriers to effective use of ACT methods professionally are removed.

The population targeted for intervention should match the population the behavior analyst has experience with or can access appropriate supervision for work with. A rich history of working with the target population will allow the behavior analyst best able to judge the relative impact that ACT can have with this population. Approximately 75% of all currently employed behavior analysts work within the autism care system, and thus it will be likely that initial uses of ACT will be with autistic persons. That is not a problem as such since there is extensive evidence that ACT can be helpful for this population. Even so, there is a wide range of persons with an autism diagnosis, and because behavior analysts have a history of working with a truncated section of this spectrum, barriers may exist. Those behavior analysts wishing to introduce ACT to staff within a work setting or to college students will also likely have experience working with neurotypical adult humans. Population experience alone is not a free pass towards ethical implementation of ACT, but it does help with noticing some of the relative gains and risks that ACT may pose for the person(s) of interest. When a new population is being suggested that the behavior analyst has no experience with, it is the ethical responsibility of the behavior analyst to review published literature on the population's unique considerations, as well as the prior work with ACT and this specific population, and when applicable, to seek supervision from those who have this experience.

Ethical or Not Ethical?

Fred Chong has spent his entire career working in a master's level behavior analysis program as a teacher. His applied work consists entirely of the special courses he teaches. For example, he has a one-credit course on public speaking skills and because speech anxiety is common for almost all students, he long-ago built-in ACT modules into the class. It was extremely successful and as a result even though this course is optional every year it fills to capacity. He's recently decided to apply what he knows to persons on the spectrum who also have difficulties speaking in public. He has no experience with this population but he says "I'm confident I can handle it."

Ethical – It is great that Fred has developed his ACT skills and applied them in an appropriate professional role.

Not ethical – Applying ACT to persons on the spectrum is not a matter of confidence, it is a matter of competence. Depending on client functioning some of what Fred knows may well apply – but some may not. A more ethical approach would be to seek out guidance and needed training with the new population and to apply his skills there in a careful, empirically assessed manner.

The presenting problem for the client should match the typical conditions treated in the past by the behavior analyst. An enthusiastic desire to do ACT now that one has read this book does not give the clinician *carte blanche* to just go out and try it with any sort of client problem. When verbal contingencies place influence on environmental four-term contingencies, a whole realm of challenging behaviors may rise up that are novel for the behavior analyst to deal with. Therefore, just because one knows ACT does not mean one knows how to use ACT for a specific presenting problem. And just as importantly, the behavior analyst must make clear not to confuse a form of behavior and the functional control that it might be operating under. Verbal aggression under pure non-verbal antecedent control might be reliably influenced by demands being presented by caregivers. Conversely, with a verbally sophisticated client, that same demand antecedent, when influenced by the presence or absence of self-generated rules such as "I am always a failure" or "I really love recess and I need to deal with my work so I can go outside later", can accelerate or suppress the probability of the escape response. A history with the former may not make the behavior analyst ready for the latter. And the absence of understanding the latter will hinder the overall treatment outcome.

In order to ethically build competency across novel problem areas, the behavior analyst will need to consult with more skilled peers in the field where there is a genuine collaboration, not simply a "bouncing off some ideas." The peer who is providing support has an ethical responsibility to the client as well the moment they start reacting to your "ideas", which necessitates a deeper relationship of collaboration duty to you and the client. Efforts to gain further education on the specific sorts of problems one plans on treating, and a reading of the published literature on how ACT has been used in similar circumstances, are additional ways to ethically foster a competency to treat a specific presenting condition.

The client must meet the necessary thresholds of language development that might indicate ACT could have a potential for working. ACT does not work for everyone. A client must have some level of established verbal skills to benefit from a verbally-based intervention. If the potential client has never spoken about a past or future event, and lives life strictly under control of programmed contingencies, ACT is not for them. At least not yet. When there is a potential for language development, the behavior analyst has an ethical responsibility to foster such growth as quickly as possible. In order to ensure these improvements in language have the necessary depth to enable comprehension, relational framing techniques must be used as the model for intervention. Interventions should start by establishing non-arbitrary relational skills of same, opposite, different, comparison, hierarchy, and temporality or contingency. Once some growth has occurred here, a move upward to arbitrary framing and cultural control can occur. Contextual control over the entire range of relational framing skills can be assessed and linked to contextual control over transformations of stimulus functions. It is possible that a concurrent treatment approach whereby RFT and ACT interventions are done synchronously but here again there needs to be some amount of already established referential verbal skills intact. Therefore, when clientele that the behavior analyst works with have varying levels of tenuous degrees of language abilities, there is an ethical responsibility for the behavior analyst to learn how to assess, and eventually treat these limitations so that ACT interventions can be maximized in effectiveness.

Ethical or Not Ethical?

Jordan Beefeater is a behavior analyst who is an expert in ACT but is "still learning" in the area of RFT. A child has been referred for aggression at school who can answer a wide variety of questions such as "what do you like to do at school?" or "what's your favorite food?" but seems to give rote answers and cannot say much about the future or what other people might be experiencing. Jordan has decided to "forge ahead anyway' figuring the rote answers are "just his diagnosis having its effect."

Ethical – It is good that Jordan has excellent skills and it is wise to assess for the level of verbal abilities.

Not ethical – It is not wise and may not be ethical to forge ahead. The rote answers may simply indicate a long history of direct training by previous behavior analysts and may not reflect the ability to engage in arbitrarily applicable relational responding. A warning sign is the inability to use temporal relations or perspective-taking relations. ACT may not be applicable in this situation until these relational framing skills improve and it may be unethical to proceed with ACT.

Access to the controlling stimuli (antecedent and consequence) is critical to improve the potential for treatment success. When the behavior analyst has the ability to manipulate the presence of these variables, greater functional control over behavior is possible. Advocacy for access is an ethical necessity because treatment efficacy is compromised without it. Take for example a teenager who is "anxious" about going to history class. For some reason whenever that student walks into the classroom, he begins to get disruptive by making loud noises to draw attention to him from other peers. The entire classroom has lost focus, and the prior interventions tried have been to remove him from the classroom to a different location. With an ACT intervention in place, the behavior analyst will need to control both the presence and removal contingencies surrounding history class. With some pre-class dialogue with the client, the behavior analyst might discuss acceptance willingness of this low preferred class ("I know you don't like History but remember you said you were willing to be here in the class for 15 minutes this time? We all have to accept the ups and downs of a school day."), as well as an orientation to this client's value of watching a class movie at the end of the day ("Make sure you defuse from your thoughts of making noises about needing to run out of the room, because if we can commit to staying just a little longer, you will move closer towards your values of watching a movie with everyone.").

When the behavior analyst can control the consequences involved in the presence or absence of class, even when a disruptive behavior starts to occur, they may be able to place a bit more verbal pressure on the contingencies using therapeutic utterances ("Remember your values"; "Stay committed"). Such statements just might be the nudge necessary to promote a bit more positive behavior and allow for additional utterances that can reinforce such attempts at remaining in the classroom ("I like how you are accepting and willing to commit to this right here, right now"; "That movie is going to be awesome, great job defusing from your thoughts of leaving the room"). If the behavior analyst is not the person making the decision as to the threshold for class removal or is unable to provide classroom supports via such ACT-based conversation in the moments the client needs to hear them, the treatment potential will likely have been marginalized. It is therefore ethically critical to advocate for influence in the very space the controlling variables for challenging behaviors are occurring. ACT treatment in a vacuum will likely produce delayed to reduced effectiveness on client well-being. When direct influence is practically impossible, there remains a rationale to have an indirect influence by consult or decree towards the other staff or stakeholders who do.

Cooperation from stakeholders can enhance or weaken treatment effects. That unsettling reality is difficult for many of us to accept as professionals. Even with our best efforts, treatment gains oftentimes in part rely on the behavior of others that we have little to no control over. With this variable factored into the treatment equation, the behavior analyst has an ethical responsibility to gauge the degree to which treatment adherence by others and the coordination necessary for treatment outcome. For example, you may have designed a treatment plan that requires the client to attend daily ACT sessions in your outpatient clinic, but that client relies on a parent to transport them to sessions. After weeks of sporadic attendance, you cannot simply hold tight to your proposed intervention model just because you think it is the best for the client. In reality, the treatment may be rarely occurring, and thus ethically speaking a different treatment approach is needed. Perhaps it may involve telehealth sessions to eliminate the driving element altogether. Perhaps it may require in-home supports, to continue the face-to-face therapeutic benefits. Yet another solution might be to transfer service delivery to the school environment, such that attendance is almost guaranteed due to the client riding the bus every day. There needs to be some flexibility on the part of the behavior analyst to compromise approach or convenience to promote a practical and effective method of service delivery.

Attendance difficulties are far from the only challenges that the behavior analyst will encounter from stakeholders. Excessive demands to speak ACT language outside of sessions, too much reliance on them for data collection, and treatment implementation that is too complex are just a few additional glitches that can mitigate treatment outcomes. Keep in mind that the ideal might be impossible, and thus settling for the practical might be necessary. You may need to learn to be patient with what you are asking caregivers to do. You do not live their life, understand the competing contingencies that are placed on them that weaken adherence, and you do not fully understand the distress that the client has on them that they experience within their shared relationship with the client.

For most readers of this text, you get to go home at the end of the day of work and take off the behavior analyst hat. When someone lives every moment of their day with a client, a child, or a sibling it is very different from simply just working with them. Be patient, be respectful, be compassionate, and most importantly, be reasonable and humble.

The most practical and ethical way to design an ACT intervention is to assume you hold the entire responsibility of making it work. That way, when stakeholders participate in the treatment process it is a bonus – not a necessity. This bonus will serve as a treatment accelerator, not a treatment requirement. And when their participation does in fact occur, you are positioned to be excited and reinforcing of their efforts – not disappointed by the lack of support

It would be remiss if we did not also note that the most important stakeholder in your ACT intervention is the client themselves. Their interest and compliance voluntary participation can definitely influence your treatment effects. Your treatment may be provoking the client and thus increasing the presenting condition that you are hoping to treat. At some point there may be the need for a critical self-appraisal. Is ACT being done because you like it, or because it has benefit for the client and they are participating in the process? When the answer is not crystal clear – there is an ethical responsibility to reassess the intervention direction.

Ethical or Not Ethical?

Charlie Haze is a senior behavior analyst who is convinced by the existing research, including his own, that ACT can be helpful in many situations but easily fails to take the perspective of others. He talks over parents' concerns and gives elegant ACT explanations instead. He has done a substantial amount of ACT research, so he often quotes back what the data suggest when he becomes aware of problems in follow-through. He is loath to work more with the school since he does not enjoy that kind of work and "there would be no need if the parents would just follow through." Recently a family dropped out of treatment for their son with autism and he found himself muttering "their loss, not mine."

Ethical – Charlie is doing worthwhile research and is applying scientific knowledge.

Not ethical – Charlie is not taking responsibility for his own client's success or failure – instead he is mentally putting the parents on the hook for that, which is dangerously irresponsible. Ethically speaking he needs to keep his eye on the lives of those he serves and either learn to work effectively with the school or to learn how to better motivate the parents.

You need to know your limits. You will have clients and presenting conditions that puzzle you. You will have staff retention problems that are beyond your comprehension. You will worry you do not know ACT well enough for it to be effective in a certain circumstances. Practice what you preach and accept the pain that comes from such unmet challenges and try to do what you can. Be ethical enough to be honest with your abilities and ask for help when you need it.

We are not advocating for you to have your hand held on every attempt at implementing ACT, rather we are simply noting that it is normal to have thoughts of incompetency or inadequacy. We are making it clear that everyone has limits. We do too. There will never come a day that you feel comfortable implementing ACT to everyone and every condition. We certainly don't.

The first step is to know where your current comfort boundaries are, and where are your aspirational boundaries. The next step is to stand firm on not exceeding your practice of ACT beyond those aspirational borders. Once clearly defined, a plan should be made to gradually move from current to target using support from others, training in ACT methods, and an openness to these learning experiences. Make sure that pride doesn't get in the way of asking for help. Approach your own professional growth with a genuine desire to grow, not as a requirement from an employer or yourself. And most importantly learn how to say no. Recognize what your threshold is for referring a case to others. Ethically when your limits are exceeded, you owe it to the client and everyone else involved to back off and facilitate support from others that may have greater expertise than you do. This should not be seen as a sign of failure, but rather of strength.

CONTINUING EDUCATION FOR THE BEHAVIOR ANALYST

Education is a lifelong direction, not something finite that is met and discarded. As with all of applied behavior analysis, ACT itself is constantly progressing and thus requires a long-term ongoing commitment to continuing education to staying abreast of the latest developments. As behavior analysts the first and foremost issue we should be examining the empirical data regarding the effectiveness or lack of effectiveness of ACT and RFT. Look first and foremost at the data being generated by behavior analysts within the scope of practice of applied behavior analysis. When gaps are revealed in that work, we all should be doing our part as best we can to close such gaps. There are several external forces that put pressure on professional behavior analysts to learn more. The use of Continuing Education Units or (CEUs) is one such mechanism. However, most CEUs can be obtained through attendance only, which opens up a wide range of less-than-optimal "attendance behaviors." Concurrently shopping online, checking social media, chattering with a friend, or even sleeping during a CEU event can still yield needed credits. We have an ethical responsibility to attend and to do our best to learn. Other peoples' lives are in our hands, and we owe it to them to pay attention, participate, and learn. What makes matters worse is the advent of telecommuting and remote conferencing tools, so now anyone anywhere can self-profess their expertise on a topic to reap enrollments in their CEUs, oftentimes when they themselves are only a short distance ahead of those that they are instructing.

Ethical or Not Ethical?

Bobby Sue has been advertising a new ACT study group online for only 20 dollars per week to any behavior analyst interested in learning more about using ACT with their clients. Bobby Sue has a fancy web presence, but a quick review of his credentials reveals that he has never published a journal article and does not retain an active client base receiving comprehensive ACT-based services.

Ethical – If Bobby Sue's group allows for peer-to-peer mentoring and the interested behavior analyst cannot find another else person offering such a service, with a clientele that could benefit from ACT, this option may be better than doing nothing whatsoever.

Not ethical – Bobby Sue is potentially taking advantage of naïve behavior analysts that are desperate to learn more about ACT. This is exacerbated by the financial rewards that can come to him and the deprivation conditions of his attendees.

The behavior analyst interested in stepping up their skill set with ACT via continuing education would best be served by listening to those behavior analysts who actually do ACT on a daily or weekly basis, and those who also publish research on ACT within a behavior analytic framework. This type of caution, at least initially, will reduce the probability of newly interested persons drifting in the wrong direction with how to apply ACT or (perhaps even worse) misunderstanding what ACT is and should be for a behavior analyst. There is also value in being mentored on the ACT processes by someone with considerable experience who can provide that individualized attention on the path towards greater competency. Here again, who the mentor is really matters, because inadequate training or supervision will only compound the behavior analyst's confusion and put at risk the appropriateness of practice.

Ethical or Not Ethical?

Morgan is looking for a new mentor to help her develop her skills with ACT. She found the email address for Rip, one of the top people in the field. He said yes to taking her on as a mentor but says he can only talk with her for one hour per month.

Ethical – Rip is extremely talented with his abilities to deliver ACT and train others. Given that Morgan is working with only a single client using ACT, and the behaviors are relatively benign, a single quality session per month of mentorship is sufficient.

Not ethical – Morgan may be compromising other potential mentors due to the perceived status of Rip and is using that relationship for personal gain. She would be much better off finding someone who could actually improve her ACT skill set, rather than to inflate her credentials via a minimal relationship.

ETHICAL DECISION-MAKING MATRIX ON USE OF ACT BY A BEHAVIOR ANALYST

The most ethical position a behavior analyst can take when implementing ACT is a stance arrived at through a thoughtful journey through a decision-making process that balances risks and benefits and upholds dignity and respect for the client and others. A wide variety of ethical choice-making procedures have been developed over the decades to guide care providers who embark upon such work. We believe the behavior analyst will be best served to competently move forward with an ACT intervention by following the eight steps we delineate here.

Step 1: Become Ethically Sensitive

Ethical awareness is not a dichotomous position. There is always room for continued growth by any professional. Furthermore, current environmental and cultural developments shape and alter the dimensions of what ethics are contained with a certain content area. For the behavior analyst there should be an effort made to learn more about the entire realm of ethics as a philosophical school of thought beyond the simplistic to-do lists (and not-to-do lists) that occupy space within introductory behavior analytic texts and regulation bodies. Varieties of ethical schools of thought exist have existed for hundreds of years.

Where do you stand – philosophically?

Difficult questions are often part of any ethical training. Have you ever thought about why?

Take the classic example of the choice of saving an old man or a child with the remaining space on a lifeboat. Who would you save and why? Would you toss yourself in the ocean to save both? Or would you freeze in place and fail to make a choice altogether?

Suppose there was a risky unproven drug that had a small chance of curing cancer. Would you take it? What if it could save a million people? Would you give that drug to your own child? Why or why not?

These sorts of questions are easy to dismiss as impractical and irrelevant. They are "hypothetical" we say. But we ask them in part to experience the discomfort involved in making such ethical choices. We know we will face ethical choices, but we can easily cover them other so as to avoid the discomfort they can produce. That's a mistake. We entertain ethical questions not because there is a "right answer" but so we can strengthen our sense of tolerance to the uncertainty that is involved in all sorts of ethical decision-making. Without that openness (yes, ACT obviously applies here) we may well pretend there is no ethical issue at hand.

The behavior analyst must also notice that their own history will place a degree of bias on their ability to solve an ethical challenge. If you have enjoyed the luxury of a privileged life where housing and food were never issues of concern, it might be difficult for you to comprehend the non-compliance of a parent in adhering to your ACT treatment regime because they are too tired from working 18-hour days to keep from being evicted from their apartment. If you have been someone distracted by every novel social cause that happens to trend on digital media, you might have failed to see how a client's history might impact their willingness to change a long-established system of beliefs. Taking the perspective of others is critical to becoming a good ACT treatment provider and understanding that this is not a luxury but rather an ethical responsibility. Your beliefs are not right, and theirs are wrong – they are just different. You do not need to agree with your client's political views, childraising practices, holiday celebrations, or religious practices. But you do need to respect them, and not disdain them due to variance from your own. Again, applying ACT processes to yourself will help.

Step 2: Recognize a Problem

With a careful educated eye to detecting when an ethical dilemma is present, the behavior analyst needs to know when such a problem is a present risk to delivering care. A wide range of problems will arise – treatment-problem match, caregiver compliance, peer dismissals of ACT, funding sources unfamiliarity, competency, scope, time, effort, and probability of treatment success all are constantly at risk of rearing up and becoming an ethically laden matter in need of problem-solving. The easiest solution is to ignore that a problem exists, but this alone is perhaps one of the largest ethical violations a behavior analyst could make. Dismissal due to discomfort with recognizing the issue is not appropriate and becomes even more egregious when the well-being of a client is at stake. When something doesn't feel right – it probably isn't right. And when someone else brings a matter to your attention that they believe has some ethical complexity to it, that alone justifies you examining the matter yourself rather than dismissing their claims out of hand.

It may be beneficial to articulate the existence of the problem in terms of the differences between the current state of affairs and the desired outcomes. For example, if a client is struggling to make progress with their existing traditional ABA programming, and the behavior analyst is uncertain what to do given they do not know ACT – the problem is not one of therapist competency. Rather the problem is best defined as client-focused whereby there is a shortcoming in treatment outcomes for this particular client and some sort of action needs to be taken in order to improve this current state of affairs. There is no need to start problem-solving at this stage in the ethical decision-making process. All that needs to happen is acknowledgement that a problem exists and to broadly frame that problem in terms of the gap between current and ideal. This general approach can be taken with any non-clinical application of ACT as well. Perhaps there is a gap between current free-throw percentages and what is expected for this specific basketball player. Reports of anxiety are increasingly plaguing court performance. Employee turnover is twice that of the closest competitor agency, and staff report feeling burnt out and unsupported. Respectively these problems should be identified as low shot percentages and high turnover rates. No appeals to possible causes should occur just yet. And only if these deviations involve an ethical matter would the decision-making process continue. In the case of the anxious basketball player, a coach's callous reaction to just practice harder might pose the risk of inflaming the condition. And with regard to staff turnover, when such "burnout" is leading to compromises in client care and therapeutic stability, an ethical responsibility and complexity may exist to do more than just pay people to stick around.

Step 3: Define the Problem

Following problem identification, the next step is to carefully define what the ethical challenge actually is. This definition should remain as objective as possible and explicitly be devoid of any judgement or bias towards a possible solution. Here the problem is articulated with its potential adverse outcomes. The lack of clinical gains made by the client is negatively affecting integration into their peer group, and a potential treatment of ACT is difficult or impossible for the current staff to deliver because they lack the competency or training to do so. The basketball player's free-throw percentages are considerably lower than others on the team because of self-reported anxious thoughts, and the coach is ignoring any solutions beyond more practice. The staff turnover is twice that of all other agencies, and client care is suffering yet management just wants to pay people more to keep them employed. Here it can be seen that the problem definition encompasses both the broad matter of deviation from current to ideal, along with the existing course of action that is occurring which is creating an ethical dilemma. Within the context of ACT and these matters, although the approach may offer a potential solution, such a solution is more complicated than just "Let's do ACT on these things because I think they might help."

Step 4: Examine Professional Standards/Laws

It is critical to examine what the professional standards and local laws are related to the ethical problem. It may be possible that you have a non-exclusive role in rendering any sort of ethical path forward if the presenting problem is beyond your privy to act upon it. In many cases you will need to notify others of what the dilemma is and seek collaboration in the problem-solving process. As a behavior analyst you have external forces that regulate your practice of the profession. In certain locales this might limit you to treating only a specific population, and in others, to a specific set of intervention techniques. You will need to make sure that you can actually participate in the role you are hoping to participate in. When your role is truncated or eliminated due to certain restrictions, you still have an ethical responsibility to help source out other support systems for the clientele involved in the problem. Furthermore, when existing restrictions are in place that seem irrational (i.e., practicing behavior analysis only with persons with autism), you have an ethical responsibility to inform policymakers about the benefits that ACT interventions may bring to persons with other sorts of disabilities, or non-clinical populations, and non-clinical populations (e.g., prevention). When no professional standard or law exists that impede you from delivering ACT and you know it can be effective, you have a responsibility to obtain the necessary repertoire to help those who seek your services. In the case of the client whose gains are minimized by a lack of a treatment approach rooted in language processes, that therapist must add the ACT skills to her repertoire. The basketball player's disclosed anxieties should be examined by a licensed therapist, and together with the behavior analyst perhaps a comprehensive intervention focusing on ACT and self-management could be designed collaboratively with the mental health professional to improve the free-throw accuracy. Finally, staff struggling with burnout might benefit from an evaluation from both a physician and human resource manager prior to constructing an intervention approach to ensure health and employment policies are intact and not put at risk by a subsequent ACT intervention.

Step 5: Describe Various Potential Courses of Action

There is often no clear perfect course of action. Rather what remains possible is a series of paths that can be chosen. None are perfect, and likely there will be a few that are completely flawed. Here a ranking of possibilities, from logical to absurd, needs to occur. The inclusion of the latter helps anchor the relative value-added nature of the less-than-perfect solutions. There should be no exclusion of ideas, list them all. An emergence of strengths and weaknesses of each action direction will be revealed.

It can help to try to generate courses of action by deliberately manipulating ACT processes. Use your perspective-taking skills to imagine the situation from the point of view of different participants in the situation and brainstorm alternatives. Identify possible values at stake and generate an alternative course of action from the point of view of each. Focus on your present-moment experience when considering the issue and see if a thought, memory, emotion, or bodily sensation stands out – and if any pretend that each such experience could specify an alternative and see what emerges (e.g., if that sinking feeling in your stomach could speak which might it suggest as an alternative? If that memory of a client you helped could be given a voice, what alternative course of action comes to mind?

The goal here is to create a broader range of alternatives – to foster useful cognitive flexibility. Brainstorming rules are usually best in this phase: don't criticize alternatives, generate alternatives.

Step 6: Consult with Others

Be willing to ask for help. In most cases your presenting dilemma has been dealt with in some manner by someone else at a different time. Rarely are you encountering the first time anything like this has ever happened. Speaking to other professionals within your organization and field can provide needed support. Find someone who is the primary person you count on for advice. Make sure that person shares a similar philosophical stance on ethics as you do. Each of us has relied on our mentors and other senior members of the behavioral field to help us navigate a wide range of ethical dilemmas. Yet don't overlook the next generation. They too have important perspectives that must be heard. Ethical review boards are often conceptualized as gatekeepers for just doing research. However, such boards often contain a wealth of experienced professionals who interact with ethical matters on a regular basis. It would be wise to add this group of people to your ethical toolbox and seek their assistance when you find yourself continuing to struggle with how to move forward with a specific course of action.

Step 7: Choose a Course of Action

The path forward is not going to be straight. You will rarely feel as if you have discovered the perfect solution that somehow no one else had ever thought of. Rather you will choose with some hesitancy and worry that maybe this path is not altogether ideal. Such feelings are natural to have. The literal discovery of an ethical problem alone suggests that a solution wasn't apparent – a dilemma existed, not a "no brainer".

It can help to focus first on the value that is most important to you in this situation and then try to focus on an alternative that moves in the direction of that value while still maintaining contact with such practical issues of the ability to implement the choice, and the benefits it will produce for others.

Step 8: Implement and Evaluate

Move forward with data. As a behavior analyst, this final step should provide some comfort. Our field is rooted in data-based decision-making, and your ethical decision-making is no different. Did your proposed path forward create the hypothesized gains in well-being? If so a continued journey with this course of action seems rational. However, if the path taken has created unsuspected challenges, or moved matters into a worse state of affairs, then it is time to regroup, move back to Step 2, and reconceptualize the entire decision-making process under this new set of information.

RISKS AND REWARDS FOR DOING ACT

The positive characteristics of verbally sophisticated humans allow for transcending the programmed contingencies, thus allowing for more successful navigation without trial-and-error learning for acquisition or elimination of every single behavior. However, there are negative characteristics of being verbal complex as well. Mental health conditions are a uniquely human tragedy, with many of such causes rooted in maladaptive language processes. ACT has extensive reach into aiding those persons struggling with mental health conditions, but such interventions have predominantly been done by mental health professionals – not behavior analysts. There is a fair amount of overlap between the behavior analyst and the mental health practitioner, however it is not exclusive. Thus, when presenting problems and/or proposed treatment is beyond a behavior analyst's experience, or scope of practice, that extreme caution may be necessary to continue a course of care. When in doubt as to if the client is experiencing mental health conditions or just exhibiting a behavioral challenge, that doubt alone necessitates a conversation with a skilled professional involved in mental healthcare.

The journey ahead that you are about to embark upon will contain a range of risks and rewards. The ultimate goal is to minimize the former and maximize the latter. However, this is not a dichotomous path moving forward. Rather there is a continuum of risk in every single choice that is made when implementing an ACT intervention. The greatest risk of all is not using ACT when there is a potential for improving the human condition. Another great risk is that you are contributing to the stagnation of the field of behavior analysis that reluctantly fails to move forward from its historical roots. A balance between risk and outcome must be made and stay at the forefront of all ethical decision-making. When embarking on treating a presenting problem that is of low risk (fear of public speaking), even a beginning ACT user might not do much harm if treatment fails. Nonetheless, when the problem is much more significant (threats of violence), treatment failure could yield much greater adverse consequences.

The choice to proceed to use ACT is an easy one. When the human condition is in need of improvement, and that human has a verbal repertoire, a science of human behavior will need to rise up to the complexity needed to make meaningful change happen. ACT is the logical vehicle to provide the necessary care and thus what remains the only decision is the degree of hesitation the behavior analyst should have with its implementation. When the presenting condition that the client seeks improvement in is best described as a clinical disorder that cannot be reconceptualized as a behavioral repertoire (i.e., schizophrenia; reactive-attachment disorder), then a behavior analyst's use of ACT is extremely risky and proceeding into such treatment may be ethically (and potentially legally) inappropriate. If that same presenting problem might involve a behavioral manifestation that can be observed and treated as a dependent variable, the relative risk is slightly reduced. In such an instance there may be added value for a behavior analyst to participate in care provision, and risk might be mitigated by the inclusion of other clinical professionals that address any mental health elements of the condition. Ethical concerns are reduced further when a presenting condition is not hypothesized as an actual mental health condition, but rather a behavioral performance deficit of some kind. Here the behavior analyst will likely play the lead or solo role in care delivery and find comfort in treatment of a condition that is more centrally located within their scope of practice. Even with such a presenting condition or comfortable population, the severity of the behavior may scale the relative risk accordingly. For example, it will be less of a risk of harm of developing an ACT intervention when working with an adult with autism who needs to be more accepting with their reactions when customers ask for paper bags for their groceries rather than plastic – the default usage modality. A rather benign treatment that focuses on acceptance rather than fusion to the thought that "everyone must have plastic" could have a positive impact on job performance where the client continues to display a pleasant demeanor to the customer. However, if that same rigidity yields extreme aggression towards fellow coworkers upon a paper bag request, the risk of implementing ACT is increased. Perhaps the lowest level of risk comes from behavioral manifestations of non-clinical populations such as staff and oneself. Within this subpopulation, implementing ACT is a low-risk endeavor. Keep in mind low risk is not the same as no risk. As it is still possible that even a basic one-hour ACT informational session to coworkers could reveal disclosure of significant psychological distress. In summary risk of doing ACT is never eliminated, but rather should be viewed on a sliding scale. This does not mean you should avoid the riskier implementations, but it does mean that there are greater ramifications that could result from inappropriate, ineffective, or even perfect implementation. This is why a careful ethical decision-making process must be followed whereby the relative risks and rewards are weighed carefully against each other before any sort of treatment begins (Figure 14.1).

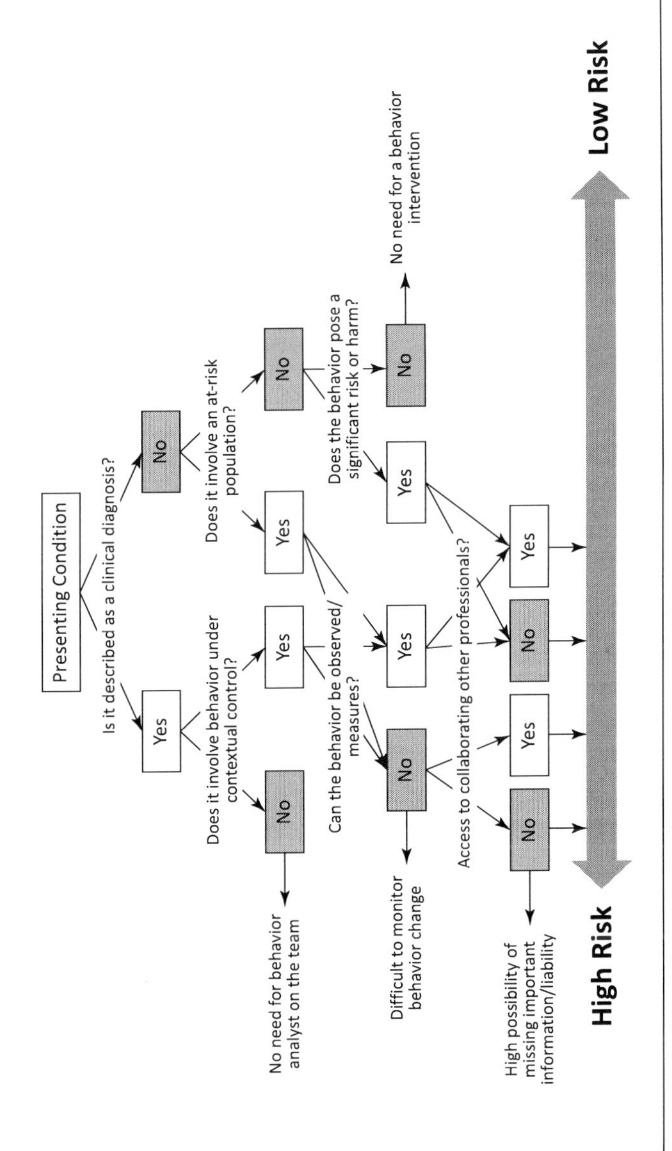

Figure 14.1 Diagram of an ethical decision-making process.

THE ROAD AHEAD

We have come to the end of our journey together, but this is hardly the end. In many ways, this is the beginning. Behavior analysis was never meant to be a small percentage of behavioral science, stuck in a remote corner. The founders of our field were incredibly bold and creative scientists and practitioners, who were not afraid to break the rules if doing so fostered human well-being. They broke the mold methodologically, philosophically, and technologically. Despite their emergence in a small, dedicated group long ago they did not aspire to be "we few; we happy few" forever. Behavior analysts aspired to be at the center of behavioral and life science and of cultural development, but not by being doctrinaire.

Skinner wrote a utopian novel and the most frequently mentioned scientist in his writings (almost never mentioned with criticism) was Sigmund Freud. Charles Fester (who with Skinner wrote the first book on schedules of reinforcement) developed a theory of depression and was himself in psychoanalysis for several years. Nate Azrin – one of the most brilliant basic animal learners ever – created treatment innovations for obsessive-compulsive behavior, chronic mental illness, and relationship enhancement that live on to this day. Todd Risley directed an entire state mental health system (in Alaska) and, after hearing one of the earlier descriptions of RFT, in 1986 told a shocked room full of behavior analysts at the University of Kansas, "this is the kind of thing we should be doing." Despite what some critics say, any fair reading of its history shows that behavior analysis was flexible and forward-looking *from day one.*

ACT is part of that tradition. Earlier in this chapter we described how the founders of applied behavior analysis (Don Baer, Mont Wolf, and Todd Risley) in 1987 explicitly laid out the outline of the development approach ACT has taken over the last four decades. It paid off handsomely by any objective measure, but it is hardly finished. And here we encounter the larger need for behavior analysts to step up.

In order to link flexibility processes to idiographic functional analysis and overt behavior, applied behavior analysts need to become far more involved in ACT development. In order to lay out and establish the relational leaning prerequisites for ACT, behavior analysts need to explore that issue with populations that are still taking advantage of language development training. There are holes in ACT development that were caused by the slow uptake of ACT within its original home of clinical behavior analysis, just as there are holes in RFT development caused by the slow uptake of RFT in basic behavior analysis. It is time to fill those holes and only dedicated behavior analysts can do so.

As ACT and RFT impact behavior analysis, they arrive not just with needs but also with assets. ACT is a validated method worldwide; it is involved in the cultural conversation in many topical areas. Popular ACT books become best sellers; ACT media for children have been viewed tens of millions of times (google "Here Comes a Thought" for an example); ACT is distributed by the World Health Organization in 21 different languages. ACT articles publish in the highest-impact scientific journals there are. RFT is raising the eyebrows of mainstream approaches in intelligence, natural language processing, and language training. There is a drumbeat of undeniable success.

We believe that behavior analysts have long passed the point when isolation is needed to maintain purity. Our field is confident in its assumptions and sure-footed in its theoretical commitments. It is time to put ACT and RFT to use inside behavior analytic practice. It will be a challenge – but that challenge is one that our field is ready for.

References

Acarturk, C., Uygun, E., Ilkkursun, Z., Carswell, K., Tedeschi, F., Batu, M., ... & Barbui, C. (2022). Effectiveness of a WHO self-help psychological intervention for preventing mental disorders among Syrian refugees in Turkey: A randomized controlled trial. *World Psychiatry, 21*, 88–95. https://doi.org/10.1002/wps.20939

Addis, M. E., & Jacobson, N. S. (1996). Reasons for depression and the process and outcome of cognitive-behavioral psychotherapies. *Journal of Consulting and Clinical Psychology, 64*, 1417–1424.

Addis, M. E., Truax, P., & Jacobson, N. S. (1995). Why do people think they are depressed?: The reasons for depression questionnaire. *Psychotherapy: Theory, Research, Practice, and Training, 32*(3), 476–483. https://doi.org/10.1037/0033-3204.32.3.476

American Psychiatric Association. (2013). Neurodevelopmental disorders. In *Diagnostic and statistical manual of mental disorders* (5th ed.). Washington, DC: American Psychiatric Association.

Andrews, P. W., Maslej, M. M., Thomson, J. A., & Hollon, S. D. (2020). Disordered doctors or rational rats? Testing adaptationist and disorder hypotheses for melancholic depression and their relevance for clinical psychology. *Clinical Psychology Review, 82*, 101927. https://doi.org/10.1016/j.cpr.2020.101927

Arch, J. J., Brown, K. W., Dean, D. J., Landy, L. N., Brown, K. D., & Laudenslager, M. L. (2014). Self-compassion training modulates alpha-amylase, heart rate variability, and subjective responses to social evaluative threat in women. *Psychoneuroendocrinology, 42*, 49–58.

Arch, J. J., Eifert, G. H., Davies, C., Vilardaga, J. C. P., Rose, R. D., & Craske, M. G. (2012). Randomized clinical trial of Cognitive Behavioral Therapy (CBT) versus Acceptance and Commitment Therapy (ACT) for mixed anxiety disorders. *Journal of Consulting and Clinical Psychology, 80*, 750–765. https://doi.org/10.1037/a0028310

Assaz, D. A., Roche, B., Kanter, J. W., & Oshiro, C. K. (2018). Cognitive defusion in acceptance and commitment therapy: What are the basic processes of change?. *The Psychological Record, 68*(4), 405–418.

Augustson, E. M., Dougher, M. J., & Markham, M. R. (2000). Emergence of conditional stimulus relations and transfer of respondent eliciting functions among compound stimuli. *The Psychological Record, 50*, 745–770. https://doi.org/10.1007/BF03395381

Axelrod, S., McElrath, K. K., & Wine, B. (2012), Applied behavior analysis: Autism and beyond. *Behavioral Interventions, 27*, 1–15. https://doi.org/10.1002/bin.1335

Baer, D. M., Wolf, M. M., & Risley, T. R. (1968). Some current dimensions of applied behavior analysis. *Journal of Applied Behavior Analysis, 1*(1), 91–97. https://doi.org/10.1901/jaba.1968.1-91

Baer, D. M., Wolf, M. M., & Risley, T. R (1987). Some still-current dimensions of applied behavior analysis. *Journal of Applied Behavior Analysis, 20*(4), 313–327.

Barlow, D. H., & Hayes, S. C. (1979). Alternating treatments design: One strategy for comparing the effects of two treatments in a single subject. *Journal of Applied Behavior Analysis, 12*, 199–210. https://doi.org/10.1901/jaba.1979.12-199

Barnes, T. C., & Skinner, B. F. (1930). The progressive increase in the geotropic response of the ant Aphaenogaster. *The Journal of General Psychology, 4*, 102–112. https://doi.org/10.1080/00221309.1930.9918305

Barnes-Holmes, D., Barnes-Holmes, Y., McEnteggart, C., & Harte, C. (2021). Back to the future with an up-dated version of RFT: More field than frame? *Perspectivas em Análise do Comportamento, 12*(1), 033–051.

Barnes-Holmes, Y., Boorman, J., Oliver, J. E., Thompson, M., McEnteggart, C., & Coulter, C. (2018). Using conceptual developments in RFT to direct case formulation and clinical intervention: Two case summaries. *Journal of Contextual Behavioral Science, 7*, 89–96.

Bateson, P. (2014). Evolution, epigenetics and cooperation. *Journal of Biosciences, 39*(2), 1–10. https://doi.org/10.1007/s12038-013-9342-7.

Beck, A. T. (1970). Cognitive therapy: Nature and relation to behavior therapy. *Behavior Therapy, 1*(2), 184–200. https://doi.org/10.1016/S0005-7894(70)80030-2.

Belisle, J. (2020). Model dependent realism and the rule-governed behavior of behavior analysts: Applications to derived relational responding. *Perspectives on Behavior Science, 43*(2), 321–342.

Belisle, J., & Clayton, M. (2021). Coherence and the merging of relational classes in self-organizing networks: Extending relational density theory. *Journal of Contextual Behavioral Science, 20*, 118–128.

Belisle, J., & Dixon, M. R. (2020a). An exploratory analysis of relational density theory: Relational resistance and gravity. *Journal of Contextual Behavioral Science, 16*, 80–95.

Belisle, J., & Dixon, M. R. (2020b). Relational density theory: Nonlinearity of equivalence relating examined through higher-order volumetric-mass-density. *Perspectives on Behavior Science, 43*(2), 259–283.

Belisle, J., & Dixon, M. R. (2021). Relational behavior and ACT: A dynamic relationship. *Behavior Analysis in Practice*, 1–12.

Belisle, J., Paliliunas, D., Dixon, M. R., & Speelman, R. C. (2019). Decreasing influence of arbitrarily applicable verbal relations of recreational gamblers: A randomized controlled trial. *Journal of Applied Behavior Analysis, 52*(1), 60–72.

Belisle, J., Stanley, C. R., & Dixon, M. R. (2017). The relationship between derived mutually entailed relations and the function of challenging behavior in children with autism: Comparing the PEAK-E-PA and the QABF. *Journal of Contextual Behavioral Science, 6*(3), 298–307.

Belisle, J., Stanley, C. R., & Dixon, M. R. (2021). *Research methods for the practicing behavior analyst.* Naperville, IL: Emergent Press.

Bernier, M., Thienot, E., Codron, R., & Fournier, J. F. (2009). Mindfulness and acceptance approaches in sport performance. *Journal of Clinical Sport Psychology, 3*(4), 320–333.

Bethay, J. S., Wilson, K. G., Schnetzer, L. W., Nassar, S. L., & Michael J. Bordieri, M. J. (2013). A controlled pilot evaluation of acceptance and commitment training for intellectual disability staff. *Mindfulness 4*, 113–121. https://doi.org/10.1007/s12671-012-0103-8

Biglan, A., & Barnes-Holmes, Y. (2015). Acting in light of the future: How do future-oriented cultural practices evolve and how can we accelerate their evolution? *Journal of Contextual Behavioral Science, 4*, 184–195. https://doi.org/10.1016/j.jcbs.2015.06.002

Birkhoff, G. D. (1931). Proof of the ergodic theorem. *Proceedings of the National Academy of Sciences, 17*(12), 656–660. https://doi.org/10.1073/pnas.17.2.656

Blackledge, J. T., & Barnes-Holmes, D. (2009). Core processes in acceptance and commitment therapy. In J. T. Blackledge, J. Ciarrochi, & F. P Deane (Eds.). *Acceptance and commitment therapy: Contemporary theory, research, and practice* (pp. 41–58). Sydney: Australian Academic Press.

Bohlmeijer, E. T., Lamers, S. M. A., & Fledderus, M. (2015). Flourishing in people with depressive symptomology increases with acceptance and commitment therapy. Post-hoc analyses of a randomized controlled trial. *Behaviour Research and Therapy, 65*, 101–106. https://doi.org/10.1016/j.brat.2014.12.014

Bowen, S., & Marlatt, A. (2009). Surfing the urge: Brief mindfulness-based intervention for college student smokers. *Psychology of Addictive Behaviors, 23*(4), 666–671. https://doi.org/10.1037/a0017127

Bricker, J. B., Watson, N. L., Mull, K. E., Sullivan, B. M., & Heffner, J. L. (2020). Efficacy of smartphone applications for smoking cessation: A randomized clinical trial. *JAMA Internal Medicine, 180*, 1472–1480. https://doi.org/10.1001/jamainternmed.2020.4055

Cardillo, R., Erbì, C., & Mammarella, I. C. (2020). Spatial perspective-taking in children with autism spectrum disorders: The predictive role of visuospatial and motor abilities. *Frontiers in Human Neuroscience, 14*, 208.

Chase, J. A., Houmanfar, R., Hayes, S. C., Ward, T. A., Vilardaga, J. P., & Follette, V. M. (2013). Values are not just goals: Online ACT-based values training adds to goal-setting in improving undergraduate college student performance. *Journal of Contextual Behavioral Science, 2*, 79–84. https://doi.org/10.1016/j.jcbs. 2013.08.002

Chawla, N., Collins, S., Bowen, S., Hsu, S., Grow, J., Douglass, A., & Marlatt, G. A. (2010). The mindfulness-based relapse prevention adherence and competence scale: Development, interrater reliability, and validity. *Psychotherapy Research, 20*(4), 388–397.

Cheron, D. M., Ehrenreich, J. T., & Pincus, D. B. (2009). Assessment of parental experiential avoidance in a clinical sample of children with anxiety disorders. *Child Psychiatry and Human Development, 40*, 383–403. https://doi.org/10.1007/s10578-009-0135-z

Chomsky, N. (1959). A review of B. F. Skinner's *Verbal Behavior. Language, 35*, 26–58.

Chomsky, N. (1972). *Studies on semantics in generative grammar.* Boston: de Gruyter.

Christopher, M. S., Neuser, N. J., Michael, P. G., & Baitmangalkar, A. (2012). Exploring the psychometric properties of the five-facet mindfulness questionnaire. *Mindfulness, 3*(2), 124–131.

Chua, J. Y. X., & Shorey, S. (in press). The effect of mindfulness-based and acceptance commitment therapy-based interventions to improve the mental well-being among parents of children with developmental disabilities: A systematic review and meta-analysis. *Journal of Autism and Developmental Disorders, 52*, 2770–2783. https://doi.org/10.1007/s10803-021-04893-1

Ciarrochi, J. Sahdra, B., Hofmann, S., & Hayes, S. C. (2022). Developing an item pool to assess processes of change in psychological interventions: The Process-Based Assessment Tool (PBAT). *Journal of Contextual Behavioral Science, 23*, 200–213. https://doi.org/10.1016/j.jcbs.2022.02.001

Colbert, D., Tyndall, I., Roche, B., & Cassidy, S. (2018). Can SMART training really increase intelligence? A replication study. *Journal of Behavioral Education, 27*(4), 509–531.

Cooper, K., Smith, L. G., & Russell, A. J. (2018). Gender identity in autism: Sex differences in social affiliation with gender groups. *Journal of Autism and Developmental Disorders, 48*(12), 3995–4006.

Cooper, R. A., Plaisted-Grant, K. C., Baron-Cohen, S., & Simons, J. S. (2016). Reality monitoring and metamemory in adults with autism spectrum conditions. *Journal of Autism and Developmental Disorders, 46*(6), 2186–2198.

Craske, M. G., Liao, B., Brown, L., & Vervliet, B. (2012). Role of inhibition in exposure therapy. *Journal of Experimental Psychopathology, 3*(3), 322–345. https://doi.org/10.5127/jep.026511

Critchfield, T. S., & Reed, D. D. (2009). What are we doing when we translate from quantitative models? *The Behavior Analyst, 32*, 339–362.

Dada, T., Mittal, D., Mohanty, K., Faiq, M. A., Bhat, M. A., Yadav, R. K., ... & Dada, R. (2018). Mindfulness meditation reduces intraocular pressure, lowers stress biomarkers and modulates gene expression in glaucoma: A randomized controlled trial. *Journal of Glaucoma, 27*(12), 1061–1067.

Daks, J. S., & Rogge, R. D. (2020). Examining the correlates of psychological flexibility in romantic relationship and family dynamics: A meta-analysis. *Journal of Contextual Behavioral Science, 18*, 214–238. https://doi.org/10.1016/j.jcbs.2020.09.010

Davies, A. W., Balter, A. S., van Rhijn, T., Spracklin, J., Maich, K., & Soud, R. (2021). Sexuality education for children and youth with autism spectrum disorder in Canada. *Intervention in School and Clinic, 58*(2), 129–134. https://doi.org/10.1177/10534512211051068

Deci, E. L., & Ryan, R. M. (2000). The "what" and "why" of goal pursuits: Human needs and the self-determination of behavior. *Psychological Inquiry, 11*(4), 227–268. https://doi.org/10.1207/S15327965PLI1104_01

Dell'Osso, L., Carpita, B., Muti, D., Morelli, V., Salarpi, G., Salerni, A., ... & Maj, M. (2019). Mood symptoms and suicidality across the autism spectrum. *Comprehensive Psychiatry, 91*, 34–38.

Dickins, D. W., Singh, K. D., Roberts, N., Burns, P., Downes, J. J., Jimmieson, P., & Bentall, R. P. (2001). An fMRI study of stimulus equivalence. *Neuroreport, 12*(2), 405–411.

Dixon, D. R., Vogel, T., & Tarbox, J. (2012). A brief history of functional analysis and applied behavior analysis. In *Functional assessment for challenging behaviors* (pp. 3–24). Springer, New York, NY.

Dixon, M. R. (2014). *ACT for children with autism and emotional challenges*. Carbondale: Shawnee Scientific Press.

Dixon, M. R. (2015). *PEAK relational training system: Equivalence*. Shawnee Scientific Press, LLC.

Dixon, M. R. (2016). *PEAK relational training system: Transformation*. Shawnee Scientific Press, LLC.

Dixon, M. R. (2019). *Peak comprehensive assessment: Administration manual*. Carbondale: Shawnee Scientific Press.

Dixon, M. R., & Paliliunas, D. (2018). *AIM accept. Identify. Move. A behavior analytic curriculum for social-emotional development in children*. Naperville, IL: Emergent Press.

Dixon, M. R., & Paliliunas, D. (2020). Clinical behavior analysis: Integrating ACT and ABA. In M. E. Levin, M. P. Twohig, & J. Krafft (Eds.), *Innovations in acceptance & commitment therapy: Clinical advancements and applications*. Oakland, CA: Context Press/New Harbinger Publications..

Dixon, M. R., Belisle, J., McKeel, A., Whiting, S., Speelman, R., Daar, J. H., & Rowsey, K. (2017). An internal and critical review of the PEAK relational training system for children with autism and related intellectual disabilities: 2014–2017. *The Behavior Analyst, 40*, 493–521. https://doi.org/10.1007/s40614-017-0119-4

Dixon, M. R., Belisle, J., Rehfeldt, R. A., & Root, W. B. (2018). Why we are still not acting to save the world: The upward challenge of a post-Skinnerian behavior science. *Perspectives on Behavior Science, 41*(1), 241–267. https://doi.org/10.1007/s40614-018-0162-9

Dixon, M. R., Enoch, M. R., & Belisle, J. (2017). Transfers of stimulus function during roulette wagering. *Journal of Applied Behavior Analysis, 50*(4), 819–824.

Dixon, M. R., Hayes, S. C., Stanley, C. R., Law, S., & Al-Nasser, T. (2020). Is Acceptance and Commitment Training or Therapy (ACT) a method that applied behavior analysts can and should use? *The Psychological Record, 70*, 559–579. https://doi.org/10.1007/s40732-020-00436-9

Dixon, M. R., Paliliunas, D., Barron, B. F., Schmick, A. M., & Stanley, C. R. (2021). Randomized controlled trial evaluation of ABA content on IQ gains in children with autism. *Journal of Behavioral Education, 30*(3), 455–477.

Dixon, M. R., Small, S. L., & Rosales, R. (2007). Extended analysis of empirical citations with Skinner's verbal behavior: 1984–2004. *Behavior Analyst, 30*, 197–209.

Donati, M. A., Berrocal, C., Bernini, O., Gori, C., & Primi, C. (2021). Measuring cognitive fusion through the cognitive fusion questionnaire-7: Measurement invariance across non-clinical and clinical psychological samples. *PloS one, 16*(2), e0246434.

Dougher, M. J., Augustson, E., Markham, M. R., Greenway, D. E., & Wulfert, E. (1994). The transfer of respondent eliciting and extinction functions through stimulus equivalence classes. *Journal of the Experimental Analysis of Behavior, 62*(3), 331–351.

Dougher, M. J., Hamilton, D. A., Fink, B. C., & Harrington, J. (2007). Transformation of the discriminative and eliciting functions of generalized relational stimuli. *Journal of the Experimental Analysis of Behavior, 88*(2), 179–197.

Dusek, J. A., Otu, H. H., Wohlhueter, A. L., Bhasin, M., Zerbini L. F., Joseph, M. G., Benson, H., & Libermann, T. A. (2008). Genomic counter-stress changes induced by the relaxation response. *PLoS ONE, 3*(7), e2576. https://doi.org/10.1371/journal.pone.0002576

Dymond, S., & Barnes, D. (1995). A transformation of self-discrimination response functions in accordance with the arbitrarily applicable relations of sameness, more than, and less than. *Journal of the Experimental Analysis of Behavior, 64*(2), 163–184.

Dymond, S., Roche, B., Forsyth, J. P., Whelan, R., & Rhoden, J. (2007). Transformation of avoidance response functions in accordance with same and opposite relational frames. *Journal of the Experimental Analysis of Behavior, 88*(2), 249–262.

Eilers, H. J., and Hayes, S. C. (2015). Exposure and response prevention therapy with cognitive defusion exercises to reduce repetitive and restrictive behaviors displayed by children with autism spectrum disorder. *Research in Autism Spectrum Disorders, 19*, 18–31. https://doi.org/10.1016/j.rasd.2014.12.014

Epstein, R. M., Siegel, D. J., & Silberman, J. (2008). Self-monitoring in clinical practice: A challenge for medical educators. *Journal of Continuing Education in the Health Professions, 28*(1), 5–13.

Eriksson, T., Germundsjö, L., Åström, E., & Rönnlund, M. (2018). Mindful self-compassion training reduces stress and burnout symptoms among practicing psychologists: A randomized controlled trial of a brief web-based intervention. *Frontiers in Psychology, 9*, 2340.

Fang, S., & Ding, D. (2020). A meta-analysis of the efficacy of acceptance and commitment therapy for children. *Journal of Contextual Behavioral Science, 15*, 225–234.

Feldner, M. T., Zvolensky, M. J., Eifert, G. H., & Spira, A. P. (2003). Emotional avoidance: An experimental test of individual differences and response suppression using biological challenge. *Behaviour Research and Therapy, 41*(4), 403–411.

Ferroni-Bast, D., Fitzpatrick, J., Stewart, I., & Goyos, C. (2019). Using the Implicit Relational Assessment Procedure (IRAP) as a measure of reaction to perceived failure and the effects of a defusion intervention in this context. *The Psychological Record, 69*(4), 551–563.

Ferster, C. B. (1973). A functional analysis of depression. *American Psychologist, 28*, 857–870.

Finn, M., Barnes-Holmes, D., & McEnteggart, C. (2018). Exploring the single-trial-type-dominance-effect in the IRAP: Developing a Differential Arbitrarily Applicable Relational Responding Effects (DAARRE) model. *The Psychological Record, 68*(1), 11–25.

Fishbein, J. N., Baer, R. A., Correll, J., & Arch, J. J. (2022). The questionnaire on self-transcendence (QUEST): A measure of trait self-transcendence informed by contextual cognitive behavioral therapies. *Assessment, 29*(3), 508–526. https://doi.org/10.1177/1073191120980061

Foody, M., Barnes-Holmes, Y., Barnes-Holmes, D., Rai, L., & Luciano, C. (2015). An empirical investigation of the role of self, hierarchy, and distinction in a common act exercise. *The Psychological Record, 65*(2), 231–243.

García-Zambrano, S., Rehfeldt, R. A., Hertel, I. P., & Boehmert, R. (2019). Effects of deictic framing and defusion on the development of self-as-context in individuals with disabilities. *Journal of Contextual Behavioral Science, 12*, 55–58.

Gates, K. M., & Molenaar, P. C. M. (2012). Group search algorithm recovers effective connectivity maps for individuals in homogeneous and heterogeneous samples. *NeuroImage, 63*(1), 310–319.

Gates, K. M., Molenaar, P. C., Iyer, S. P., Nigg, J. T., & Fair, D. A. (2014). Organizing heterogeneous samples using community detection of GIMME-derived resting state functional networks. *PloS one, 9*(3), e91322.

Ghezzi, E. L., Houmanfar, R. A., & Crosswell, L. (2020). The motivative augmental effects of verbal stimuli on cooperative and conformity responding under a financially competing contingency in an analog work task. *The Psychological Record, 70*(3), 411–431.

Gifford, E. V., Kohlenberg, B., Hayes, S. C., Pierson, H., Piasecki, M., Antonuccio, D., & Palm, K. (2011). Does acceptance and relationship-focused behavior therapy contribute to bupropion outcomes? A randomized controlled trial of FAP and ACT for smoking cessation. *Behavior Therapy, 42*, 700–715.

Gilsenan, C. M., Yi, Z., Hinman, J. M., Barron, B. F., & Dixon, M. R. (2022). Using relational training to improve performance during acceptance and commitment training sessions. *Behavior Analysis in Practice, 15*(1), 179–191. https://doi.org/10.1007/s40617-021-00574-8

Gilsenan, C. M., Yi, Z., Hinman, J. M., Barron, B. F., & Dixon, M. R. (2021). Using relational training to improve performance during acceptance and commitment training sessions. *Behavior Analysis in Practice*, 1–13.

Gilsenan, C. M., Yi, Z., Hinman, J. M., Barron, B. F., & Dixon, M. R. (2022). Using relational training to improve performance during acceptance and commitment training sessions. *Behavior Analysis in Practice, 15*(1), 179–191.

Ginsburg, S., & Jablonka, E. (2010). The evolution of associative learning: A factor in the Cambrian explosion. *Journal of Theoretical Biology, 266*, 11–20.

Glassman, L. H., Forman, E. M., Herbert, J. D., et al. (2016). The effects of a brief acceptance-based behavioral treatment versus traditional cognitive-behavioral treatment for public speaking anxiety: An exploratory trial examining differential effects on performance and neurophysiology. *Behavior Modification, 40*(5), 748–776. https://doi.org/10.1177/0145445516629939

Goldberg, S. B., Tucker, R. P., Greene, P. A., Davidson, R. J., Wampold, B. E., Kearney, D. J., & Simpson, T. L. (2018). Mindfulness-based interventions for psychiatric disorders: A systematic review and meta-analysis. *Clinical Psychology Review, 59*, 52–60.

Gooding, A., & Gardner, F. L. (2009). An investigation of the relationship between mindfulness, preshot routine, and basketball free throw percentage. *Journal of Clinical Sport Psychology, 3*(4), 303–319.

Grossman, P., Niemann, L., Schmidt, S., & Walach, H. (2004). Mindfulness-based stress reduction and health benefits: A meta-analysis. *Journal of Psychosomatic Research, 57*(1), 35–43.

Habib, R., & Dixon, M. R. (2010). Neurobehavioral evidence for the "near-miss" effect in pathological gamblers. *Journal of the Experimental Analysis of Behavior, 93*, 313–328. https://doi.org/10.1901/jeab.2010.93-313

Hahs, A. D., Dixon, M. R., & Paliliunas, D. (2019). Randomized controlled trial of a brief acceptance and commitment training for parents of individuals diagnosed with autism spectrum disorders. *Journal of Contextual Behavioral Science, 12*, 154–159. https://doi.org/10.1016/j.jcbs.2018.03.002

Hanley, G. P., Iwata, B. A., & McCord, B. E. (2003). Functional analysis of problem behavior: A review. *Journal of Applied Behavior Analysis, 36*(2), 147–185.

Hannon, G., & Emily P. Taylor, E. P. (2013). Suicidal behaviour in adolescents and young adults with ASD: Findings from a systematic review. *Clinical Psychology Review, 33*(8), 1197–1204. https://doi.org/10.1016/j.cpr.2013.10.003

Harmon, T. M., Nelson, R. O., & Hayes, S. C. (1980). Selfmonitoring of mood versus activity by depressed clients. *Journal of Consulting and Clinical Psychology, 48*, 30–38. https://doi.org/10.1037//0022-006X.48.1.30

Harris, R. (2019). *ACT made simple: An easy-to-read primer on acceptance and commitment therapy*. Oakland, CA: New Harbinger Publications.

Hawking, S., & Mlodinow, L. (2010). *The grand design*. New York: Bantam.

Hayes, S. C. (1984). Making sense of spirituality. *Behaviorism*, 99–110.

Hayes, S. C. (1986). The case of the silent dog: Verbal reports and the analysis of rules. A review of K. Anders Ericsson and Herbert A. Simon, "Protocol analysis: Verbal reports as data." *Journal of the Experimental Analysis of Behavior, 45*, 351–363. https://doi.org/10.1901/jeab.1986.45-351

Hayes, S. C. (Ed.). (1989). *Rulegoverned behavior: Cognition, contingencies, and instructional control*. New York: Plenum.

Hayes, S. C. (1993). Analytic goals and the varieties of scientific contextualism. In S. C. Hayes, L. J. Hayes, H. W. Reese, & T. R. Sarbin (Eds.), *Varieties of scientific contextualism* (pp. 11–27). Reno: Context Press.

Hayes, S. C. (2019). *A liberated mind: How to pivot toward what matters*. New York: Penguin/Avery.

Hayes, S. C., & Brownstein, A. J. (May 1985). Verbal behavior, equivalence classes, and rules: New definitions, data, and directions. Invited address presented at the Meeting of the Association for Behavior Analysis, Columbus, OH.

Hayes, S. C., & Brownstein, A. J. (1986). Mentalism, behaviorbehavior relations and a behavior analytic view of the purposes of science. *The Behavior Analyst, 9*, 175–190.

Hayes, S. C., & Hayes, L. J. (1989). The verbal action of the listener as a basis for rule-governance. In S. C. Hayes (Ed.), *Rulegoverned behavior: Cognition, contingencies, and instructional control* (pp. 153–190). New York: Plenum.

Hayes, S. C., & Hayes, L. J. (1992). Some clinical implications of contextualistic behaviorism: The example of cognition. *Behavior Therapy, 23*, 225–249. https://doi.org/10.1016/S0005-7894(05)80383-1

Hayes, S. C., & Hofmann, S. G. (2017). The third wave of cognitive behavioral therapy and the rise of process-based care. *World Psychiatry, 16*(3), 245.

Hayes, S. C., & Hofmann, S. G. (2018). (Eds.), *Process-based CBT: The science and core clinical competencies of cognitive behavioral therapy*. Oakland: Context Press/New Harbinger Publications.

Hayes, S. C., & Sanford, B. (2014). Cooperation came first: Evolution and human cognition. *Journal of the Experimental Analysis of Behavior, 101*, 112–129. https://doi.org/10.1002/jeab.64

Hayes, S. C., & Strosahl, K. D. (2004). *A practical guide to acceptance and commitment therapy*. New York: Springer.

Hayes, S. C., Barnes-Holmes, D., & Roche, B. (Eds.). (2001). *Relational frame theory: A post-Skinnerian account of human language and cognition*. New York: Kluwer Academic/Plenum Publishers.

Hayes, S. C., Bissett, R., Korn, Z., Zettle, R. D., Rosenfarb, I., Cooper, L., & Grundt, A. (1999). The impact of acceptance versus control rationales on pain tolerance. *The Psychological Record, 49*, 33–47.

Hayes, S. C., Bond, F., Barnes-Holmes, D., & Austin, J. (Eds.). (2006). *Acceptance and mindfulness at work: Acceptance and commitment therapy, relational frame theory, and organizational behavior management*. Binghamton: Haworth.

Hayes, S. C., Devany, J. M., Kohlenberg, B. S., Brownstein, A. J., & Shelby, J. (1987). Stimulus equivalence and the symbolic control of behavior. *Mexican Journal of Behavior Analysis, 13*, 361–374.

Hayes, S. C., Hofmann, S. G., & Ciarrochi, J. (2020). A process-based approach to psychological diagnosis and treatment: The conceptual and treatment utility of an extended evolutionary model. *Clinical Psychology Review, 82*, 101908. https://doi.org/10.1016/j.cpr.2020.101908

Hayes, S. C., Hofmann, S. G., & Stanton, C. E. (2020). Process-based functional analysis can help behavioral science step up to the challenges of novelty: COVID–19 as an example. *Journal of Contextual Behavioral Science, 18*, 128–145. https://doi.org/10.1016/j.jcbs.2020.08.009

Hayes, S. C., Hofmann, S. G., Stanton, C. E., Carpenter, J. K., Sanford, B. T., Curtiss, J. E., & Ciarrochi, J. (2019). The role of the individual in the coming era of process-based therapy. *Behaviour Research and Therapy, 117*, 40–53.

Hayes, S. C., Lattal, K. A., & Myerson, W. A. (1979). Strength of experimentally induced phobic behavior in rats: Avoidance versus dual-component formulations. *Psychological Reports, 44*(3), 891–894.

Hayes, S. C., Merwin, R. M., McHugh, L., Sandoz, E. K., A-Tjak, J. G., Ruiz, F. J., ... & McCracken, L. M. (2021). Report of the ACBS task force on the strategies and tactics of contextual behavioral science research. *Journal of Contextual Behavioral Science, 20*, 172–183.

Hayes, S. C., Strosahl, K. D., & Wilson, K. G. (1999). *Acceptance and commitment therapy: An experiential approach to behavior change.* New York: Guilford Press.

Hayes, S. C., Strosahl, K. D., & Wilson, K. G. (2011). *Acceptance and commitment therapy: The process and practice of mindful change.* New York: Guilford Press.

Hayes, S. C., Strosahl, K., & Wilson, K. G. (2012). *Acceptance and commitment therapy: The process and practice of mindful change* (2nd edition). New York: Guilford Press.

Hayes, S. C., Strosahl, K. D., Bunting, K., Twohig, M., & Wilson, K. G. (2004). What is acceptance and commitment therapy? In *A practical guide to acceptance and commitment therapy* (pp. 3–29). Springer.

Hayes, S. C., White, D., & Bissett, R. T. (1998). Protocol analysis and the "silent dog" method of analyzing the impact of self-generated rules. *The Analysis of Verbal Behavior, 15*, 57–63.

Hayes, S. C., Wilson, K. W., Gifford, E. V., Follette, V. M., & Strosahl, K. (1996). Experiential avoidance and behavioral disorders: A functional dimensional approach to diagnosis and treatment. *Journal of Consulting and Clinical Psychology, 64*, 1152–1168. https://doi.org/10.1037//0022-006X.64.6.1152

Haynes, S. N., O'Brien, W., & Kaholokula, J. (2011). *Behavioral assessment and case formulation.* New York: Wiley & Sons.

Hersh, M. N., Ponder, R. G., Hastings, P. J., & Rosenberg, S. M. (2004). Adaptive mutation and amplification in Escherichia coli: Two pathways of genome adaptation under stress. *Research in Microbiology, 155*, 353–359. https://doi.org/10.1016/j.resmic.2004.01.020

Hoffman, D. (2019). *The case against reality: Why evolution hid the truth from our eyes.* New York: Norton.

Hofmann, S. G., & Hayes, S. C. (2018). The history and current status of CBT as an evidence-based therapy. Chapter in Hayes, S. C. & Hofmann, S. G. (Eds.), *Process-based CBT: The science and core clinical competencies of cognitive behavioral therapy* (pp. 7 –21). Oakland: Context Press/New Harbinger Publications.

Hofmann, S. G., & Hayes, S. C. (2019). The future of intervention science: Process based therapy. *Clinical Psychological Science, 7*(1), 37–50. https://doi.org/10.1177/2167702618772296

Hofmann, S. G., & Hayes, S. C. (2020). *Beyond the DSM: Toward a process-based alternative for diagnosis and mental health treatment.* Oakland: Context Press/New Harbinger Publications.

Hooper, N., Dack, C., Karekla, M., Niyazi, A., & McHugh, L. (2018). Cognitive defusion versus experiential avoidance in the reduction of smoking behaviour: An experimental and preliminary investigation. *Addiction Research & Theory, 26*(5), 414–420.

Hooper, N., Sandoz, E. K., Ashton, J., Clarke, A., & McHugh, L. (2012). Comparing thought suppression and acceptance as coping techniques for food cravings. *Eating Behaviors, 13*(1), 62–64.

Hyde, J. S., Bigler, R. S., Joel, D., Tate, C. C., & van Anders, S. M. (2019). The future of sex and gender in psychology: Five challenges to the gender binary. *American Psychologist, 74*(2), 171.

Iacoboni, M. (2009). Imitation, empathy, and mirror neurons. *Annual Review of Psychology, 60*(1), 653–670. https://doi.org/10.1146/annurev.psych.60.110707.163604

Ivancic, M., & Belisle, J. (2019). Resolving barriers to an applied science of the human condition: Rule governance and the verbal behavior of applied scientists. *The Analysis of Verbal Behavior, 35*(2), 196–220.

Iwata, B. A., Dorsey, M. F., Slifer, K. J., Bauman, K. E., & Richman, G. S. (1982). Toward a functional analysis of self-injury. *Analysis and Intervention in Developmental Disabilities, 2*(1), 3–20. https://doi.org/10.1016/0270-4684(82)90003-9

Iwata, B. A., Dorsey, M. F., Slifer, K. J., Bauman, K. E., & Richman, G. S. (1994). Toward a functional analysis of self-injury. *Journal of Applied Behavior Analysis, 27*(2), 197–209. https://doi.org/10.1901/jaba.1994.27-197

Jablonka, E., & Lamb, M. J. (2014). *Evolution in four dimensions: Genetic, epigenetic, behavioral, and symbolic variation in the history of life* (2nd ed.). Cambridge, MA: MIT Press.

Jeffcoat, T., & Hayes, S. C. (2012). A randomized trial of ACT bibliotherapy on the mental health of K-12 teachers and staff. *Behaviour Research and Therapy, 50*, 571–579. https://doi.org/10.1016/j.brat.2012.05.008

Jessel, J., Hanley, G. P., Ghaemmaghami, M., & Metras, R. (2019). An evaluation of the single-session interview-informed synthesized contingency analysis. *Behavioral Interventions, 34*(1), 62–78.

Ju, W. C., & Hayes, S. C. (2008). Verbal establishing stimuli: Testing the motivative effect of stimuli in a derived relation with consequences. *The Psychological Record, 58*, 339–363.

Juvin, J., Sadeg, S., Julien-Sweerts, S., & Zebdi, R. (2021). A systematic review: Acceptance and Commitment Therapy for the parents of children and adolescents with autism spectrum disorder. *Journal of Autism and Developmental Disorders, 52*, 124–141. https://doi.org/10.1007/s10803-021-04923-y

Kanfer, F. H., & Grimm, L. G. (1977). Behavioral analysis: Selecting target behaviors in the interview. *Behavior Modification, 1*, 7–28.

Kanfer, F. H., & Saslow, G. (1965). Behavioral analysis: An alternative to diagnostic classification. *Archives of General Psychiatry, 12*, 529–538.

Kavaklı, M., Ak, M., Uğuz, F., & Türkmen, O. O. (2020). The mediating role of self-compassion in the relationship between perceived COVID-19 threat and death anxiety. *Journal of Clinical Psychiatry, 23*(Supp: 1), 15–23.

Kazdin, A. E. (2000). Perceived barriers to treatment participation and treatment acceptability among antisocial children and their families. *Journal of Child and Family Studies, 9*(2), 157–174.

Kelly, A. C., & Carter, J. C. (2015). Self-compassion training for binge eating disorder: A pilot randomized controlled trial. *Psychology and Psychotherapy: Theory, Research and Practice, 88*(3), 285–303.

Kessler, R. C., Angermeyer, M., Anthony, J. C., De Graaf, R. O. N., Demyttenaere, K., Gasquet, I., ... & Üstün, T. B. (2007). Lifetime prevalence and age-of-onset distributions of mental disorders in the World Health Organization's World Mental Health Survey Initiative. *World Psychiatry, 6*(3), 168.

Kestner, K. M., & Peterson, S. M. (2017). A review of resurgence literature with human participants. *Behavior Analysis: Research and Practice, 17*(1), 1–17. https://doi.org/10.1037/bar0000039

Kircanski, K., Lieberman, M. D., & Craske, M. G. (2012). Feelings into Words: Contributions of Language to Exposure Therapy. *Psychological Science, 2012;23*(10), 1086–1091. https://doi.org/10.1177/0956797612443830

Klimley, A. P. (1993). Highly directional swimming by scalloped hammerhead sharks, Sphyrna lewini, and subsurface irradiance, temperature, bathymetry, and geomagnetic field. *Marine Biology, 117*(1), 1–22.

Krapfl, J. E., & Nawas, M. M. (1970). Differential ordering of stimulus presentation in systematic desensitization. *Journal of Abnormal Psychology, 75*(3), 333–337. https://doi.org/10.1037/h0029351

Lawlor, K. B., & Hornyak, M. J. (2012). Smart goals: How the application of smart goals can contribute to achievement of student learning outcomes. *Developments in Business Simulation and Experiential Learning, 39*, 259–267.

LeBlanc, L. A., Taylor, B. A., & Marchese, N. V. (2020). The training experiences of behavior analysts: Compassionate care and therapeutic relationships with caregivers. *Behavior Analysis in Practice, 13*(2), 387–393.

Levin, M. E., Hayes, S. C., & Waltz, T. (2010). Creating an implicit measure of cognition more suited to applied research: A test of the Mixed Trial—Implicit Relational Assessment Procedure (MT-IRAP). *International Journal of Behavioral Consultation and Therapy, 6*(3), 245–262. https://doi.org/10.1037/h0100911

Lewinsohn, P. M. (1974). A behavioral approach to depression. In R. J. Friedman & M. M. Katz (Eds.), *Psychology of depression: Contemporary theory and research* (pp. 157–178). Oxford, UK: John Wiley & Sons.

Liberman, Z., & Shaw, A. (2019). Children use similarity, propinquity, and loyalty to predict which people are friends. *Journal of Experimental Child Psychology, 184*, 1–17.

Liebal, K., Behne, T., Carpenter, M., & Tomasello, M. (2009). Infants use shared experience to interpret a pointing gesture. *Developmental Science, 12*, 264–271.

Lionello-DeNolf, K. M. (2021). An update on the search for symmetry in nonhumans. *Journal of the Experimental Analysis of Behavior, 115*(1), 309–325. https://doi.org/10.1002/jeab.647

Lipkens, G., Hayes, S. C., & Hayes, L. J. (1993). Longitudinal study of derived stimulus relations in an infant. *Journal of Experimental Child Psychology, 56*, 201–239.

Lippman, L. G., & Meyer, M. M. (1967). Fixed interval performance as related to instructions and to subjects' verbalization of the contingency. *Psychonomic Science, 8*, 135–136.

Little, A., Tarbox, J., & Alzaabi, K. (2020). Using acceptance and commitment training to enhance the effectiveness of behavioral skills training. *Journal of Contextual Behavioral Science, 16*, 9–16. https://doi.org/10.1016/j.jcbs.2020.02.002

Longmore, R. J., & Worrell, M. (2007). Do we need to challenge thoughts in cognitive behavioral therapy? *Clinical Psychology Review, 27*, 173–187.

Lovibond, P. F., & Lovibond, S. H. (1995). The structure of negative emotional states: Comparison of the Depression Anxiety Stress Scales (DASS) with the Beck Depression and Anxiety Inventories. *Behaviour Research and Therapy, 33*(3), 335–343. https://doi.org/10.1016/0005-7967(94)00075-U

Lowe, C. F. (1979). Determinants of human operant behavior. In M. D. Zeiler & P. Harzem (Eds.), *Advances in analysis of behavior: Vol. 1. Reinforcement and the organization of behavior* (pp. 159–192). Chichester, UK: Wiley.

Lowe, C. F., Beasty, A., & Bentall, R. P. (1983). The role of verbal behavior in human learning: Infant performance on fixed interval schedules. *Journal of the Experimental Analysis of Behavior, 39*, 157–164.

Luciano, C., Gómez-Becerra, I., & Rodríguez-Valverde, M. (2007). The role of multiple-exemplar training and naming in establishing derived equivalence in an infant. *Journal of Experimental Analysis of Behavior, 87*, 349–365.

Luciano, C., Törneke, N., & Ruiz, F. J. (in press). Clinical behavior analysis and RFT: Conceptualizing psychopathology and its treatment. In Twohig, M. P., Levin, M. E., & Petersen, J. M. (Eds.), *Handbook of acceptance and commitment therapy*. New York: Oxford University Press.

Lundgren, T., Luoma, J. B., Dahl, J., Strosahl, K., & Melin, L. (2012). The bull's-eye values survey: A psychometric evaluation. *Cognitive and Behavioral Practice, 19*(4), 518–526.

Luoma, J. B., Hayes, S. C., & Walser, R. D. (2007). *Learning ACT: An acceptance & commitment therapy skills-training manual for therapists*. Oakland, CA: New Harbinger Publications.

Luoma, J. B., Hayes, S. C., & Walser, R. D. (2010). *Learning ACT: An Acceptance & Commitment Therapy skills-training manual for therapists*. Oakland, CA: New Harbinger Publications.

Luoma, J., Hayes, S. C., & Walser, R. (2017). *Learning ACT: An acceptance & commitment therapy skills-training manual for therapists* (2nd ed.). Oakland, CA: Context Press and New Harbinger Publications.

Luoma, J. B., Kohlenberg, B. S., Hayes, S. C., & Fletcher, L. (2012). Slow and steady wins the race: A randomized clinical trial of Acceptance and Commitment Therapy targeting shame in substance use disorders. *Journal of Consulting and Clinical Psychology, 80*, 43–53. https://doi.org/10.1037/a0026070

Maisel, M. E., Stephenson, K. G., Cox, J. C., & South, M. (2019). Cognitive defusion for reducing distressing thoughts in adults with autism. *Research in Autism Spectrum Disorders, 59*, 34–45.

Mandavia, A., Masuda, A., Moore, M., Mendoza, H., Donati, M. R., & Cohen, L. L. (2015). The application of a cognitive defusion technique to negative body image thoughts: A preliminary analogue investigation. *Journal of Contextual Behavioral Science, 4*(2), 86–95.

Markham, M. R., Dougher, M. J., & Augustson, E. M. Transfer of operant discrimination and respondent elicitation via emergent relations of compound stimuli. *The Psychological Record, 52*, 325–350 (2002). https://doi.org/10.1007/BF03395434

Marshall, E. J., & Brockman, R. N. (2016). The relationships between psychological flexibility, self-compassion, and emotional well-being. *Journal of Cognitive Psychotherapy, 30*(1), 60–72.

Matson, J. L., Tureck, K., & Rieske, R. (2012). The Questions About Behavioral Function (QABF): Current status as a method of functional assessment. *Research in Developmental Disabilities, 33*(2), 630–634.

McHugh, L., & Stewart, I. (2012). *The self and perspective taking: Contributions and applications from modern behavioral science*. Oakland, CA: New Harbinger Publications.

Miller, M. B., Meier, E., Lombardi, N., Leavens, E. L., Grant, D. M., & Leffingwell, T. R. (2016). The valued living questionnaire for alcohol use: Measuring value-behavior discrepancy in college student drinking. *Psychological Assessment, 28*(9), 1051.

Moffitt, R., Brinkworth, G., Noakes, M., & Mohr, P. (2012). A comparison of cognitive restructuring and cognitive defusion as strategies for resisting a craved food. *Psychology & Health, 27*(sup2), 74–90.

Molenaar, P. C. M. (2013). On the necessity to use person-specific data analysis approaches in psychology. *European Journal of Developmental Psychology, 10*, 29–39. https://doi.org/10.1080/17405629.2012.747435

Molenaar, P. C., & Campbell, C. G. (2009). The new person-specific paradigm in psychology. *Current Directions in Psychological Science, 18*(2), 112–117.

Moore, J. (2007). *Conceptual foundations of radical behaviorism*. Hudson, NY: Sloan Publishing.

Moran, O., Almada, P., & McHugh, L. (2018). An investigation into the relationship between the three selves (Self-as-Content, Self-as-Process and Self-as-Context) and mental health in adolescents. *Journal of Contextual Behavioral Science, 7*, 55–62.

Neff, K. D., & Vonk, R. (2009). Self-compassion versus global self-esteem: Two different ways of relating to oneself. *Journal of Personality, 77*(1), 23–50.

Neuringer, A. (1986). Can people behave "randomly?": The role of feedback. *Journal of Experimental Psychology: General, 115*(1), 62–75.

Neuringer, A. (2002). Operant variability: Evidence, functions, and theory. *Psychonomic Bulletin and Review, 9*, 672–705.

Neuringer, A. (2012). Reinforcement and induction of operant variability. *The Behavior Analyst, 35*(2), 229.

Nevin, J. A. (1992). An integrative model for the study of behavioral momentum. *Journal of the Experimental Analysis of Behavior, 57*, 301–316.

O'Reilly, A., Roche, B., Ruiz, M., Tyndall, I., & Gavin, A. (2012). The Function Acquisition Speed Test (FAST): A behavior analytic implicit test for assessing stimulus relations. *Psychological Record, 62*, 507–528 (2012). https://doi.org/10.1007/BF03395817

Oldenburg, B., Van Duijn, M., & Veenstra, R. (2018). Defending one's friends, not one's enemies: A social network analysis of children's defending, friendship, and dislike relationships using XPNet. *PloS One, 13*(5), e0194323.

Olfson, M., & Marcus, S. C. (2010). National trends in outpatient psychotherapy. *American Journal of Psychiatry, 167*(12), 1456–1463.

Orlando, R., & Bijou, S. W. (1960). Single and multiple schedules of reinforcement in developmentally retarded children. *Journal of the Experimental Analysis of Behavior, 3*(4), 339–348. https://doi.org/10.1901/jeab.1960.3-339

Page, S., & Neuringer, A. (1985). Variability is an operant. *Journal of Experimental Psychology: Animal Behavior Processes, 11*(3), 429.

Paliliunas, D. (2021). Values: A core guiding principle for behavior-analytic intervention and research. *Behavior Analysis in Practice, 15*, 115–125. https://doi.org/10.1007/s40617-021-00595-3

Palmer, D. C. (1991). A behavioral interpretation of memory. *Dialogues on Verbal Behavior, 261*, 279.

Parry-Cruwys, D. E., Neal, C. M., Ahearn, W. H., Wheeler, E. E., Premchander, R., Loeb, M. B., et al. (2011). Resistance to disruption in a classroom setting. *Journal of Applied Behavior Analysis, 44*, 363–367.

Pearson, A., Ropar, D., & Hamilton, A. F. D. (2013). A review of visual perspective taking in autism spectrum disorder. *Frontiers in Human Neuroscience, 7*, 652.

Perez, W. F., de Almeida, J. H., Soares, L. C., Wang, T. F., de Morais, T. E., Mascarenhas, A. V., & de Rose, J. C. (2020). Fearful faces and the derived transfer of aversive functions. *The Psychological Record, 70*(3), 387–396.

Pilecki, B. C., & McKay, D. (2012). An experimental investigation of cognitive defusion. *The Psychological Record, 62*(1), 19–40.

Plumb, J. C., Stewart, I., Dahl, J., & Lundgren, T. (2009). In search of meaning: Values in modern clinical behavior analysis. *The Behavior Analyst, 32*, 85–103. https://doi.org/10.1007/BF03392177

Polk, K. L., & Schoendorff, B. (2014). *The ACT matrix: A new approach to building psychological flexibility across settings & populations*. Oakland, CA: Context Press/New Harbinger Publications.

Pratt, L. A., Brody, D. J., & Gu, Q. (2017). Antidepressant use among persons aged 12 and over: United States, 2011–2014. *NCHS Data Brief*. Number 283. National Center for Health Statistics.

Pryor, K. W., Haag, R., & O'Reilly, J. (1969). The creative porpoise: Training for novel behavior. *Journal of the Experimental Analysis of Behavior, 12*(4), 653–661.

Raes, F., Pommier, E., Neff, K. D., & Van Gucht, D. (2011). Construction and factorial validation of a short form of the self-compassion scale. *Clinical Psychology & Psychotherapy, 18*(3), 250–255.

Ren, Z., Zhao, C., Bian, C., Zhu, W., Jiang, G., & Zhu, Z. (2019). Mechanisms of Acceptance and Commitment Therapy: A meta-analytic structural equation model. *Acta Psychologica Sinica, 51*(6), 662–676. https://doi.org/10.3724/SP.J.1041.2019.00662

Ritzert, T. R., Forsyth, J. P., Berghoff, C. R., Barnes-Holmes, D., & Nicholson, E. (2015). The impact of a cognitive defusion intervention on behavioral and psychological flexibility: An experimental evaluation in a spider fearful non-clinical sample. *Journal of Contextual Behavioral Science, 4*(2), 112–120.

Roche, B., Barnes-Holmes, D., Barnes-Holmes, Y., Smeets, P. M., & McGeady, S. (2000). Contextual control over the derived transformation of discriminative and sexual arousal functions. *The Psychological Record, 50*(2), 267–291.

Rosenfarb, I., & Hayes, S. C. (1984). Social standard setting: The Achilles' heel of informational accounts of therapeutic change. *Behavior Therapy, 15*, 515–528. https://doi.org/10.1016/S0005-7894(84)80053-2

Sahdra, B. K., Ciarrochi, J., Parker, P. D., Marshall, S., & Heaven, P. (2015). Empathy and nonattachment independently predict peer nominations of prosocial behavior of adolescents. *Frontiers in Psychology, 263*. https://doi.org/10.3389/fpsyg.2015.00263

Sahdra, B. K., Shaver, P. R., & Brown, K. W. (2010). A scale to measure nonattachment: A Buddhist complement to Western research on attachment and adaptive functioning. *Journal of Personality Assessment, 92*(2), 116–127.

Sanchez, A. L., Cornacchio, D., Poznanski, B., Golik, A. M., Chou, T., & Comer, J. S. (2018). The effectiveness of school-based mental health services for elementary-aged children: A meta-analysis. *Journal of the American Academy of Child & Adolescent Psychiatry, 57*(3), 153–165.

Sanford, B. T., Ciarrochi, J., Hofmann, S. G., Chin, F., Gates, K. M., & Hayes, S. C. (2022; in press). Toward empirical process-based case conceptualization: An idionomic network examination of the process-based assessment tool. *Journal of Contextual Behavioral Science., 25*, 10–25. https://doi.org/10.1016/j.jcbs.2022.05.006

Schlinger Jr, H. D. (2017). The importance of analysis in applied behavior analysis. *Behavior Analysis: Research and Practice, 17*(4), 334.

Schlund, M. W., Hoehn-Saric, R., & Cataldo, M. F. (2007). New knowledge derived from learned knowledge: Functional-anatomic correlates of stimulus equivalence. *Journal of the Experimental Analysis of Behavior, 87*(2), 287–307.

Schneider, S. M. (2012). *The science of consequences: How they affect genes, change the brain, and impact our world*. Amherst: Prometheus Books.

Schusterman, R. J., & Kastak, D. (1993). A California sea lion (zalophus californianus) is capable of forming equivalence relations. *The Psychological Record, 43*, 823–839.

Segers, M., & Rawana, J. (2014). What do we know about suicidality in autism spectrum disorders? A systematic review. *Autism Research, 7*(4), 507–521.

Seligman, M. E. (1972). Learned helplessness. *Annual Review of Medicine, 23*(1), 407–412.

Shimoff, E., Catania, A. C., & Matthews, B. A. (1981). Uninstructed human responding: Sensitivity of low-rate performance to schedule contingencies. *Journal of the Experimental Analysis of Behavior, 36*, 207–220.
Shin, J. Y., Kim, S. W., Roh, S. G., Lee, N. H., & Yang, K. M. (2016). Congenital insensitivity to pain and anhidrosis. *Archives of Plastic Surgery, 43*(1), 95–97. https://doi.org/10.5999/aps.2016.43.1.95
Sidman, M. (1960). *Tactics of scientific research*. Boston, MA: Authors Cooperative.
Sidman, M. (1971). Reading and auditory-visual equivalences. *Journal of Speech and Hearing Research, 14*, 5–13.
Sidman, M. (1989). *Coercion and its fallout*. Boston: Authors Cooperative.
Sidman, M. (1994). *Equivalence relations and behavior: A research story*. Boston: Authors Cooperative.
Sidman, M. (2008). Reflections on stimulus control. *The Behavior Analyst, 31*(2), 127–135.
Sidman, M., & Tailby, W. (1982). Conditional discrimination vs. matching to sample: An expansion of the testing paradigm. *Journal of the Experimental Analysis of Behavior, 37*(1), 5–22.
Singh, N. N., Lancioni, G. E., Karazsia, B. T., Myers, R. E., Kim, E., Chan, J., ... & Janson, M. (2019). Surfing the urge: An informal mindfulness practice for the self-management of aggression by adolescents with autism spectrum disorder. *Journal of Contextual Behavioral Science, 12*, 170–177.
Singh, N. N., Lancioni, G. E., Manikam, R., Winton, A. S., Singh, A. N., Singh, J., & Singh, A. D. (2011). A mindfulness-based strategy for self-management of aggressive behavior in adolescents with autism. *Research in Autism Spectrum Disorders, 5*(3), 1153–1158.
Singh, N. N., Lancioni, G. E., Winton, A. S. W., et al. (2007). Individuals with mental illness can control their aggressive behavior through mindfulness training. *Behavior Modification, 31*(3), 313–328. https://doi.org/10.1177/0145445506293585
Singh, N.N., Lancioni, G.E., Winton, A.S.W., Singh, A.N., Adkins, A.D. and Singh, J. (2009), Mindful staff can reduce the use of physical restraints when providing care to individuals with intellectual disabilities. *Journal of Applied Research in Intellectual Disabilities, 22*, 194–202. https://doi.org/10.1111/j.1468-3148.2008.00488.x
Singh, N. N., Lancioni, G. E., Winton, A. S., Singh, A. N., Singh, J., & Singh, A. D. (2011). Effects of a mindfulness-based smoking cessation program for an adult with mild intellectual disability. *Research in Developmental Disabilities, 32*(3), 1180 1185. https://doi.org/10.1016/j.ridd.2011.01.003
Singh, N. N., Wahler, R. G., Adkins, A. D., Myers, R. E., & Mindfulness Research Group. (2003). Soles of the feet: A mindfulness-based self-control intervention for aggression by an individual with mild mental retardation and mental illness. *Research in Developmental Disabilities, 24*(3), 158–169.
Singh, R. S., Watford, T. S., Cotterman, R. E., & O'Brien, W. H. (2020). A pilot study of acceptance and commitment therapy for sexual minorities experiencing work stress. *Journal of Contextual Behavioral Science, 16*, 25–29.
Skinner B. F. (1957). *Verbal behavior*. New York: Appleton-Century-Crofts.
Skinner, B. F. (1938). *Behavior of organisms*. New York: Appelton-Century-Crofts.
Skinner, B. F. (1945). The operational analysis of psychological terms. *Psychological Review, 52*, 270–276.
Skinner, B. F. (1948). *Walden II*. New York: MacMillan.
Skinner, B. F. (1953). *Science and human behavior*. New York: The Free Press.
Skinner, B. F. (1957). *Verbal behavior*. New York: Appleton-Century-Crofts.
Skinner, B. F. (1966). An operant analysis of problem solving. In B. Kleinmuntz (Ed.), *Problemsolving: Research, method, and theory* (pp. 225–257). New York: Wiley.
Skinner, B. F. (1969). *Contingencies of reinforcement: A theoretical analysis*. New York: Appleton-Century-Crofts.
Skinner, B. F. (1971). *Beyond freedom and dignity*. Boston, MA: B. F. Skinner Foundation.
Skinner, B. F. (1974). *About behaviorism*. New York: Alfred A. Knopf.
Skinner, B. F. (1981). Selection by consequences. *Science, 213*, 501–504.
Skinner, B. F. (1989). The origins of cognitive thought. *American Psychologist, 44*(1), 13–18. https://doi.org/10.1037/0003-066X.44.1.13
Skinner, B. F. (1990/1999). Can psychology be a science of mind? In V. G. Laties & A. C. Catania (Eds.), *Cumulative record* (pp. 576–584). Cambridge, MA: B. F. Skinner Foundation.
Slothuus, R. (2010). When can political parties lead public opinion? Evidence from a natural experiment. *Political Communication, 27*(2), 158–177.
Stockton, D., Kellett, S., Berrios, R., Sirois, F., Wilkinson, N., & Miles, G. (2019). Identifying the underlying mechanisms of change during Acceptance and Commitment Therapy (ACT): A systematic review of contemporary mediation studies. *Behavioural and Cognitive Psychotherapy, 47*(3), 332–362. https://doi.org/10.1017/S1352465818000553
Stoddard, J. A., & Afari, N. (2014). *The big book of ACT metaphors*. Oakland, CA: New Harbinger Publications.
Sturmey, P. (2020). *Functional Analysis in Clinical Treatment*. New York: Elsevier.
Sweeney, M. M., & Shahan, T. A. (2013). Behavioral momentum and resurgence: Effects of time in extinction and repeated resurgence tests. *Learning & Behavior, 41*(4), 414–424. https://doi.org/10.3758/s13420-013-0116-8
Szarko, A. J., Houmanfar, R. A., Smith, G. S., Jacobs, N. N., Smith, B. M., Assemi, K., Piasecki, M., Timothy, K., & Baker, T. K. (2022). Impact of acceptance and commitment training on psychological flexibility and burnout in medical education. *Journal of Contextual Behavioral Science, 23*, 190–199.

Tanner-Smith, E. E., Durlak, J. A., & Marx, R. A. Empirically based mean effect size distributions for universal prevention programs targeting school-aged youth: A review of meta-analyses. *Prevention Science, 19*, 1091–1101 (2018). https://doi.org/10.1007/s11121-018-0942-1

Taylor, B. A., LeBlanc, L. A., & Nosik, M. R. (2019). Compassionate care in behavior analytic treatment: Can outcomes be enhanced by attending to relationships with caregivers? *Behavior Analysis in Practice, 12*(3), 654–666.

Thorndike, E. L. (1898). Animal intelligence: An experimental study of the associative processes in animals. *Psychological Review Monographs Supplement, 2*(4), i–109. https://doi.org/10.1037/h0092987

Tikkanen, R., Fields, K., Williams, R. D., & Abrams, M. K. (2020). *Mental health conditions and substance use: Comparing U.S. needs and treatment capacity with those in other high-income countries.* New York: Commonwealth Fund. https://doi.org/10.26099/09ht-rj07

Tol, W. A., Leku, M. R., Lakin, D. P., Carswell, K., Augustinavicius, J., & Adaku, A. (2020). Guided self-help to reduce psychological distress in South Sudanese female refugees in Uganda: A cluster randomised trial. *Lancet Global Health, 8*(2), E254–E263. https://doi.org/10.1016/S2214-109X(19)30504-2

Tomasello, M., Hare, B., Lehmann, H., & Call, J. (2007.). Reliance on head versus eyes in the gaze following of great apes and human infants: The cooperative eye hypothesis. *Journal of Human Evolution*, 52(3), 314–320. https://doi.org/10.1016/j.jhevol.2006.10.001

Tversky, A., & Kahneman, D. (1992). Advances in prospect theory: Cumulative representation of uncertainty. *Journal of Risk and Uncertainty, 5*(4), 297–323.

Twohig, M. P., Hayes, S. C., & Masuda, A. (2006). A preliminary investigation of acceptance and commitment therapy as a treatment for chronic skin picking. *Behaviour Research and Therapy, 44*(10), 1513–1522.

Twohig, M. P., Shoenberger, D., & Hayes, S. C. (2007). A preliminary investigation of acceptance and commitment therapy as a treatment for marijuana dependence in adults. *Journal of Applied Behavior Analysis, 40*(4), 619–632. https://doi.org/10.1901/jaba.2007.619-632

van Steensel, F. J. A., Bögels, S. M., & Perrin, S. (2011). Anxiety disorders in children and adolescents with autistic spectrum disorders: A meta-analysis. *Clinical Child and Family Psychology Review, 14*, 302. https://doi.org/10.1007/s10567-011-0097-0

VanBuskirk, K., West, L., Malcarne, V., Afari, N., Liu, L., Petkus, A., & Wetherell, J. L. (2012). Confirmatory factor analysis of the valued living questionnaire in a Black American sample: Implications for cognitive research and practice. *Cognitive Therapy and Research, 36*(6), 796–805.

Venebra-Muñoz, A., Corona-Morales, A., Santiago-García, J., Melgarejo-Gutiérrez, M., Caba, M., & García-García, F. (2014). Enriched environment attenuates nicotine self-administration and induces changes in ΔFosB expression in the rat prefrontal cortex and nucleus accumbens. *Neuroreport, 25*(9), 688–692.

Vidic, Z., & Cherup, N. P. (2022). Take me into the ball game: An examination of a brief psychological skills training and mindfulness-based intervention with baseball players. *International Journal of Sport and Exercise Psychology, 20*(2), 612–629.

von Neumann, J. (1932). Proof of the quasi-ergodic hypothesis. *Proceedings of the National Academy of Sciences, 18*(1), 70–82. https://doi.org/10.1073/pnas.18.1.70

Wang, D., Hagger, M. S., & Chatzisarantis, N. L. (2020). Ironic effects of thought suppression: A meta-analysis. *Perspectives on Psychological Science, 15*(3), 778–793.

Weil, T. M., Hayes, S. C., & Capurro, P. (2011). Establishing a deictic relational repertoire in young children. *The Psychological Record, 61*, 371–390.

Weiner, H. (1970). Instructional control of human operant responding during extinction following fixed ratio conditioning. *Journal of the Experimental Analysis of Behavior, 13*, 391–394.

Welzl, H., D'Adamo, P., & Lipp, H. P. (2001). Conditioned taste aversion as a learning and memory paradigm. *Behavioural Brain Research, 125*(1–2), 205–213. https://doi.org/10.1016/S0166-4328(01)00302-3

Wenzlaff, R. M., & Wegner, D. M. (2000). Thought suppression. *Annual Review of Psychology, 51*(1), 59–91.

Whelan, R., & Barnes-Holmes, D. (2004). The transformation of consequential functions in accordance with the relational frames of same and opposite. *Journal of the Experimental Analysis of Behavior, 82*, 177–195. https://doi.org/10.1901/jeab.2004.82-177

Whiting, S., Pamula-Neal, H., Miller, J. R., & Dixon, M. R. (2022). Effects of preferred and non-preferred concurrent activities during self-control training in a school for Autism. *International Journal of Psychopathology and Psychiatric Diagnosis, 1*(1), 44–49.

Whitney, D. G., & Peterson, M. D. (2019). US national and state-level prevalence of mental health disorders and disparities of mental health care use in children. *JAMA Pediatrics, 173*(4), 389–391.

Wicksell, R. K., Kemani, M., Jensen, K., Kosek, E., Kadetoff, D., Sorjonen, K., Ingvar, M., & Olsson, G. L. (2013). Acceptance and commitment therapy for fibromyalgia: A randomized controlled trial. *European Journal of Pain, 17*, 599–611. https://doi.org/10.1002/j.1532-2149.2012.00224.x

Wilson, K. G., & Dufrene, T. (2009). *Mindfulness for two: An Acceptance and Commitment Therapy approach to mindfulness in psychotherapy.* Oakland, CA:: New Harbinger.

Wilson, K. G., & Hayes, S. C. (1996). Resurgence of derived stimulus relations. *Journal of the Experimental Analysis of Behavior, 66*, 267–281. https://doi.org/10.1901/jeab.1996.66-267

Wilson, K. G., & Murrell, A. R. (2004). Values work in acceptance and commitment therapy. In S. C. Hayes & Strosahl (Eds.). *A practical guide to Acceptance and Commitment Therapy* (pp. 120–151). New York: Springer-Verlag.

Wilson, K. G., Sandoz, E. K., Kitchens, J., & Roberts, M. (2010). The valued living questionnaire: Defining and measuring valued action within a behavioral framework. *The Psychological Record, 60*(2), 249–272.

Wolf, M. M. (1978). Social validity: The case for subjective measurement or how applied behavior analysis is finding its heart 1. *Journal of Applied Behavior Analysis, 11*(2), 203–214.

Wood, J. V., Perunovic, W. Q. E., & Lee, J. W. (2009). Positive self-statements: Power for some, peril for others. *Psychological Science, 20*, 860–866.

Yadavaia, J. E., & Hayes, S. C. (2012). Acceptance and commitment therapy for self-stigma around sexual orientation: A multiple baseline evaluation. *Cognitive and Behavioral Practice, 19*(4), 545–559.

Yi, Z., & Dixon, M. R. (2021). Developing and enhancing adherence to a telehealth ABA parent training curriculum for caregivers of children with autism. *Behavior Analysis in Practice, 14*, 58–74. https://doi.org/10.1007/s40617-020-00464-5

Yu, L., McCracken, L. M., & Norton, S. (2016). The Self Experiences Questionnaire (SEQ): Preliminary analyses for a measure of self in people with chronic pain. *Journal of Contextual Behavioral Science, 5*(3), 127–133.

Zettle, R. D. (2005). The evolution of a contextual approach to therapy: From comprehensive distancing to ACT. *International Journal of Behavioral Consultation and Therapy, 1*(2), 77.

Zettle, R. D., & Hayes, S. C. (1986). Dysfunctional control by client verbal behavior: The context of reason giving. *The Analysis of Verbal Behavior, 4*, 30–38.

Zettle, R. D., Gird, S. R., Webster, B. K., Carrasquillo-Richardson, N., Swails, J. A., & Burdsal, C. A. (2018). The self-as-context scale: Development and preliminary psychometric properties. *Journal of Contextual Behavioral Science, 10*, 64–74.

Zettle, R. D., Hayes, S. C., Barnes-Holmes, D., & Biglan, T. (Eds.) (2016). *The Wiley handbook of contextual behavioral science*. Chichester, UK: Wiley/Blackwell.

Zettle, R. D., Petersen, C. L., Hocker, T. R., & Provines, J. L. (2007). Responding to a challenging perceptual-motor task as a function of level of experiential avoidance. *The Psychological Record, 57*(1), 49–62.

Zlomke, K. R., & Dixon, M. R. (2006). Modification of slot-machine preferences through the use of a conditional discrimination paradigm. *Journal of Applied Behavior Analysis, 39*(3), 351–361.

Index

Page numbers in **bold** denote tables; those in *italics* denote figures.